Process of Speech

PROCESS of SPEECH:
Puritan Religious Writing & Paradise Lost

BOYD M. BERRY

The Johns Hopkins University Press

BALTIMORE AND LONDON

The Johns Hopkins University Press, Baltimore, Maryland 21218
The Johns Hopkins Press Ltd., London

Library of Congress Catalog Card Number 75-36933
ISBN 0-8018-1779-X

Library of Congress Cataloging in Publication data will be
found on the last printed page of this book.

The illustration on the cover and the title page, which depicts a
subversive pope agitating politically, is adapted from a woodcut
that appears on the title page of Lewis Hughes's *A looking-glass
for all true hearted Christians* . . . (London, 1642). By permission
of the Harvard College Library.

TO SARA

who has reservations about the egoism of a poet
and in many other ways has helped me to keep
some balance.

Contents

Acknowledgments

During the long haul when this book was being written and rewritten I have had a lot of help from many friends. Frank Huntley at the University of Michigan asked me what sermons had to do with literature, and Warner Rice did what he could patiently to give my first thoughts some shape and kindly to encourage my explorations. Students at Indiana University listened to me talk about Milton, Puritanism, and the seventeenth century, and then they talked and wrote back. They not only sat in my classes; during the time when much of my thinking coalesced they were trying, as they saw it, to revolutionize our society. They taught me something about what a revolutionary era feels like and where literature might fit into one, about why a man like George Fox might have visions, dress oddly, and preach love, about the attractions of theoretical and long-winded analysis for revolutionary thinkers, about the conservative nature of my own discipline, and about many other things important to the writing of this book. I should like to give a long list of their names, but because these friends do not always appear in my grade books, the list would be too long and I might forget some.

Other friends helped in other ways. David Bleich, Murray Sperber, and Lee Sterrenberg helped raise my political and psychological consciousness. Peter Lindenbaum threshed out Milton with me. Mel Plotinsky, Leo Solt, Gerald Strauss, and Don Gray read my manuscripts or listened. Rudolph Gottfried kindly commented on matters large and minute. James Thrope, Ted Tayler, and a lot of other people at the Huntington Library pitched in. Joseph Summers followed the book for years, always with fine observation. Stanley Fish did a lot of things, perhaps the most important being to keep my spirits up.

A substantial portion of Chapter 12, "Puritan Soldiers in *Paradise Lost*," was published under the same title but in somewhat modified form in *Modern Language Quarterly* 35 (1974) and appears here by kind permission of the editors.

The University of Michigan granted me a fellowship which first took me to England, Indiana University granted a faculty summer research fellowship in 1967, and the William Andrews Clark Memorial Library at UCLA made me a summer fellow in 1968 and enabled me to meet and work with half a dozen excellent students of Milton. Staff of the Clark Library, the Huntington Library, Harvard University Library, and the British Museum made life pleasant for me. Among many fine typists I wish to mention Liz Frederich and Gail Sarno.

A Note on Texts

One of my aims in this book has been to allow seventeenth-century preachers to make their points in their own words and then to show how their preoccupations can have immediate interest today. To these ends, I have preferred to modernize or to use modernized editions; the arbitrary spelling and punctuation of texts by men like Stephen Marshall, relatively unknown to most readers, often represent only the convenience of the printer anyway. However, although I have modernized spelling and most punctuation, I have not altered the seventeenth-century practice of using italics both for emphasis and to indicate quotations. Where a man cites many brief texts rapidly, modern quotation marks (here, perforce, often within quotation marks) make his phrasing seem choppy. Further, preachers quoted from more than one translation of the Bible, often from memory, and occasionally, one suspects, gave their own translation of Greek or Hebrew; the modern paraphernalia of quotation marks makes a sharp distinction between one's own and quoted words, while for many preachers the words of the Bible often seemed their own words as well. Nor did they quote, with our sense of "scholarly accuracy," from a single, established text.

However, nineteenth- and twentieth-century editions are obviously more accessible to most readers than unedited originals, and where I had a choice, I chose the modern text for the reader's convenience. Although many modern editions retain the original spelling, I have not modernized them. Thus we have the anomalous situation in which Marshall's words appear in modern guise, John Milton's in the original spelling. The text I chose not only gathers all Milton's writing together in one place but is more likely to be available to my readers than any particular, modernized version of his poetry I might select. To have modernized this text would have involved me in interpretative questions beside my point. Unhappily, some modern editions seem to me more distracting and difficult to follow than the original, yet I followed them. Since students of literature, at least, will probably have greater interest in those writers who merited modern editions over the years than they will in "lesser lights" like Marshall, perhaps the oddity of having the latter appear in more modern form than the former can be justified by my initial aim.

Process of Speech

Introduction

Paradise Lost is a poem in the Puritan style. As the thesis of this study, that proposition will surprise or offend few. Indeed, one might wonder that I devote an entire book to elaborating it. We often refer to the "Puritan epic" and generally acknowledge that Milton was a Puritan. Indeed, some students of Milton, typified by William Haller and A. S. P. Woodhouse, have become renowned exponents of Puritanism in their own right. Why then flog a seemingly dead horse?

There are several reasons, the most essential being that while many have tacitly assumed the proposition, no one has really ever demonstrated it. Because the Puritans distrusted art and rhetoric as mere human invention, they wrote and preached in a style which (quite arbitrarily and artificially) emphasizes intellectual content and dismisses form; Puritan preachers implicitly tell us, in their habitual ordering of words, sentences, and arguments, to pay attention to the ideas, not the way they are presented.[1] Students of Puritanism, responding to that direction, often practice "history of ideas," and like the Puritans themselves derive the "marrow of Puritan divinity" from their sermons. Consequently, when they turn to Milton's poetry, their categories are doctrinal and intellectual rather than formal. The problem is made much more complex, however, when we realize that Milton was no ordinary Puritan. Students of the history of ideas hit a brick wall particularly when they turn to Milton, because the "doctrines" which he articulated in his theoretical theological tract, *De Doctrina Christiana,* are very far from orthodox Puritanism. Thus, although we often instinctively feel that Milton was a Puritan and the poem Puritanic, we cannot, so long as we practice conventional history of ideas, "prove" it. Between the "marrow of Puritan divinity" and the verbal texture of his doctrinally idiosyncratic *Paradise Lost* there lurks a vast abyss, and no one has set out systematically to build a bridge over it.

Drawing the blueprint for this methodological bridge is not simply a rarified venture. Admittedly, in many respects it will connect only castles in the air. Yet it is also a bridge over troubled waters. The history of seventeenth-century England is the tale of a society falling systematically apart. The twenty years of civil war and political turmoil between 1640 and 1660 simply made overt and obvious a spirit of contention, bickering, and strife which had informed most of the words men wrote down during the previous forty years. Revolutions, Lawrence Stone succinctly reminds us, do not spring up like Topsy.[2] This one was preceded by a great deal of controversy. I am not entirely sure why seventeenth-century Englishmen were so contentious nor do I propose here to trace out the causes of their bickering. But, to appreciate the sublimity of *Paradise Lost,* we have to re-

1

member and understand the battles which raged in the intellectual streets and byways.

England was nominally a protesting, because Protestant, society during the seventeenth century. Men of quite different sensibility lodged under the broad umbrella of English Protestantism, bound together by certain elements of Christian doctrine and a common distaste for Roman Catholicism. It is quite possible, therefore, to talk about the writing of an intellectual regicide like John Milton in the same breath that we discuss the work of a royal favorite like John Donne. Both were in important ways writing to protest against the things of this world (as Christian poets generally do), both had a marked antipathy toward Rome, both looked intently to the Day of Judgment, when the mess of this world would be finally cleaned up. As Protestants, both indulged in a great deal of transcendental speculation about that glorious other place, the *locus amoenus* of Christian apocalypse. Protestors generically feel ill at ease in the world they inhabit; that is the basis of their protest and the root of their impulse to construct a better place.

But, despite all the common Protestant ground which united these Englishmen, there were intensely disputed differences between religious man and man in that controversial age. One way of categorizing those differences is to notice that some Englishmen were far more "advanced or radical Protestants" than their fellows. C. S. Lewis used that phrase to refer to "Puritans,"[3] but it has the much wider significance of recalling that in any society, some men are more at home than others with the things of this world. John Donne, for example, sought actively to fit himself into the established order of things in this world, and finally succeeded; John Milton, on the other hand, felt himself "Church-outed by the Prelats."[4] In a society coming apart, these differences will, obviously, be relatively pronounced, and it is upon these differences that I wish primarily to focus. Students of literature have already given us a good and extensive account of many of the similarities of our period, of the "world pictures" which bound men, of the overarching Christian tradition, of the unity of the thought and training of any "seventeenth-century reader" or "common expositor."[5] These studies explain particularly well how religion solaced Englishmen of that era; they do not account quite so well for the reasons men craved that solace so intensely, for they tend to ignore the fact that Christian doctrine furnished the words and categories—the intellectual vehicle— which men rode to the battlefield and the horrors of strife.[6] While *Paradise Lost* must have provided Milton considerable relief from the pangs of twenty devastating years, involving blindness, marital and more public strife as well as political and ideological anguish, and while I shall keep the nature of that solace squarely at the center of my analysis, I wish nevertheless to come at the poem from a study of the contemporary controversy out of which it was written. That means seeing the poem as part of a force at once destructive, oversetting many sorts of established order, and meliorative, aiming at the reform and recreation of a better life. Particularly the first part of that proposition may frighten the timid, who would prefer to think of poetry simply as sweetness and light, but it seems the only interpretation fair to the poet who could not praise a fugitive and cloistered virtue, a man who may have been the only genuine radical activist in the history of English letters.

To argue that *Paradise Lost* is an utterance in the Puritan style is to suggest that it was written by a troublemaker. The conservative bias of literary studies (and I use the word "conservative" in the broadest sense) makes that point difficult for many to swallow. Of course the Puritans often seem at the least unlovely, and at the worst nasty, suspicious, overweening, boring, grim, prim, and sour. It is not surprising that lovers of Milton's mighty lines would shrink from saying that their poet's teeth were set on edge, that he was weaned on a Puritan pickle. Moreover, protestors do often combine distaste for this world with radical optimism that it can be set right. In their age, the Puritans demonstrate this general truth, acquiring a new optimism, markedly in contrast with the last expressions of their establishment adversaries, and marching steadily, even cheerfully, out to make the supreme gesture of confidence—a revolution. But this matter runs deeper. Students of verbal icons must have difficulty appreciating an iconoclast. Indeed, one of the things of this world to which protestors frequently object is language itself. Reformers of any age commonly employ a realistic, antirhetorical aesthetic to "debunk" the establishment. To the extent that protestors are not confident about their place in this world, they are equally unsure about words. The angel Raphael makes that kind of distinction when he recalls that God's acts are immediate but that human "process of speech" is bound by "time and motion" and cannot adequately represent them (*Paradise Lost* [hereafter PL], 7:176-78). Literary studies are conservative, in part, because they assume that words are trustworthy and the process worth investigation.

A Puritan epic is therefore a sort of oxymoron. The values of a poet or singer, who deals by trade in words, clash with the values of the advanced or radical Protestant. That fact has made some students of Milton ill at ease. Milton seems immensely confident about his words and his ability securely to use them. Indeed, his fictive angel follows his maker and creates magnificent lines. Often Milton's verbal dexterity is traced back to humanistic training and intellectual background, which was, like Puritanism, an innovative intellectual movement of its age; as new responses to much the same world, the two shared many things in common.[7] But they differ in one or two critical points: humanism cultivates confidence in verbal dexterity as a support to political authority. The gracious orator trains himself to advise kings. In clear contrast, the iconoclastic Puritans cultivated a plain style to break down the facade of authority and expose the corruption which words concealed. Unless we are willing to argue that Milton responded incoherently to the crises of his time, we may find it well to question the notion that Milton deployed the graces of a courtier and kingly advisor in the task of attacking the king. Rather, I wish to argue, his verbal dexterity was, at least in part, the aesthetic counterpart and expression of a newly emergent, radical optimism, a poetic parallel to the pragmatic acts of a Puritan making a revolution.

Puritan writing is simultaneously immensely exciting and profoundly dull. The latter, more frequently remarked characteristic derives principally from the fact that Puritans talked too much. Despite their attacks upon rhetoric, many Puritan preachers remark even in the published versions of their sermons that they have turned over the hourglass while they beg their auditors to have patience. Relatively conservative preachers—Andrewes, Laud, or Donne, for example—preach far fewer pages. Verbal giantism afflicts not only the form of individual Puritan sermons but the whole endeavor of Puritan theologizing over the course of the seventeenth century. Puritan theologians in effect spent their time inflating a single thesis into a mammoth, systematic work, refining arguments, spinning out implications, clarifying assumptions, weaving an ever more tightly constructed web out of a few central propositions. Puritan writing on any topic tends therefore to be profoundly repetitious; a short, pioneering essay typically gets expanded, by later expositors, into a series of 700-page tomes during roughly half a century.[8] At the same time, however, the urge for self-consistency which produces this sort of monumental repetition also makes Puritan writing extraordinarily vital. Puritan thinking about church polity, for example, underlay the military tactics of the New Model Army and the methods the Puritans used to rear their children. A slight quibble concerning ecclesiology therefore may produce dramatic, concrete acts in the home or on the street or at war. The airy speculations these men pursued could and often did eventuate in blood.

To put the point more theoretically, Christian theology was a broad framework within which men could contend sharply: it furnished the language and categories with which seventeenth-century Englishmen threshed out what they perceived to be the burning questions and answers about their world and their lives. Douglas Bush remarked that "it is hardly possible to exaggerate the importance of the sermon in the seventeenth-century world" and went on to enumerate the main social functions which sermons performed—mass communication, political agitation, entertainment, etc.[9] In addition, the language and categories of sermons—which were the language and categories of theological summas as well—were the means by which Englishmen argued politics, economics, anthropology, geography, history, military theory, and natural science. Sermons are, if anything, more exciting than summas because the preacher in the pulpit confronted the daily events of passing history and, inspired or appalled, might more easily be drawn into making revealing statements of his belief in response to them. Summas (of which the Puritans produced an inordinate number) tend to be cooler and more balanced, the underlying tendencies of the thought muted, while sermons, in their occasional extravagance, let us see whither those tendencies were headed.

Perhaps the point is sufficiently obvious, but I want to emphasize doubly that theological thinking and writing constituted the overwhelmingly most important way of talking about the world between 1600 and 1640. Even to phrase the point in that way may obscure the importance of Christian expression. When we write about the seventeenth century we sometimes suggest that really, secular matters—politics and economics, history and anthropology, natural science or psychology—were and eternally are the most important of men's concerns and that seventeenth-century English-men simply had a quaint way of addressing themselves to these matters. I am not claiming that these men were extraordinarily religious—no doubt they varied among themselves markedly in this respect. What I am claiming is that, just as we "place" a stranger in a bar by the way he uses and re-sponds to various words and phrases having to do with politics, economics, racial matters, and the relationship between the sexes, for example, so one could "place" a seventeenth-century Englishman by the way he talked Christian doctrine. That is what a dominant intellectual framework and language provides—the stage for contention and confrontation. If any mode of analysis touches upon, illuminates, or defines the burning ques-tions of the time, it will spawn fights and identifiable factions. Abraham Wright thought he could "place" his contemporaries within their factions when in 1656 he collected his *Five sermons in five several styles or waies of preaching;*[10] his contemporaries did it when they fought wars with words or guns in Christian language; and I wish to do so here as a way of showing the vitality and excitement of theological prose, and as a means of locating *Paradise Lost* in its time.

Quite apart from matters of mere excitement, however, there are three additional reasons for pursuing this thesis. First, it permits me to consider and unite theological prose and religious poetry within a single intellectual framework or method of analysis. Second, by speaking of a Puritan style (defined in part by its opposite) I can group theological writers of the early seventeenth century into a flexible yet coherent arrangement and can account for the differences among members of either party as well as among all Englishmen. Third, by defining a specific kind of religious sensi-bility which informs *Paradise Lost* (as opposed to demonstrating how it conforms to the general Christian consensus), I can draw together certain seemingly unrelated aspects of that poem into a coherent pattern and can account for certain anomalies by showing how they resemble and fit in with some less unusual aspects of the whole. To demonstrate these things, however, I must first pause and say a word about my use of the term "style."

Style is habitual or preferred choice. Whether or to what extent the choice is conscious or unconscious does not affect my argument. When we describe a writer's style and distinguish it from that of other writers, we are saying that the writer chooses to do one thing rather than another or to do it one way rather than another, and we are saying that the sum of his choices forms a consistent and characterizable pattern. Basically, we are engaged in rudimentary statistical surveys, even if we do not formally count, for we are suggesting that if we tabulated every instance in which an author made a particular decision—for example, to use Latinate rather than Anglo-Saxon diction, periodic rather than nonperiodic sentence structure, pastoral rather than urban imagery—a clear-cut pattern, of statistical signif- icance, would emerge. Every writer is faced with an almost infinite number of options in casting even a single sentence; when we describe a writer's style, we instinctively pick those orders of choice or decision which seem likely to differentiate him from other writers. We don't look at all the op- tions and choices because many of them are common to most writers; for example, the fact that an author does *not* invert the normal subject, verb, object ordering common in English will hardly help us to see his idiosyn- cracies.

The simple counting of options and choices, the simple description of a writer's style, interest me far less than the way in which the patterns of choice either express or determine (I do not care which) the writer's per- ception and/or ordering of the world. To write a sentence is to order words and phrases, but it is also to take a stand concerning the nature of the uni- verse. If we believe that the medium is the message, we might put it that the form into which we cast our words and phrases is the form of our ideas about the universe. Or we may feel that the mere act of playing with words generates our thoughts. If we take a romantic view of writing, we will speak of verbal choice expressing the writer's deeper intellectual or emotional predispositions. If we are more classically minded, we will speak of words"fitly embellishing" the prior ideas. I am not interested in which way we articulate the connection between matter and manner, however. My point is simply that the texture of words and the texture of ideas are interrelated and inseparable, and hence that the concept of habitual or pre- ferred choice need not be confined to our consideration of verbal matters.

Let me make the point another way. My working hypothesis is that man is primarily a logical or coherent or consistent being. Indeed, we can't begin to describe a writer's style if we don't believe that, for we can only speak of the characteristics of a style if we assume that in any given kind of situation a man will by habit prefer to act or order events in a way consistent with every other instance of that situation he encounters. His style or logic is either to exceed speed limits or conform to them, run stop signs or pause for them, choose one sort of word or another, cast one syntactic pattern or another, etc. True, there are situations when even the most law-abiding of us exceed speed limits or ease through stop signs, that is, when we decide not to do what we prefer or do by habit. And we recognize these exceptional moments when we talk about a style, noticing tensions, special effects, emphases achieved by deviation from the ordinary pattern. Moreover, there are some situations which we don't care very much about; we don't form habits or develop preferences about these matters, just as some men so blissfully ignore speed limits that they sometimes conform to and sometimes exceed them. If, in writing, a man will meet a situation one way one time and another way another time so that his choices form no clear pattern of preference, we simply ignore that facet of his style, assuming that it was not important to him either. Further, we may recognize public pressures at work upon an author's style, just as many of us will tend to conform to the speed limit if the vast majority of our fellow travellers are so doing. We commonly speak of how an author participates in the predominating style of his age, for example. But throughout we assume, as we engage in stylistic analysis, that the most interesting aspect of human personality is self-consistent, with an inner logic which is self-coherent and all its own.

My analogy between driving a car and writing is calculated to recall a further aspect of the self-consistency of the human personality: we tend to meet different kinds of situations and make different orders of choice in ways which are also consistent. A reckless driver may well be reckless with syntax, choose daring images, and (unless he has mixed feelings about his own style) preach a certain abandonment in other areas of life. True, if he is ambivalent about this characteristic, he may drive too fast and preach a go-slow politics or love-making to assuage his conscience. Either way, however, there is a connection between the way he performs diverse tasks. Thus, to take some literary examples, it is easy to see how Hooker handled his choices of syntax, of the ordering of ideas, and of legal entities: parallelism predominates in all. Similarly, E. M. W. Tillyard could argue that Elizabethan authors habitually preferred to employ certain kinds of metaphor (e.g., the Great Chain of Being), perceived certain kinds of order in the universe (hierarchic), and argued in certain logical patterns (analogic, or by drawing out correspondences)—all three kinds of behavior cohering in a unified pattern or style which evoked for him an Elizabethan world picture. It would follow from this that we can expect to find the same sorts of consistency being manifested in the myriad choices and patterns which one makes when constructing a theological argument.

To write Christian theology is to attempt an impossible description systematically. Theology is a description rather than an arbitrary manipulation of doctrine. When we way, for example, that Calvin "set God at a greater distance from man than most theologians," we forget that no serious theologian would approve of the blasphemous idea that man can push God around. We may feel, if we are men of lesser faith, that if a Calvinist talks about God as if he were a punishing avenger, he does so for psychological reasons (he wants to be a punishing avenger himself, perhaps) or for controversial strategy (his opponents think of God in much more kindly terms), etc. But I feel we ought to accord seventeenth-century theologians this virtue at least, that they set out to talk about the world as they thought they truly saw it, and that consciously at least they did so in good faith. They may indeed have been shoving God around, unconsciously; advanced or radical Protestants began to shove the paternal authority of the king quite consciously over the edge. But if, in several ways, Puritans unconsciously attacked father figures, consciously, at least, they must have felt in their bones that God was simply a long way away.

The description of God is de facto impossible. As a consequence, a serious theologian walks a very dangerous tightrope. Christian doctrine is a web of paradox ideally binding logically opposed or disparate entities together; one must deal with trinity and unity, free will and divine providence, eternity and human time, sin and salvation, justice and mercy, to name only some of these entities to be fused in paradox. Differences in theological outlook amount to differing ways of treating these oppositions or differing ways of formulating the paradoxes. The more balanced a theologian, the more successfully he does this; conversely, the less successful he is, the more he will fall off the tightrope. When matters of faith are matters of life and death, to stumble may mean the gallows. Writing theology is, in times of religious contention particularly, dangerous, but even in the most serene eras, a misstep means heterodoxy. Yet, since the description of God is impossible, all men stray from the wire one way or another. Theological style, then, is nothing less than the way in which men, by habit or preference, fall off the tightrope.

The essence of the Puritan style is a quest for a permanent, fixed, static, even rigid order. This drive so permeates all of their many activities that one suspects that it was almost compulsive, which is not surprising when we reflect how many changes were occurring in the world about them. The Puritans cast themselves as being dissatisfied with the status quo, as being discontented with the world they saw about them, and hence their first desire was to formulate some plan which was unchanging and worthy of their approbation. Their first impulse was to systematize doctrine in summas; they did the same thing in their bipartite sermons, extracting "doctrines" before they applied them to "uses" in this world.[11] They increased the distance between God and man in order to keep God clear of all the mess they saw about them, and in talking about him they emphasized his stability and permanence. Their historiography was, as I shall show in section 1, correspondingly rigid, for as they diminished the importance of the historical Jesus who for other theologians came as a god/man into this impermanent world of space and time, they appealed either to "God," who dispensed justice and mercy throughout all time, or they spoke of the "lamb slain from the beginning" whose sacrificial status was not determined by the transitory nature of a chronological matrix. They were especially taken with Sabbath-keeping (section 2) because on the one hand it had been ordained at creation (time's passage had not tainted its permanence), and on the other it provided a model for the "eternal resting day" or final Sabbath of the millennium when time will "stand fixt," in Milton's phrase. Their typological analysis (section 3) was improgressive and eschatological; the way Christ had completed or fulfilled some types was of less moment to Puritan thinkers than the equality they saw between themselves and the typical patriarchs. England was Sion in sermon after Puritan sermon; the English almost literally *were* the ancient Israelites, since time and change did not affect God's relationship with his peculiars. And the Puritans hoped, at least in their more optimistic hours, to complete the eschatological types by erecting the New Jerusalem in England. Hence their concern for the "calling and conversion of the Jews," and the analogic quality of badly managed Puritan typology. Reflecting this myriad quest for static fixity was their prose itself, cast into rigidly "methodized" systems and redolent of such terms as "justification," "sanctification," "salvation," and "damnation." All turn a potentially transitive act into a solid, manageable noun. Similarly, just as the Puritan's Christ had not effected a major change of direction in time and the course of human history by completing types and instituting a new dispensation, so (to turn to "uses" in this world) the Puritan hero could not expect to operate transitively and decisively upon the universe about him. Caught in a series of repeated trials and little "progress," he could resist temptation and manifest his faith, but he could slay few dragons. Puritans most heavily emphasized the stable arrangements made by God at the creation and the final fixity of the end, rhapsodizing upon paradise lost and paradise regained; there was no Aristotelean "middle" to human history, to theology, or to their art;[12] Christ did not mediate, for the Puritans, between God and man, just as he did not reverse the course of history. And there was little mediation in Puritan art as well. In contrast, Donne, the court preacher, believed that the Church mediated between "sign" and "thing signified," and Herbert thought that a poetic and pious person might "spell" the hieroglyphs of nature and of art; Ross has shown how liturgical views and aesthetic principles mesh in much the same way.[13] Puritans, however, were suspicious of both liturgy and aesthetics for much the same reasons. Fluid and fallible, rhetoric was not suitable for nailing down doctrine and driving home uses.

Milton was a Puritan in his own way. Typical was his apparently private exercise in theological systematization, the *De Doctrina Christiana;* idiosyncratic was the way he overtly subordinated the Son to the Father as a way of playing down his historical mission, the way he brought God on stage to give us the Word for once and for all, and the way he created one of the most omniscient of all narrative voices in literature (if I may modify an absolute) which deals or at least seems to deal in eternal truth. Typical was the manner in which he represented the second person of the Trinity making his mediatorial gesture before time *begins* and the millennialist preoccupation with beginnings and endings, the sanctification of the Sabbath at creation and its glorious recurrence in the last Sabbath. More personal was the immensely anachronistic apparatus of the poem, which swirls back and forth through time and eternity in a nonlinear, achronologic movement and the "foreshadowing" which dampens slightly the decisiveness of the heinous act. Typical was the way in which God oversees and manages all (for example in the war in heaven) from his throne "fixt for ever firm and sure" (PL, 7:586), and the way in which the virtuous angels and regenerated men make gestures of faith which testify to their commitment but do not seriously and transitively alter the world around them. More purely Miltonic is the way God's acts are represented as flowing out into a world which they activate, so that even the decisiveness of God's creative gestures are muted by the response of the creatures. Typical is the way Milton, in defiance of all chronological considerations, portrays Adam as the first Christian, and the way in which the poem moves our focus first away from this world and then, in the final books, back to the practical applications or "uses" in this world. Miltonic is the artistry with which all of this is accomplished.

Such a brief sketch of the Puritan style in operation may seem bald and reductive, particularly because I have advanced it without considering a different theological style. It indicates not the actual, tentative way Puritans worked out their theology but some of the extremes toward which their writing tended; contrastive definition will, in the first three sections, help me to show relative emphases implicit in a theological proposition and allow me to work somewhat more delicately. However, one can see that even such a brief statement of the essence of Puritan style connects various theological topics with doctrinal emphases, structural ordering, and verbal style.

Perhaps, after so much theory and abstract summary, a concrete example of analysis will help to cement both the nature of my method and some of the conclusions toward which I am arguing. Let us, then, contrast the way Calvin either ignored or de-emphasized the entrance of God into the lives of men with Luther's formulation of these matters: to obtain a fair yet manageable sample of Calvin's choices, I shall notice how Calvin kept Christ from entering intimately into men's lives when he constructed his historiographic theories, discussed Christian conversion, and edged toward a Zwinglian view of communion.

Historiographically, Calvin tended to de-emphasize the coming of Christ in two ways. On the one hand, as François Wendel points out, while Calvin took into account the humanity of Christ, yet he stressed the divinity over the humanity, whereas Luther had characteristically laid greater stress on the humanity. Calvin "dismissed anything tending towards the deification of man, even in the person of Jesus Christ," and consequently tended to ignore Christ's humanity, while for Luther the humanity of Christ had been so important that he "finished by admitting the ubiquity not only of the divine, but also of the human nature of Christ."[14] Secondly Calvin played down the difference which Christ's coming in time made in men's lives. He quoted Augustine with approbation that "the children of the promise (Rom. 9, 8) reborn of God, who obeyed the commands of faith working through love (Gal. 5, 6) have belonged to the New Covenant since the world began."[15] Luther also had recognized a "Church of the Word" extending back in human history even to Adam, but he habitually defined "the Word" as "the promise of Christ's advent," and hence for him the Old Testament Church was a church anticipating the decisive historical moment of Christ's coming.[16] Calvin did not employ this promissory explanation and since in his view the "new covenant" had been established "since the world began," it is clear that "new" had little temporal meaning as he uses it; his "new covenant" does not alter or replace in time the "old covenant," nor is it tied, even by a promise, to the advent of Christ in this world. Since Christ entered time by assuming his humanity and enters the lives of men by offering the "new covenant," to talk in these ways about sacred history was to de-emphasize the entrance of God into men's lives.

When Wendel refers to Luther's belief in the ubiquity of Christ's human nature, he alludes indirectly to Luther's theory of consubstantiation. Calvin's views on communion are difficult to trace. However, it seems likely that Zwingli's "memorial" interpretation, as opposed to Luther's theory of consubstantiation, derived from and expressed more explicitly tendencies latent in Calvin's thought. Zwingli held that during communion an alteration might occur in the participant, but that alteration occurred because the participant remembered Christ's loving deeds, not because Christ was in any sense physically present in the elements. For Luther, Christ was literally and physically present in the elements—because he is ubiquitous—and hence he literally and physically enters men's lives during communion to effect an alteration.[17]

Thirdly, Luther's conversion was a matter of great moment in his life, whereas Calvin spoke infrequently of his conversion and never located it in time with anything like the historical precision of Luther. In what Wendel terms his unique reference to his own conversion, Calvin calls it a "sudden conversion," but then goes on to say that God "subdued and brought my mind to a teachable frame," that he acquired "some taste and knowledge of true godliness," and "was inflamed with so intense a desire to make progress therein, that although I did not altogether leave off other studies [he had been studying law] I yet pursued them with less ardour." For all the "suddenness" of his "conversion," Calvin's life style, as reflected in his studies, seems to have altered only gradually.[18] His conversion, in other words, does not seem to represent the abrupt about-face, datable with any precision, that Luther's was; his general silence on the subject suggests that the historical alteration did not interest him nearly as much as it did Luther.

These examples are far from exhaustive; I pick them because of the diversity of topics, because they are few enough to manage briefly, and because the issues raised will figure in the first three sections of this study. Few and diverse as they are, they suggest a clear pattern of preference characteristic of each man and visible in the whole work of each. Calvin, we know, perceived a great gulf between God and sinful man, and in these examples we see how he describes God as having little shared experience with us; Luther tends to join God and man in communion and what was for him a vivid experience of conversion. Calvin adored God for his unimaginable mercy in crossing the gulf, Luther for the way he establishes bridges of communication between us and him. Calvin, scornful of "mere human invention" employed in describing God (particularly by his Roman Catholic opponents), felt that human communication about God was, as a bridge across the gulf, suspect, and he worshipped a truth which words cannot express but which abstract theological formulation can best approximate. Luther tried more directly to communicate the experience of God's communication with him and did not rely so heavily on the impersonal forms of systematic divinity. Even these three apparently rather minor doctrinal choices or preferences not only cohere but fit smoothly into the texture of the whole theology of each man.

My assumption that a man's behavior shows an inner coherence or personal logic is not, of course, startling. Erik Erikson employed it when he considered diverse aspects of Luther's activity from a theological, political, and psychoanalytic perspective and traced out how the ego transforms "instinctual energy into patterns of action, into character, into style—in short, into an identity."[19] Similarly, Edmund Wilson drew together Ben Jonson's choices in the ordering of plot, episode, character, image, verbal texture, "humor," and in his reliance upon classical learning in order to define his "anal erotic" personality.[20] To take one other example of scholarly work on the seventeenth century, Charles Mauron has conflated the plays of individual seventeenth-century French dramatists to define the "personal myth" of the poet being expressed in each.[21] Suggestive as a methodological approach is the collaboration between Richard Ohmann and Norman Holland on the texture of Victorian prose, for there linguistic behavior was linked through psychological analysis to various other structures and choices in nonfictional as well as fictional prose.[22]

It should come as no shock then that I apply the term "style" to patterns of intellectual as well as verbal behavior and choice. The single word embodies that unity or core of identity from which coherent patterns of preference and habit operating in diverse situations spring. While it may be true that in a general way my use of the word owes something to the disciples of Freud, a man like Lancelot Andrewes provides, in his exposition of Scripture, a model for my method. Andrewes's sermons are glorious explications of the divine style as it functioned in prose and poetry. Admittedly, Andrewes thought (along with all his contemporaries) that the words of the Bible were divinely inspired, not the works of men; yet the claim that Andrewes was the greatest preacher in an age of magnificent pulpit oratory still rests upon the thoroughgoing way he drew a theological "message" from an analysis of diction, syntax, and structuring, or "spelled" the "hieroglyph" of the text. The text "incarnated" theology in a very physical and highly formalistic sense for him, and hence he could press on every jot and tittle to show the self-consistency of the divine nature at work formally as well as intellectually.

Despite a "Puritan" phase which reminds us that "Calvinism" was not the sole property of the reforming wing of the English religious community, Andrewes emerged as an "establishment" preacher whose work naturally found its way into The Library of Anglo-Catholic Theology. His views about divine expression did not go uncontested, even in his own age. For example, the angel Raphael was markedly less certain than Andrewes that words do express the divine style. Explaining to Adam how he will narrate the story of creation in book seven of *Paradise Lost,* Raphael points out:

Immediate are the Acts of God, more swift
Then time or motion, but to human ears
Cannot without process of speech be told.   [7. 176–78]

Raphael's specific problem is that God's timeless plan took immediate effect; he was not bound by the human "days" which Genesis employs to accommodate the mystery of creation to our human understanding. Furthermore, Milton wanted to paraphrase and expand upon the account of Genesis, and Raphael's quibble helps him to justify that procedure. Yet it simply takes time to say (or write or read or listen to) the words necessary to represent his acts, and we may mistakenly attribute that duration to the acts themselves. This sort of difficulty (as well as the feeling that one must justify expanding upon Genesis) could only occur to a man with a style resembling Calvin's more nearly than Andrewes's or Luther's. To comment upon the discrepancy between divine style and human process of speech is to reveal a well-developed sense of the vastness of the gulf between God and man; the suggestion that words will not mediate between the two implies that theological mediation will be less likely also. Raphael, of course, is far from an utter doubter; he goes on, as did his creator, to tell the story of creation in magnificent poetry. Milton was never an ordinary Puritan, particularly when he crafted things out of words. Yet Raphael's doubt would not have occurred to Andrewes with the force it does to the angel, and that difference, with all its theological, social, political, and psychological implications, is central to my analysis.

Indeed, it should become clear that, in a sense, I am partially defying the Puritan preachers and doing what they implicitly and habitually tell me not to do. Rhetoric, they thought, was "mere human invention," and so they labored to create the impression that they did not themselves use it. Of course they did and of course like all writers they created a style. If my assumptions about the human personality and the coherence of any piece of writing are not unusual, it is perhaps this disinclination to take Puritan writing at face value which distinguishes my analysis from previous studies of Puritan prose (particularly those which find it devoid of style and of no literary interest). On the other hand, Raphael's phrase, "process of speech," furnishes me part of my title because it articulates something about the very humanity and limitation of utterance; perhaps in Raphael's view "process of speech" is limited and of less value than the immediate acts of God simply because it is human. Yet if so, it is a limitation we all labor under. At any rate, Raphael here articulates and calls our attention to the fact that speech is a process extending over time.

If we press a bit further with my brief sketch, we might say that Calvin's and Raphael's styles cohere around a disinclination to be where they presently are (in this world of sorrows) and an inclination to be elsewhere, out of this world, with God, who does not easily come into this world (and thereby may himself express their preference not to be here). I do not care to speculate why some men have such a style, why they are ill at ease with this world and its process of speech, why they become truth-seeking "realists" who debunk rhetoric and refuse, as Thoreau did not, to take any man's word for his deed. Obviously, if one manifested an extreme form of this style, one would be a sort of revolutionary, eager to escape the present situation by straining toward somewhere else—utopia. One would think that truth lodged in that somewhere else, and that if one could go there and learn it, one could make this world of sorrow over in its image. In

Christian terms, one would focus upon the "otherness" of God, would be highly interested in Eden, and would turn one's face toward the millennium (which is the return of paradise and Eden) where all things will be set right once and for all in the kingdom of the saints. Calvin was not, as it happens, such a complete revolutionary. He was not much interested in Revelation or eschatology,[23] and he devoted a great deal of his energy to organizing a community here below in Geneva. But, it does seem to be true that, for some reason, a group of men appeared in seventeenth-century England who developed Calvin's style in such an extreme direction, and it was the presence of these men which created the combative tone which reigned throughout our period.

John Donne, whose public religious profession aligned him with a conservative establishment very much at home (as all conservative political establishments are) in this world, will provide an instructive, contrastive example. Donne manifests an acute sense of personal sin and a fondness for eschatology—two traits which would seem to align him with Puritanism; his religious sensibility often strikes us as in a loose way "Puritanic." Yet Donne always kept one foot securely on this earth, even when ascending to an "*O altitudo!*" and it is that fact, perhaps, which helps us to understand why his politics were implicitly conservative. Consider his sonnet "At the round earths imagin'd corners" where the "Puritanic" eschatological preoccupations and personal sense of sin both emerge clearly.

> At the round earths imagin'd corners, blow
> Your trumpets, Angells, and arise, arise
> From death, you numberlesse infinities
> Of soules, and to your scattred bodies goe,
> All whom the flood did, and fire shall o'erthrow,
> All whom warre, dearth, age, agues, tyrannies,
> Despaire, law, chance, hath slaine, and you whose eyes,
> Shall behold God, and never tast deaths woe.
> But let them sleepe, Lord, and mee mourne a space,
> For, if above all these, my sinnes abound,
> 'Tis late to aske abundance of thy grace,
> When wee are there; here on this lowly ground,
> Teach mee how to repent; for that's as good
> As if thou hadst seal'd my pardon, with thy blood.[24]

Initially, Donne speaks as if in the voice of God, much, perhaps, as Milton brings God on stage in book three to lend a note of authority, and the picture of the Day of Judgment is unforgettably vivid. In the sestet, however, Donne begins to drop back from this cosmic vision, because of his sense that "above all these, my sinnes abound"; the pivot is completed fully in line 12, where Donne juxtaposes "there" with "here on this lowly ground" and prays for repentance in this life and time. The final thought, that repentance is "as good / As if thou hadst seal'd my pardon, with thy blood" sounds the eschatological note again, evoking the seals opened in Revelation to certify those washed in the blood of the lamb. The point, however, is tentative; "as if" was a phrase Milton did not much use. Eschatologically read, the tentativeness reinforces and echoes Donne's willingness to live in the uncertainties of this life "here" because only in due course of time will he arrive "there." Certainly there is a straining for the eternal, unchanging, beatific vision, very much as we find it in Puritan prose, and there is an intense sense of sin; on the other hand, there is a considerable confidence expressed in the efficacy of repentance here, and a final willingness to live on this earth, since it is, after all, all we really have except faith and hope.

The practice of writing theology is a fine example of very complex human behavior and it is a mistake to expect that the results can be easily or simply classified and analyzed. The Puritans, for example, were not merely otherworldly nor (despite all the Puritan propaganda) were the preachers of the Laudian establishment simply "secure sinners." The longer the Puritans elaborated upon a theological system which emphasized (or at least seemed to emphasize) faith over works, the farther they were, paradoxically, driven toward reintroducing the importance of works. Perhaps we are dealing here with some law of human nature according to which the farther an initial philosophical action is pressed, the more firmly intellectual reaction occurs; however that may be, a whole series of such paradoxes evolved in Puritan thinking; after initially producing mountains of systematically transcendental prose, the Puritans turned downward to set this world aright. And just as the more faithful and abstract they became, the more working and concrete their final thoughts, so the more completely they exorcised Christ from the center of their theology and history, the more they were driven to reintroduce a glorious, eschatological hero—King Christ or Lord Jesus. Having laid out with such loving, compulsive care that mind of God so incredibly different from wormlike, fallen man, they began to suspect that they, although still human, could and did see as God does, and then that they could indeed and did in fact begin to unfold his plan for England. Just as, in individual sermons, they first preached "doctrines," then applied them to the world in "uses," so they first developed an all-encompassing ideology which "explained" the things which concerned them most, then elaborated upon and applied it on the battlefield and in politics. Donne's sonnet might seem at first glance "Puritanic" from this point of view, since it first leaps transcendentally upward out of this world of time and space to God and the end of time, and then in the second part turns its attention back down to earth. But the mood and tone which inform this pattern are not Puritanic. For the poem is initially assertive and confident where the Puritans were most tentative, and it finally becomes tentative in tone at just the point where Puritans developed a new, confident optimism.

It should now begin to be clear why I choose to consider theological writing and *Paradise Lost* together and why I define style as I do. First, I can set the poem within the context of the dominant intellectual activity of its age. Second, I can consider two seemingly different kinds of activity— the writing of polemic and of poetry—to see what sorts of consistency emerge in men's choices. Third, in considering seventeenth-century theology, I am dealing with a series of choices made in an area of great moment to the writers, and hence those choices should be more revealing than those made in an area of less conscious concern. If men care deeply about something, they will have strong, sharply marked preferences and habits when they confront or deal with it. The three add up to this: my conception of style allows me to relate or bring together two kinds of highly wrought pattern central to the lives of the writers and to the concerns of their age.

One further assumption and one methodological strategy should be noted here. The assumption is that everything I have said about style as it operates in theological writing can be said with equal truth about style as it operates in poetry, where we are, if anything, more immediately and acutely conscious of the writer making choices. The strategy is to apply the psychological model of the individual personality to a group of men. The analogy between the behavior of a single man and the behavior of a group of men has its obvious limitations, but these, recognized fully, constitute a positive asset when one is trying to classify the extensive and confused mass which is seventeenth-century theological thought and writing. It gives us a way to handle the diversity which we can see within the unity of Puritanism. Because individual men are not interchangeable parts and the members of any party are not mass-produced robots, their individual habits and idiosyncracies cannot be overlooked. The problem is somewhat diminished when I think of style as personal expression on an infinite number of levels of activity. A single man may or may not articulate one doctrine or set of doctrines, one ideology or political program, one ecclesiastical policy or habit or worship, etc.; he may be *more* or *less* a Puritan. Further, this kind of stylistic analysis allows me to account for the historical diversity which differentiates early from later Puritans, permitting me to see them as members of the same developing group.

John New warned us fully about the dangers and difficulties of distinguishing between one group of seventeenth-century theologians and another, before he so delicately drew some distinctions.[25] There are two main sources of difficulty. In the first place there was a great degree of homogeneity in the theological views of seventeenth-century Englishmen. Were that not true, we could not speak of the language of Christian doctrine as being the most important language of the age. All men were agreed that

God was the creator of the universe, that he was a God of Justice—punishing the sins of naturally sinful man—and a God of Mercy—saving out of his "mere mercy" those who were truly repentant. Original sin, predestinate election, and the literal truth of the Bible were fundamentals. True, a man like Jeremy Taylor questioned the doctrine of original sin, and a John Goodwin or a John Milton could query the doctrine of predestinate election, but these men were exceptional, in the first place, and in the second, to summarize their views as briefly as I have done does violence to the complexities of their positions.[26] Still, both New and I would freely admit that many students of the period have presented it as utterly homogeneous, and there is considerable basis in fact for that argument.

Secondly, the implications of any great innovation are never entirely apparent at the time of discovery or breakthrough, and it generally takes men some time to work out those implications for themselves. Henry VIII, for example, seems to have held the view, which strikes us with hindsight as extraordinary, that he could simply transfer ecclesiastic power from Rome to the *fidei defensor* without disrupting any other element in the texture of religious life.[27] The really major innovations of history are therefore often followed by a period in which the implications of the change are explored; we have been exploring Marx and Freud for most of a century now, consolidating the gains, rendering the mental leaps into systematic structures, unravelling the implications. The seventeenth century was just such a period of consolidation, elaboration, and analysis following the great leap of the early Reformers. As a consequence, theological writing of our period exhibits at once a great sameness over time—infrequently going beyond the terms of the initial innovation—and chronological development—as the elaboration and analysis drew to completion and perfection.

Not only did the elaboration of Protestant theology produce more and more radical Protestants as the years passed, but others, initially inclined to reform matters in the Church, later found that they did not want to reform this or that specific matter, or reform as many matters as their more radical brethren kept uncovering. Thus the theological homogeneity was apparently greater during the early decades of the century than, for example, it was after 1640. I say apparently, because Tudor and Stuart control of the press had the effect of creating an intellectual pressure cooker; observing the outer surface, we see little enough going on, with the exception of a few spurts of escaping steam. The lid was taken off, in 1640, to reveal an already seething stew which finally boiled over the pot. But, setting that control aside, we can say that in general the longer the controversies of our period lasted, the less homogeneity obtained in English theological writing. The few exceptions to the general homogeneity of Christian doctrine I have mentioned above—Taylor, Goodwin, Milton (and admittedly there were others)—wrote rather late in our period, it is worth noting.

The kind of stylistic analysis I am engaged in handles both of these difficulties very nicely by simply admitting the limits of the analogy between a single man and a group of men. On the one hand, it allows us to see the commonly and generally accepted fundamentals as areas where men did not exercise individuating choice. On the other, it allows us to account for the varieties of doctrine, ecclesiology, and practice which blossomed late in our period, particularly among the sectaries, as well as the differences between early and late Puritans. Indeed, it allows us to understand those oddities of Milton's belief that seem to separate him from Puritanism or, at the very least, make it difficult to argue that Milton was doctrinally a Puritan, as the fullest expression of certain tendencies in the Puritan style of regarding and representing the universe. My method seeks to dissolve that brick wall which students of Puritanism customarily hit when they turn to apply their analysis to Milton.

Part I: DOCTRINES

Section One: Bowing at the Name of Jesus

And being found in fashion as a man, he humbled himself, and became obedient unto death, even the death of the cross. Wherefore God also hath highly exalted him, and given him a name which is above every name: That at the name of Jesus every knee should bow, of things in heaven, and things on earth, and things under the earth; And that every tongue should confess that Jesus Christ is Lord, to the glory of God the Father.
—*Philippians 2.8-11*

Chapter 1: ANTIPAPAL AGITATORS: THE DYNAMICS OF A CONTROVERSY

In *Paradise Lost,* Milton dramatized a reading of the text from Philippians (enunciated in his *De Doctrina*), which in at least one important way resembles the Roman Catholic much more closely than the Protestant interpretation. Like papal apologists at the seminary at Rheims, this radical Protestant poet stated that Christ was exalted "partly of his own merit,"[1] a view which first Protestant champions and later antiestablishment Puritans had questioned in print for more than half a century. This apparent anomaly can only be explained by a careful study of the unfolding history of controversy over these words and the process whereby a battle between Rome and the apologists of the English Church turned into an internecine affair between Puritans and members of the Laudian establishment.

Because this is the first controversy I take up, let me point out that, generically, controversies are generated by protestors whose habits of setting groups of men at odds with each other is matched by an intellectual habit of pulling ideas apart. Specifically, advanced or radical Protestants started the fight over this text at the same time they severed God from man and, as a parallel, Christ's divine from his human nature. Secondly, controversy crystalizes out differences, reveals assumptions and implications, and in the process allows men to see and understand more clearly what they think; if differences of opinion are in many ways unfortunate, they do have the value of making positions and options clear to men who must decide. In a general way, the whole bulk of Puritan theologizing had much this self-revelatory effect; specifically, this controversy beautifully illustrates the way Puritans uncovered ideas at the same time they were advancing an apocalyptic rather than a liturgical (magical) reading of these verses. Generally, protestors feel that they have to start fights because they are unhappy about the way things are in this world; the Puritans embodied that truth in theological doctrine during their discussion of these words, for they casually expressed their disaffected otherworldliness by subordinating the carnality of Christ's passion to the overarching sovereignty of the Father. Finally, as the history of this controversy abundantly illustrates, the mere process of controverting doctrines or ideas can have an immensely reassuring effect, even upon the unhappy and disaffected. Once they could see with blinding clarity what they believed (and what that belief implied),

the Puritans became noticeably more happy about the world they had revealed to themselves. Milton came of intellectual age precisely at the moment when Puritans were evolving this new optimism. Ever advancing the
frontiers of Puritan thought, he logically extended this optimistic drift by
arguing that some human actions can (pace Puritan orthodoxy) be meritorious. That he gained this sense of merit as a result of the dynamics of
Puritan controversy rather than from the pages of Roman Catholic sources
becomes clear when we notice all of the other myriad ways in which his
dramatization of this text exemplifies and expresses the Puritan point of
view.

Our text for this chapter, the epistle for Palm Sunday in the *Book of
Common Prayer,* is for two reasons a good point of departure. It was,
first of all, the principal proof text in a controversy, initially waged by the
champions of English Protestantism against Roman Catholic adversaries,
which developed into a dogfight between Puritans and members of the
Laudian establishment. Its history, therefore, shows us how the Puritan
platform of the mid-seventeenth century was rooted in and a radicalization
of Protestant argument of an earlier era. Secondly, Christ is, for any Christian theologian, the center of his thought. The ways he talks about Christ
radiate out into his discourse on all other matters. It seems wise to begin
at that center in this first chapter, and record how men developed polarized
ways of talking about Christ.[2]

Many of the differences between the Roman Catholic and Protestant
English conceptions of Christ emerged in the way translators "Englished"
a single conjunction. The Catholic seminary at Rheims rendered the Vul-
gate phrase *"propter quod et Deus exaltavit"* as "For the which thing God
also hath exalted him"[3] while James's authorized committees, in reply,
translated αιὸ κὰι ὁ Θευξ αυνου υπερυφωαευ as "wherefore God also hath exalted him." "Wherefore," probably something of a compromise since it
was the work of a committee, diminishes or partly obscures the sense of
causal, chronological linking which Rheims's "for the which thing" emphasizes. The most advanced or radical Protestants who attacked the Catholic
version, men like the almost nonconforming Thomas Cartwright, probably
would have preferred even less causality than the word "wherefore" implies. If these differences seem slight, nonetheless they were the stuff of
theological war. The reason is simple; insofar as one emphasized the causal
and chronological connection between Christ's act of humiliation and
God's act of exalting him, one seemed to attribute *merit* to Christ and his
submission; in contrast, as the Catholic annotator upon this text observed,
"Calvin doth so abhor the name of merit in Christian men toward their
own salvation, that he wickedly and unlearnedly denieth Christ himself to
have deserved or merited anything for himself" (p. 529). The battle was
on. Calvin did emphasize the unimaginable mercy of God in descending to

save poor sinners and to stress that love even further he underscored man's total inability to merit anything through his own actions. To attribute merit to Christ was to attribute merit to a being with at least a partly human nature: "the expression, *for this cause,* denotes here a consequence rather than a reason," Calvin argued, because "it would otherwise follow, that a man could merit Divine honours, and acquire the very throne of God—which is not merely absurd, but even dreadful to make mention of." God was not compelled by any causal "reason" to exalt his Son. "For it is the design of the Holy Spirit, that we should, in the death of Christ, see, and taste, and ponder, and feel, and recognize nothing but God's unmixed goodness, and the love of Christ toward us."[4] To posit a causal connection between Christ's gesture of humiliation and God's gesture of exalting him was to diminish the force of God's gesture of "unmixed goodness" and to imply that Christ may have humbled himself for personal gain rather than love of us. "This passage has given occasion to sophists, or rather they have seized hold of it, to allege that Christ merited first for himself, and afterwards for others . . . ," Calvin sneered. "Who does not see that this is a suggestion of Satan—that Christ suffered upon the cross, that he might acquire for himself, by the merit of his work, what he did not possess?" (p. 59). In short, positing a causal connection here reduced the effect of God's love and impugned Christ's motives. From Thomas Cartwright's point of view, Calvin endeavored "to hold men wholly in the consideration of the love of Christ towards them, in that he will have all that, which either he did or suffered, to be carried to the price of our redemption only. Wherefore to say that Christ by his works merited for himself is to diminish the love of God and of Christ toward us."[5]

The idea that to attribute merit to Christ was to attribute merit to men may strike one as odd logic; after all, many theologians feel that Christ was more than man. Yet that was unmistakably the position which Calvin's English disciples took. "Calvin," William Fulke observed, "as zealous of the glory of God, to whom only our salvation is to be ascribed, abhorreth the name of merit in any man toward his own salvation."[6] Cartwright added bluntly: "That Christ according to his manhood deserved not the glory whereunto he was exalted is an evident plain doctrine" (p. 499), and Fulke went on to spell out the logic, arguing that from the Catholic annotator's "opinion it followeth that a man may merit divine honor and the throne of God himself, which is blasphemous" (p. 627).

One could only make the "blasphemous" argument, "dreadful to make mention of," by splitting Christ's humanity from his divinity. In their eagerness to attack Rome and strain after controversial gnats, that is precisely what these radical Protestants did, projecting the theological fragmentation which resulted back upon their opponents. The glory of exaltation is "due to our Savior Christ's divinity and not merited by his suffering

in his humanity" was the way Fulke put it, offering as proof "his prayer,
John 17.5. Glorify me O Father with that glory which I had with thee before the world was made" (p. 627). Cartwright argued that "unless you
will make the cause come after the effect," you must argue that the "works
that [Christ] wrought cannot be causes of his felicity." Rather, Christ was
"chosen and predestinate unto it before the beginning of the world, when
he had deserved nothing" (p. 500). He referred his readers to Augustine,
who taught that "God's *election or reprobation, is never made in regard
of works foreseen and to come.* And even in this very cause of our Savior
Christ, [Augustine] teacheth that he was chosen of God, not in regard of
works, but of grace" (p. 500). Andrew Willet, the most moderate and
thorough of the antipapal writers, arguing that "all glory that Christ hath,
was from everlasting due to his person, because he is the eternal Son of
God," and noting that "this glory was due unto Christ so soon as he was
incarnate by the right of his Godhead," concluded that "he merited not
his glorification by his death." To argue that Christ merited his exaltation
would be to argue that "he also merited the hypostatical union"; however
"his humanity deserved not to be united to the Godhead." Hence, Willet
concluded in a balanced way, "the divine glory which Christ hath, was not
merited, but his own it was from the beginning, which glory the human
nature in Christ is made partaker of, not for any merit, but because it is
united to the Godhead in the same person."[7] One nature was joined to the
other because it was a "partaker" of that other nature; overall, however, the
human nature certainly did not merit anything at all.

Before I go on to show how the microscope of systematic theology magnified these matters into a vast web of distinctions, let me pause to comment on two ways in which these controversialists had already begun to
split the divine from the human nature of Christ in an effort to emphasize
God's overarching mercy and keep Christ's motives pure; Calvin had been
involved in much the same gesture when he split God off from man. These
advanced or radical Protestant controversialists tended, when speaking
about Christ's love, to deny his humanity, conflating him rather with the
Father as "pure deity": thereby they moved the mediator and his gesture
away from man. Secondly, they emphasized that Christ was divine before
the world began; thereby they moved the issue of Christ's submission and
his exaltation out of the matrix of chronological, human history or away
from man in a historical sense. These tendencies became habitual mental
gestures for a later generation of Puritan theologians and flowered in
Milton. As a mature poet, he would focus almost exclusively on the divine
nature of "the Eternal Son" in one great poem and upon his human nature
in another; thereby he poetically segregated, as Woodhouse would put it,
nature from grace or divine from human, in good Puritan style.[8] Clearly
in line with these tendencies is the shape of book three of *Paradise Lost,*

where the Son (who has not yet achieved his human names, given him in time), submits and is exalted before the story of the world begins in the poem. Since we, as readers, have not experienced the events of the fall, the Son's gesture remains "uncaused" in our minds. And if that fact makes the Father's talk about "justice" seem gratuitously harsh and unpleasant—as indeed it has for countless students of the poem—it also makes the Son's gesture the more magnificent because so clear of any recognizable human motive. That is, Milton incarnates Puritan theological tendencies in his poem by placing the events of book three before his version of creation and before the story of the fall, "before the world began." Moreover, in doing so, Milton achieves a remarkably compelling portrait of the Son and his *motiveless* love, even if that emphasis comes at the expense of making the Father seem unpleasant and even unloving.

Not only did the anti-Catholic English split Christ's motives for humbling himself from his act, but they also sneered at the Catholics' motives for humbling themselves in bowing at the name of Jesus. In their view, physical actions could be "masks" for hypocrisy or simple ignorance and error. Cartwright put the matter in his characteristically blunt way when he charged the Roman Catholics that "this suppleness of your knees, in *bowing at the name of Jesus,* is nothing but a mask to hide the starkness and numbness of all the joints of your soul. . . . For it is well known, that your knees, which are camel-like in the courtesy which you give unto this name, are jointless and elephant-like in your obedience unto his precepts" (p. 500). A somewhat more sophisticated, less openly hostile way of attacking motive was adopted by Fulke, and quoted or paraphrased by Willet: "capping and kneeling at the name of Jesus is of itself an indifferent thing, and therefore may be used superstitiously as in popery, where the people stoop at the sound of the name when it is read, not understanding either what it meaneth, or what is read concerning him." While genuflection is indifferent, "due reverence may be yielded to our savior without any such outward ceremony of capping and kneeling" (Fulke, p. 628; Willet, p. 411). Cartwright as well pointed out that Catholics, responding to the sound of the name only without understanding the meaning of the Latin, might give the same reverence to other biblical characters named Jesus as they give to Christ. The Catholics argued, in Fulke's words, that they did not "honor those things nor count them holy for their matter, color, sound, etc., but for respect and relation they have to our savior ," but Fulke replied that such a distinction between physical reality and spiritual intent was "too short a cloak to cover your idolatry." Much the same argument, he noted, had been advanced by the ancient, idolatrous Israelites on behalf of their golden calf and Jeroboam's calf. "It is not sufficient to say, such things bring us to the remembrance and apprehension of Christ by sight, hearing and use of the same signs." Indeed, he opposed this use of objects, which may be perceived by the senses, to "religion and God's service" (p. 628). Willet took the moderate position that the English Church neither bound "any of necessity to use this reverence to the name of Jesus as the Papists do . . . neither do we judge and condemn those that do use it, being free from superstition, and grounded in knowledge, and careful not to give offense; for superstition and offensive ignorance is not in any case to be defended" (p. 411).

The Protestant propagandists, in short, portrayed the Catholics as reverencing the things of this world rather than higher and spiritual matters, ignorantly or erroneously bowing to the wrong Jesus because they know no Latin, or hypocritically hiding evil motives under physical acts. Virtue goes hand in hand with truth, error with hypocrisy. The intellectual's bias is clear in these remarks. Indeed, even the Established Church's theory of "matters of indifference," which Willet makes moderating use of, emphasizes intellect, for the proper use of bowing (as opposed to its improper use) depended on right understanding. Motive is guided by knowledge, in the Protestant view, and both motive and knowledge are without question more important than physical actions or things. Hence, the Protestants always wanted to be "grounded in knowledge," wrote long, potentially tedious theological tracts, and split such fine hairs. In effect, they severed motive from action, then exalted the spiritual over the fleshly. Aesthetically and philosophically, they became iconoclasts, smashing the images to which people bowed; however, iconoclasm can have political and economic implications as well. The seemingly arcane question of bowing at the name of Jesus eddied out into, or fitted in with, much larger, much more pragmatic and homely matters of behavior.

Attacking the practice of physically bowing at the name of Jesus went hand in hand with denying that Christ had merit. Both positions tended to sever Christ's divinity from his humanity. It is well to explore this fragmentation a bit further, however, even at the risk of repetition, because in attacking the physical, liturgical gesture, Protestants began to choose which of several was that "name above all names." Moreover, when they chose names, they chose a tone of voice as well. The question was, what was that highest name? Defenders of genuflection argued that it was Jesus. Opponents noted that Jesus was a name given him in time as he was a man; a name like Christ, denominating his eternal office, was greater. Gervase Babington initiated a line of argument which linked the name Jesus almost exclusively with his humanity, Christ with the eternal office of mediator: "how could that name be a name above all names, which so many had as well as he?" he queried, referring to other biblical personages who had the name of Jesus. "Therefore needs by name must be meant some other thing . . . even power, authority, rule and government, which is in Christ above all others. Secondly, this title [of Christ rather than Jesus] showeth his office, for it signifieth anointed."[9] Titles of office, moreover, are more important than personal surnames; "for whether is greater, *Henry,* a proper name common to many of his subjects, or King, a name of office, peculiar to him; *Mary,* or Queen; *John,* or Earl and Lord? As then *Henry* and *King* be, so is *Jesus* and *Christ.*" Babington supported his thesis with two texts, Luke 2.11 and Matthew 1.16, where, he argued, the angels announced not only the birth of "*a Jesus, or a savior,*" but added, for distinction and elevation, "which is Christ the Lord." In other texts, he notes, men objected to Christ's calling himself Christ, but not to his calling himself Jesus. In short, Babington began to suggest that the two names, Christ and Jesus, might be distinguished one from the other, that they named somewhat different entities and had different values. The manner in which he conducts this argument, if repetitious, is illuminating: "In the tenth of *John* they would have stoned him for saying he was the Son of *God,* and called it blasphemy, but they did not for the name of *Jesus.* In *Luke* they demand of him, *Art thou the very Christ,* not art thou *Jesus,* for they so called him, without offense: and when they heard this answer they rent their clothes, thereby declaring how far greater it was to be *Christ,* than to have the literal name of *Jesus*" (p. 246). While Babington distinguished, very carefully, between the names of Christ, without separating, verbally, the natures of Christ, a less balanced, more combative writer could in making the same argument seem verbally to sever the persons. Thus, for example, when Cartwright charged the Roman Catholic practice was "pernicious in regard to the suspicion that it may move of the inequality of the persons in Trinity" (p. 500) because it seems to accord greater honor to the Son, he could only do so really, by first severing them himself.

If advanced and radical Protestants preferred a Christ to a Jesus, there were other names they thought highly of also. William Whitaker queried his Roman Catholic opponents, "will you never once stir your caps or bow your knees when God is named? Is this your religion?"[10] The term God is, of course, ambiguous to a trinitarian; Willet quoted a remark by Fulke which shows the ambiguity, while attacking the "superstitious" Roman practice of "sitting and not veiling at the name of Christ, Emanuel, God the Father, the Son, and the Holy Ghost, and bowing only at the name of Jesus" (Fulke, p. 628; Willet, p. 411). Cartwright was of much the same opinion that "there ought to be no other honor or reverence given unto [the name Jesus], than unto the name of Christ, of Lord, of God" (p. 500). Yet if "God" refers to the Father, Son, and Holy Ghost, it is highly unusual to find any theologian referring to "God the Son" and so, when we hear the word "God," we are most likely to think of "the Father." A phrase like "God so loved the world that he gave his only begotten Son"— a phrase important to a theologian who wishes (like Calvin and his followers) to exalt God's love—makes the equation between "God" and "Father" as opposed to "Son" explicit. It would be an impossible task to prove that Puritans used the term "God" (common enough in all theological writing) more often than non-Puritans or that they used it oddly, in contexts which clearly seem to discuss only the Son. It is my impression that both assertions are true, but the statistical evidence requisite to prove it would take a lifetime to assemble. However, insofar as both are true, they suggest that the Puritans not only shunned "Jesus," but talked about the Son in ways which made him seem unusually like his Father.

If so much is speculative, there is some much firmer verbal evidence. When Babington linked the name above all names with the attributes of "power, authority, rule, and government" he uttered a Protestant commonplace. Moreover, he mentioned attributes which pertain primarily to the Father and which will operate most clearly on the Day of Judgment. If the Catholics interpreted this text liturgically, the Protestants pressed on the millennial implications when paternal justice would conclude. Fulke pointed out the difference between the liturgical orientation of the Catholic annotator and his own understanding that the text "pertaineth to the subjection of all creatures to the judgment of Christ, when not only Turks and Jews, which now yield no honor to Jesus, but even the devils themselves shall be constrained to acknowledge that he is their judge" (p. 628). Paul had argued that Christ came to set us free from the bondage of the Law, but these Pauline theologians could, in heat, easily describe him as "judge." And if for many theologians Christ is the suffering servant, for Cartwright, in contrast, his name should signify first and foremost "his authority, and whatsoever is glorious and excellent within him"; similarly, the word "knee" does not refer to "the member of the body, whereby men give a signification of reverence towards the persons whom they honor, but (by a borrowed speech) the subjection and bending of all creatures unto the infinite power of Christ" (p. 500). The "kneeing and curtsying here spoken of is performed as well by the wicked and disobedient as by the holy and obedient spirits" (p. 501); Cartwright is not interested in loving adoration but rather in subjection by external compulsion and the constraining power of God. Babington wound up his remarks with some revealingly jubilant, authoritarian phrases: to Christ's "rule and government shall be subject angels in heaven, men in earth, and devils under the earth. This is to bow the knee to him, and this is for him to have a name above all names" (p. 245).

The Puritans, remarked New, were "always giving God the glory";[11] thereby he evoked both a central theological bias of their writing and their marked preference for singing psalms of praise. The note had been struck as early as Luther's Protestant battle hymn with its initial image of massive power: a mighty fortress is our God, strong and sure, as Puritan preachers reiterated, to save. If that trait emerges clearly in all this talk about Christ the judge as well, it is important to notice further how smoothly it gets

conjoined with talk about the millennium and paternal justice. God created
the world as his first exercise of power and he will recreate the "New
Heav'n and Earth, wherein the just shall dwell" again when "God shall be
All in All" (PL, 3:335, 341). If our instinct is to think that these phrases
refer primarily to the Father and to suspect paternal bias, the Puritan emphasis upon the eternal mercy of Christ, its function even "before the
world began" at once provides some trinitarian color for their statements
and links the Son in another way with the Father's attributes.

It is not, therefore, very surprising that when a liberal-minded, mildly
reformist young man, trained by a Puritan pastor and a notable Presbyterian tutor, set out to write of the morning of Christ's nativity, he would
portray his babe as manifesting a muscular power to "controul the damned
crew" ("On the Morning of Christ's Nativity," l. 228). Admittedly, it was
not a very Puritanic thing to sing of God's entrance into this world and
time, as Martz has already suggested;[12] the reformist Puritans didn't like
this world and preferred to keep their ideals well removed from it and to
stress the "eternal" aspects of the Son. I shall later point out how this
logically eventuated in attacks even upon Christmas. What we have first
to realize is that Milton's sensibility had not yet fully taken shape and
that he was always his own sort of Puritan. Still, even while attempting
this non-Puritanic poetic gesture, Milton manifests Puritanic stresses and
emphases; several critics have been struck by and have remarked upon the
babe's almost physical, cosmic strength. In Milton's manger he is not help-
less and the object of pity; rather he suggests even then the "power and
authority" he will exercise when "time will run back and fetch the age of
gold" (l. 135). The center of this poem pivots on millennial expectations,
and the latter phrase beautifully exemplifies the tendency to scramble
chronology which commonly functions in "eternal" poetic visions. It is
matched by the temporal ambiguity of the first "this," which points two
ways simultaneously in "This is the Month, and this the happy morn"
(l. 1). That atemporal ordering of events persisted in Milton's writing, embedded deeply in the structure of *Paradise Lost*.

The Puritans preferred to think about Christ who was eternal and so un-
contaminated by the things of this world, because Jesus suffered and humbled himself. If the divine movement of downward love began with the
nativity, it reached its nadir (from the Puritan point of view) at the crucifixion. A poet like George Herbert could happily contemplate that moment, in such a poem as "Easter-wings," because Easter signified for him
a conjoining of diverse things: sin and salvation, death and resurrection,
God and man, sign and thing signified. "With thee let me combine" to rise,
he sings in a poem which, even in its shaping becomes a thing of this world.

Lord, who createdst man in wealth and store,
    Though foolishly he lost the same,
        Decaying more and more
            Till he became
                Most poore:
                With thee
            O let me rise
        As larks, harmoniously,
    And sing this day thy victories:
Then shall the fall further the flight in me.

My tender age in sorrow did beginne:
    And still with sicknesses and shame
        Thou didst so punish sinne,
            That I became
                Most thinne.
                With thee
            Let me combine
        And feel this day thy victorie:
    For, if I imp my wing on thine,
Affliction shall advance the flight in me. [13]

Milton, in contrast, could not finish his Passion poem, and what he did write was dismal; the subject didn't suit him, and he never seems to have managed to set right what he began in youth. Herbert's "Easter-wings" is much closer to Richard Crashaw's hymn on the nativity both aesthetically and theologically. If Herbert hopes to "combine with" and thereby imitate God, Crashaw's babe "lifts earth to heaven, stoopes heav'n to earth." [14] The theological two-way street is matched by a feeling that one can move one's attention from the things of this world to an "*O altitudo!*" If the shape of Herbert's poem and the falling and rising tone which it generates catches the spirit of the event it celebrates, Crashaw's focus moves from an event in time—the manger—to an eternal significance, in ways which Martz has outlined. Milton, in contrast, paints a cosmic view, in the Nativity Ode, then focuses down on the manger. And in his poem, all movement is from top down; there is no countervailing ascent, lifting, and flight from this world. God comes to save man, but man cannot raise himself, can hardly even be raised to meet him. Man sinks into the things of this world unless first he has had the cosmic vision, traced out the mind of God and the absolute, purified reality; then a man can, as a reformist, come back into this world to set it square with God's plan. Doctrine must, however, precede use; the eternal, divine vision must be tapped before one has a platform for reform. And the best model for reform is the kingdom of the saints, that state which will emerge after time is destroyed, that state which mirrors the first paradisical state before time began. For then God's might is most manifest as he, in a top-down gesture, constrains all creatures to participate in perfect harmony.

Chapter 2: THEOLOGICAL MATTER EQUALS CONTROVERSIAL MANNER: SOME ANOMALOUS PURITANS

So far I have quoted five men of diverse religious sensibility and outlook all talking much the same language, making much the same points, and striking much the same tone in opposition to Rome. All of them were, in their age, "advanced or radical Protestants," since all took up arms against the worldwide popish conspiracy, which some Englishmen believed threatened their nation. Not all Englishmen did. Many still followed the old ways quietly in isolated parishes; some were, like Thomas Campion and the seminarists at Rheims, more militant in defense of Catholicism. Many simply drifted into the new church, a few felt strongly that it was an improvement, and a very few felt so strongly that they sat down to write books about the problem, as Cartwright, Fulke, Willet, Whitaker, and Babington did. It is not surprising that five men who made that choice made other choices in unison. They were all engaged in an attack upon a prior figure of authority, participating in that oedipal guerrilla warfare aimed at a papa and his papacy which was the Reformation, and so they all sound a bit strident and aggressive, like sons attacking their fathers. Their sneering, jibing, complaining tone fits together, psychologically, with something which seems nearly its opposite—hymns to paternity and their good father in heaven. Oedipally aggressive men often value fatherhood highly; indeed, they often seem to knock down a father-figure in order that they may themselves become fathers. Quite obviously, the Father was the center of Puritan theology, which we often term "paternal" and "patriarchal." As they began to dissolve the Son, clothe him in paternal adjectives and attributes, and "give God the glory," they initiated a process which would flower fully in Milton's explicit subordination of the Son to the Father as well as in the de-Christianized deism of more prominent Restoration theologians. The first step in that process was to sever the humanity of Christ from his divinity, the Son from the Father, and divine mercy from divine justice, in a

controversy which severed Catholics from Protestants. By the end of the
process, most of Christ's humiliation, suffering, and servantship had been
squeezed out of him and he emerged a glorious champion fit to represent
the aims of these aggressive men.

But, if these antipapal controversialists were in many ways alike, set
off from the generality of Englishmen by their controversial spirit, they
were also different. Thomas Cartwright was the most advanced or radical
(as well as the most strident and curt in tone) for he came very close to
nonconformity with even the English Protestant establishment and during
the same period that, for example, William Perkins was hacking out the
main outlines of Puritan "federal theology," established an essentially
"Presbyterian" church on an island away from the English mainland.[1]
Such men were ahead of their time; Cartwright's book on this controversy,
emblematically, was published in 1618, thirteen years after he died. They
were pressing Protestant principles farther than more solidly conforming
members of the English Church (Willet is a pre-eminent example because
of his encyclopedic moderation) were yet willing to go. The effects of
what men like Cartwright and Perkins did would become apparent, like
Cartwright's book itself, only after the fact. Setting up little islands of
church discipline and Puritan theological analysis was, as these men wrote,
outside the mainstream of English Protestant activity; but it would not
remain isolated for long.

Before I record that shift, let me consider some "Puritans" who were
less "advanced or radical" contemporaries of these five. Thomas Adams
and Henry Airay did not attack Rome; moreover, they spoke a slightly
different language from the antipapal controversialists and made slightly
different points. I have to consider these men here because they did make
an interrelated series of choices which differed from our assertive quintet.
I thus begin a series of contrastive exercises which are essential to my aim
of documenting not only what choices were open to theological writers
but what happened when men opted for one or another theological style.
Airay and Adams are especially interesting because Adams has often been
termed by scholars not simply a Calvinist but even a Puritan preacher while
Airay was, in his own time, suspected of "preciseness." In many ways these
men were both "Puritanic" as were many English Protestants; Calvin
appealed to a wide range of English theologians. But the differences in
doctrine, tone, and controversial fervor allow us to distinguish these men
as less "advanced or radical" than Cartwright, Fulke, Whitaker, Willet, and
Babington while at the same time helping us to see more clearly through
contrast what it was to be a thoroughgoing Puritan.

When Thomas Adams turned his attention to our controversial point,
he focused upon the unimaginable mercy of God in saving poor wretched
sinners (as any Calvinist would); however, he chose to develop that con-

ception of sin into a rhapsody honoring Christ as a Jesus or Savior from sin. He chose, in short, to extol the name Jesus above all names, "a principal name, both in regard of God and of us," and naturally and smoothly moved on to other, un-Puritanic propositions. [2]

Adams shows that he was fully aware that earlier theologians had linked the name Jesus with mercy and suffering, Christ with power, dominion, and glory. He understood the choices and options open to him. Although God has many titles which may seem more glorious, "yet he esteems none of them like this [Jesus]." The other names "have in them more power and majesty but not so much mercy, not so much of that wherein God delights to be magnified above all his works; and indeed, the greater mercy, the greater glory." Here he merely twists the Puritanic concern for God's glory around slightly, connecting it with mercy. Hence, Jesus is "a principal name," a name above all names, "in regard of God" (p. 1199).

It is also a principal name in regard to us because "we have no other name to hold by." He works from the chronology of sacred history when he argues that "there is goodness and greatness enough in the name Jehovah; but we merited so little good and demerited so much evil, that in it there had been small comfort for us. But with the name *Jesus,* there is comfort in the name of God, without it none" (p. 1200). Jehovah is, of course, the name of the deity in the Old Testament, and it was only when God came into time and became Jesus that the terror of the law was mitigated. Calvinism is clearly a "comfortable" doctrine, as its exponents claimed, when it shows how God "will interpose *Jesus* whom he loves betwixt his wrath and our sins which he hates." With a neat turn of words, Adams shows how mercy surpasses justice; "as *suprema lex, salus,* so *supremum Nomen, Jesus;* the highest, the sweetest, the dearest to us of all the names of God is the name Jesus" (p. 1200). "*Salus*" is higher than the wrath of *lex talionis* just as Jesus is higher than Jehovah. Jesus then emerges as the name above all names in an argument focused on mercy rather than dominion and power and rooted in the chronological matrix of sacred history.

Choosing a name and striking a tone was no whimsical matter; it called for some theological argument. Adams, for example, felt he ought to rebut the view that Christ is as great a name as Jesus. Being anointed or "a Christ," he said, was not unique to Jesus; other men had been anointed as well, and for that matter "God cannot be anointed." Moreover, Christ was anointed to the end that he might "be a savior; *Jesus* is therefore the end, and the end is always above the means" (p. 1203). Considerable splitting of the divine attributes had to have preceded this argument, which also shows how quickly men came to agree that a particular name (as Christ or Jesus) implied particular attributes.

Just as he picked out the name Jesus to exalt, so Adams praised physically bowing at that name; the two choices fitted together. A long, Cal-

vinistic disquisition on sin eventuates, at the end of his sermon, in a
meditation on our first "duty" that "we learn to hold this name in high
respect and reverence," particularly by bowing when we hear it read.
While "the heart is indeed *primum mobile,*" the seat of those motives
which were so important to Cartwright, Fulke, Whitaker, and Willet, yet
"that queen walks not abroad without her train"; God "created corporal
organs to express without, the mental devotion that is within." Motive
reigns still, in this formulation, but, articulated in a monarchical rather than
reformist metaphor, it functions differently from the way it works in more
Puritanic writers. For it leads to a physical gesture, bowing, enjoined by
God upon us with "an oath; shall we offer to make him forsworn, giving
him no more reverence than the seats that hold us?" (p. 1203). Since motive is still queen, Adams can smoothly controvert the Catholic practice of
bowing at the sound rather than the sense of the name, and indeed, his
whole meditation attempts to demonstrate what the proper sense is. Still,
while unmistakably Protestant, Adams's remarks are in a much different
spirit, striking a tone and advancing doctrines which testify to a feeling of
homeliness about things in this world and a slightly elitist complacency
about the subordination of "her train" to the "queen."

Let me admit that, in all likelihood, had Fulke, Whitaker, or Willet set
about to defend the right use of bowing, they would probably have sounded
indistinguishable from Adams; indeed, in his more conciliatory passages,
Willet actually does. There is small doubt that Adams, had he focused on
the Catholic Church, might well have reviled it and its idolatrous practices
in exactly the same language the controversialists had; he might well have
paid a great deal more attention to names like Christ, Lord, and God—as
well as to the attributes of power, dominion, and glory—than he does here.
The umbrella of matters of indifference allowed men to go several ways
while holding many views in common. My point, which Adams's "Puritan"
reputation allows me to show in a striking way, is this: once a man chose
to move in one direction rather than another (to praise bowing rather than
Puritanically attack it, for example), a whole series of other choices were,
in effect, ready made for him. Language and theological thought matched.

Henry Airay, who produced what was probably the most lengthy Calvinistic commentary on our text, was not a contentious man. "I do not
here dispute the question, which commonly hence is moved, whether
Christ by his death and passion deserved this exaltation into glory for
himself or only for us" he remarked at one point.[3] Christopher Potter, his
pupil, editor, and memorialist, said Airay "misliked all busy disturbers of
the Church's peace and quiet . . . conformed himself to her seemly ceremonies and injunctions . . . [and was] zealous and fervent, not turbulent
and contentious." Yet he was "so sincere and unrebukable, that by some
(partly by occasion of these *Lectures*) he was defamed for preciseness"

(sig. A3 $^{\text{r and v}}$). Precise or Puritanic he was in his conviction that Christ came for us, not himself, and that popish genuflection was evil, idolatrous, ignorant, and silly. He quoted phrases like "the bare and outward capping and kneeling at the name of Jesus" (p. 354) from the controversialists while dismissing Roman practices, and like them he linked the name above all names with "glory, and honor, and majesty, and dominion over all things created" while emphasizing Christ's eternal nature: "for as before so after, and as after so before he was and is called the wisdom of God, the power of God, the true light of the world." These, and a very long list of other names the Son had before time; these were not given "unto Christ after his resurrection" (p. 345).

Still, Airay was not contentious and he came in time to enjoy at least some of the things of this world, becoming vice-chancellor of Oxford shortly before he died. He was appreciated by Potter, who ultimately became a close ally of Laud and stresses the "seemly ceremonies" of the Church (sig. A3^{r}) which were to become so important to Laud's reign. It is not therefore surprising that Airay declined to dispute points and extracted from his texts lessons in Christian piety rather than theological bludgeons and polemical armament. His tone matches his "unrebukable" yet "not turbulent and contentious" personality and contrasts with the fiery utterance of controversial writers. The difference between Airay's writing and that of the controversialists, especially when set against what biographic information we have,[4] suggests that a man's temperament was expressed by the kind of theological writing he undertook; Airay did not undertake to dispute, he wrote a softer sort of argument, and he fitted in relatively smoothly even with proto-Laudians.

If Airay did not participate in fragmenting controversy, if he did not split God from man, Christ's humanity from his divinity, Catholic from Protestant, or Puritan from Anglican, he differed from the controversialists as well by turning their basically eschatological reading of our text away from the millennium and back onto the day-to-day life of his readers. That is, he was not so utterly repelled by the things of this world as to experience an overpowering urge to think only about utopia; indeed, he took other men's utopian thoughts and brought them back down to earth. Taking, for example, the spiritualized reading of bowing at the name—"subjection and worship which all creatures ought continually to perform and which all creatures shall perform to Christ in that day" (p. 353)—Airay focuses not upon the eternal "shall" but on the daily "ought." What will happen in the final day should happen always, every day, now. "Here then is a duty prescribed, necessarily to be performed of every Christian, which is to glorify him who is exalted into the heights of glory, both in our bodies and in our spirits . . . to worship him, and to glorify his name, even to be hearers and doers of his word, to obey his will, to walk in his laws, and to keep his commandments. Not the bare and outward capping and kneeling at the name of Jesus, but principally obedience unto his will, that is named, is the honor which here he accepteth of us" (p. 354). When Airay first suggests, here, that worship is to occur in our bodies as well as in our spirits, he sounds very much as if he advocated physical bowing. Lack of contentiousness, in other words, seems at first to fit with submissive genuflection. But, as we read on we see that bowing is beside the point—truly a matter of indifference: "To obey his will is better than capping and kneeling or all outward ceremonies whatsoever" (p. 354).

If Airay differed from the controversialists by writing down-to-earth exposition—both by eschewing the fancy footwork of theological distinction-making and by turning eschatological speculation back to here and now—he was, as the last remark shows us clearly, a deep-dyed Calvinist, Protestant, and in many ways a Puritan; the charge of "preciseness" which Potter recalls did not arise from thin air. For Airay shows us what happens when an advanced or radical Protestant attempts to imitate Christ. From Thomas à Kempis on, the *imitatio* involved humiliation, service, and a childlike love. Airay is eager that we "subject ourselves unto his will" and become "doers of the word" (p. 355) but if the word was given before the fall, before time began, it is hard to imitate Christ in any very clear way; moreover the verb "subject" reminds us that the Puritan Christ exercised "power and dominion." Thus Airay's adept does not imitate the actions of Christ—serving the poor, humbling himself, etc.—so much as he conforms himself to and imitates a cosmic, timeless, peaceful, static order of perpetual adoration. Airay comes as close as a Puritan can to an imitatio; the distinctive form into which he casts the life of the adept, represented in curiously diffuse language for all his down-to-earth quality, indicates one of the characteristic limits of Puritan thought.

We can see something of the problem in Airay's choice of diction. When he turns to what we ought to do, he employs noun phrases—"obedience unto his will"—of an abstract and theoretical nature; we do not even obey; we show obedience. Other verbs—glorify, worship, be hearers and doers—function as nouns modifying yet another noun—duty—in a static, copula-laden sentence. Finally, when we do find a verb which we can act out, it tells us to "subject ourselves" to a power outside ourselves. Vigorous action and the really forceful powers lie outside the faithful, if Airay's diction can tell us anything, while we have little opportunity to act ourselves.

I shall from time to time draw similar points from the verbal constructions which the Puritans employed, although to do so systematically is impossible, given the vast bulk of their writing. Here I would like to connect Airay's habits of style with the Calvinists' fascination with concepts—election, reprobation, sanctification, justification, salvation—rather than with actions—electing, reprobating, sanctifying, justifying, saving—and argue that this sort of diction, which of necessity involves the writer in casting sentences around static, copulative verbs, coheres perfectly with their emphasis upon Christ's eternal nature. The drama upon the cross was less important to them than the theological truths and concepts it acted out. The implication that God is (in some peculiar way) especially all-powerful, the Puritan habit, in short, of always giving God the glory, meshes neatly with Airay's diction, which mutes the possibility of godly acts; the wicked can cap and kneel, we must do something much less vigorous and clear-cut. The tendency to ignore the drama of the cross, the scholarly habit of abstraction, and the emphasis on God's overarching power at the expense of man's ability to act, all reflect the Puritan predilection for an eternal vision and an eternal peace. Just as these men contended with "papa" in order properly to adore their Father, so they fought fiercely for an existence free of contention. Nowhere is the second paradox more beautifully framed than in Marvell's "Bermudas," where the sturdy rowers "kept the time" by hard work and songs about an existence in which they would not even have to pick the fruit they would eat.

I am not saying that the Puritans were never "down to earth," that they took no interest in this world, nor that they saw no conflict about them. Obviously, they took strict account of themselves and their neighbors (too strict an account from the point of view of Ben Jonson and his fellows) and they were willing to strike a blow, either literal or verbal, in the battles of the Lord. Joan Webber has observed that "radical Puritan" prose was "timebound" while "conservative Anglican" prose was always moving toward eternity.[5] Yet it seems that, before they turned their attention to this world, they first pursued an eternal vision. Only after that vision did they descend to reform this world, just as their God descended from on high. The absence of a two-way street between God and man (that is, the radical Protestant insistence upon faith rather than works) required that all motion be from the top down; that habit of mind even obtained in the order in which they preached the separate points of their sermons, for they always began with the abstractive process of deducing "doctrines" (which are eternal) and then moved on to apply those doctrines to specific "uses" in this world. Ultimately they cared a great deal about this world, but only when they approached it with the theoretical statement of the eternal nature of God—approached it, in short, from as close to God's timeless point of view as they could. One of the many things which the "epic voice" of *Paradise Lost* first does is to soar, with his song, above this fallen world so that he can see God looking down from heaven and can present things as God sees them. If, as Joseph Summers so beautifully shows, the muse's method in the first twenty-six lines involves much motion,[6] that motion swirls back and forth through time in an ascending pattern; only after this gesture can the narrator "get down to hell" and begin his story.

Chapter 3: THE CONSERVATIVE REACTION

Apparently the Puritans consolidated their theological position by the first decades of the seventeenth century in silence—or so it seems from this distance. Licensing of books no doubt played a big part in producing that quietness, but the Puritans must have kept busy. We know something about their activities from peripheral comment; we can learn a good deal more about it by noticing that a conservative reaction to Puritan positions was being articulated by members of the ecclesiastical establishment by about this time. Adams's and Airay's moderate views, different as they were, were hardened by John Boys and Lancelot Andrewes, liturgical engineers of the Laudian Church, into such a reaction as early as the first two decades of the century. These two advanced a positive case for genuflection, physical bowing, Christ's humanity and suffering, and a liturgical rather than an eschatological interpretation of the text. Between them, they came to deny that bowing was a matter of indifference and to assert, in Andrewes's words, that it was a positive "duty of the text." As fixtures of the establishment—Boys produced the standard explication of the liturgical scriptures and Andrewes was one of the jewels among the bishops—they participated in and enjoyed the things of this world, including its Church Militant, physical objects and gestures, Christ's entrance into this world and time, and the divine service now, rather than the judgment then. They furnish a striking contrast to the sort of speech and thought we have been considering, and complete the process of setting the stage for an angry, self-consciously polarized confrontation between Puritan and Anglican.

Boys, writing before 1610, yet clearly after the burst of controversy with Rome and Cartwright's radical Puritan experiment, did not debate whether Christ merited for himself at all, avoiding thereby the distinction between temporal sequence and eternal nature. He borrowed little of the Calvinist's polemical diction and he wrote in a tone even less dogmatic than that of Airay. Indeed, he "conjoined" diverse and even opposed opinions, as when he explained what the phrase "a name above all names" meant: "sometime *name* signifieth in scripture power" and "sometime name is used for honor and fame."[1] He offered scriptural examples for both these alternatives and said that, really, both were worthy of our consideration. Indeed, there were still other possible interpretations of the phrase. "S. *Ambrose* thinks that the Father gave this name to Christ as God, *Jerome,* the Greek *Scholia, Theophylact,* and many more, that he gave this name to Christ as man; other, and that most fitly, conjoin both opinions. . . . And so much is implied in the clause following, *that at the name of Jesus every knee should bow.* Christ is an appellative, *Jesus* is his proper name; now Jesus is Emanuel, *God with us,* as *S. Matthew* doth expound it in his Gospel; as *God,* then his glory was from all eternity, but as *with us,* it was in time manifested unto us" (p. 122). Boys's method here is the opposite of controversial; he articulates alternatives and then draws them together since they are most fitly "conjoined." Indeed, he is not simply joining interpretations and avoiding controversy; rather, he is making a theological point by joining God and man. That is, he so interprets the name Jesus as to draw the reader's mind forcibly to the name Emanuel, which semantically joins God with man. When he interprets the name Christ or "anointed" as an "appellative" and Jesus as the "proper name," he stresses, like Adams, the Son's participation with man "in time" as an Emanuel and de-emphasizes that eternal office for which he was anointed. He neither splits theological position from theological position through controversy, nor Christ's human from his divine nature, nor God from man.

In addition, he chooses to exalt the name Jesus because, like Adams, he thought it referred to suffering and humility rather than authoritative power and glory: "that contemptible name *Jesus,* as Pilate scoffingly, *Jesus Nazarenus rex Judaeorum,* is now so preached and praised as that it is a name far above all names" (pp. 122–23). Here he selects an illustrative example in which Jesus appears as a name to be reviled, an example drawn from the context of the crucifixion or lowest point of his suffering. Thereby he exalts humility and suffering, which he feels all Christians do when that name is "preached and praised." True, Boys thought a name might indicate power, as the controversialists had, but he notes that "in the name" may mean "through his power and help" (p. 122). To formulate God's power that way is quite different from celebrating "power and glory" which constrains all creatures to bow; divine power becomes an agent which helps *us* to do something, mediates so that *we* may act. If Boys does not compel us to choose one single interpretation of the text but rather invites us to embrace them all, his Christ does not authoritatively compel all the world to bow through the exercise of his power upon them, but rather, as mediator, acts through them and provides "help." His Christ is not only suffering but, as syntactic agent, a servant, and Boys's noncontroversial tone and manner matches exactly his theological conception. Like his Jesus, Boys was himself providing a service when he set out to explicate the liturgical scriptures for his Church and his nation.

It is not surprising, given the marked difference between on the one hand Boys's views about theological matters, his prose style, and his liturgical concerns and on the other the Puritans' doctrines, style, and eschatological bias, that Boys edged toward the position that we must bow to the name during divine service rather than at the last day. Genuflection is "an

harmless yet not fruitless ceremony, which may be well used, and not to
be misliked" (p. 123), he thought. First he states the case for "indifference," it is "harmless," then counters the tendency of the controversialists'
aggression, it is (negatively) "not fruitless" and (more positively) "may be
well used" and finally "not to be misliked." If he spends three phrases
working his way up to his point and then phrases that point in a distinctly
negative and conciliatory way characteristic of his tone and his theology,
the fact remains that the "submissiveness" of both tone and thought
eventuates in the belief that we must submit ourselves physically to God by
bowing at his name.

Lancelot Andrewes took a much firmer line than Boys and expressed it
in the most concrete diction of any commentator in this controversy, distinctive when compared to other writers yet typical of his preaching style
throughout. "God requireth a reverent carriage, even of the body itself; and
namely, this service of the knee, and that to His Son's Name." The require-
ment was no matter of indifference but a "duty of the text."[2] Truth (here
reverence for Jesus) must express itself physically just as Andrewes's
method of analysis and prose style were both extremely physical. Andrewes
strikes us as one of the great expositors of Scripture because he regarded
the text as an almost physical emblem expressing truths intellectually, verbally, and even visually. Stylistically, Andrewes had the habit of investing
his own words as well as those from Scripture with a similar physical life
and existence independent of their meaning.

For example, as early as the "sum" which sets out the plan of the sermon, Andrewes begins to focus upon the key conjunction, *"propter quod."*
Although he had been deeply involved in the authorized translation of
1611, he ignored its "wherefore" on Easter Sunday 1614 and emphasized
causality here and (by repeating the phrase as a dominant rhetorical peg)
throughout his sermons: "'For this cause, God hath exalted Him,' saith the
Text; 'Him,' that is, Christ. And, 'for this cause' are we now here, to celebrate this exalting" (p. 323). The "cause" in the first clause refers quite
clearly to Christ's past action. The "cause" in the second, parallel clause
can refer either to Christ's resurrection (which is the reason that Christians
gather for worship at Easter) or to us (as we conform ourselves to the pattern of Christ through bowing). The ambiguity is central to the sermon; the
text, as Andrewes explicates it, manifests a pattern of descent and ascent,
of humiliation and exaltation (the rhetorical parallelism, involved in repeating "for this cause," serving to heighten the paradoxical nature of
what happened to Christ) and, further, a pattern in which we place ourselves parallel to Christ in his humiliation. Aware of the studied ambiguity
in just this short, early phrase, we can then go on to see that the four parts
of the rest of the sermon fit together into two patterns—manifesting divine
descent and ascent as well as drawing a parallel between God and man.

The first of the four parts focuses on the "cause" of Christ's exaltation—
his humiliation—while the second, third, and fourth concern his exaltation.
Andrewes sees that arrangement physically expressed in the text itself:
"That of His humbling was dispatched in one verse; This, of His exalting
hath no less than three. So the amends is large, three to one." Moreover,
the physical structure expresses theological truth: "For *non sicut delictum,
sic donum,* saith he elsewhere, so here, not as His humbling, so was His
exalting, but more" (p. 328). In addition, if we break the last three sections down, we see a balanced parallel between Christ and us; section two
considers Christ's personal exaltation, three and four the exaltation of his
name. His name is exalted by the bowing of knees (section three) and by
the confession of tongues (section four). Since we bow (and thereby humble ourselves) and exalt ourselves (by confession) we follow, in sections
three and four, the downward, then upward movement of humiliation and
exaltation which Christ followed in sections one and two. Were we to divide the two stanzas of Herbert's "Easter-wings" evenly in two, the four
half stanzas would physically represent the patterns of this sermon, patterns which Andrewes finds both semantically and physically expressed in
his text as well as in gestures: "What better way, or more proper, than by
our humility to exalt Him Who for His humility was exalted?" he queried
in his transition from section two to three (p. 333). And he ended his sermon by tracing out the parallel between Christ's exaltation and our own:
"but of us, 'I hope for better things,' that by our humble carriage and obedience . . . we will set ourselves some way to exalt Him, in this His day
of exaltation; which, as it will tend to His glory, so will He turn it to matter of our glory, and that in His kingdom of glory. . . . That so we may
end, as the text ends"—exalted (p. 343).

If we do end as the text does, then the text itself becomes a sort of map
or pattern of our Christian lives as well as an almost physical emblem of
Christ's humiliation and exaltation and of the three to one ratio between
them. Yet, more fundamentally, the four parts of this sermon simply plod
after the order of the text itself, phrase by phrase. When we perceive the
diverse orders in Andrewes's sermon, we come to understand the skill with
which Andrewes explicates Scripture, for in effect, by elaborating upon the
order of the text, Andrewes has revealed not one but two emblems or
physical patterns in it (i.e., the two orders or patterns in his exposition).
That is the essence of Andrewes's exegetical method here and throughout
his preaching.

Bits of the text become, in Andrewes's hands, a curious sort of thing,
leading an existence almost independent of scriptural context and seman-
tic meaning. *"Propter quod"* which is "the *axis* and *cardo,* the very point
whereupon the whole text [and Andrewes's sermon] turneth" (p. 325)
gets transformed in this way. For example, to underscore the immensity

of Christ's humiliation, Andrewes breaks it down in the first section into eight points or "extensives, and intensives" which "put together, will I trust make up a perfect *propter quod*" (pp. 327-28). To much the same effect, Andrewes earlier pointed out that "for one of mean estate to be humble, is no great praise. . . . But, *in alto nihil altum sapere:* . . . for the King of Kings, for Him, to shew this great humility, that is a *propter quod* indeed" (pp. 325-26). The effect of talking about "a *propter quod*" is not simply to transform it into a sort of noun with a kind of physical existence. By gathering the "extensives, and intensives" together in it, Andrewes almost physically compresses the extremity of Christ's humiliation and the mystery of his magnificent descent into that entity. The gesture of humiliating himself becomes "a *propter quod*" in deed. Paradoxically, while the phrase semantically suggests a logical connection between two actions, the logic Andrewes labors to expound is illogical. Such a great exaltation could only occur to one who humiliated himself so inconceivably. A "*propter quod,*" then, expresses a divine mystery in a concrete noun.

In the second section, Andrewes plays the same trick with the Latin preposition "*super.*" Christ's personal exaltation "hath a *super,* whither or whereunto" (p. 328), while concerning Christ's name, Andrewes speaks "of the giving first, And then of the *super,* of it" (p. 330). If "*propter quod*" expresses the immensity of Christ's humiliation, "*super*" shows the greatness of his exaltation: "*Super* is not thither only, but above and beyond it. From death to life; nay, *super,* more than so. Not to Lazarus' life, to die again, but to life immortal. . . . From shame to glory? only that? Nay, *super,* 'to the glory of the Father,' that is, glory, that shall 'never fade,' as all here shall" (p. 329).

Not only does Andrewes thus construct physical signs of the "extensives, and intensives" or find truths in the ratio between the number of verses in each part of the text, but he uncovers rhetorical patterns expressive of those truths in scriptural syntax. For example, he makes an almost Euphuistic period of our text when he points out how humiliation and exaltation "answer one another: For *humiliavit* there, here is *exaltavit;* For *Ipse* there, *Deus,* 'God' here; For *Ipse Se, Deus Ipsum;* 'He humbled Himself;' 'God exalted Him.' For *humiliavit usque* there, here is *exaltavit super.* For *factus obediens* there, here *factus Dominus.* For *mortem Crucis,* 'the death of the cross' there, here is 'the glory of God the Father'" (p. 328). Students of prose style often argue that a man like Andrewes repudiated the extreme parallelism of Euphuistic periods for a tougher, more crabbed "Senecan amble," but in Andrewes' case, at least, the tough texture derives from eliding much of two parallel utterances (even to the extent of producing one-word sentences) and employing parallelism, as here, to heighten paradox or logical opposition rather than logical likeness. Yet Andrewes's world and utterance rest upon a profound sense of parallelism, both syn-

tactic and theological; theological parallelism opens the way for Andrewes
to suggest, as Puritans really could not, that we imitate or conform ourselves to the prior pattern of Christ, or that our lives can parallel his.

If Christ's person was exalted to a *super,* so also was his name—above
all names. That topic leads Andrewes, in the third section, from Christ to
"our duty" which parallels him: "God, though He have so exalted it, yet
reckons it not exalted, unless we do our parts also, unless our exaltation
come too" (p. 333). We exalt Christ by a corporal, physical act, necessary
to express reverence. It is on this point that Andrewes overtly attacks the
Puritan view of worship. We declare our esteem for Christ's name, show
that we believe it is above all names, by bowing our knees and confessing
with our tongues. "Now, these are outward acts, both. So then; first we
are to set down this for a ground, that the exalting of the soul within is
not enough. More is required by Him, more to be performed by us. He
will not have the inward parts only, and it skills not for the outward members, though we favour our knees, and lock up our lips. No, mental devotion will not serve, He will have both corporal and vocal to express it by"
(p. 333). What is within must and can only come out through a physical
gesture. To express our motives, we must physically incarnate them, just
as God incarnates his truths in Scripture. Not to bow at the name of Jesus
is as wicked as not bowing "at the holy mysteries themselves." Andrewes
refers to the Eucharist and shows the sacramental implications of his argument when he says that it is "where His name is, I am sure, and more than
His name, even the body and blood of our Lord Jesus Christ" (p. 335).
Despite an early "Puritan phase" in his life, Andrewes is very far, in stressing a real presence in the Eucharist, from Zwinglian, memorialist views of
this important point. Advocating genuflection, then, leads Andrewes naturally, smoothly, and logically away from an "advanced or radical" Protestantism.

If Andrewes moves here toward a conservative position on the Eucharist,
he also repeatedly invokes politically conservative, hierarchical structures
in his preaching—as we might expect of a bishop seriously considered for
the headship of his Church. A good example, rooted in physical reality yet
spiritual in effect, emerges in his discussion of the fact that we must employ
both our knees and our tongues to exalt Christ. "Not only the upper parts,
the tongue in our head, but even the nether also, the knee in our leg" must
testify to his glory (p. 333). The tongue, linked with intellection through
physical location in the head, is "a peculiar we have more than the beasts;
they will be taught to bow and bend their joints, we have tongues besides
to do something more than they" (p. 337). Two things are striking here.
That "dominion and power" which the Puritans saw as constraining the
creatures to bow forms only part of Andrewes's conception of God; more
mercifully, he has created us rational and with tongues, and thereby given

us "a peculiar" which permits us to act directly as mere animals cannot. By placing man hierarchically above the animals, Andrewes implicitly accords him a greater ability to act in this world. Secondly, however, Andrewes says that even the lesser, animalistic part of us must express our reverence to Christ; if it can indeed do so, it must not be so very horrid after all. Here is very incarnation indeed, of a sort with which few Puritans could be at all comfortable. Andrewes was sufficiently at home in this world that he could, seemingly, exalt even its baser parts.

The rest of the sermon need not detain us here, delightful as it may be. His conclusion, however, where he asks that we end as the text ends, again shows how, as Andrewes draws his points together, he insists upon corporal signs. The end of text and sermon is "a Lesson, even His *Discite a Me;* and it is a pattern, even His *Exemplum dedi vobis,* to commend unto us the virtue of the text, the *propter quod* of the feast, even humility; *hoc erit signum,* it is His sign at Christmas. As His sign then, so His *propter quod* now at Easter" (p. 342). The lesson, pattern, and sign are, clearly, expressive of humility—are, as they apply to us, bowing at the name of Jesus and confessing his lordship with our tongues. Christ expressed humility by being born as he did—in his incarnation—and by suffering as he did—on the cross. In Andrewes's world of essentially parallel order, we must clearly conform ourselves to Christ's example as nearly as we can, imitate him, both by being humble and by expressing that humility in a corporeal gesture. This knowledge Andrewes draws from another sign—Scripture—itself a pattern, and expresses through various signs—the literary devices basic to his style.

Andrewes, then, presents a sharp and complete contrast to those men who attacked bowing. He stresses a causal relation between Christ's action and God's, and, at least on a verbal level, a parallel causal relation between Christ's actions and man's. He dwells at length on Christ's humility, not his power and glory, and he interprets the physical gesture of bowing not as a possible mask for hypocrisy, not as a mere or "bare outward" gesture, but as in itself significant. Thus, while his reformed training led him to say "the name is not the sound but the sense" (p. 336), he did not emphasize the distinction between the "sound" of the name of Jesus and the "signification" since all his thought and art were dedicated to the proposition that they are one.

Chapter 4: SELF-CONSCIOUS CONTROVERSY AND PURITAN OPTIMISM

By the time of Andrewes's sermon, controversy over bowing at the name of Jesus had become internal to England. Those who sided with Andrewes's view that bowing was a "duty of the text" and those who opposed that notion were beginning to agree upon one thing: the ceremony was no longer a matter of indifference. Puritans (and by that time we may speak of them confidently) damned all bowers and bowers later damned all Puritans. The exclusion of the middle and the intense polarization of positions may be seen in the series of tracts on this subject which began to appear openly in the mid-thirties. William Prynne, fire-breathing protestor against the Church of Laud, contributed several pamphlets arguing that bowing of all sorts was forbidden, and his views were supported by an anonymous writer in 1641 and William Wickins in 1660. Prynne was answered by Giles Widdowes and William Page.[1] The argument was lengthy and recapitulated much of what we have already seen; the shortest way with all these dissenters will be to focus on the differences between William Prynne and William Page. The manner in which they repeated the verbal distinctions and theological emphases of earlier writers, and the way in which they exaggerated those differences as they simplified and self-consciously polarized the issues were both common to the whole lot.

Prynne could assert more clearly and bluntly than Cartwright the arguments developed against Rome because that dispute had been settled for some thirty or forty years when he wrote; the qualifications which Willet's encyclopedism once expressed had disappeared for much the same reasons, as Prynne rode roughshod over the paradigms and flattened out the delicate web of Christian paradox. Unlike Airay and Boys, he loved to dispute not wisely but too well. He announced confidently that he could and would *disprove* that bowing was a "duty of the text" or even a matter of indifference.[2] He took over the eschatological interpretation of Philippians 2. 9, denying *any* liturgical significance *at all,* and he took over the authoritarian diction used in describing a millennial Christ. He opened, for example, by asking "whether the text of the *Phil.* 2.9.10.11. on which they ground this ceremony or will-worship be not in the judgment of all divines both ancient and modern a prophecy of the joint subjection of all angels, saints, devils, and reprobates to the supreme Lordship and dominion of

Christ, not now in the Church, in time of divine service and sermons, but hereafter, when they shall all appear before Christ's tribunal to be judged by him" (p. 1). We notice immediately the confidence and the radical simplifying involved in appealing to "all divines both ancient and modern," the easy way he distinguished and held in polarized opposition the liturgical and eschatological readings, his language of constraining power and dominion, and his sense of Christ as paternal judge. He hated the idea that the name Jesus, which was after all *"imposed on our Savior's humanity only at his circumcision and not given to his deity, but to his human nature, in the very beginning of his humiliation"* should be considered *"a name above every name* . . . [or] the true, chief, yea proper name of God and of Christ's divinity, as the patrons of this ceremony affirm" (p. 3). Here he casually splits Christ's humanity from his divinity, links the former with circumcision and suffering, and in a single suggestive phrase links "God and . . . Christ's divinity." The process of fragmenting Christ's natures runs to its logical conclusion here, for the "chief" name becomes, in Prynne's repetitious heaping up of adjectives, the "true" and "proper" name. To talk about a chief name is to emphasize one aspect of Christ over another; to talk about a true and proper name is to reduce relative emphasis to absolute doctrine. Christ is no longer primarily eternal but almost purely eternal.

Prynne savaged the name Jesus, "a name that was principally given unto Christ in regard of his humiliation and passion, . . . the only *name by which all the Evangelists* style him, *in relating the history of his passion, the very lowest degree of his humiliation* . . . [or] when they mention either his death, his sufferings, or debasements, . . . *the only name that was written over his head upon the cross"* (quoted by Page, pp. 41–42). The extreme iconoclasm, which led Prynne to attack another book because it had a cross on the title page (crosses, he remarked, are the special province of Jesuits), emerges clearly here; one suspects that, angry and combative as he by temperament was, Prynne craved a hero who displayed those qualities rather than meekness, submission, and suffering love. The text from Philippians, by contrast, refers for him to a "name expressing Christ's exaltation, his sovereignty and glory."

In short, Page was absolutely correct when he remarked that Prynne's "mind runs all on power, and greatness, and majesty, and sovereignty." He added that "God's ways are not like our ways; you, like the world, prefer for greatness, God for goodness; he honors and respects names of pity and mercy more than names of power and majesty" (pp. 51–52). That is, Page and Prynne agreed upon the terms of the argument and self-consciously linked one name with a tone and whole set of associations, the other with a different tone and opposed set of assumptions. In effect, rules for writing and setting tone had developed, clear and self-evident because so well threshed out in previous controversy. Page preferred the name Jesus for three reasons: "First, . . . it is an humble and lowly name," second, "to us Christians, because it is unto us a gracious and saving name" without which we would be lost, and third, because the Jews mocked and scoffed at it (pp. 30–31). His taste and sensibility differed from Prynne's, but he chose his terms from exactly the same list Prynne used.

Prynne took over the old trick of asking whether other names might not be as important as Jesus. When he proposed *"the natural only begotten Son of God,"* Page made another shrewd comment about Prynne's habits of mind. "The Son of God" was a name given "before all time," whereas the most important name was "acquisite and purchased . . . in the fullness of time; for Christ merited this name by dying for us." That is, Page overtly links Prynne's position with a taste for eternity, his own with a taste for the chronological time of this world as well as of Christ's suffering. When Prynne proposed Emanuel as an alternative name to Jesus, Page had a bit more difficulty answering him, for Page's entire position centered on the fact that God came into time and space and mercifully joined his nature to ours. "I must confess indeed that *Emanuel* is a very gracious name of Christ," he admitted (p. 63). But, he added, "God may be with us in judgment as well as in mercy" and there is a great "difference between *Emanuel* and *Jesus,* between *God being with us* and *God saving us*" (pp. 63–64). That is, Page, if he does not quite split the Deity, clearly attributes "salvation" to Jesus' mercy and suffering and opposes it to the judgmental function which would operate at Prynne's last "tribunal."

If these exchanges show us clearly the effect of the long controversy against Rome and the refining of doctrine which intervened between it and this full-blown, intra-English dispute, we can see other effects as well. For example, Page wished to argue that a physical gesture or action was necessary to express an inner state, just as Andrewes had, yet he had to "grant that this bowing is principally intended at the last day, and then is the only time when this scripture shall be truly fulfilled" (p. 74). He also had to "confess that by bowing is meant subjection" (p. 73). Controversy with Rome had established so much, Page was himself a conciliatory man intellectually as well as religiously, and eschatological speculation was rife in his time. Still, he builds onto that advanced and potentially radical position much of what Andrewes had asserted. Granted that subjection was required by the text, still it was "not the inward without the outward, but rather the inward as it is expressed by the outward" (p. 73). Further, proper bowing "I take to be a bowing not only of subjection but of gratitude and thankful remembrance; so that when I put off my hat or bow my knee at the name of *Jesus,* I do not only acknowledge his power and sovereignty over me, but I do also call to mind and in all humbleness acknowledge that inestimable favor he hath showed me in this name *Jesus;* so that my bowing of body and soul unto his name is a real thanksgiving unto him. And in our thanksgiving unto God I hope you will allow bowing" (pp. 76–77). Granted further that bowing "is principally intended at the last day," he still queries "is there no intent that any should bow in the meantime? It is literally to be fulfilled then; may it not, nay must it not therefore be a-fulfilling now, and so go on by degrees to be more and more verified?" (pp. 74–75).

We can observe several things in these statements. Page seems the sort of man to "put off his hat" with ease and delight, a courtesy Prynne was constitutionally incapable of, and the sort to "hope that you will allow" bowing. That was Sir Thomas Browne's plea, who could not "stand in diameter and swords point" with even Roman Catholics since "there is between us one common name and appellation." "Naturally inclined to that, which misguided zeale termes superstition," Browne loved "to use the civility of my knee, my hat, and hands, with all those outward and sensible motions, which may express or promote my invisible devotion."[3] Few were so completely willing to dissolve controversy and to say a good word for Rome as Browne was. Perhaps that was because Browne published his book, after a pirated version had appeared in 1642, the year King Charles entered the military field against his Parliament. The process of social polarization, at work through the first decades of the century, had about gone to completion, and Browne seems to have wished to dissolve such controversies by laughing men out of their paper wars. No man could hope to succeed in that venture; no doubt the desperateness of the social and political situation helps to account, on the one hand, for Browne's extravagance, his willingness to be reconciled even with Rome, and, on the other hand, for the fact that *Religio Medici* articulates an extremely tentative, fideistic scepticism together with reconciliation.

In his book, Prynne begins with rhetorical questions and concludes with hammering assertions, while Page in contrast ends with rhetorical questions and a tentative tone. To put it another way, Prynne would disprove and thus intellectually destroy his opponents, while Page would solicit him in much the same submissive tone and spirit he would solicit the mercies of his Jesus. As an expression of religious sensibility, Page's book is, on the face of it, much more appealing than Prynne's assertiveness. Yet Page's tentativeness, which Browne could turn into scepticism, is the expression of a man with relatively less self-esteem than that implied by Prynne's cockiness. Prynne is moving toward the belief that all the world agrees with him, as we see when he makes the outrageous statement that "all divines both ancient and modern" support his view and then goes on to provide in his margins the footnotes which would, were an inquisitive reader to check them, prove him wrong.

As the polarization implicit in this controversy was perfected over time, the extreme positions begin paradoxically to resemble each other again. Prynne, Page, and Browne are in quest of unanimity of belief, but Prynne optimistically has begun to assume that his is the universally held view, while Page partially and Browne more openly are forced to undercut and even to deny their own positions in the hopes that strife and bickering could somehow be dissolved. If Prynne is unlovely in his hybris, as indeed he was, Browne is troubling when he seems willing to dissolve or even to begin to betray his own views so as to accommodate those of his enemies and thereby prove that he has none.

Page's remarks also serve to remind us how far the eschatological bias and millennial vision inhering in "advanced or radical Protestantism" had spread. Prynne suffered from the sort of hybris he did in part because the Puritan position had indeed come of age, and its adversaries had perforce to reckon with and in some cases admit the force of it. The English Church had become firmly Protestant, as Joseph Summers has indirectly reminded us by showing a "low" and Calvinistic element in George Herbert's poetry.[4] Protestants seem to have been interested in the millennium because then what they thought to be the meddling influence of the Roman Church would be ended once and for all; no more priestly mediation, for then we shall see face to face. When we look at the poetry of such men as John Donne or Henry Vaughan, the first raised a Catholic and ultimately a bright light of the establishment under Laud, the second an extremely tentative Royalist and Anglican during the years of war and protectorate, we detect an overt, moderately developed, apocalyptic note. Ecclesiast as he is, Donne can still easily soar to the "world's imagin'd corners" and sound the trumpet of the Day of Judgment which will mark the end of the Church Militant. And Vaughan "saw eternity the other night."

Yet, if apocalyptic visions were, on the one hand, a cornerstone of Protestant agitation and, on the other hand, a not unexpected response to a fluid, rapidly changing, and potentially frightening society, that motif may be handled in a variety of ways. Donne, who for all his spiritual hypochondria and fascination with death could pull back from the Day of Judgment "there" to repent "here on this lowly ground," seems relatively happy and comfortable in this world and in the sacramental efficacy of acts and gestures made in it. Page too, a decade before the wars, focused not so much on a blinding and instantaneous resolution and clarification of all the tensions of his world and prophecies of the next as on a chronologically ordered "fulfilling now" which can "go on by degrees to be more and more verified." If, like Airay and Donne, he drops back from a millennial vision into the here and now, he also differs from the more Puritanic or precise expositors in important ways. Airay first contemplated the final, crystal-clear, and unambiguous revelation of the prophecy and then projected the undiminished clarity and eternal stasis of that final

vision back upon men's daily lives. He did not add "thanksgiving"—a human
and humane response—to "subjection"—an eternal, passive, eschatological
state—as Page does. Page, in short, sees man steadily working up, by degrees, over time, to the final vision, and he is content to remain in the uncertainties and partialities of this sin-, space-, and time-bound world. He
quotes Calvin to Prynne, "a man whose authority you will not easily deny,"
to support his argument that the text speaks of the progressive fulfillment
of prophecy over time (p. 75).

But Prynne and the other, finally unbending opponents of bowing had
by then, in their confidence, marched right past their old master, Calvin,
to draw ever more fully "advanced or radical" propositions from his first
fruits. They exaggerated what had once been "advanced or radical" tendencies in Calvin's less completely polarized world, and hardened what had
been for Calvin a somewhat tentative predisposition, balanced in his writing by other pulls, into a fully revealed, self-consciously stated, simplistic,
and optimistic orthodoxy. Attracted by the blinding clarity of the last
days, no doubt at first out of rebellion and fear, then in a kind of confidence which could flatten out Christian paradox into a simple, obvious,
rigid orthodoxy, Prynne and his Puritanic fellows would finally not grant
Page's quiet plea that he be allowed to bow in thanksgiving. There was no
unambiguous and unequivocal prescription for bowing in the Bible, and
therefore it did not exist. Matters of indifference were, for Prynne, "will-
worship," the gracious middle way was wicked, just as the middle way of
Emanuel, of God combining mediatorily with man and man with God,
appealed to Puritans less than the dominion, power, glory, and subjection
of the last tribunal. It was only a short step from that position to the joy
with which the young John Milton could sing of the final triumph:

> Then all this Earthy grosness [we shall] quit,
> Attir'd with Stars, we shall for ever sit,
>   Triumphing over Death, and Chance, and thee O Time.
> ["On Time," ll. 20–22]

Such a note rings out not only in "On Time," but also in "At a Solemn
Musick" and the Nativity ode, all written about the time the controversy
over bowing had gone to self-conscious completion.

In contrast to the young Puritan's exuberance, Henry Vaughan would,
in the year after his king was beheaded, feel himself permanently stuck in
this world, like the cloud in "The Showre," sullied and ultimately damaged
by his sojourn here below.

> 'Twas so, I saw thy birth; That drowsie Lake
> From her faint bosome breath'd thee, the disease
> Of her sick waters, and Infectious Ease.

But, now at Even
Too grosse for heaven,
Thou fall'st in teares, and weep'st for thy mistake.

Ah! it is so with me; oft have I prest
Heaven with a lazie breath, but fruitles this
Peirc'd not; Love only can with quick accesse
    Unlock the way,
    When all else stray
The smoke, and Exhalations of the brest.

Yet, if as thou doest melt, and with thy traine
Of drops make soft the Earth, my eyes could weep
O're my hard heart, that's bound up, and asleep,
    Perhaps at last
    (some such showres past,)
My God would give a Sun-shine after raine.[5]

He had tried the wars for a few years, we now believe, then as the combat continued, retreated to Wales; when his political world caved in, he underwent a poetic "conversion" and could catch glimpses of

The way which from this dead and dark abode
    Leads up to God   ["The World," ll. 53–54]

but never quite achieve that exultant certainty of Milton.

These several versions of apocalypse briefly exemplify a rather complex series of historical changes in tone and outlook which Christopher Hill has captured briefly in the story of Antichrist in the writings of seventeenth-century England.[6] It is at once a terrible and a cheering tale, which begins in intense fear and ends in confidence. Militant English Protestants had at first exorcised their own demons by rolling them up in one ball, and through a massive psychosocial projection, established Antichrist at Rome, where, at considerable distance, he menaced England. But then, as Englishmen fell out among themselves, he came like Grendel from his mere ever closer. To Presbyterian and Parliamentary opponents of the king, he seemed to have crossed the Channel to advise the king; then, to the Independents, he seemed to have joined the Presbyterians and "new forcers of Conscience." Finally, for some radicals in the 1650's, he was "in us." Of course, he always had been. Men create such monsters out of fear and dissatisfaction, out of the personal anxieties which fuel protest. Up to a certain point, the ability of a Donne or a Page to pull back from the whole, absolute, compulsive scenario of Antichrist and eschatology testifies to an ability to cope with such fears. But on the other hand, as Hill's tale suggests, at a certain point psychological projection seems to have accomplished what it was, however inadequately, first created to do; it seems to have reassured protestors sufficiently that they could begin to take new, independent steps on their own. To be able self-consciously to face one's fears and limitations and the constraints under which one operates is to exhibit bone deep self-confidence. When we no longer have to blame another, when we can tacitly admit that in the past we made up a monster so that we could blame him absolutely, we are well on the way to coping positively with our situation. The immense amount of abuse which anti-Roman, English controversialists hurled at Antichrist had made him sufficiently familiar that their protesting heirs could finally take that next, positive step.

When, in 1650, Vaughan was somewhat frantically wishing that "My God would give a Sun-shine after raine," he was stuck in that tentativeness which we have seen developing in Page and Browne—a tentativeness which he would at least partially overcome by his volume of 1655. I shall follow out the development of conservative thought and art later on, having briefly suggested it here with the admittedly somewhat untypical example of Vaughan. My main point now has to do with the young John Milton, coming of intellectual age, with generous, liberal, and humane impulses, precisely at a time when the ways of talking about the religio-political establishment in England had taken quite definite shape, and the rules for writing had become fixed. This made it easy for Milton to begin to think and write about his society, and that ease must have fostered his own sense of confidence.

The home from which Milton came had undergone a microcosmic reformation when his father deserted the old faith of the grandfather; Milton was almost literally a child of reform. When he left home and began that universal search for a way to express himself, his feelings and hopes and dreams, controversy had crystalized out clear, distinct, self-consciously adopted patterns of thought. Being almost uniquely articulate, he of course found his own idiosyncratic ways of talking. But no man makes up for himself his whole way of talking and living; we do borrow and learn from others. By the time Milton went to Cambridge, there were in effect two languages ready at hand for talking about bowing at the name of Jesus and a whole host of similar controversies. He did not have to thresh out for himself the words and ideas and tones, but rather faced the relatively easy choice—to adopt the old, conservative ways of talking or adopt the new, liberal, and reformist ways of talking. Articulating his liberal impulses was therefore relatively simple and free of strain, and hence Milton's tone, even while castigating his enemies, tends on the whole to be somewhat easier and less vituperative than Prynne's as well. True enough, finding such ready-made, verbal tools at hand could be slightly misleading. For example, Milton obviously thought for some time that he was a Presbyterian, presumably because it was the Presbyterians of his undergraduate days who took the most viable reformist position and adopted a publicly tolerated tone nearest to his own. Events were to prove that the tools did not quite match the job Milton ultimately wished to undertake, and it is in part a measure of his own, indiosyncratic articulateness that he ultimately did forge a new, distinct, personal language and doctrine. And, of course, forging that language did involve new strains, which we can see, it seems to me, in the relatively lumpish and opaque prose of such late products of his Presbyterian phase as *Of Reformation*.[7] Beginning roughly with the divorce tracts, the prose seems to flow much more smoothly as Milton sloughed off old views and words which no longer quite fitted his vision and struck out for himself. Still, despite those new problems in finding a style, one must wonder whether Milton didn't always preserve a certain degree of confidence from those early days when it must have seemed that he could adopt a style which others had already created for him. If he smashed the king's image, he was not primarily a carper, or perhaps his carping, Prynne-like moments were more than balanced by much more lovely stuff. He did not have vituperatively to assail the will-worship of Rome or Laud in the manner of Cartwright or Prynne because they had already done so for him. He could go on to extend protest in increasingly more liberal and radical directions, until he could confidently assert that Christ merited his exaltation just as man can merit divine favor. That was not a return to the old, Roman Catholic theology, however, but rather the fullest expression of Puritan confidence in the world and in man himself.

Moreover, his confidence blossomed in a characteristically Puritanic way. When in the 30's and 40's Puritans addressed themselves seriously to the possibility of making a revolution, they effectively betrayed (as almost all revolutionaries do) their own ideological base. If God does all and men are abject sinners, how can one reasonably undertake to reform society? The illogic of the venture need not detain us, common as it is;[8] my point here is that it is confidence which destroys logic and ideology. And, at much the same period, Milton was personally forging new theological views, among them (as I will exemplify in the next section) a most positive, almost anti-nomian optimism centered on the idea of Christian liberty. In terms of our text and controversy here, this new optimism was expressed in the apparently un-Puritanic notion that Christ did in some way merit his exaltation.

Book three of *Paradise Lost* articulates this new and radical Puritan reading of the text from Philippians after the Son volunteers to humiliate himself by descending to earth. Both humiliation and exaltation are outside of time, both occurring (here is book three) as time first begins, or implicitly at the apocalypse. It is the eternal Son who humiliates himself here, not a Jesus on the cross in time, blood, and sweat. He fits himself verbally into a pre-existent plan and a cosmic order outside himself, by using "me" rather than "I," and thereby shows his motive is not to be exalted. More

striking, however, than these common elements of the Puritan conception
of Christ, the Son clearly merited his exaltation and, more generally, men
seem capable of meriting something as well. When the Father responds to
the Son's mediatorial gesture, he thrice uses the word merit. The Son's

                                        merit
    Imputed shall absolve them who renounce
    Thir own both righteous and unrighteous deeds,
    And live in thee transplanted, and from thee
    Receive new life.   [3:290-94]

The Son has

                            been found
    By Merit more then Birthright Son of God,
    Found worthiest to be so by being Good,
    Farr more then Great or High.   [3:308-11]

The Father verbally transfuses power to the Son, first by articulating what
the Son will do:

                        because in thee
    Love hath abounded more then Glory abounds,
    Therefore thy Humiliation shall exalt
    With thee thy Manhood also to this Throne;
    Here shalt thou sit incarnate, here shalt Reign
    Both God and Man, Son both of God and Man,
    Anointed universal King.   [3:311-17]

And then he flatly states: "all Power/I give thee." Having done so, the
Father orders the Son to

                        reign for ever, and assume
    Thy Merits; under thee as Head Supream
    Thrones, Princedoms, Powers, Dominions I reduce:
    All knees to thee shall bow, of them that bide
    In Heaven, or Earth, or under Earth in Hell.   [3:318-22]

These lines accord with Milton's equally bald statement in *De Doctrina*
that the Son achieves his exaltation "partly by his own merits, partly by
the gift of the Father" (bk. I, ch. 26; pp. 440-41); speaking more generally
concerning man he exclaimed, "Since we are not mere puppets, some cause
at least should be sought in human nature itself, why some men embrace
and others reject this divine grace" (bk. I, ch. 4; p. 186). The sense of
merit is strengthened in the poem by the Father's remark that the Son is
"found" good; he can only be so found (twice in two lines) by God, who
must therefore recognize his merit; moreover, men seem to be able to "re-
nounce" their deeds and to "live."

More conventionally Puritan is the emphasis upon the last days; "all knees" shall bow then, rather than during weekly service. In addition, the Father stresses the judicial and glorious aspects of the Son (despite his comment that the Son merits his exaltation "by being Good,/Farr more then Great or High"). The Son shall be "attended gloriously"; the Father says he will

> send
> The summoning Arch-Angels to proclaime
> Thy dread Tribunal.   [3:324-26]

All the creatures shall hasten to the "general Doom," when, the Father promises, the Son shall "judge/Bad men and Angels" who will "sink/Beneath thy Sentence" (3:328-32). Hell will be filled and closed, and the world shall burn as the Son exercises "all Power." In such a passage, when the Father says he will "reduce" the creatures, we may think he intends to constrain them by force or (as Satan would see it) diminish them, although (knowing Latin as he does) he clearly plans to lead them back under the headship of Christ. That liberal reading of the word "reduce" reminds us, when we think about it, that all this emphasis upon glory and judgment occurs in a passage largely dominated by love, which re-emerges when the Father concludes with the saints and "New Heav'n and Earth." It is the first instance of that oft-repeated phrase which will bring the millennium to our mind throughout the poem, and it is accompanied, as all loving and merciful gestures are in *Paradise Lost,* by cosmic music which shall also reign when the millennium commences with joy and gold. Set in this loving context, the references to Philippians and to the justice and glory and power stand out, clearly deriving from the style of Puritan exegetes.

The Puritan emphasis upon the right apprehension of truth, important in their controversy with Rome, fuses with the Puritan distrust of works in this passage. The Father suggests that to be "good" the Son and those men who will be saved must recognize and act out their true nature through expressive definition. Thus the Son is to "assume [his] Merits," which is what he has already done when he volunteers to express divine love easily, naturally, without prompting, so that all may see and know. In addition, virtuous men will recognize their own nature as well as the relatively insignificant position they occupy in this God-centered world, when they "renounce/Thir own both righteous and unrighteous deeds." The Son has already syntactically renounced his efforts. One of the most striking things about what Summers calls "the voice of the redeemer" is the manner in which it selflessly subordinates the speaker as the object to an action deriving from an actor outside himself—God. Thus the Son, as Summers notes employs "me" as well as the "I" which Satan uses almost exclusively in his acceptance speech in book two;[9] thereby the Son gives up the role of actor and doer:

> on mee let thine anger fall;
> Account mee man   [3:237-38]

the Son exclaims at the height of his gesture, and his selfless motives, of
such concern to Puritans, embedded in syntax, contrast to the style of
Satan's politic egoism.

The difference between Son and Satan marks, in another way, the fact
that the consult in hell involves delusion and false appearances, the consult
in heaven, realism. For the Son's gesture as well as Eve's later one is most
correctly expressed in the objective case. They are not acting like heroes
in epics we know; they do not act upon, to change, other entities outside
themselves; they are not manipulative. Rather, they place the Son and Eve
within the context of God's ultimate and Puritanically conceived plan and
the bonds of human relationship; they subordinate themselves to the
source of all power and all true heroism and its reflection in right marriage.
They recognize the very Puritan emphasis laid upon the vast difference between creature and Creator and the fact that in this God-centered world
one can only stand.

Hence we see the eternal Son of God given when time has just begun for
us, humbling himself verbally, rather than upon the cross in time, through
selfless motives of verbal subordination to the eternal decree of his own
nature. The gesture occurs, within the poem, before the fall which we,
seeking causal relationships, may expect to have occasioned it. God says his
grace is prevenient, but the ordering of the poem and placing of this scene
show it. Neither the Son's humiliation nor his exaltation has been caused.
Once we have read the scene, we have seen the terms of Christian salvation
completed and our world become "New Heav'n and Earth," have seen the
word given in more than one way. True to the Puritan vision, there is no
"*propter quod*" in all the scene.

In subsequent chapters I shall more fully argue that the millennial expectation of a "New Heav'n and Earth" was the essence of this new, radical,
ideologically illogical Puritan optimism. Provisionally, then, I shall observe
here that Milton's radically Puritanic temperament emerges most clearly,
in book three, when he connects the conventional Puritan emphasis upon
the Son's dominion, power, glory, and authority with a loving, positive,
liberal, and confident hope for the millennium. If "New Heav'n and Earth"
sounds like a bell throughout *Paradise Lost* to impel us forward to the
glorious future, it is fitting that that bell first sounds in a passage owing
much to the grim overtones of Puritan controversy. Like a good Puritan,
Milton poetically gives God all the glory; as a supremely confident and
articulate radical Puritan he does so gloriously.

Section Two: Puritan Sabbatarianism and the Attack on Christmas

Remember the Sabbath, to keep it holy.—*Exodus, 20.8*

Chapter 5: THE SABBATH REST: THE ROCK OF AGES

"Whatsoever is said or written by the prophets, Christ, or the Apostles, it is none other thing but the interpretation and exposition of these ten words or ten commandments," began the radical, reforming bishop, John Hooper, in his commentary of 1548 on the Ten Commandments.[1] No doubt, as John Milton would have been the first to observe, Christ would have been greatly surprised to hear that he was expounding the Ten Commandments when, for example, he allowed his disciples to gather grain on the Sabbath. But that was what Puritan divines argued, elaborating on Calvin's timeless definition of "the covenant made with all the patriarchs" which, although historically distant from us, "is so much like ours in substance and reality that the two are actually one and the same."[2] They extended Hooper's thesis into the rigorous Sabbatarianism to which for some odd reason a great many Englishmen cheerfully submitted themselves during the seventeenth century and later. No single text sparked such a voluminous controversy in England during the seventeenth century as this, the fourth commandment. There were so many books written on it that when, in the nineteenth century, Robert Cox compiled his bibliography of Sabbatarian literature, what he anticipated would be a work of one volume mushroomed into two.[3] The sheer volume of books on this topic attests to the political impact it had and requires that we examine it.

Puritan Sabbatarianism was, as Patrick Collinson has shown, consistent with the larger trends of Reformed theology from whence it naturally sprang, a particular expression of more pervasive intellectual tendencies.[4] It was not simply "a bit of English originality" or "the first and perhaps the only important English contribution to the development of Reformed theology" in the sixteenth century, as M. M. Knappen earlier argued,[5] because it was neither very original nor confined strictly to English theologians. Yet there is no disputing the fact that the English were, relatively, far more interested in this basically lifeless problem than other Reformed theologians and poked it into a blazing controversy of intense political heat while other Protestants basically let it smoulder.

In short, Christopher Hill has asked the proper questions: why was there so much interest in this subject and why was that interest so strong among the English?[6] His concern with the economic implications of theology allows him to explain Sabbatarianism as a way of regulating working hours and regularizing the process of political indoctrination. Nascent capitalists needed an efficient work force and Sabbatarianism ensured that employees could work six full days uninterrupted by holidays and festivals. Systematically enforcing a rest on the seventh day prevented workers from being overworked but in addition provided Puritan preachers a regular platform for the "spiritual business" of theological indoctrination. If so much accounts for the seemingly unusual concern about Sabbatarianism in a society where a sort of proto-capitalism was beginning to emerge, it does not explain why the English were particularly attracted to it. At times Hill seems to assume that revolution was somehow predestined to occur in England and hence that the process of indoctrination had to be facilitated there; that assumption seems less than verifiable. He also suggests a connection between Sabbatarianism and a certain "Judaical" interest among the English (pp. 202–6) and while it still remains unclear why the English came to think of themselves as God's peculiars, still Sabbatarianism did fit smoothly in with that tendency to identify with Israel.

Analysis of this controversy, then, leaves us with a basic puzzle, a puzzle I frankly shall not attempt to solve. If we cannot really say what caused this interest, we can on the other hand see how that interest reveals more openly the historiographical paradigms implicit in the controversy over bowing at the name of Jesus. We can, secondly, see how the steamroller of Puritan analysis flattened complex arguments into superlogical simplicity— seventh-day Sabbatarianism on the one hand and Milton's antinomian plea for Christian liberty on the other. For if the causes of Puritanism baffle us, there is another puzzle about this controversy as well. John Milton rejected the Puritan interpretation of the Sabbath in his mature work and again he did so for distinctly Puritanic reasons. We can see the mechanics of this anomaly slightly more clearly than we can in the case of bowing at the name of Jesus, because Milton initially took what seems to have been an "orthodox" Puritan position on the Sabbath and then, driven to advance and radicalize Puritan thought, reversed his doctrinal position as he moved ever closer to fully radical Puritan thought. Finally, this controversy permits us to see Puritan iconoclasm effectively removing Christ from this world and, to an amazing extent, from theological speculation.

The controversial process which polarized Englishman from Englishman occurred quickly and early in the case of Sabbatarianism. Whereas the dispute over bowing took almost half a century to develop into crystalline clarity, the first theoretical statement of the Puritan doctrine of the Sabbath appeared from the pen of Nicholas Bownd in 1595.[7] It had been preceded, as Collinson rightly notes, by much verbal discussion among the precise brethren; presumably unpublished manuscripts circulated from hand to hand, and Bownd's father-in-law, Richard Greenham, had already published one partially doing the job. Yet Bownd articulated a full-blown theory, and by 1618 when James I published his *Book of Sports,* the controversy had been sufficiently cultivated that James caused a furor among what Hill calls the "industrious sort." Because I have already analyzed the apocalyptic dynamics of controversy and because the issues stood fully revealed so early, I shall simply select four works—Bownd's pioneering work of 1595, John Sprint's treatise of 1607, the highly popular exposition by John (Decalogue) Dod in 1612, and Thomas Shepard's late contribution of 1649; to consider the countless other tracts listed by Cox would be simply to repeat what was an immensely repetitious analysis. Discussion of the Puritan Sabbath was ahistorical in the sense that during fifty years the Puritans elaborated upon but did not develop, alter, or change the essential doctrines. It was ahistorical in other ways as well, and it is to matters of historiography that I wish now to turn.

When John Dod echoed Hooper's basic position that "there is no good duty which God bound *Adam* to perform but is comprehended and commanded in one of these [ten commandments]; and there is no sin that we are bound to abstain from and eschew which is not forbidden in some of these ten words," he implicitly emphasized the achronologic strain of Christian historiography.[8] For centuries Christian theologians had sought to account simultaneously for *chronos* and *kairos*—for the linear, minute by minute process of human history which we perceive here below and for the great circle of eternity which God sees in his timeless vision. C. A. Patrides has outlined the ways in which these two schemata were traditionally fused; the paradox of the line and the circle, developed especially by Augustine, had flowered forth in, to city only the most obvious example, the medieval dramatic cycles. Typically, the eternal circle is generated through meditation on the temporal line; a specific temporal moment or sequence is transcended or transmuted in an *"O altitudo!"*[9] Men in the seventeenth century were generally agreed, despite party differences, that the story of "the Jews of old" "pennes and sets us down," as Herbert put it in "The Bunch of Grapes."

> Joy, I did lock thee up: but some bad man
>   Hath let thee out again:
> And now, me thinks, I am where I began
>   Sev'n yeares ago: one vogue and vein,
>   One aire of thoughts usurps my brain.
> I did towards Canaan draw; but now I am
> Brought back to the Red sea, the sea of shame.
>
> For as the Jews of old by Gods command
>   Travell'd, and saw no town;
> So now each Christian hath his journeys spann'd:
>   Their storie pennes and sets us down.
>   A single deed is small renown.

Gods works are wide, and let in future times;
His ancient justice overflows our crimes.

Then have we too our guardian fires and clouds;
        Our Scripture-dew drops fast:
We have our sands and serpents, tents and shrowds;
        Alas! our murmurings come not last.
        But where's the cluster? where's the taste
Of mine inheritance? Lord, if I must borrow,
Let me as well take up their joy, as sorrow.

But can he want the grape, who hath the wine?
        I have their fruit and more.
Blessed be God, who prosper'd *Noahs* vine,
        And made it bring forth grapes good store.
        But much more him I must adore,
Who of the Laws sowre juice sweet wine did make,
Ev'n God himself being pressed for my sake.[10]

Israel's search for Canaan prefigures ("let[s] in future times") the Christian search for salvation, and the repetition of searches begins to generate a cyclic view of history. Yet Herbert's poem is first of all firmly rooted in chronos before it spirals into kairos; the Jews searched for an *earthly* paradise, they were the objects of God's "ancient justice," they were famous for "murmurings": for three stanzas, Herbert's speaker is in much the same frame of mind as the ancient Israelites; he concludes the third by repining:

                Lord, if I must borrow,
        Let me as well take up their joy, as sorrow.

It is not an entirely sensible request, since that joy was earthly, and the speaker successfully moves beyond it, in the fourth and final stanza, by realizing that "I have their fruit and more," since Christ "of the Laws sowre juice sweet wine did make." That is, Christ is conceived to have added something important to the old dispensation—mercy—and the poem embodies the implicit sense of historical progress (out of which the spirals arise) by showing a speaker who progresses spiritually in time as well. Identifying literally with Israel may be a beginning but it is not the end of Herbert's meditation; one must progress beyond justice to mercy and thereby attune oneself to the progress of sacred history.

Donne also generated circles out of straight lines. In the first prayer of his *Devotions upon Emergent Occasions* (a book strongly rooted in a historical and even minutely chronological matrix) he asked: "O Eternall, and most gracious God, who, considered in thy selfe, art a *Circle*, first and last, and altogether; but considered in thy working upon us, art a *direct line,* and leadest us from our *beginning,* through all our wayes, to our end,

enable me by thy grace, to looke forward to mine end, and to looke backward to, to the consideration of thy mercies afforded mee from my beginning, that so by that practise of considering thy mercy, in my beginning
in this world, when thou plantedst me in the *Christian Church,* and thy
mercy in the beginning of the other world, when thou writest me in the
Booke of life in my Election, I may come to a holy consideration of thy
mercy, in the beginning of all my actions here." [11] Although Donne first
glances briefly at the eternal reality of the circle as he articulates the whole
of the paradox, he then drops back to the linear structure of his autobiography "from our beginning, through all our wayes, to our end" and generates a pattern of repeated (and hence cyclic) beginnings and endings, first
"in this world" and then in "the other world." God is a circle "first and
last, and altogether," but Donne focuses on the "first" part of the pattern—
on the "beginning"—and eschews consideration of his end; if that is a
result of his fear that he might die, it is also expressive of a less than millennial concern as well. A consideration of endings would produce more
immediately circular structures (since as Frank Kermode has pointed out,
there are generally concords between beginning and ending); [12] a tendency
to disregard the historical ending goes hand in hand with a certain theological and psychological comfort about the things of this world—goes hand
in hand with the way, having articulated the paradox, Donne drops back
from the eternal verity to contemplate his life here below.

Perhaps a more telling example is Donne's "Hymne to God my God, in
my sicknesse," for in that poem Donne was actually writing near his own
"ending" and so therefore was more inclined to focus on "endings." And
the poem is much more obviously circular than his emergent devotions,
confirming Kermode's theory.

> Since I am comming to that Holy roome,
>   Where, with thy Quire of Saints for evermore,
> I shall be made thy Musique; As I come
>   I tune the Instrument here at the dore,
>   And what I must doe then, thinke here before.
>
> Whilst my Physitians by their lore are growne
>   Cosmographers, and I their Mapp, who lie
> Flat on this bed, that by them may be showne
>   That this is my South-west discoverie
>   *Per fretum febris,* by these streights to die,
>
> I joy, that in these straits, I see my West;
>   For, though theire currants yeeld returne to none,
> What shall my West hurt me? As West and East
>   In all flatt Maps (and I am one) are one,
>   So death doth touch the Resurrection.

Is the Pacifique Sea my home? Or are
　　The Easterne riches? Is *Ierusalem?*
Anyan, and *Magellan,* and *Gibraltare,*
　　　All streights, and none but streights, are wayes to them,
　　Whether where *Iaphet* dwelt, or *Cham,* or *Sem.*

We thinke that *Paradise* and *Calvarie,*
　　Christs Crosse, and *Adams* tree, stood in one place;
Looke Lord, and finde both *Adams* met in me;
　　As the first *Adams* sweat surrounds my face,
　　May the last *Adams* blood my soule embrace.

So, in his purple wrapp'd receive mee Lord,
　　By these his thornes give me his other Crowne;
And as to others soules I preach'd thy word,
　　Be this my Text, my Sermon to mine owne,
　　Therefore that he may raise the Lord throws down.[13]

Donne produced, as any dying man might, an obviously circular poem. But
what seems to me distinctive about him is that, after the first, timeless
vision of the future when "I shall be made thy Musique" his meditation
turns to linear objects—"flatt Maps." In order to "thinke here before"
about "what I must doe there," Donne has recourse to fallen, partial representations of circular reality.

　　　　　　　　As West and East
　　In all flatt Maps (and I am one) are one,
　　So death doth touch the Resurrection.

The edges of a map touch only when one so rolls the map that a linear object becomes spherical. Human limitation and sinfulness is embodied in
maps; they are flat while the reality is curved; twisting the map alters its
fallen use, perhaps, but it also makes the map more nearly "true." After
working out through this geographic conceit, Donne remarks, historiographically:

　　We thinke that *Paradise* and *Calvarie,*
　　　Christs Crosse, and *Adams* tree, stood in one place.

The spatial juxtaposition of these two places amounts to an achronological
juxtaposition of two widely separated events in human history. But, if our
maps are flat when the world is really round, are we correct when we
"think" these things? Probably, although the doubt still lingers how we
are to take this proposition and the circular thinking involved. However
that may be, it seems clear that Donne achieves his effects primarily by
clashing a linear perception of space and, by extension, time against a
circular, almost divine vision of the "truth" about reality.

John Milton, in contrast, had a much more obvious inclination to drive directly toward the circle before descending to the contemplation of chronos. The point is not that he considers one instead of the other, but rather that he considers them in a particular order and for clear strategic reasons. The first five lines of *Paradise Lost,* referring as they do to events both before and after the close of history, are only one notable example of the optimistic way Milton moves directly to see and write with divine timelessness; the habit informed even such early poems as the Nativity Ode, "On Time," and "At a Solemn Musick." Characteristically, in *Paradise Lost* a review of chronology comes at the *end* of the poem, in the last two books, and I shall have something to say later about a looping movement even there. Instinctively, Milton preferred to focus on moments when "time stands fixt," for only from such an elevated perception could he descend to reform the world and fix the times. The few works by Herbert and Donne, representative of their authors, must suffice for the present to illustrate the mechanics of what was a conservative, established, ecclesiastic habit of writing. If Patrides' analysis of this venerable historiographic tradition helps us to understand the texture of Donne's or Herbert's typology and poetry, his argument concerning Milton's place in that tradition is weakened by his failure to consider the splitting and fragmenting pressures of life and thought in seventeenth-century England. Milton was much more nearly a radical, reforming Puritan than conservative establishmentarian, and his handling of history reflects that difference.

Controversial pressure split chronos from kairos, just as it split Jesus from Christ and/or God the Father (as I have shown in section 1), body from soul, God from man, and Royalist from Roundhead. The Puritan attack upon the establishment cracked the old threads binding the two historical schemata together and the conservatives were busy yoking them back together in defense. God sees more truly than men, both parties were agreed, and because the Puritans were super-realists athirst for the purified vision of "Truth" as it really was, because, that is, they wanted to see as nearly as possible in the way God sees, they moved instinctively first to the cyclic view, descending only afterwards to redeem fallen time through godly acts or revolution. They could only begin to attempt the latter *after* they had achieved the former; "doctrine" had to precede "use," and doctrine was timeless.

It is not surprising, when we think about it, that less protesting members of the Established Church in seventeenth-century England advanced what we can call a pedagogic theory of Christian history quite similar to the one Patrides has described. The view was, by the time these men expounded it, venerable, inherent, for example, in Irenaeus's comment that before the advent of Christ men were "infantile" and "unaccustomed to, and unexercised in, perfect discipline." The process of history had instructed men and improved their spiritual perception, particularly through the fulfilling of types and prophecies. God had called men "to the things of primary importance by means of those which were secondary; by things temporal, to eternal; and by the carnal to the spiritual; and by the earthly to the heavenly. . . . By means of types they learned to fear God."[14] Paul had made a contribution when he remarked that the Law "genders to bondage" (Gal. 4.24); Christ came to set men free in Christian liberty by abrogating the old requirements. In other words, God established a dispensation which progressively raised men out of the process of history and prepared them for eternal circularity and direct apprehension of God in Christ. Linear temporality generated spiritual ascent, both as men's interests and expectations became more spiritually elevated and as the types were fulfilled over time. Dod summarized this pedagogic theory, of which he disapproved, in terms which strongly emphasized the effects of the passage of time: "the Jews were children of Christ and weaklings, and therefore they had need of a Sabbath; but we are past babes, we are men grown and have more knowledge, we are stronger than they" (pp. 127-28). Dod did not think we "are stronger than they" at all; we still needed a Sabbath to raise our thoughts above mundane routine just as even Adam had. Whereas in the pedagogic view the Law had merely been one temporary step in God's immutable plan, a step beyond which men progressed as time passed and revelation became clearer and clearer, for Dod that Law, man's condition, and the contents of God's plan were also immutable. For Puritans, process of history had had minimal effect upon the lot of man.

A man happy and successful in any "establishment," be it political, economic, academic, or religious, is a man relatively at ease with and able to operate with the things of this world. A retrospective yet progressive view of history comes naturally to him, for it assures him (or expresses his assurance) that the history of the world has produced his oyster. It is not surprising that he wishes to conserve these things which history and his own efforts have brought forth, that he resists extending his notions of progress into the future, that he becomes what we call conservative. Nor is it surprising that protesters, men less at ease with and constitutionally unable to work within the established order of things, evoke a much more static, sociological, cyclic, and future-oriented view of human history. Life within the established order does not provide a sense of stability for such men's lives, and so they seek for one outside of this world.

Thus, for example, one of the central motifs of the Puritans' reverence for the Sabbath was an unusually prominent emphasis upon God's immutability and by extension upon the unchanging nature of his eternal plan. Neither God nor his design were affected, altered, or contaminated by the process of history. The root of Sabbatarian theory is the most un-Pauline conviction that the fourth commandment binds modern Christians just as it bound the ancient Jews. God could not lie and, they confidently believed, he was a plain-speaking God. He stated unambiguously what he wished us to do, indeed he even fixed it in stone, and it followed that since his word and plan were immutable, he meant that injunction to be eternal and as long during as rock. He and his word provided something stable to hang onto in this dark swirl of human error. Here we may see how the Puritan habit of removing the Son from time, of asserting that he was eternal and of playing down his suffering here below is a mental gesture, a way of giving God the glory, analogous to insisting on the unchanging permanence of his plan. If this world is corrupt, the Puritans craved something "fixt forever firm and sure" outside of it upon which to fasten their hopes.[15]

This disinclination to talk and write about historical change manifested itself in another way. The Sabbatarians argued that the Sabbath had been kept before the Ten Commandments were written down, that it had been kept from the very beginning by Adam; and they finally pushed its institution back even further in time by claiming that Adam kept the Sabbath because he wished to follow a model laid down by God when he rested during and thereby instituted the Sabbath in the first great week of creation. That was to remove the institution of and authority for the Sabbath from human history entirely and was a manner of arguing which again cohered obviously with the Calvinistic emphasis upon the eternal nature of the Son and the de-emphasis of his entrance into time. Christ was the lamb slain from before time; the Sabbath was the resting day instituted before time.

The response of anti-Sabbatarians to this sort of speculation is illuminating. They termed it, shortly, "Judaical." John Prideaux said he wished "to explode their *errors,* who either seem to tend on the one side to *Atheism* or on the other side to *Judaism.*"[16] John Pocklington, whose sermon was publicly burnt by the Puritans in London during the Commonwealth, argued on the verbal level that the Hebrew word Sabbath was itself Judaical and totally inappropriate to the Christian holiday. To that effect he asked, "What shall we think then of Knox and Whittingham and their fellows, that in their letter to Calvin depart from the constitution, ordinance, and practice of the Apostles and apostolic men and call not the day the Lord's day, or *Sunday,* but with the piety of Jeroboam make such a day of it as they have devised in their own hearts to serve their own turn, and anabaptizing it after the mind of some Jew hired to be the god-father thereof, call it the Sabbath."[17] His remarks on the theological implications of Puritan diction became conventional anti-Sabbatarian arguments; the Puritan Sabbatarians were fixated on Herbert's "Jews of old" and wouldn't progress beyond them. And the Puritans more or less agreed, choosing sides by choosing "Judaical" words and concepts. Diction and dogma, again, match. "Sabbath" was a Puritan word, "Judaical," to the establishment; "Sunday" and "Lord's day" were Christian and less favored by the Puritans.[18]

Men of Prideaux's and Pocklington's persuasion saw Christ's ministry as the center of a progressive history and the conclusion of a clearly defined historical period. Pocklington quoted Tertullian to connect Christ bowing to death on the cross with his anti-Sabbatarian argument: "it is manifest, therefore, that that cannot be moral nor perpetual that began but with Moses (as Saint Justin Martyr says) and ended with Christ, when he nailed all the ceremonial law to his cross with those words, *consummatum est,* it is finished" (p. 17). The period of Mosaic dispensation began occasionally, "but with Moses," and ended with that bowing in humiliation which we must imitate in the liturgy. It was not "perpetual" nor established at creation, but commanded at Sinai; later still, Christ had replaced the old with the new. Establishment anti-Sabbatarians, in other words, conceived of God's immutable plan as incorporating within itself elements of historical change; the plan itself was unchanging, but the contents were occasional, temporary, and fluid.

A hint as to why the Puritans tended to squeeze the process out of history and fasten almost compulsively upon the eternal verities of God's doubly immutable plan (immutable, that is, both in form and content) may be gathered from a clear-cut change which occurred in the purely formal arrangement of their books on this subject. Theoretical speculation upon the Sabbath seems to have derived originally from a very practical Puritan aim—to purify daily life as they saw it in this world about them. The first tracts were hardly theological at all, except by implication. Humphrey Roberts's *An earnest complaint of divers vain, wicked and abused exercises practised on the Saboth day* (1572) and John Northbrooke's *Spiritus est vicarius Christi in terra. A treatise wherein dicing, dauncing, vaine playes or enterluds with other idle pastimes, &c., commonly used on the Sabboth day, are reproued by the authoritie of the word of God and auntient writers* (1577?) attack practices which they do not like. In 1595, Nicholas Bownd provided some theoretical underpinnings (about half of his work) before he went on to resolve practical cases of conscience. Dividing one's attention about equally between theory and practice remained conventional for several years after Bownd, but by mid-century, Puritan treatises dropped practice altogether and concentrated purely on abstract speculation. That is, Puritan Sabbatarians began by attacking corrupt practices in this world, but in order to clean the mess up, they had first to systematize their belief; in the process of systematizing, they moved their discussion right out of this world of practical concerns and ascended to the plane of pure theory. The logical extension of that transcendent movement was made by Milton, who cheerfully ignored what

he considered to be the petty practice of keeping the rigorous Puritan
Sabbath. He returned to the original Pauline notion that the Law genders
to bondage (Gal. 4.24), but he did so, we can see from his analysis, by
passing through Puritan Sabbatarianism and only then going beyond it to
meditate on eternal rest.

Dod began his exposition of the Ten Commandments, as I have pointed
out, with just such a theoretical, methodological section explaining how
there is a natural instinct "written and engraven in every man's conscience"
to follow the timeless law. "Every man" and his conscience dwell outside
of time and history, for Dod's parallel syntactic construction (relying exclusively, to repeat an earlier point, on copulative verbs) not only tosses
us into the same categorical basket with Adam but places us in a relationship parallel to Adam's under the law. Dod embodies the same proposition
in a two-page catalogue of illustrative examples—all drawn from the Old
Testament—which he so applies as to show that "we must hence learn with
all reverence to hearken unto them and willingly to hear the admonitions
and rebukes that are contained in them, whosoever we be" (p. 5). "Whosoever," like "every man," covers a lot of historical ground, as Dod uses
it, since it extends back to Adam and down to us too.

The Puritan's habit of pursuing sociological rather than historical analysis, of focusing, that is, upon the ways in which "all good men in all times"
are bound together under the same timeless dispensation, rather than upon
the evolution of the Christian dispensation over time, jibes neatly with
their habit of removing "the Eternal Son of God" from time. Early in his
book Dod explicates the name "Jehovah" in ways which show these inter-
connections. Jehovah, he says, "signifieth the essence of God," and that
essence is "expressed in *Hebrews* 13.8., *Christ yesterday, and today, and
the same for ever*, and *Revel.* 1.4., *He that was, and is, and is to come.*"
Since the name Jehovah has connotations of wrath and fire and particularly of judgment, glossing it so casually with these texts and not those
from Exodus which explicate the name calls our attention to the similarity
between Dod's language and the anti-Roman controversialists' habit of
linking Christ with God the Father when they disputed about bowing.
Essential to both is an anachronistic habit of mind, common enough in
Christian apologetic, but unusually prominent in the writing of Puritans
who sought to express God's timeless vision of the world. And, it is timelessness which Dod next emphasizes, both formally and intellectually: the
name Jehovah "declareth first God's eternity whereby he differs from all
creatures, whereas men and angels, though they be everlasting and so shall
have no ending, yet they be not eternal for they had a beginning from him
as other things had, but he from none. Also power, and wisdom, and mercy,
and justice, and such other things which are properties in men and angels,
in him are natures; in us they are weak and imperfect, in him absolute and

perfect" (p. 14). Grammatically, these two sentences segregate "eternity" from the other attributes of God, which trail weakly off into "such other things," while Dod's argument separates God from man. One attribute stands alone and requires elaboration while the rest get lumped indefinitely together with little comment. Even if we merely count words, we can tell easily which attribute interested Dod most. In addition, however, the sentence segregates "eternity" from God's other attributes intellectually as well as formally. For Dod feels he can most completely and clearly separate God from man (as Puritans always sought to do) in terms of his eternity; men and angels share the other attributes partially which God has absolutely. There is, then, both a doctrinal and syntactic segregation of that single attribute from the others in a sentence segregating God from man.

Dod attempted to avoid sounding literally "Judaical" when he stated that we must "keep this law spiritually" in our "inward parts." The ancient Israelites keep the letter, but we must do more; the laws of men constrain only "the hand and the tongue and the foot" but God's law affects our "inward parts," our "heart," and the "inward motions of the soul" (p. 8). Like "bare capping and kneeling," Dod distrusts "such a love only as is declared by the outward behavior of the body" and he spiritualizes the law here in precisely the terms in which Puritan commentators turned liturgical bowing into an eschatological prophecy.

Most telling, perhaps, are Dod's remarks about the way he and his fellow Puritans read the Bible, for they show how emphasizing God's "eternity" fitted in with the "patriarchical" tone of Puritan writing. One consequence of God's "eternity," according to Dod, is that "if God is the same for ever and that in his dealing to his children," if he has in the past used his "power . . . and wisdom . . . and mercy for their comfort," then "he will do the same for us also." "He being Jehovah, the same for ever without any change, he must deliver us also when we call upon him" (p. 15). Many a Puritan battle cry would eventuate from such a restatement of Calvin's doctrine of the covenant. "Unless we believe that God is Jehovah, and immutable, all the histories of the Scripture are made unprofitable unto us" (p. 15). Now there are certain histories, recorded in the New Testament, which Dod seems to ignore completely here. Obviously he is trying to argue that the Old Testament is an open rather than a closed book to Christians and that the decalogue still binds us. But he has a most unusual way of putting that thought, referring as he does to "*all* the histories of the Scripture" yet clearly ignoring the history of Christ's ministry; his minor slip of tongue illuminates clearly the spirit in which Puritans read their Bible as well as the pages to which they instinctively turned. In the Puritan view, England was an "elected nation" because it was "peculiar" to God as Israel had been; the patriarchs and prophets formed the core of Puritan

reading and thought, as anachronism and exegesis came together in triumphant assertion: "Whatsoever good thing he did for them, he will do the
like for us" (p. 16). That was the sounding brass from which Parliamentary
and New Model trumpets would be cast.

The thread binding these expressions together is a sort of historical
and doctrinal immobility which paradoxically underlay stirring calls to
arms. That immobility was expressed through the systematizing or methodizing efforts of Puritan theologians, through their insistence that on the
Sabbath men memorialized God's first "rest" from the work of creation
by resting from their workday labors and through their hope that the
weekly Sabbath prefigured that eternal rest when all human labor in this
messy and threatening world would cease. John Sprint ticked off, as briefly
as any Sabbatarian, the Puritan application of Dod's theoretical remarks to
the specific practice of keeping the Sabbath; he summarized the collective,
reformed position or "mean" view and "harmony of judgment" on it:

> 1. That the fourth commandment is partly moral and perpetual, and
> partly ceremonial, proper to the Jew, and quite abolished. 2. That the
> ceremonial of that law stood in the seventh day's rest from the creation,
> the strictness of that rest, the shadowing of Christ to come and rest in
> the grave which was performed on the Sabbath day, and Jewish cere-
> monies and sacrifices tied unto their observations of it. 3. That the pub-
> lic worship of God, preaching and hearing of the word, administering
> and receiving of the sacraments and prayer, together with the works of
> mercy, giving rest to servants and to cattle upon a certain and defined
> day (to which some add the limit of the time—one day of seven), is the
> moral of the fourth commandment and of the law of nature belonging
> to us as well as to the Jews. 4. That the Apostles of Christ did themselves
> translate the Jewish Sabbath into the Lord's day. 5. That this translation
> by the Apostles is to be proved and concluded directly out of those
> places of *Act.* 20.7, *I Corin.* 16.1, *Rev.* 1.10. 6. That this alteration was
> therefore made both to put a difference between the Jews and Chris-
> tians as also in memorial of our Savior's resurrection. 7. That the primi-
> tive churches, Fathers, and Christian princes did in their several times
> always observe and cause to be observed the Lord's day with all holy
> solemnity and godly reverence. 8. And lastly, that the Lord's day is by
> no means to be condemned, but hath well and rightly been observed by
> themselves and others, heretofore from the Apostles and hereafter to
> the world's end, above all other days, seeing it is the received and con-
> firmed manner, the which must needs be better and more fit than any.[19]

It is essential to understand the terms of this summary before we can see
the immense immobility which it embodied. The fourth commandment
is at once "moral and perpetual" and yet "ceremonial," temporary, and

"abolished." The "ceremonial" part, wiped out by the process of history and therefore of little interest, is that part of the commandment which was specifically "Judaical" even to Puritans. The moral and perpetual part, unchanging and binding all good men in all times, concerns "public worship" (preaching the word and administering the sacraments made up the whole of the conventional Protestant definition of the church), was confirmed by the apostles, "primitive churches, Fathers, and Christian princes," and will remain in force in its "received and confirmed manner" until "the world's end." Historical process has, admittedly, had its effect on the Sabbath; the apostles, those touchstones for Protestant practice, had "translated" the Sabbath of the seventh day into the Christian "Lord's day" or Sunday, and there were specific texts which seemed to enjoin that change. There is a difference between Christian and Jewish practice, a result of historical change, but "all good men" in the Christian Church, all really good "Fathers" and "Christian princes" have steadfastly supported the keeping of the Lord's day, although (it goes without saying) bad churchmen have also tried (with frightening success) to corrupt that practice. That is, if Puritans tried to anchor their Sabbath securely by tracing it back beyond the bounds of time, if they used that timeless base to project a stable future in the millennium, and if they appealed to the stability of God's specific word made concretely manifest in the rock of the two tablets, they tried to do much the same thing for the Christian Sunday after it had been altered from the Jewish Sabbath.

Sprint appended to his summary a list of three propositions which were still debated among the "godly learned" who accepted the broad harmony.

> First, whether the keeping holy of the seventh day or any one day of every seven be part of the moral law of God and be perpetually to be observed. Secondly, whether the Lord's day or first day of the week (called commonly our Sunday) be established *jure divino,* by the will and ordinance of Christ instead of the Jewish Sabbath, and do tie the conscience. Thirdly, whether the Church of God might have chosen at the first another day or hath yet authority or Christian liberty to abrogate or alter the Lord's day into any other certain or uncertain day, or whether it be not of necessity to be continued to the end of the world. [P. 7]

Here the process by which doctrines solidified may be seen briefly at work. Sprint and his brethren, who were "in this point of the more strict sort," believed that there was a positive, moral injunction to keep one day in seven—that was the moral and perpetual commandment—while keeping the seventh day had been ceremonial. They believed there was a positive biblical injunction to change from worshipping on the seventh to worshipping on the first day—as positive as the commandment on Sinai or at creation. The command to alter the day was "jure divino," it was not the result of arbitrary alteration or ecclesiastical authority; Sunday was no matter of indifference, as (among many others) Charles supposed. The king thought "it will not be found in Scripture where Saturday is discharged to be kept or turned into the Sunday," and he was right; the Puritans had made that injunction up, precisely in order to circumvent Charles's conclusion that "it must be the Church's authority that changed the one and instituted the other."[20] Establishment anti-Sabbatarians even speculated that the Church might have instituted any day of the week; if Wednesday was as good as Sunday, however, then the whole Sabbath business became utterly arbitrary, and the Puritans could not stand that thought. So they developed the view that God had positively said "keep one day in seven" *and* "change from the seventh to the first day." The way they fabricated a divine injunction reveals just how desperate they were to establish their practice on something as granitelike as the Law of Sinai. "Jure divino" was the club by which they beat down the worldly claims which ecclesiasts made for the authority of the church.

That was what Bownd had been up to when he argued that the Sabbath was instituted "from the beginning, when God rested from creation, and has been, is, and will always be a seventh day." The Sabbath "ought still to be continued with us" just as "from the beginning" for "so soon as the day was, so soon was it sanctified, that we might know that as it came in with the first man so it must not go out but with the last man" (pp. 5-6). That was what Dod was getting at when he argued that "the keeping of the Sabbath day holy is a moral law and bindeth us and all men, to the end of the world, as much as it did the Jews afore Christ" (p. 132). Millennial expectation confronts and opposes ecclesiastic authority. God (or a Puritan) speaks from outside time for all time; the Church simply follows his injunctions and awaits the end of time.

John Milton disagreed with much that the Sabbatarians had to say, from reasons as diverse as his radical habits of mind, his antinomian claims for the power of holy poetic utterance, his arguments concerning divorce, and his insistence upon Christian liberty. I wish later to comment more fully on the ways in which he diverged from Puritan orthodoxy on this point and the means by which we may account for it. Here I wish only to notice that Milton was fundamentally a Puritan in his conception of the Sabbath, however he diverged from orthodoxy in details. His first controversial comments concerning the Sabbath occurred in *The Reason of Church-Government Urg'd Against Prelaty* when he wished to argue that Old Testament injunctions concerning priests and Levites did not support episcopacy: "The whole Judaick law is either politicall, and to take pattern by that, no Christian nation ever thought it selfe oblig'd in conscience; or morall, which containes in it the observation of whatsoever is substantially, and perpetually true and good, either in religion, or course of life. That which is thus morall . . . the Gospell, as stands with her dignity most, lectures to us from her own authentick hand-writing." The Gospel is more than the Law and perfects it, yet what is moral needs no perfection and is taught (as Hooper had stated more flatly) both by the Gospel and by the Law. History purified God's dispensation, and therefore, although the Church "retain[s] the morality of the Sabbath, [yet] she does not therefore imitate the law her underling, but perfect[s] her" (CE, 3: 197). The offices of the "ministers of the Gospell, succeeding those in the law, as the Lords day did the Sabbath," are polished or perfected versions of Old Testament patterns (CE, 3: 206).

Later, in *De Doctrina,* Milton came explicitly to reject much of the Puritan position, yet even there he began by saying that the time of worship under the Law "was the SABBATH, that is, the seventh day, which was consecrated to God from the beginning of the world, *Gen.* ii.2,3" (II, vii; Yale ed., p. 705). References to the Sabbath in *Paradise Lost* are also minimally Puritan and few in number. After the sixth day, the creative Son ascends:

> And now on Earth the Seventh
> Eev'ning arose in *Eden,*
>
> .   .   .   .
>
> when at the holy mount
> Of Heav'ns high-seated top, th'Impereal Throne
> Of Godhead, fixt for ever firm and sure,
> The Filial Power arriv'd, and sate him down
> With his great Father
>
> .   .   .   .
>
> and from work
> Now resting, bless'd and hallowd the Seav'nth day,
> As resting on that day from all his work,
> But not in silence holy kept   [7:581-94]

The angels sing with the music of the spheres, and "Thus was Sabbath kept" joyfully in heaven. Raphael seems to have understood that the Sabbath was for rest (although perhaps the Father simply arranged for him and his cohorts to act as if they did); at any rate, he and the other guardian angels leave their post outside the gates of hell and reascend to heaven "Ere Sabbath Eev'ning" since their trip upward was "no journey of a Sabbath day." I shall return to the other Puritan aspects of Milton's views on the time of worship, but here we can see that he associated it with creation and believed that there were certain "moral and perpetual" elements of that first rest and the hallowing of it which occurred at the close of creation.

Dod and Bownd agreed that since the Sabbath was instituted at creation,

Adam had to keep it in Eden; Milton demurred on this point, yet he did paint a startling picture of Adam surprisingly like Dod's and Bownd's. According to Bownd, Adam, had he not fallen, *"should have kept that day holy above the rest,"* while he pursued some "honest calling and work" on the other six (p. 5). Dod queried: "if he had need of this [commandment] . . . because his calling . . . would yet partly have withdrawn his heart [from God]. . . , then what need have we! and how far is our necessity greater?" (p. 129). Both are suggesting that Adam was potentially fallen before the fall, that he resembles us much more closely than he differs from us, that he ran the risk of getting so interested in his calling on the six days that he might ignore God altogether unless checked on the seventh. To much the same effect, Millicent Bell argued that no fall occurs in *Paradise Lost* because Adam and Eve were flawed by a potentiality for sin right from the beginning of the poem.[21] Both kinds of argument suffer from a certain inflexibility and absoluteness of phrasing. Dod and Bownd seem to be arguing that, if Adam was good, and if all good men in all times have kept the Sabbath, then Adam must have kept the Sabbath for the same reasons we do. Bell begins by expecting some absolute distinction between unfallen and fallen man, some utterly pure model of perfection, and when she does not find it in *Paradise Lost,* she reacts by stating equally absolutely that no fall occurs there.

Both positions might well profit from the sort of qualification which Bownd himself offered, that *"Adam* was perfect and needed no ceremony to lead him to Christ, because he did not need to believe in Christ, being himself perfect and holding his happy estate not by faith in Christ's merits but by confidence in God's word" (p. 127). That is, Adam both resembles us (because he has the potential for sin) and differs from us (in not having realized it). In Dod and Bownd, then, we find the Puritan notion that a common dispensation binds all good men in all time pushed about as far back as it can go, and we can see the sociologists' impulse, essential to that argument, embodied in what Bell calls the "foreshadowing" of sin in Milton's poem. Bell and Dod forget what Bownd and H. V. S. Ogden remembered to add: that moral "perfection" may include the unrealized potential for sin.[22] But Bell does suggest something important about *Paradise Lost* and the Puritan roots of Milton's vision. There are important ways in which Adam and Eve do not change over time, for Milton paints a psychological portrait of the two in the early books which makes the ways in which they later fall characteristic of their personalities. And when Eve makes her fateful suggestion that the two separate and fears lest "th' hour of Supper comes unearn'd"(9:225), she is paying too much attention to their "calling and work." Milton has very carefully made it clear that Adam and Eve *must* pleasantly labor to restrain an Eden "tending to wild." He posits a setting which requires they act like the "industrious sort," and the

point of this poetic strategy seems to be to remind us that, like us, Adam
and Eve simultaneously had to keep busy and had to avoid becoming too
interested in their business. It is precisely the economic tension which
Hill points out in the theory of the Sabbath, which increased and regular-
ized the time in which men could work yet restrained them during the
seventh day from overdoing.

As John Parish observed some time ago, Milton's Adam was the first
Christian.[23] To mention only one way in which, even before his lapse, he
provides models of Christian conduct, he sets us an example of unpremeditated worship before he falls and he undergoes the entire process of regeneration necessary (as Milton argued in *De Doctrina Christiana*) for salvation after the fall. Parish points us to a specific habit of portraying Adam
which far from all Christians follow; his list of analogues might be supple-
mented from seventeenth-century sources by a whole host of *specifically*
Puritan commentators. Thomas Hayne, for example, created a little deathbed speech for his Adam which he felt was scripturally based on or derived
"from his story."

> O my sons, gather you together and hearken unto the words of your
> father Adam, the last that ever he shall speak unto you. I was void of
> salvation and enjoyed not happiness by disobeying, which disobedience
> I then practiced when I hearkened to the persuasion of Heva and did eat
> the forbidden fruit. I then felt the heavy judgments of God against sin
> and saw my nakedness, whereof I was ashamed. Thereby I brought
> death upon all my posterity, which curse had continued if the mercy of
> God had not removed it by offering a blessing in the seed of the woman.
> I have ruled you all the days of my life as a father, that you may learn
> to choose governors which resemble fathers in behavior. I have instructed
> you to love and obey their government; you must know that as my sal-
> vation resteth upon belief in the seed of the woman so must yours. But
> the house of Cain, despising this and hating Abel, a figure of him who
> by dying shall overcome the power of the serpent, will cause the flood
> to destroy the earth. Few shall embrace this doctrine, for though eight
> be saved by the ark, yet seven only shall keep sincerely the belief in the
> promise of the seed of the woman. My days have been long with the
> rest of your fathers, but the end of all flesh is come upon me; for out
> of the earth I came, and to the earth I must return.[24]

Here we find Adam "void of salvation" before or just at the fall (the implication being that he has undergone the standard Christian process of regeneration since), and able to assert that Abel will be a type of "him who
by dying shall overcome the power of the serpent." Hayne is representing
overtly what many commentators like Dod and Bownd implied: Adam
must have been the first Christian since all good men in all times were saved

by Christ in the same way. The Adam of the medieval lyric lay bound in sin "four þowsand wynter."

> Adam lay I-bowndyn, bowndyn in a bond,
> Fowre þowsand wynter þowt he not to long;
> And al was for an appil, an appil þat he tok,
> As clerkis fyndyn wretyn in here book.
>
> Ne hadde þe appil take ben, þe appil taken ben,
> Ne hadde neuer our lady a ben heuene qwen;
> Blyssid be þe tyme þat appil take was,
> þer-fore we mown syngyn, '*deo gracias*'.[25]

Hayne's and Milton's Adam in contrast can sing "deo gracias" *with us*, either on his deathbed (for Hayne) or in book twelve of *Paradise Lost!* He can rejoice to see Christ's day and the New Jerusalem because he is nearly related to the Adam of Bownd and Dod who kept the Sabbath lest he forget God in Eden. Historical process does not operate in the world view of men who see Adam that way; the harrowing of hell, that device of the old, authoritarian church for rescuing Adam and the patriarchs, was a nonevent for them. It was, on the one hand, part and parcel of the hated Roman Catholic doctrine of purgatory (hated originally, it would seem, for primarily economic reasons); it represented the extreme nadir of Christ's descent (and humiliation); and it suspended those excellent patriarchs in the flux and messiness of human history, provisionally awaiting the process of time. Worldliness, worldliness, all was worldliness about the harrowing of hell. The Puritans quickly turned that historical event in time into a psychological and sociological constant.

Hence, advanced or radical Protestants pushed out and away from that central cluster of events surrounding the cross; they moved backward in time, de-emphasizing historical change and proposing that Adam was the first Christian. "No action of Christ doth of itself sanctify any time," argued Thomas Shepard; if we did not believe that, we should be forced to "keep as many holy days every year as we find holy actions of Christ recorded in scripture, as the superstitious crew of blind Papists do at this day." From this sort of position, which Milton would logically extend in dismissing even Puritan Sabbath-keeping, Shepard can explain why, given that God's commands are eternal, the day of worship had been changed. Echoing the language of the dispute over bowing, Shepard argues that "the Lord Christ in the day of his incarnation and birth did not enter into his rest, but rather made entrance into his labor and sorrow, who then began the work of humiliation," and so, by implication, Christmas should not be celebrated as a holiday; moreover, "in the day of his passion, he was then under the sorest part and feeling of his labor, in bitter agonies upon the cross and in the garden," and so Good Friday is no holiday either. "And hence it is that none of those days were consecrated to be our Sabbath or rest-days which were days of Christ's labor and sorrow." In contrast, Christians ought to celebrate the first day in memory of his victorious resurrection, "the day of Christ's rest from the work of Redemption," which neatly parallels, syntactically and doctrinally, the original Sabbath or God's "rest from the work of creation."[26] Resting remains constant over time and prefigures the final rest when our situation in the kingdom of the saints will become fixed and constant as well—a beatific, eternal, triumphant peace and rest from our struggles in time.

In the medieval lyric, the fortunate aspects of the fall are revealed through the process of history. In *Paradise Lost,* those same aspects are made clear through a change in Adam's perception of historical events and through the reader's assessment of those changes. True, there is change in the poem. Stanley Fish's entire argument about what happens to the reader is based on the assumption that the poem is a unified process with beginning, middle, and end.[27] Bell was wrong that Adam and Eve do not change; if their psychology remains constant, their moral position does not. And in book twelve, Michael speaks of how mankind has been "disciplin'd/From shadowie Types to Truth" over time. Yet at the end of the poem, Adam remarks upon how Michael's speech has

Measur'd this transient World, the Race of time,
Till time stand fixt: beyond is all abyss,
Eternitie, whose end no eye can reach.   [12:554-56]

Books ten, eleven and twelve each form a loop or epicycle within a larger loop (the entire poem), and as Adam treads these loops, his spiritual progress is not steady and progressive so much as a series of backward and forward motions. Within the loops of each book there are lesser loops or cycles much as Summers has noted, which mirror in microcosm the loop of all human history: time after time, an initial peace is broken by a fall, then restored by God.[28] The historical episodes which Milton there recounts are not firmly tied together in any chronological matrix; any one event does not influence the following events. Moreover, certain crucial events all end with references to the millennium when time will indeed "stand fixt" and become what Puritans always wanted it to become—a sort of rock of ages.

Let me focus briefly on the story of Noah, which completes a loop begun in the first lines of book eleven—a loop of regeneration. Adam undergoes a decisive change of perception here while learning about a story with obvious apocalyptic overtones. During the course of the book he has made numerous errors, scrutinized carefully already by Fish, concerning the nature of death, the sexy marriages of the Sons of God and the Daughters of

Eve, and military and political prowess. When he first sees the flood, the
narrator queries:

How didst thou grieve then, *Adam,* to behold
The end of all thy Ofspring, end so sad,
Depopulation; thee another Floud,
Of tears and sorrow a Floud thee also drown'd,
And sunk thee as thy Sons.   [11:754–58]

And Adam laments in precisely the same mistaken vein:

Let no man seek
Henceforth to be foretold what shall befall
Him or his Childern, evil he may be sure,
Which neither his foreknowing can prevent,
And hee the future evil shall no less
In apprehension then in substance feel
Grievous to bear.   [11:770–76]

His response is profoundly "natural," that of a father for natural children,
and is focused upon loss and punishment. The narrator, entering into
Adam's spiritual state, misleads us slightly when reporting that it is the
"end of *all* thy Ofspring" and Adam goes on in the same pessimistic rut
to say that he is sure that the few in the boat will also die. He focuses on
evil so persistently that Michael must point out that a few do escape. Adam
then rests assured that mankind shall persist and simultaneously he ceases
to be preoccupied with punishment:

Farr less I now lament for one whole World
Of wicked Sons destroyd, then I rejoyce
For one Man found so perfet and so just,
That God voutsafes to raise another World
From him.   [11:874–78]

The language might with ease be applied to Christ and the millennium, and
book eleven ends with a reference to that time when fire will Puritanically

purge all things new,
Both Heav'n and Earth, wherein the just shall dwell.   [11:900–901]

Up to this point, all the "changes" have been occurring in Adam's head
rather than in historical events. The apocalypse is the only objective change
(which has not, let us recall, ever occurred), and that change will destroy
chronos.

Adam goes beyond "natural" to "supernatural" responses, conforms
himself internally to the basic pattern of the universe (God consistently
brings good or greater good out of evil), as he recognizes the fortunate

aspects of the flood. The process inevitably concludes on a distinctly millennial note. That pattern, sharp and well defined in the case of this episode, informs almost all of them. The cycles of unredeemed history in book
twelve each individually contain a reference to the promise of the Seed,
which as Milton handles it is a promise of the "New Heav'n and Earth."[29]
The most famous and most commented-upon episode, in all likelihood, is
that which recounts the crucifixion. The references to the cross are minimal, both in terms of the bulk of the entire poem and in terms of the episode itself. For Michael, in recounting that bit of sacred history, does not
(as an established ecclesiast and conservative Anglican would) stop at the
cross; he devotes six and a half lines to it (12:413-19) then moves through
the resurrection and the acts at the apostles, to ascend finally with the
Son as he shall

> resume
> His seat at Gods right hand, exalted high
> Above all names in Heav'n; and thence shall come,
> When this worlds dissolution shall be ripe,
> With glory and power to judge both quick and dead,
> To judge th'unfaithful dead, but to reward
> His faithful, and receave them into bliss,
> Whether in Heav'n or Earth, for then the Earth
> Shall all be Paradise, far happier place
> Then this of *Eden,* and far happier daies.   [12:456-65]

Here Milton works in an eschatological reference to the name above all
names with a preview of those millennial days, far happier, when time
shall indeed stand fixt. When Adam, in response, speaks of "all this good"
which God shall "of evil produce," he is probably also speaking millennially.
The Son undergoes a process of descent and ascent. Like the story of Noah,
this bit of history is simply a different version of a basic, cyclic pattern.
Spiritual perceptions change (as Adam's do in both these instances) but
history shows very little variation and no linear progress. Creating loops and
cycles but not spiraling up to them *out of lines,* Milton participates in a
Puritan taste for improgressive history and yearns, as his Puritan brethren
did, for the moment when time shall stand fixt.

Chapter 6: RADICAL SABBATARIANISM: SEVENTH-DAY WORSHIP OR CHRISTIAN LIBERTY

The Puritans manifested an immense rage for order and orthodoxy as they wrung immensely "logical" doctrine and rigorous "orthodoxy" out of what has generally been a paradoxical and polysemous web. The major effect of their manner of analyzing a problem was to uncover assumptions and realize tendencies. It is not therefore surprising that two radical extensions of their thinking, both unacceptable to the orthodox, although for quite different reasons, emerged with startling clarity during the middle of the seventeenth century: seventh-day Sabbatarianism and an almost antinomian appeal to Christian liberty. The first accentuated further the rigor and rigidity of the Law and the inflexibility of historical process and of God's commands. The second pushed the Puritan emphasis on election so far that certain adepts began to claim special freedoms or new dispensations, and appealed to the Puritan's preference for "inward" rather than "outward" worship while bringing the millennium closer to men. The first logically extended the Puritans' intellectual rigidity and compulsiveness about order; the second embodied the free-flowing, revolutionary spirit of optimism which came to a head during the Wars and got expressed in such diverse contexts as Parliamentary preaching, Quaker doctrine, and Milton's prose and poetry.

Despite their rage for systematic and logical order, the Puritans were profoundly inconsistent on two points concerning the Sabbath: they refused to follow the ahistorical implications of their scriptural analysis to its logical conclusion—celebrating the seventh day ordained on Sinai and at creation—and they believed that the process of history had not only perfected the Sabbath day into Sunday but that it had also perfected their own theological arguments. The first of these inconsistencies is instructive in many ways: it shows first whither Puritan thought tended, for when Puritans combated seventh-day Sabbatarianism, they had to reverse directions both logically and rhetorically, emphasizing change where before they emphasized eternity and rest. Secondly, that about-face provides yet another, clearly focused example of how theological argument matched literary style in controversy. Thirdly, if the apparent inconsistency between what they urged on behalf of the Christian Sabbath and what they urged against the seventh-day Sabbath shows whither the Puritan's logic tended, it also allows us to see how a man like Milton might emerge from Puritan intellectual surroundings denying the keeping of the Puritan Sabbath.

The key to the Puritan attack on seventh-day Sabbatarianism lies in their distinction between moral commandments which are perpetual, and ceremonial commandments which fade with time. Sprint's definition of the fourth commandment as "partly moral and perpetual, and partly ceremonial, proper to the Jew, and quite abolished" was essential to his attack upon what he called that "extremity of opinion . . . that the Jewish Sabbath of the seventh day in the week from the creation is never to be abolished."[1] When he outlined what he called that "Jewish" or "Anabaptist" position, he showed how, in effect, it simply extended Puritanic, Sabbatarian logic and rhetoric, for, he said, its proponents argued from "the precedence of the Sabbath before the law and before the fall . . . the perpetuity of the moral law . . . the perpetuity of the covenant . . . the memorial and meditation of the works of God" (p. 2). These were, of course, the arguments which "orthodox" Puritan Sabbatarians advanced on behalf of their doctrine against conservative opponents; the seventh-day Sabbatarians simply flattened a somewhat complex position into logical consistency by making no distinction between what was perpetual and what was "a shadow of things to come, and . . . abolished" (p. 3). They apparently read more literally than even their Puritan brethren, argued that everything in the commandment was perpetual, and applied the Sabbatarian arguments to the day as well as the significance of keeping the day.

When Puritan Sabbatarians set out to rebut seventh-day Sabbatarians, then, they faced a super-Puritanic opponent, a set of men who stole their language, their intellectual method, and their fondness for literal interpretation of the Scripture, who realized their own dreams and fantasies, and who wrote in what was essentially their own theological spirit. For the seventh-day Sabbatarians not only squeezed the last little bit of change and movement out of the Puritan doctrine of the Sabbath—the change from the seventh to the first day—but they also completed a kind of methodical and systematic elaboration which the Puritans themselves might have celebrated as their own contribution to intellectual progress. Perry Miller has remarked upon what we might call a rage for orthodoxy among Puritan divines, a habit of bringing method and order to a set of theological propositions and of building upon past writers.[2] Intellectually, the Puritans were not innovative or original so much as conformist; they were not leaders so much as led. Two facts illustrate that: the fact that Sabbatarianism was the single contribution of English Puritanism to Reformed theology (despite the fact that English Puritans wrote voluminously about theological matters) and the fact that even Puritan tracts on the Sabbath, aside from minor changes of focus and a historical tendency to talk more about theory and less about practice, are as like as peas in a pod. Rather than innovating, Puritans refined previous arguments, brought system to a previously articulated position, drew out implications and elaborated arguments within a framework of thought already at hand.

Indeed, it was that systematic elaboration which they themselves defined as intellectual progress. When Sprint turned to consider certain "points of difference among the godly learned" within the broad, eight-point "harmony of judgment," he explained those differences by pointing out that the "former sort and company of reverend and godly writers (for the most part) living in the times next above us" who asserted the "more remiss and weaker judgment" were conditioned by the "opposition that they bare against the Papists." Once the Roman adversary had been vanquished and Protestant could sit down with Protestant to work out the finer parts of their theory, doctrinal acuity sharpened and a "more sincere and strict" interpretation emerged, "God (as it were) rewarding the diligence and pains of every age with the revealing of some part of truth" (pp. 7–8). In such a scheme of things, no man and no doctrinal position can escape the march of time; Sprint himself fell victim to it when forty-two years later Thomas Shepard derided the "many arguments heaped up and multiplied" which "seem of great weight, while they want an adversary" preaching seventh-day Sabbatarianism, yet turn out to be "light" when put to the test; Shepard footnoted Sprint's book as an example of early, facile optimism. Shepard's intellectual superiority derives largely from the fact that a Mr. Bradbourne had begun recently to preach the seventh-day doctrine. Historical process allows Shepard "to accept that little light which God gives us in greater as well as of such light as he is pleased to lend us in smaller matters" just as Sprint had benefitted from "the revealing of some part of truth" in his own age by new, Protestant opponents.[3]

This small example must serve, given the limitations of this study, to illustrate what has been more largely documented by other scholars; the Puritans, who were the religious innovators of their age, did not so much innovate as methodize and solidify and elaborate upon a few great intellectual breakthroughs of the early Reformers. That observation will first remind us that the sixteenth and early seventeenth centuries produced a great deal of backward-looking intellection based on traditions and precedents,[4] and second will allow us to see how intellectual method and theological doctrine reflect each other and form a part of the Puritan's quest for an almost concrete permanence in this ever-changing world. The elaborate, Ramistic schemata prefixed before William Ames's *Marrow of sacred divinity* and countless similar works may seem, of themselves, to have no theological or intellectual content; the brackets and bipartite branches may seem merely a curious way of organizing that content, but they are not. For the bipartite patterns match the bipartite vision of the Puritan universe—God and man, sin and salvation, life and death, eternity and time, soul and body, Christ and Antichrist, doctrine and use. And secondly, however fortuitous that resemblance may be, once one can diagram a position, that position is also fixed forever firm and sure. Indeed, since we are to look at such a scheme rather than read through it, it offers a way of avoiding the effects of process of speech upon the reader over time. Puritanic elaboration upon and systematization of a few central precepts amounts, then, to the process of working out such schemata and creating an immensely coherent and self-consistent pattern which extends out from the center into every aspect of life in this universe. The contribution which any single Puritan divine made to theological "knowledge" might amount to little more than a second branch on one of these diagrams or a new bracket; yet each bit was "useful" because it further methodized the system and permitted that all-inclusive diagramming which the most wide-ranging theologians, like Ames, performed. Putting in an additional bracket or branch fixed one more part of the scheme in a settled relationship with the whole.

One might well ask why the Puritans felt such a compulsive rage for order, system, and orthodoxy, and the answer seems to lie ready at hand: their analysis of human nature was dour indeed and was matched by a potentially revolutionary impulse to change things as they were and men as they saw them. They saw this world as more bad than good, as potentially chaotic rather than orderly, as frightening rather than reassuring. It is not surprising that they sought for something to hang onto in such a world and that they would remove that something from or define it out of this world. Systematizing doctrine about a systematic and eternal God is logical behavior for such men, and it would seem that the exercise served the purpose for which it was undertaken. For, at the same time that Puritans brought more and more of the world within the branches and brackets of their diagrams, they also became more confident and assertive about their beliefs. Sprint again exemplifies in miniature how his sense that God had progressively allowed Puritan theologians to see more and more clearly in each succeeding year was matched by an increasing stridency and assertiveness of tone. He begins his book in an amiable, understanding, moderate frame of mind and tone, speaking of a broad "mean" position, of "harmony," and of "judgments" and "opinions." He can patiently explain the reasons why he dissents from former writers, and speak relatively of the "more sincere" and "more remiss and weaker judgment." But when he arrives at his peroration, at the end of his analysis, he is talking about serious, almost cataclysmic differences, about truth and falsehood rather than difference of opinion. He need no longer explain the sinfulness of Sabbath-breakers because they are so obviously wicked and he will not speak relatively but rather in terms of black and white about clearly polarized views.

And thus (*O reader*) according to the model of my present strength, thou hast the truth of the Christian Sabbath proposed and confirmed to thy conscience; a doctrine harmless, true and holy, making thee holy and preparing thee to heaven, agreeing to the Scripture, to right reason, to common civility, and even to civil policies; a doctrine conforming us to the commandment of God, yea even to his blessed and holy image; a doctrine bringing much glory unto God and benefit to man, knowledge to the ignorant, sense unto the hardened, direction to the willing, discipline to the irregular, conscience to the obstinate, comfort to the conscienced, and bringing none inconvenience in the world; a doctrine that addeth face, fashion, growth and firmitude unto a church, strength and comely order to a commonwealth, giving propagation unto the Gospel, help and vigor to the laws, ease, honor, and obedience unto the governors, unity and quiet to the people, and lastly, certain happiness and blessing to them all. For the which doctrine whosoever argues, pleadeth for GOD, for his glory, for his worship, for his commandment and will, for his Word, his sacraments and invocation; for the Law, for the Gospel, for Moses and the Prophets, for CHRIST and his Apostles, for the upholding and flourishing estate of the Church and commonwealth, of schools and universities, and of the faithful ministry of Christ. In a word, they plead for the wearied body's rest, for the evil conscience's quiet, for the sound practice of godliness and mercy, in a certain, settled and constant order, and so by consequence, for heaven itself.

The contrary judgment worketh contrary effects. For it depriveth GOD of his honor, the Church of religion, the commonwealth of order, the body of rest, the soul of instruction, the life of direction, the word of attendance, the ministry of reverence, and draws along a world of inconveniences and mischiefs besides. For it plainly breedeth sloth and scandal in the ministry, neglect and mere contempt of ministry in the people; confirming blindness and superstition in the ignorant, quenching the zeal of the more forward, strengthening the hands of the more wicked, and giving liberty to them that are too apt to take it of profaning of the Sabbath day of God. It hinders the courses of the Gospel, depriveth of the means of godliness; it defaceth the beauty and cuts in two the very sinews of the Church, enlarging Satan's horrid kingdom and power of darkness by giving strength to atheism, Papism, and carnalgospeling, abolishing the universities by inevitable consequence, and shaking the frame and fabric, yea poisoning up the vital powers of the very commonwealth; and in a word drawing on confusion, irreligion, barbarism, God's curse and utter desolation on them all. [Pp. 35–36]

Just these two paragraphs, while they cap a movement which extends through the entire work, comprise a microcosm of it. The diction heats up as Sprint turns from what he likes to what he hates.

Such an increase in heat and assertiveness operates not only within Sprint's book and its individual paragraphs but over the history of the controversy as a whole. Bownd had begun the whole theoretical enquiry on a modest note, pointing out that his was a tentative essay. A very fine divine had written a much more excellent work, he recalled, but he died before publication and Bownd consented to carry on. He acknowledged himself "subject unto" error and "most willingly" submitted "unto the Church of God, by it in all things to be censured and reformed."[5] There was a great deal of controversy about the matter of the Sabbath (there is not "any one point of our religion that is so in controversy among the learned of all sorts"), an observation which probably reflects Bownd's private conferences with like-minded, Puritan friends rather than the topics which bishops of the Established Church found themselves forced to discuss; yet Bownd writes not to settle controversy but as a "spur to the godly learned, to take more pains in so worthy an argument and to publish abroad that which I know some have in their hands" (p. 30). Alas, they did, not always with the spirit of moderation which Bownd shows. We have seen Shepard terming the views of early Sabbatarians "light," and his diction was (like Sprint's) far more hostile when he contemplated those he more actively hated. After Bownd's book, the Sabbath of the English Church was broken. It was only a matter of time, once Englishman had fallen out with Englishman, that Puritan would fall out with Puritan. They could only do so after they had developed immense confidence in the knowledge which they were so massively systematizing. Seventh-day Sabbatarianism could only rear its ugly head after the categories of Puritan doctrine had hardened and Puritan confidence had bloomed.

Orthodox Puritan attacks upon the seventh-day Sabbatarians provide one of the clearest examples of how language and theological doctrine cohered. When the Puritans were forced to assert that an important change had occurred in human history (the change from the seventh-day Sabbath to the first, Christian "Lord's day"), they began instinctively talking about the cross and a whole host of other topics which they normally avoided. At the same time, they handled these arguments and Christocentric diction awkwardly, revealing their basic commitment to or preference for a solid rock of ages. Dod evoked ideas of historical progress when he explained how the day of worship had been changed from the seventh to the first day: "now that a greater and more excellent work [than the creation of the world] was done, namely, the redemption of the world [through Christ], it was reason that the greatest work should carry the credit of the day."[6]

Shepard stressed the importance of an action in time over the claims of
an immutable theological truth when he wrote that while "Christ was a
Lamb slain from the foundation of the world meritoriously but not actually
. . . [and] risen again in the like manner from the foundation of the world
meritoriously but not actually," still it was not "meet that this day should
be changed, until Christ Jesus had actually finished, (and not meritoriously
only) the work of redemption and restoration" (p. 9). That sentence,
while it does admittedly introduce the despised term Jesus, might in many
respects be taken as a précis of *Paradise Lost*. Bownd, in contrast, explicitly evoked the cross and the center of traditional Christian history, rather
than circumlocuting his way around them, when he told of how Christ "submitted himself to the observation of the least ceremony [of the law] . . .
till at his death he cried out, *It is finished, when the veil of the Temple rent
in twain from the top to the bottom:* to show that all types and figures
were abrogated and taken away" (p. 9).

   All three of these representative utterances, so foreign in tone, effect,
and focus from conventional Puritan fare, still rely on static verbal and
syntactical structures. They all employ copulative verbs extensively. Shepard's key words—"meritoriously" and "actually"—which form the basis of
his distinction, modify past participles which function as adjectives
and are elided passive constructions. Sprint makes his point through a
string of adjectives—"moral," "perpetual," and "ceremonial"—which point
to nouns as the root of the construction; he hardens his position by using
the noun "perpetuity" as well. All three employ several key nouns made
from verbs, the activity of the verb thereby squeezed out: "work," "establishment," "observation," "creation," "redemption," "foundation," and
"restoration." And passive constructions, finally, are common ways to
represent even divine acts: "is abolished," "were abrogated and taken
away," "was done," and "should be changed." Seymour Chatman has
adroitly pointed to the theological significance of past participles in Milton's participial style;[7] God implicitly controls these actions even when he
is not named. I wish to add that that element of Milton's style resembles
important elements in Puritan writing.

   To much the same effect, Bownd spoke of our "very special *seventh day*,
that now we keep in the time of the Gospel" (p. 35) which, because it is
not literally a seventh but rather a first day is "very special" indeed. Shepard said we must observe "not *that* Sabbath only, nor yet a Sabbath merely
when man sees meet: but . . . *the Sabbath*, i.e. such a Sabbath as is determined and appointed of God, (which may therefore be either the first or
last of the seven days)" (p. 5). Rebutting the seventh-day Sabbatarians,
Shepard rests his distinction on a difference in adjectives—"that," "a," and
"the"—to signal first the old Sabbath, then the conservative ecclesiast's
flexible holiday, then the true Puritan Sabbath. Both men explicitly call

our attention to the real difficulty they have making this sort of distinction once they have started writing in the Puritan style, for both have to append explanations to their points—an admission that the points are themselves unclear. Bownd added that our "very special *seventh day*" is "not the same as it was from the beginning" as a way of signalling that "seventh day" is used metaphorically rather than literally, and Shepard tacked on his parenthetic clause. Both men achieve a sense of "perpetuity" even while trying to portray change; they do so by using a single, unchanging term and modifying it. Bownd's "very special" awkwardly signals that the new "seventh day" is metaphorically different from the old, literal one; Shepard builds his point around the word "Sabbath" by changing adjectives.

The Puritans, then, had at this critical point to assert historical change, and in the process they began talking about Jesus, the cross, submission, etc. Yet at the same time, their prose retains a certain historical and verbal inflexibility and suggests something about the Puritan distrust of metaphor as well. Bownd's "very special *seventh day*" is metaphoric as is Shepard's "*that* Sabbath." Now metaphor transmutes the world, introduces a shape-shifting element in the verbal and philosophic process, creates uncertainty out of ambiguity. If one is nervous about this world and the changes involved in historical process, if one is dedicated to nailing this universe firmly down through the superlogical and methodizing effort of writing a theological summa, if one must squeeze the words of Scripture to extract the precious drops of doctrine which lurk therein, disregarding the form of the utterance in the process, one will remain uncomfortable with metaphoric language as well. And when one is forced, as the Puritans were in rebutting seventh-day Sabbatarianism, to deal in metaphor, one will use it awkwardly, stiffly, inflexibly, and in such a way that further explanation is required. In part, of course, that further explanation is merely an overt signal to the reader that the author is using metaphor; it is a verbal gesture very like the Puritan habit of labeling "similitudes" in their margins when they used them. It warns the reader not to take what the author is saying "literally." But it is, in these two instances at least, necessary to explain as well because the metaphors don't work. Shape-shifting and metamorphic writing was foreign to the Puritan sensibility, which saw quite enough shape-shifting in this world and indeed wanted to fix some of that motion forever firm and sure. Giving God the glory was not a metaphoric process.

It is difficult to reconstruct the position of the seventh-day Sabbatarians in any more than general outline. There are few seventh-day tracts still extant and one wonders whether the Puritans either weren't unduly nervous (and spent more time controverting this doctrine than was warranted) or overzealous in suppressing it. Certainly seventh-day Sabbatarianism must have acutely embarrassed the Puritans, for it proved what their enemies in the religious establishment had always been saying—Puritan Sabbatarianism tended toward "Judaism." The intensity of their embarrassment may be gauged not only by their strident tone but also by such awkward attempts as those made by Nathaniel Holmes (*An essay concerning the Sabbath, or the Sabbath-day's rest from controversy* . . . , 1673), Thomas Chafie (*A brief tract on the Fourth Commandment* . . . , 1692), and John Smith (*The doctrine of the Church of England concerning the Lords day* . . . , 1694) to juggle astronomy and play with calendars to prove that the original seventh day and the Christian Sunday were actually one and the same. This desperate attempt to dodge controversy and forge unity of belief where there was none won few adherents, but it shows clearly how the Puritans clung to their sense of immutability, for if the theory worked, it proved that the original institution of the Sabbath at creation was still firmly in force and that Christ had not really changed anything at all.

The absurdity of trying to prove, in the ways that these men set out to argue the case, that Saturday and Sunday were actually the same day testifies to the manner in which seventh-day Sabbatarians merely finished the Puritanic job of flattening out paradox and removing the process from history. John Milton understood clearly how the new positions had developed, and he did not like what he saw. He asserted warmly that "our consciences must not be ensnared by the allegation of a divine command, borrowed from the decalogue. . . . If we are to use the decalogue as a guide in fixing the time of our public worship under the gospel, it will certainly be much safer to select the seventh day, according to the express commandment of God, rather than the first day, which has nothing to recommend it beyond mere human conjecture" (*De Doctrina Christiana*, II, vii; Yale ed., p. 714). Milton firmly believed that we must follow all and any divine commands and must regulate our lives wholly according to them; he decried in good Puritan fashion "mere human conjecture" upon which ecclesiasts based their claims for liturgical efficacy. The decalogue, however, was not in his view binding on Christians who enjoy Christian liberty and are freed from the bondage of the Law. Moreover, neither Christ nor his apostles positively enjoined Puritan Sabbatarianism, despite the Sabbatarian pretense that they had, and those who attempted to prove that they had were building castles in the air. The Puritan position tends logically to seventh-day Sabbatarianism and any orthodox Puritan who chooses to accept the terms of that fallacious argument will be "safer" keeping the seventh day than imagining that he has a positive injunction to keep the first day. Milton's radical mind can entertain the seventh-day Sabbatarian position hypothetically with great ease before it moves on to make its own point. Since there was, in Milton's view, no positive new dispensation, the entire Puritan position comes tumbling down, and Milton freed men to follow their liberated and elevated consciences.

Central to Milton's thinking about the Sabbath are two unmistakably

Puritanic notions: that we ought to guide our lives jure divino since God speaks plainly and his behests are to be followed, and that we cannot imitate God. The Israelites were commanded to keep the Sabbath, but either this command was restricted to them explicitly, or (where the commandment was a "sign to distinguish the Israelites from other nations") the need for it had ceased. To those who argue that the Sabbath was the day on which God rested, Milton answers slyly: "True, and with reason, for he had created heaven and earth—no small task. If they insist that we are to imitate him in his rest . . . let them also insist that . . . we imitate his work" (II, vii; p. 709). Thus, the need for the Sabbath evaporated, and "though it became the practice of the church to make this change, she did not obey any divine command, for there was none any longer, but merely gave evidence of her own freedom of action (either freedom of action or madness—one of these it was). For whether my opponents hold that this commandment of God's has been abrogated or not, it is equally dangerous and equally reprehensible for them to alter it in any way. If it has not been abrogated, then by changing it they, in effect, abrogate it, and if it has they, in effect, revive it. It is up to them to show us what moral excellence there can possibly be in the number seven" (II, vii; p. 710). (The last sentence, slightly beside my point, illustrates a waggish spirit which Carey's translation brings out.) At first Milton may seem to have agreed with Charles that the Church could exercise its authority (Sumner's translation was particularly misleading here). But that is clearly not the point Milton was making, for the Church cannot abrogate God's command any more than it can revive what God has abrogated. The Church operated in a complete vacuum and exercised choice as best it was able (proposing a number which in itself has no moral significance because the church had no moral basis for what it did) but that is far from ecclesiastic authority to alter what had been divinely ordained.

Equally Puritanic was the rigor with which Milton scrutinized Genesis and the early chapters of Exodus, looking for a place where the patriarchs were commanded jure divino to keep the seventh day. Unlike orthodox Sabbatarians, he could not find one, although he was willing to admit that the command might have been passed by word of mouth and not recorded: "But it is not known, because there is nothing about it in scripture, whether this [commandment] was ever disclosed to Adam or whether any commandment about the observance of the Sabbath existed before the giving of the law on Mount Sinai, let alone before the fall of man" (I, x; p. 353). He agreed with the Sabbatarians that God had enjoined the keeping of the Sabbath on the Israelites "as a memorial of God's completion of creation on the seventh day" (II, vii; p. 705), but he could not accept their notion that the patriarchs had been self-consciously aware of the commandment (whether or not they all adhered to it) before it had been given on Sinai;

that is, it was not clear to Milton that the fourth commandment simply
confirmed what those patriarchs already knew they should do. William
Ames, among many others, had been forced to admit that during the time
of the patriarchs "the observation of this day was for the most part neg-
lected," yet he still asserted that they knew better.[8] Patriarchal neglect of
the Sabbath "ought no more to make the first institution doubtful than
polygamy of the same times can show that the sacred laws of wedlock were
not equal in time with the very first marriage" (p. 285). Milton disagreed
with both extrapolations backwards from Sinai; moreover, he seems to
have believed that Christian liberty not to keep the Sabbath and to live
polygamously was equivalent to patriarchal practice.[9] We are not positively
bound jure divino (since we are freed from the decalogue) and (Scripture
being silent on both matters) neither were the patriarchs bound.

What emerges from Milton's remarks is a tripartite division of history.
The first period seems to have extended from Creation to the giving of the
decalogue; the second from Sinai to Christ; the third, of Christian liberty,
from Christ to the millennium. Now, to divide history into three parts is
not an uncommon activity for Christian theologians, although it tends to
emerge most clearly in millennial thinking. Norman Cohn provides a host
of medieval examples, deriving from Joachim.[10] Basically the scheme runs
like this: once life (thought, practice, or what have you) was good; then it
got corrupted for a period, but finally it was (or shall be) changed back
to original purity. Frequently associated with such a historical scheme, as
Cohn again profusely illustrates, is an antinomian claim that the adept is
superior to other men—elect, superhuman, divinely inspired, or God himself. The most advanced, overt, or "far gone" versions of this scheme set
aside the Christian dispensation and conventional morality. The prophet
is a "new Christ" freed to follow his whims; to Cohn's many examples
(pp. 148-86) we can add James Nayler who, during our period, rode into
Bristol on the back of an ass. Thereby he simply acted out overtly George
Fox's more restrained notion that Christ dwells in us.[11] Less overt still,
yet in the same vein, was the posture Milton tacitly assumed in the prose,
those frequent claims to special inspiration which he shared with the narrator of *Paradise Lost,* and particularly the astonishingly superhuman tone
and vision he wrote into his "epic voice."

The classic antinomian, millennial paradigm, as it emerges from Cohn's
analysis, is not necessarily Puritan, since it has sprung up from time to time
since the very first ages of the Christian dispensation, but it is advanced
or radical Protestant (in a sense much looser than C. S. Lewis intended) and
does quite obviously bear marked resemblance to certain elements in Puritan thought—elements heavily guarded or checked among the orthodox so
as to appear latencies or tendencies rather than full-blown beliefs. It generally involves a prophet bringing a new, third dispensation with strong com-

munal overtones, both financial and sexual. This dispensation liberates men from previous regulations and, in extravagant cases, abrogates Christ's teachings much as Christ had earlier surpassed the Old Testament. Election and assurance of that holy state figure prominently, for the dispensation only obtains for men who are indeed pure and regenerate in heart. *Paradise Lost* amounts, in effect, to such a further dispensation, for one must wonder why such biblical poets as Milton and Du Bartas write if the Bible is, as they believed, sufficient and clear. It is clearly a third dispensation much preferable to those of Jan of Leyden or the other lunatics whom Cohn reports on, and it has few of the dangerous social implications which they do. Yet from early age, Milton appears to have felt himself specially called or elected to an elevated role of prophetic seer, much in the mode of Cohn's medieval millenarians.

The tripartite scheme of history inherent in Milton's analysis simultaneously projects little change in the course of history (as Puritan historiography generally does) and provides a vehicle for linking Sabbatarianism with issues of divorce, something Milton instinctively did from his earliest polemical writings onward. If the patriarchs lived under much the same, liberated models which we liberated Christians do (i.e., if the last age recapitulates the first), then history records how men simply departed from, then returned to, old pure ways of living. The dark period under the Law is basically a temporary exception to the rule that all good men in all times live under the same dispensation, and the patriarchal note is simply struck more forcibly than in more conventional Puritan writing. Curiously, this scheme almost implies that the fall occurred not in Eden with the apple but on Sinai under the Law. Milton embodied this notion most overtly in the curious tenth chapter of the first book of *De Doctrina,* "Of the Special Government of Man before the Fall: Dealing also with the Sabbath and Marriage," which juxtaposed an analysis of patriarchal Sabbath practices with a discussion of patriarchal polygamy and Milton's theory of divorce. Here he countered Ames's theory that the patriarchs knew enough not to neglect the Sabbath or take more than one wife, yet fallibly they had.[12] Milton believed that Christ freed men from the rigors of an Old Testament bondage to what were, for Ames, the "sacred laws of wedlock" as well as to the Sabbath. In advancing the case for polygamy, Milton also sought to justify the patriarchs: "polygamy is either marriage or fornication, or adultery—for the apostle recognizes no halfway state between these. Let no one dare to say that it is fornication or adultery: the shame this would bring upon so many patriarchs who were polygamists will, I hope, prevent anyone from doing so. For God will judge *fornicators and adulterers,* whereas he loved the patriarchs above all, and declared that they were very dear to him" (I, x; p. 366). Those who live in Christian liberty are equally "very dear to him" and may live under the same terms as the patriarchs whom Milton thus rescues from sin and obloquy. All this discussion testifies to a strong, Puritanic interest in the patriarchs, of course, but it seems very odd to find it in a chapter purporting to discuss arrangements "before the fall" unless, and this seems the only possible solution to the riddle, Milton thought, with at least a corner of his mind, that the patriarchal age was basically unfallen. The Law, then, would seem to have marked the fall and to have initiated the second age.

Milton agreed with Ames's Puritan analysis of the connection between Sabbath doctrine and marriage practices. As early as *Of Reformation* he had attacked the bishops for trying to "despoile us both of *manhood* and *grace* at once" and to "effeminate us all at home." "Liberty consists in manly and honest labours, in sobriety and rigorous honour to the Marriage Bed," yet Englishmen were "by *Bishops* the pretended *Fathers of the Church* instigated by publique Edict, and with earnest indeavour push't forward to gaming, jigging, wassailing, and mixt dancing." The *Book of Sports* attacked "that day which Gods Law, and even our own reason hath consecrated, that we might have one day at least of seven set apart wherein to examin and encrease our knowledge of God, to meditate, and commune of our Faith, our Hope, our eternall City in Heaven, and to quick'n, withall, the study, and exercise of Charity" (CE, 3:52–53). This is a standard and apparently orthodox Puritan attack on the *Book of Sports;* it advances the notion that God's Law enjoins us to set apart one day in seven (which, we have seen, Milton dropped) and apparently moves from the Sabbath to "the Marriage Bed" by way of the "jigging, wassailing, and mixt dancing." In *The Reason of Church Government* he urged "our Magistrates" to "take into their care, not only the deciding of our contentious Law cases and brauls, but the managing of our publick sports, and festival pastimes, that they might be, not such as were autoriz'd a while since, the provocations of drunkennesse and lust, but such as may inure and harden our bodies by martial exercises . . . and may civilize, adorn and make discreet our minds" (CE, 3:239–40). What these examples show is that Milton not only took over the connection between Sabbath and marriage from such Puritans as Ames, but was capable, in his early prose, of making conventional Puritanic statements about the subject. His views of the Sabbath were of Puritan extraction, in short, and although he matured these views into what was an explicitly anti-Sabbatarian position, they were always firmly rooted in Puritan thought rather than establishment anti-Sabbatarianism.

It seems likely that Milton's defense of divorce and the rebuttals he felt impelled to add to his first tract helped to radicalize his views of the Sabbath. James T. Johnson has demonstrated how Milton radicalized Puritan attitudes toward marriage. Of the three traditional ends proposed for marriage—propagation, avoidance of sin, and mutual society—the Puritans laid their strongest emphasis upon the last. Milton spiritualized this emphasis upon society, creating thereby an intellectual basis from which he might claim a special dispensation for "higher ends."[13] This inherently antinomian impulse, which appeared to his enemies to be no less than an urge for free love, operated equally strongly and equally spiritually in his views about the Sabbath, where Christian liberty freed men from the rigors of an old command. Milton was not alone in his imaginatively freewheeling extension of Puritan habits of mind, and it is well to recall some of the precedents and analogues to his Sabbath theories before we go farther.

Heinrich Bullinger, far from an antinomian, held that the Sabbath was a time for "spiritual business" and William Tyndale extended the sense of a "higher calling" on the Sabbath so as to exclaim that "we be lords over the Sabbath" and can change the day to any in seven, so long as some time for spiritual reckoning were set aside. Tyndale was hardly an antinomian either and no more was Richard Byfield, seventy years later, when he urged that on the Sabbath a servant served not his earthly master but was rather "God's servant to be free from" mundane orders. Byfield recognized the socially disruptive implications of such a remark and qualified it, in a muddled sort of way, by saying that such a servant was still "in his master's power," but he stuck with the contention that on the Sabbath such a man served "higher ends." Roger Williams pushed things much farther when he argued that the "magistrate might not punish the breach of the Sabbath, nor any other offence which was a breach of the First table" and thereby undercut earthly, governmental authority severely.[14] Shepard, no antinomian, still remarked how in New England some men went beyond Sabbatarian rigor "because the internal and spiritual Sabbath is all in all" (p. 2). Extreme forms of Puritan iconoclasm could be turned upon Sabbatarian orthodoxy; John Owen incurred the wrath of John Eliot, apostle to the Indians, for doing something quite like that. Owen taught that "duties in their performances drawn out unto such a length as to beget wearisomeness and satiety, tend not unto edification, nor do any way promote the sanctification of the name of God in the worship itself" since the "spiritual edge of the affections of men . . . ought to be whetted, and not through tediousness in duties abated and taken off."[15] He was ambiguous concerning "sports and such like recreations" and willing to quote secular, legal, rather than scriptural precedents. John Wells had made much the same point. The Quaker Robert Barclay pushed Owen's thought a bit farther, arguing that the Sabbath ought to be kept inwardly every day rather than outwardly, formally, and in a special time (Cox, 2:70–71). John Brayne had articulated the antinomian position on the Sabbath clearly and openly as early as 1653 by postulating a double order in the world. The unregenerate ought to be bound by the restrictions of the Mosaic Law while the regenerate were freed by Christ. This situation was timeless: "As in the beginning, God divided government, committing some to Moses in the

judicials, and others to Aaron in the ceremonials . . . so . . . now . . .
Moses and Christ . . . rule and govern the world by: 1) Moses in the
world or state, under the covenant of works, also the servant of Jesus
Christ, ruling for him because he is not of the world; 2) Christ in the
Church, among the saints or believers, under the new covenant of grace,
among whom the Lord is, being one of them" (Cox, 1:245). Thus the regenerate claim a special dispensation from the rules which govern the ordinary world. If Christ is "one of them" or, as the Quakers put it, "dwelling"
in the regenerate, then these men are only that small step away from pro-
claiming themselves to be gods devoted exclusively to "higher ends." Members of the "lunatic fringe" which developed from Puritan revolutionary
preaching acted out that sense of superiority by consciously flaunting the
Sabbath of those Puritans from whom they sprung. Hill (p. 213) records
that the Diggers began planting St. George's Hill on the Sabbath to testify
to their special liberty, while Gerard Winstanley published the first number
of *Mercurius Aulicus* on the Sabbath as well. These were gestures which
would shock only Puritan Sabbatarianism; it is clear that antinomian anti-
Sabbatarianism in seventeenth-century England defined its intellectual
roots in Puritanism precisely by rejecting them.

It is not therefore surprising that when Milton in *De Doctrina* outlines
the several reasons why God imposed his Sabbath commands upon the
Israelites as a way of establishing their peculiarity, he lists most of the arguments which Puritan Sabbatarians advanced for celebrating their Sabbath.
The Sabbatarians were correct that God commanded the Israelites to keep
the Sabbath "as a memorial of God's completion of creation on the seventh
day," "because God wished this to be a sign to distinguish the Israelites
from other nations," "that the slaves and cattle might have a rest," "in
remembrance of their liberation from Egypt," and finally "as a shadow or
type of things to come" namely, "of that Sabbath rest or eternal repose in
heaven, which all believers are commanded to strive for through obedience,
following the example of Christ" (II, vii; pp. 705-7). But these commandments were particular to the Israelites, in Milton's view, much as Brayne
had thought that the "judicials" were, and did not bind regenerate Christians: "It is certain, then, that under the law the Sabbath was imposed only
upon the Israelites, and that the intention was to distinguish them from
other nations by this very sign. It follows that we who live under the gospel and are, as I proved in my first book, quite freed from the law, must
be emancipated above all from this law about Sabbath-observance, because
the distinction upon which it was founded has been removed" (pp. 707-8).
"Paul also makes it quite clear that God has not instituted, in its place, any
particular day for his worship." Just as "there was certainly no special
place designated for public worship under the gospel" so "it would be un-
reasonable to expect the other particular, time, to be laid down either"

(p. 708). Christian liberty frees us from the old, paternal dispensation; there had always been an element of oedipal tension involved in the change of the Old for the New Testament. When Milton equated that "old" paternal dispensation precisely with Puritan Sabbatarian doctrine, he showed us who his intellectual fathers were. In forging his new, radical views of the Sabbath, Milton simply moved beyond what was initially a Puritan view of the world to assert with clear, millennial overtones that "if any Sabbath-rest still remains for us under the gospel, then it is a spiritual and eternal one, and the observance of it belongs not to this life but to the next" and with an antinomian appeal to liberty, that public worship is not obligatory, but "spontaneous, not enforced, otherwise we shall be brought out of one Egypt and into another" (pp. 710-11).

That reminds us of the Father's comments about Adam and Eve in book three of *Paradise Lost.* They were not constrained to obey but left free fully to testify to their faith in God. Christian liberty parallels prelapsarian freedom; we regain under Christ what we lost under the fall. The patriarchs practiced polygamy as we still may, and since Milton can find no evidence that they kept the seventh-day sabbath, it would seem that probably they did not keep it. They also lived a model which Christians might follow. Thus, there is a certain timeless continuity to Milton's analysis very Puritanic in effect. There was a middle period when Israel was to be distinguished from other nations but now we have, as it were, "reverted" to Christian liberty. Within this roughly tripartite analysis of history, Milton's Adam qualifies as the first Christian and provides the fullest and best examples of "unpremeditated" worship, in *Paradise Lost,* before the fall. Surely we are to follow that inspired model in our daily lives. But how can we follow that "pure" and "unlapsed" model if we are ourselves fallen? The answer seems to be that Adam is not, even before the fall, so different from us as we might expect. The Sabbath rightly celebrated in Christian (and Adamic) liberty points to an internal and timeless state, the prefiguration of the millennium. Beginning and end show "concords" (to use Kermode's phrase—see chapter 5, n. 12) and we Christians, testifying at the very least to our Christian liberty, herald the advent of the end. In *Paradise Lost* Milton incarnated his own, inherently antinomian, essentially Puritanic views of worship: the true Christian is not bound by either space or time in his worship which should flow in unpremeditated strains to the glory of the eternal Sabbath.

In connecting Milton with overt antinomians like Nayler, I run the risk of oversimplifying and reducing Milton's thought. Merely to abstract some "underlying impulse" from a man's writing does violence to the personal ways in which he articulates that impulse, and it is the form of articulation, the manner of expression, which primarily concerns the literary critic. There is a great difference between acting as though one were God, openly

stating a doctrine which links one with God, and tacitly embodying in a
narrative voice an almost divine point of view. Similarly there is a great
difference between actually maintaining a harem and arguing, as Milton
did, that a harem might be permissible, or between cutting off a king's head
and writing in defense of the *idea* of cutting off a king's head. Milton always took the intellectual's stance concerning these and a host of related
attitudes, impulses, or fantasies.

Our individual reading of seventeenth-century history will determine
whether we believe that Milton was correct in his impulse to disrupt the
fabric of society in which he found himself (although perhaps crippled by
an intellectual's failure of nerve) or wrong to contend against the things of
his world (yet perhaps redeemed by a spiritualizing and intellectualizing
cast of mind). My point is not to solve that riddle nor simply to point out
the antisocial underpinnings of Milton's thought; rather, having done the
latter, I wish to focus on what was uniquely Milton's response and shaping
of those impulses, for that will be first to locate Milton roughly in the political scheme of things in his age and then to point out what was idiosyncratic to his thought and art. It is well then to remark that one trait which
marks out Milton's habits and style was his tendency to intellectualize,
spiritualize, or restrain these antinomian claims.

One further example from *The Reason of Church-Government Urg'd
Against Prelaty* will show what was essential to Milton's sensibility in operation. After attacking the bishops and their *Book of Sports* and after urging
the magistrates to have a care for "the managing of our publick sports,"
Milton adds that national edification to "justice, temperance and fortitude,"
"wisdom and vertu" might be achieved "not only in Pulpits, but after
another persuasive method, at set and solemn Paneguries, in Theaters,
porches, or what other place, or way may win most upon the people to
receiv at once both recreation, & instruction." He goes on to apologize for
not having written such magnificent literary works as might instruct and
exalt the nation. He finds himself "in a troubl'd sea of noises and hoars
disputes" and the work he intends requires more than "some vulgar Amorist, or the trencher fury of a riming parasite." It can only be wrought "by
devout prayer to that eternall Spirit who can enrich with all utterance and
knowledge, and sends out his Seraphim with the hallow'd fire of his Altar
to touch and purify the lips of whom he pleases" (CE, 3:240–41). Milton's
hopes, coolly considered, are staggering. He wishes to surpass Moses and
attain that fluent utterance which Isaiah evoked in his vision. His writing
will equal the Bible; hard work is, of course, necessary, Milton adds, but
first must come this purifying and elevating experience. And Milton feels
it is accessible to him as he contemplates the writing of that "sacred record"
of "God's mercies to [his English] Zion" which Stephen Marshall would
call for before Parliament in 1645. He takes "these British Ilands as [his]

world" and thereby elevates himself and his mission in ways men commonly do when faced with "hoars dispute." No longer able to abide what he sees about him, he will elevate his own claims by writing for "the honour and instruction of my country" (CE, 3:236-37). The selfless task will relieve the pressures on the self and the result will equal or surpass the Bible just so far as England, with its millennial hopes, was expected by many (Milton among them) to surpass the history of the whole world.

When we read that "sacred record" in *Paradise Lost*, we find that the claims have matured and become more extensive. Milton is no longer willing (perhaps, out of frustration, no longer able) to take only England as his world, and so he creates a cosmic creator and has the blinding hybris to bring him on stage, to be commented upon by his own narrative voice. In evoking Isaiah and Moses, so early in *The Reason of Church-Government,* Milton signals that Puritan view of timeless history and that Puritan taste for patriarchal paternity. His song will be a new beginning and a new creation, hearkening back to, yet going beyond his precedents. By adding "recreation" to the instruction of a Puritan ideologue's "Pulpit," Milton also proposes to go beyond his intellectual fathers by charming the nation into goodness. Similarly, his doctrine of the Sabbath, rooted as it was in Puritan Sabbatarianism, was far more charming than Puritan orthodoxy; based on his plea for Christian liberty, that charm functioned as part of Milton's antinomian appeal to be personally superior even to his Puritan antecedents—an appeal which, on the verbal level at least, was probably justified. There is no doubt that few prefer reading a Puritan sermon to reading *Paradise Lost.*

Chapter 7: KEEPING CHRIST OUT OF CHRISTMAS

Sabbatarianism served, as Hill points out, to regularize the hours during which men worked (see above, chapter 5). Festivals and holy days of the Roman Church interfered with the steady pursuit of one's vocation during the six days. Thomas Shepard, for example, was not only denying the importance of chronological historicity when he argued that "no action of Christ doth of itself sanctify any time" (see above, p. 80); if for the Puritans, even the God-man could not act out historic moments, the contrary view of his ministry might force us to "keep as many holy days every year as we find holy actions of Christ recorded in Scripture, as the superstitious crew of blind Papists do at this day." The Puritans' work ethic was at odds with the irregularity of working hours caused by holidays. More to my purpose, however, the Puritans' historical iconoclasm extended even to Christmas and Easter; in 1647 Parliament ordered: "For as much as the feast of the nativity of Christ, Easter, Whitsuntide, and other festivals, commonly called holy days, have been superstitiously used and observed, be it ordained, that the said feasts, and all other festivals, commonly called holy days, be no longer observed as festivals."[1] "Judaizing" took the Puritan Christ out of Christmas and these central, seemingly essential festivals out of Christian practice.

Indeed, Puritan theologizing presents us with one of those glorious paradoxes which inform so much of Renaissance and Reformation thought. The Puritans, dedicated above all to the study of theology, very nearly drove the theos out of their intellectual world. These men, who so reverenced God and the mystery of his predestinate election, demystified religion and iconoclastically shattered its mysteries. Like the men who wrought the Copernican revolution, they acted from a sense of intellectual or spiritual claustrophobia which brought instant agoraphobia in its wake. Outlawing Christmas was one of the most overt ways they took to secularize religion and de-Christianize their belief and practice.

The idea of the Puritan Sabbath went hand in hand with the attack on Christmas. John Collinges, a Puritan preacher of Norwich, and Edward Fisher, spokesman for the establishment, traded blows over the Sabbath and Christmas in Fisher's *A Christian caveat to the old and new Sabbatarians . . .* (London, 1653) and Collinges's *Responsoria ad erratica piscatoris: or, a caveat for old and new prophaneness* (London, 1653). It was Collinges who saw the connection between Fisher's book on the Sabbath and Allan Blayney's *Festorum metropolis . . .* (London, 1652), a lengthy, ecclesiast's celebration of Christmas. As Cox says, "the Sabbath question having been so fully discussed by others . . . he thinks it needless to devote more than a short space . . . to that subject."[2] Collinges concerns himself with such matters as proving that "the Lords Day is not of human, but Divine institution, and so of greater right than Christmas-day" (ch. xxii) or that "the Lords Day . . . [is] of greater antiquity than Christmas" (ch. xxiii). Collinges's way had been prepared by Dod's remark that the Christian Sabbath has a "singular excellency, and however times change, never changeth"; in contrast *"Easter* and *Pentecost,* and the other feasts of like kind," are "indeed abrogated, as being ceremonies, not written in the tables of stone as this was" (p. 136). Similarly, Daniel Cawdrey had set out to rebut Henry Hammond's *Practical Catechism,* in which Hammond moved smoothly from the fourth commandment to the celebration of Christmas. Concerning the *"Institution* of Feasts (particularly this of Christmas)," Cawdrey wrote, "the Scripture is neither obscure nor silent, . . . [but] speaks aloud against it, both in the Law, the fourth Commandment, which requires peremptorily but one of seven for God, *allowing* six for men's occasions, and also in the *Gospel,* which clearly speaks against *observation* of days (except the Lord's day, the Christian Sabbath) whether *Jewish, Heathenish,* or *Christian. Festivals* of old were part of the *ceremonial yoke* upon the *Jews,* and therefore to give the Church a power to institute *holy days,* is to reduce the yoke again." Cawdrey was attacking the ecclesiasts' position that the Church has its own authority to fill in the gaps in divine dispensation at will; Christmas was just such a gap, in the view of men like Fisher, Blayney, and Charles I. Charles had argued that "the celebration of this Feast [Easter] was instituted by the same authority which changed the Jewish Sabbath into the Lord's day or Sunday" and that authority was "the Church's." Cawdrey was quite willing to admit that the Church instituted the celebration of festivals of its own authority rather than jure divino; that was the whole problem with them, from a theological point of view. Cawdrey also goes to the extent of implying strongly that God not only said "keep one day in seven" but added "and no more than one." The Church has no legitimate power to change what God decrees. "Christian liberty," in Cawdrey's odd view, means following the decalogue.[3]

When Christopher Hill attributes secular, economic motives to the Puritan Sabbatarians, he does not entirely malign them. Christmas was, to the conservative churchmen, quite literally a way of reintroducing God into this fallen world; in deed he came to save us on this day and we ought in our deeds to conform to his joyous pattern of conduct. Hence Christmas was for them a time of profound joy and their sermons, reverberating with the related, joyous theme of Easter, manifest some of the richest meditations upon the coming of Christ, the fullest elaborations of his suffering here below, the densest explications of such names as Emanuel and Jesus, the most successful yoking of God and man. On the other hand, the Puritans rejoiced when, by a quirk of the calendar, the monthly fast for December 1644 fell on the 25th of the month and God providentially "buried this *feast in a fast*."[4] The Puritans were unwilling, as I have shown, to squeeze quite all the change out of Christian history; they resisted the "Judaizing" tendencies of seventh-day Sabbatarianism even when it meant talking about change, the cross, and the suffering Jesus. But they were surprisingly willing to forego the festivals like Christmas and Easter which would seem almost essential to Christian thought and worship. I have remarked how getting rid of the notion of "Jesus" eventuated smoothly in Milton's theological subordination of Son to Father and the deism of Restoration divines; here, in the debate over Christmas, we can see historical iconoclasm producing much the same effect, secularizing religion by removing the central nexus of Christian thought from this world.

In exploring that point, let us first sample the conservative establishment's sense of joy at Christmas. The holiday must have deeply appealed to these men because it so obviously served to counter the Puritan tendency to define Christ out of this world. It was a fleshly holiday, both in the way it was celebrated and in the theological issues connected with it. John, preached Lancelot Andrewes, following a patristic commonplace, soared like an eagle beyond the *"in principio"* of Genesis, then swooped down to alight on "flesh." "He dwelt not long aloft, he knew it was not to purpose; *Verbum Deus* is far above our reach. *Verbum caro*, that concerns us" and on Christmas we "celebrate the contents of the text, that the Word being made flesh this day came to dwell among us."[5] Andrewes implies historical progress and raises an implicit challenge to Puritan divines. If *"verbum deus"* really is beyond our comprehension (and Puritans would perforce have to agree), does it really make sense to pursue that word so forcibly and hope to attain to an understanding of it so rigorously as Puritans did? Of course, a conservative never desires to go "above our reach" and the Puritans as revolutionaries were overreaching. Andrewes sees John settling for what he can attain—*verbum caro*—the things of this world.

"Betwixt the *Word* and the *Flesh* there is μέγα χάσμα, a vast disproportion and infinite distance, in that one would think two natures so different should not be married together and dwell like two mates under one roof," exclaimed Richard Gardiner. The pressure of Protestant thought had emphasized that distance: *"Verbo quid sublimius?* What is there more transcendent in glory than the *Word? Carne quid vilius?* What more contemptible than the flesh?"[6] Christmas incarnated an answer to the dilemma, an illogical mystery of joy (Anglican rationalism often eventuated in fideistic scepticism), for God did not conform himself to the logic of the Protestant analysis; rather he came to suffer in this world and thereby dignified it so that men could legitimately and even hopefully talk about it. Simply to charge the establishment with worldliness (as the Puritans did) overlooks the psychological pressures at work upon its members. If one cannot talk legitimately about this world, if the flesh is simply vile, what can one talk about except dreams, fantasies, transcendent gestures? For a member of an establishment, in contrast, at home in his world, Christmas was indeed a time of joy.

That is not to say that the Anglicans ignored the troubles of this world. Indeed, they focused acutely on Christ's suffering. When he talked about the phrase "made of a woman," Andrewes twice insisted that Christ "passed not through her as water through a conduit pipe, as fondly dreameth the Anabaptist" (1:53; compare 1:140). He had really acquired the taint of human nature, he had not "a body framed for Him in heaven" which was somehow exempt from our disease. William Jones added: "Further by being *made of a woman,* of a Lord he became a servant, of eternal he was made temporal, of infinite he became an infant, of high he became low, of incomprehensible local, of intelligible, sensible."[7] The Anglicans were willing to face that suffering which eventuated on the cross, were willing to talk about the diminution of the divine as the Puritans were not. In a curious way, the Puritans were less able to confront the sin of this world than were the Anglicans; they segregated nature from grace, as A. S. P. Woodhouse noted (see chapter 1, n. 12), as well as the human from the divine in Christ. If that kept God pure, mighty, and glorious, it also offered a slightly soft way to avoid talking about the troubles of this world. In contrast, the Anglicans could face that trouble and still rejoice with John Boys: "Let all people rejoice, for that he who was *in the beginning* and . . . *an everlasting father,* in the fullness of time *was made of a woman and wrapped in swaddling* clothes. For he who was *the word* became an infant not able to speak one syllable. For that he who was *with God* did vouchsafe to *dwell among us.* . . . For that he who *was God,* and therefore most mighty, became *flesh,* and so most weak."[8]

Boys's phrases show concern for the suffering Jesus and willingness to bow to him running together with a progressive historiography, for Boys makes in effect a set of before-and-after comparisons rooted in the fact that "of eternal he was made temporal." Andrewes saw that historical pattern in scriptural syntax: "And indeed, this day's news it was ever *evangelium spei,* ever in the future tense before. Even the very last before this to the blessed Virgin, *Ecce concipies* (Luke 1.31), 'Thou shalt conceive'— 'Shalt.' So it was yet to come. This is the first in the present tense; not 'is to be born,' 'is to be sent,' 'is to come,' but *natus est, missus est, venit,* 'is born,' 'is sent,' 'is come.' . . . This is *evangelizo gaudium,* 'this is joy indeed' " (1:69).

John Day probably articulated the importance of time most sharply of any preacher, however, when he elaborated upon God's mercy and heightened the temporal aspect of Christ's coming very nearly into melodrama: "Even in this nick of time, this very, very instant, when there was but as a step between ourselves and eternal death, not only a pardon comes from heaven to forgive us all, even all that is past, but the *chariots* and *horsemen* of Israel, our true Elias, Jesus Christ, to have us up to God, and there to place us with his Father in that everlasting and heavenly kingdom."[9] Such a view of history, obviously, leads men to celebrate historical anniversaries; events in time have sufficient significance to be remembered. Moreover, that view of history generates the pedagogic interpretation of typology. Like Boys, Andrewes also stressed that Christ came "in the fullness of time." "And well also might it be called 'the fullness of time' in another regard. For till then all was but in promise, in shadows and figures and prophecies only, which fill not, God knows. But when the performance of those promises, the body of those shadows, the substance of those figures, the fulfilling of all those prophecies came, then came the 'fulness of time,' truly so called. Till then? it came not; then it came" (1:49).

The pedagogic view of history was essentially joyful because an event in time had altered man's relationship to God. The Jews argue, said Boys, that *"God gave his law to Moses his faithful servant,* and he will never change nor alter it for another." But, "true Christianity reads a contrary lecture, namely, that the ceremonies of the law were *primo mortales, postea mortuae, postremo mortiferae.* So that to leave Christ for them, or to join Christ with them is the plain way to destruction." He quoted Augustine to buttress his attack on the Puritan Sabbatarians' way with the decalogue: "the Jewish ceremonies afore Christ came were alive; when he suffered on the cross they were dead, and now they be buried." The Jews and the Puritans, in his view, created a false glory for God: "Nothing in earth, or under earth, or in heaven, or in the heaven of heavens is so glorious as he, no name else that is named, in which or by which we can be saved, but only the name of *Jesus Christ"* (p. 55). The echoes from Philippians, the references to the cross, bowing, and Jesus fit smoothly with a joyful sense of linear, historical progress and an unfolding dispensation of instructive types and antitypes.

As he had with bowing at the name of Jesus, Andrewes hardened the Established Church line about Christmas, finding what seemed a positive, biblical injunction for celebrating it in the text, "your father Abraham rejoiced to see my day" (John 8. 56). Almost immediately, Andrewes began to rebut Puritan objections to the feast of the Nativity; Abraham rejoiced: "Him we find here doing that which we now are about; seeing and rejoicing at the sight of Christ's day" (1:118). Such joy is "nothing displeasing to our Savior Christ, for it is spoken by Him to the praise of Abraham that did it, and to the dislike of the Jews that did it not" (1:118). The text, then "is against them that have a spleen at this feast; that think they can joy in Him well enough, and set His day by; nay, and abrogate it quite; and in so doing they joy in Him all the better. Nay, love Him, love His feast. Joy not in it, nor in Him neither" (1:119). These Puritans object to keeping Christmas lest " 'observing days and times' they should seem to Judaize. It falls out quite contrary. For who are they whom Christ here blameth? Are they not Jews? And wherefore blameth He them? for not doing as Abraham. And what did Abraham? Rejoice on His day. So upon the point it will fall out that not to rejoice on His day, that is indeed to Judaize, and they little better than these Jews that follow them in it" (1:119–20). Perhaps even more than their Sabbath doctrine, the Puritans' attack on Christmas seemed, to the establishment, "Judaical."

The ways men behave are always open to multiple interpretation. If the Anglicans could, in one way, confront the sins of this world which their Jesus suffered (while the Puritans averted their gaze in a way which John Donne understood yet finally went beyond in "Goodfriday, 1613, Riding Westward") we might equally charge the Anglicans with self-complacency or even masochism. Meditation on Jesus suffering on the cross might eventuate in that surreal, quasi-mechanical, precious and "merciless love" which Crashaw's speakers practice. More sedate or steady conservatives reacted against Protestant patriarchalism in a way which easily generated hierarchial thinking; Donne thought we might become godparents to the baby Jesus in one Christmas sermon and, in another, that God "calls you [the laity] *children*" under the care of the pastor;[10] the plea for political-religious authority derives from the sense that Jesus provided a humane model which we can all aspire to but, because of a certain hierarchy in the world, can never quite attain. Moreover, the established preachers could spin out of their meditations upon *caro* some most strikingly worldly notions. Gardiner suggested that the incarnation resembled "the pagans, *ob hoc simulacra finxerunt, ut in ipsis erroribus oculis cernerent, quod colebant,* that they might be more sensible of their gods, made their gods sensible, carving their portraitures in wood and stone according to the erroneous Idea of their own imaginations. And so our Savior knowing he was a long time the *Desire of all Nations* resolved at this due time to fulfill their desire and in some measure to vouchsafe his presence to the world" (p. 12). That was, in all respects, a very secular argument, and the worldly, fleshly overtones of it suggest why Puritans might have taken umbrage at "the *knowledge* which the ignorant people learned by some men's *Christmas sermons*," a knowledge "slender indeed, nothing but a *superficial . . . notional,* carnal knowledge of one *Jesus* (as that *Roman* deputy spake) that was born at that time, to give men *liberty* to *feast* and be merry" (Cawdrey, p. 146). Sermons about the nativity were not about "*verbum caro*" in the Puritan view; they were about carnal knowledge, sinful flesh. Secretly they probably wished Christ had passed through the virgin like water through a pipe, since they seem to have been in search of an invincible hero. At any rate, flesh being sinful they shunned it and its day, preferring the Sabbath, the memorial of Christ's transcendence of the flesh and, more important, an echo of the first peace of creation and a prefiguration of the final peace of the millennium when they too would transcend flesh.

In contrast to an Anglican Christmas sermon, which was especially eloquent and joyous, the idea of a Puritan Christmas sermon is oxymoronic. Three curious specimens, preached only as a result of a quirk of the calendar, survive from the four given before Parliament in 1644: Thomas Thorowgood's and John Langley's before Commons, and Calamy's before the Lords. Calamy took as his text "a house divided against itself cannot stand" and meditated upon the divisions in the nation and between God and man; such a Puritan interest in splitting the world apart conflicted directly with the idea of joining God and man in the baby Jesus. His sermon is a lengthy example of Puritan political analysis, a providential account of God visiting nations who do not repent, concluding with a plea for national repentance and unity.[11]

In the penultimate paragraph he turns this plea into what sounds almost like a parody of a Christmas sermon, except that Calamy meant what he said too seriously to intend humor: "We have divided ourselves from God by our sins, and God hath divided us one from another. Let us beseech the Lord Jesus Christ to come once more into the world by his spirit of power! Let us not despair of his coming. For he is *deus in monte*. He is our peace now the *Assyrian* is in the land, *Mic.* 5.5. And when he comes he will come as a conqueror to subdue his enemies under his feet" (p. 40). Here we have Christ coming, as he so often does in Christmas sermons, but what a Christ he is—*deus in monte*, "a conqueror to subdue his enemies under his feet"— who will come "by his spirit of power." He will come, in other words, as that apocalyptic figure of authority, dominion, power and glory to whom all knees shall be compelled to bow. He will not come as a babe in a "cold, and not too cleanly, manger" for whom we might with Donne stand godfather.[12] As *deus in monte* he is simultaneously an Old Testament avenger pitted against the "Assyrian" and an eschatological victor; Calamy looks backward into history past the manger to Sinai and forward to glorious victory, but never at a Jesus humiliated in time.

Having in this way recalled the most common theme of the Christmas sermon, Calamy does finally deign to mention Christmas explicitly in his concluding paragraph.

> This is the day which is commonly called *the feast of Christ's nativity* or *Christmas day,* a day that hath been heretofore much abused to *superstition* and *profaneness.* It is not easy to reckon whether the superstition hath been greater or the profaneness. I have known some that have pre-

ferred *Christmas day* before the *Lord's day* and have cried down the
Lord's day and cried up *Christmas day.* I have known those that would
be sure to receive the sacrament upon Christmas day, though they did
not receive it all the year after. This and much more was the superstition
of the day. And the profaneness was as great. Old father *Latimer* saith
in one of his sermons, that the devil had more service in the twelve Christmas holy days (as they were called) than God had all the year after.
Seneca saith of his time *olim December mensis erat, nunc annus est.*
There are some that though they did not play at cards all the year long,
yet they must play at Christmas, thereby, it seems, to keep in memory
the birth of *Christ.* This and much more hath been the profanation of
this feast. And truly I think that the superstition and profanation of
this day is so rooted into it as that there is no way to reform it but by
dealing with it as Hezekiah did with the brazen serpent. This year God
by a providence hath buried this *feast in a fast,* and I hope it will never
rise again. You have set out (Right Honorable) a strict Order for the keeping of it and you are here this day to observe your own Order, and I
hope you will do it strictly. The necessity of the times are great. Never
more need of prayer and fasting. The Lord give us grace to be humbled
in this day of humiliation for all our own and *England's* sins, and especially for the old superstition and profanation of this feast, always remembering upon such days as these *Isa.* 22. 12, 13, 14. [Pp. 40–41]

Here Calamy pits keeping Christmas against observing the Puritan Sabbath
and repudiates the joy of Andrewes's feast with the prayer of a fast. Ex-
cepting only the play upon feast and fast, Calamy's plain prose has an entirely different, unadorned texture from that of Donne and Andrewes, just
as the texture of his religious vision differs so sharply from theirs.

Langley in his *Gemitus columbae: The mournfull note of the dove* . . .
preached in the Puritan paranoid strain, pointing out how few and weak are
the truly faithful, the turtle doves, and how great and wicked the beasts
that assault them (from Oxford). He glanced at the Christmas story only
once in the entire length of his sermon when he was exhorting Parliament
to vote more money for clergy and thereby "to set up lights in every dark
corner of the kingdom"; to do so would be to promote peace:

When Christ the light of the world, came into the world, there was a
great hush, calm and peace throughout the world. That prophecy was
fulfilled, that *the nations should break their swords into plowshares and
their spears into pruning hooks,* and the other, *the wolf shall dwell with
the lamb, the leopard shall lie down with the kid, and the calf and the
young lion and the fatling together.* They shall not hurt or destroy in all
my holy mountain, *for the earth shall be full of the knowledge of the
Lord as the waters cover the sea.*

> When Christ comes into the heart of a man, he changeth it into a
> meek, quiet, sweet, peaceable temper.[13]

Not only is this the only reference to the nativity in Langley's otherwise
Old-Testament-flavored sermon, but in addition he exploits the peace of
the season for a two-pronged political proposition; first he asks for increased
funds for his colleagues and then justifies the request by suggesting that
preachers will make men peaceable citizens living in the spirit of the manger.
More important, if at Christ's birth the peaceful prophecies were fulfilled,
they were not fulfilled permanently, as the state of war current in England
at that time so bitterly showed. The coming of Christ was not, therefore,
the decisive pivot and center of history but a momentary lull prefiguring
the final, Sabbatical peace.

The only preacher of the three seriously to deal with the fact of Christmas was Thomas Thorowgood. Asked by Parliament to preach, he initially
felt unworthy, yet dutifully began to prepare himself: "and I found presently my lot was cast upon that very day which the providence of heaven
had designed to fall on Christmas day, as it is named yet, the *Metropolitan*
of all the *festivities.*"[14] Not only was Thorowgood more obviously aware of
preaching upon Christmas than Calamy and Langley, but his sermon manifests at once both attraction to and repulsion from the festival. This is obvious even in his choice of text from Philippians 4.5—"Let your moderation
be known unto all men, the Lord is at hand." The first part of the text, on
moderation, was appropriate to the Christmas season of reconciliation,
yet foreign to the Puritan taste for "zeal" and commitment. Consequently,
Thorowgood balanced moderation against an eschatological expectation
which is both highly Puritanic and threatening. Preaching moderation to
a pack of zealots was a tricky business, as Thorowgood very clearly understood; he began most gingerly to open his text by apologizing for it:

> It is God's word that I have read; let no man's zeal be hot against it, or
> me; and how meet it is for this time, this very time, judge not till you
> have heard. My thoughts were not fastened here without some difficulty;
> I considered again and again and as often prayed that I might speak a
> word in season. It must be affirmed, there is all the reason in the world
> you be even now incited to zeal, wisdom, magnanimity, and present reso-
> lution; but *inclusive,* there is no Christian grace, I know, but you would
> be acquainted with it and *grow up into Christ in all things and be estab-*
> *lished in every good word and work.* But that I may in time take off all
> prejudice, I shall not speak of *moderation* in the sense of politicians and
> the world, but as it is a Christian grace and not inconsistent with holy
> zeal. . . .
>
> If yet to any apprehension the first clause seems a cooler, the second
> will show it seems so only, and my *moderation* doth not make a medley

of religion nor complies with any transgression, but it is a blessed and a watchful virtue, living always in God's sight and in expectation of judgment to come; it quencheth no man's zeal, only it makes it burn fair and shine more clear. [Pp. 1–2]

When he dedicated his sermon to Parliament, as it was being published, Thorowgood took a second opportunity to suggest that moderation was a virtue not very much extolled before that body: "for now, as dedications have been made to you of zeal, righteousness, magnanimity, perseverance, etc., so the world shall see you patrons of moderation also" (sig. A2^V). Thorowgood was doubly defensive; he was preaching on a topic very much in the spirit of the hated Christmas season, and he was correct that Parliament had not been instructed in moderation. His nervous and defensive opening paragraphs show the difficulty any Puritan preacher faced when he sought to "speak a word in season" on December 25.

Thorowgood touches on most of the important Puritan objections to keeping Christmas. First, it interfered with the proper keeping of the Sabbath, which "is a *noli me tangere,* you must not otherwise meddle therewith than to sanctify it yourselves and command that by all others it be sanctified. . . . you have power; 'tis most happily improved for the Lord and the day of the Lord; there is reason and religion your *moderation* should be known and shown to the other festivities, not only because of their abuse, superstition, and other evils, but of their increase—the holy week of Lent crept into the rubricated calendar in these days" (p. 16). God has helped Parliament moderate the excesses of superstitious, prelatical holy days; now "the providence of heaven is here become a moderator, appointing the highest festivity of all the year to meet with our monthly fast and be subdued by it. For Chrysostom doth well call the day of Christ's nativity the Metropolis and chief of all other festivals; for indeed from this arose all the other dedications in the name of Christ and his Apostles which else had not been known in the world; those be the children of that mother, and who is not abundantly satisfied with the hand of God upon them altogether" (pp. 16–17). In addition to popish abuse of holidays, however, "'tis probable enough we never yet kept right the day of Christ's nativity . . . , learned men supposing it very unlikely that such a general taxation should be made through the peaceable world in the depth of winter" (p. 17). Not only is the date uncertain, but history suggests it was invented to make "a medley of religion" also: "It was Gregory's counsel that the pagan feasts should by degrees be changed into Christian holy days, that they might the more easily be drawn to Christianity; and some write expressly that our Christmas festivities, in respect of time and manner of celebration, came from the Saturnals of the Gentiles" (p. 17). In addition, Christmas had been a time of "scandalous" behavior, of riot, and unChristian excess, indeed of little work and much merriment. In celebrating it in this way, the nation had been most sinful: "Go hence therefore and examine, and bewail, and consider; God's providence hath made this day, this very day, the head of all that jocundity, a day of humiliation; do not miscall it; let it be so to every one of us, for our own, the national transgressions it hath been formerly guilty of in those days; and if the Lord, *who is at hand,* had called any of us out of the world when we were busy in those foolish, vain and un-Christian usages, we may now tremble to think how unfit we had been to meet the Lord Jesus coming in the clouds" (p. 26). Still, even if Christmas has been sinful and over merry and may have inspired an apocalyptic judgment on the land, Thorowgood can see some worthy features annexed to the old customs: "Let us repent of riot and excess, but let the neighborhood and charity of those times at least in some time of the year be continued; sure I am that some, who had withered hands all the year beside, did at that season stretch them out to the poor" (p. 18). Clearly, the Christmas theme of "moderation" was one Thorowgood at least partially liked.

Thorowgood's ambivalence toward Christmas informs the structure of his sermon, which falls roughly into two parts. The first treats of moderation and the moderating of the excesses of Christmas; the final third of the sermon (pp. 21–33) treats of repentance inspired by the second coming of Christ; if the fact that the Lord is at hand "in Saint Paul's days . . . was an argument of and to repentance, it should much more accelerate us thereunto, upon whom the Lord is nearer now by sixteen hundred years" (p. 24). At one point, Thorowgood neatly bound together the nativity, the Puritan Sabbath, the beginning and the apocalyptic ending of all human history, focusing in true Puritan fashion on the light which lies beyond it:

Though this day of Christ's birth be thus overcome by our monthly fast, yet our Savior's nativity hath and shall have its commemoration, not only in the day solemnized for his resurrection, in which is involved all the complement and consummation of Christ's doing and suffering and exaltation, but further, the Lord's day is thought to be the very determinate day of the week when Christ was born; for those that mention the privileges of that elder brother, the first day of the week, say it was not only the first day of the world, no night went before it, but it shall be the last day and no night shall come after it, and that it was the very day of Christ's birth and baptism, etc. [P. 18]

The tensions within his sermon and the peculiar fusions he does achieve mark Thorowgood's piece as that rare bird—a truly Puritan Christmas sermon.

As a young man, John Milton celebrated at least one Christmas that we know about. The Nativity Ode was a youthful venture in a most un-Puritanic mode by a sensibility which would only later emerge as radically

Puritan. In commenting upon it, Louis Martz recalled the difficulties which Puritans had with "meditation." By "meditation" Martz there means a mental gesture of the sort which Richard Crashaw made when he wrote on Christmas, a spiritual progress from a physical and temporal locus (the "cold, and not too cleanly, manger") up to an eternal moment of mystical participation in kairos.[15] Martz finds the fullest exposition of that mental gesture in ultraconservative, Roman Catholic sources, and it is no wonder that a Puritan like Milton might have difficulties adapting to such a foreign sensibility.

These difficulties are intimately related to and expressed by Puritan attitudes toward Christmas, a word which Milton used only eight times during the course of his entire authorial career, according to the Index to the Columbia edition of his works (which is, admittedly, somewhat selective). Six of the eight instances cluster in the *History of Britain,* reporting medieval events; one occurs in *The Brief History of Moscovia.* Christmas was not, by Milton's account, a joyous or even pleasant day in early English history; in two different years the Danes accomplished "by *Christmas* the circuit of thir whole years good Deeds" of pillage and rapine (CE, 10:263); the irony seems to be at least partially at the expense of Christmas. Christmas day 1017 "was an ill Feast for Edric" indeed; Canute murdered him (CE, 10:276). William the Conqueror was crowned on the day as the English people prepared to submit themselves to a rank and imported tyranny (CE, 10:315). Milton, in short, did not like to use the word Christmas and when he did, often found himself reporting horror stories.

The contrast which Martz has drawn between Crashaw's and Milton's handling of Christmas motifs is instructive, even if it is not quite representative of the contrast between Anglican and Puritan sensibilities. Crashaw was not a conservative Anglican but an ultraconservative Roman Catholic when he polished his "Hymn on the Nativity,"[16] and Milton was probably as yet unrecognizable as a Puritan when he wrote his Nativity Ode. Crashaw had been extruded from English society and politics by the civil wars while aesthetically he had turned to Italian rather than English sources of inspiration. He did not surpass his father's evident Protestantism but rather escaped from it to die, like his verse (a sport in the literary history of his nation) abroad. Milton, who would indeed advance beyond his father's microcosmic, domestic reformation, had hardly begun to do so. He wrote long before he had taken his first step toward commitment—being "Church-outed by the Prelats." And even that step was, when he made it, probably ambiguous; it was only in later life, when his political and theological alignments had been more fully worked out, that Milton advanced a political interpretation of not having taken his degree. When he left the University, it is quite likely he was thinking more about his vocation as poet than

about bishops. All before him lay the period when he would adopt orthodox Puritan doctrine concerning, e.g., predestination, the Sabbath, the
relative unimportance of merit, and even farther in the future was that
time when he would subsequently reject (in concert with other advanced
and radical Protestants of his age) these orthodoxies and develop his own,
advanced, ultra-Puritanic views, articulated in *De Doctrina.* But as he
penned his ode, he had presumably not worked out very many of the implications of his father's Protestant gesture of rebelling against the Roman
religion of *his* father.

Since, however, men do not develop randomly, since we are orderly
and order-imposing creatures who respond to the apparently random nature
of the universe in self-coherent ways, since our development occurs out
from or around stable cores of personality, identity, or life-style, it is not
surprising that a man who finally emerged as just such a radical Puritan
would, even in his unformed youth, display certain tendencies which initially would make him feel "at home" intellectually and emotionally in
Puritan thought. That he was, as yet, unformed becomes clear when we
realize that he undertook, in the Nativity Ode, a clearly un-Puritanic task;
that poem is, therefore, an excellent place to turn to see how his unformed
sensibility instinctively responded. For, although it is an un-Puritanic exercise in some ways, the Nativity Ode is nevertheless undergirded and sustained by decidedly Puritanic habits of thought and art.

The difference between Milton's and Crashaw's Christmas poems is not
that one focuses only on time, the other only on eternity. Both poems consider both. What distinguishes them, rather, is the process of thought and
speech by which they move their focus and our attention from time to
eternity. Crashaw begins in time and opens out to eternity; Milton swirls
divinely above time and then finally descends into it. Crashaw's shepherds
are coming *away* from a particular place at a particular time (the manger,
just before dawn) and that is the essential rhythm of the poem as a whole.
Their naiveté, which contributes to the infantile "sweetness" of tone, facil-
itates this kind of development; they first report, in their limited way,
what they saw, then speculate on more sophisticated things of the "world"
and its courts and kings, and finally ascend to the ultimate theological
sophistication of "our own best sacrifice." The poem creates a sort of eternal present by expanding its focus, elevating its vision, and sophisticating
our perceptions in a smooth process from chronos to kairos. Milton also
creates an eternal present, but he does so, initially, through an ambiguous
temporal reference. "This is the Month, and this the happy morn" arrests
our attention, as Daiches remarked,[17] and also points two ways, to "now"
and to "then." Tenses of verbs ebb and flow as our attention is zoomed
cinematically through a welter of historical instants related thematically,
theologically, or verbally rather than chronologically or logically. Move-

ment is predominantly downward rather than ascending—which suits the
nature of the subject—and toward the manger rather than away from it.
Muse and speaker approach with a present. Christ, on "this . . . happy
morn . . . Our great Redemption from *above* did bring": the "meek-ey'd
Peace" is "sent *down*" by God (ll. 45–46) and "the mighty *Pan*/Was kindly
come to live with [the shepherds] *below*" (ll. 89–90, emphasis mine). In
the future, "Truth, and Justice then/Will *down* return to men" (ll. 41–42)
and the poem finally settles down, in the concluding lines, upon the
manger.

Moreover, Milton's speaker is uniformly and fully sophisticated in theological and historical matters from the very beginning; he knows all about
the events of sacred history and the eternal, divine decrees and he conde-
scends to the rude shepherds, slightly, from his amazingly lofty position.
He can evoke the creation and the millennium, the giving of the Law on
Sinai and the scourging of the demons, and he knows that the significance
of human history is limited. If Crashaw focuses upon the crucial midpoint
of human history and moves gradually out into the future, Milton focuses
the central section of his poem particularly on the beginning and ending
of time,

> when of old the sons of morning sung,
> While the Creator Great
> His constellations set,   [119–21]

and when

> Time will run back, and fetch the age of gold.   [135]

Nature, which

> heard such sound
> Beneath the hollow round
> Of *Cynthia*'s seat, the Airy region thrilling.
> Now was almost won
> To think her part was don,
> And that her raign had here its last fulfilling.   [101–6]

But Nature does not have a right understanding of the times (she is, after
all, only natural) and the speaker's and our enthusiasm for the final descent
of "Truth, and Justice then" must be similarly checked by the reflection
that

> wisest Fate sayes no,
> This must not yet be so,
> The Babe lies yet in smiling Infancy,
> That on the bitter cross
> Must redeem our loss.   [149–53]

That bitter historical event intervenes between us and the millennium as does "the wakeful trump of doom" (l. 156). Neither nature nor time is yet fulfilled by this event, for Milton is preoccupied by that eternal vision when

> at last our bliss
> Full and prefect is,
> But now begins.   [165–67]

Something of joy is here in this day; yet the joy is partial because of the cosmic view, theological sophistication, and eternal orientation of the speaker. From the low vantage point of Crashaw's shepherds, in contrast, it is much easier to ascend to a sense of final consummation.

The difference between Milton's consistently cosmic vision, sophisticated theological point of view, lofty tone, and elevated diction which condescend and descend to things of this earth, and Crashaw's time-bound shepherds, rude, low, and humble, may be neatly and briefly illustrated by the ways in which the two poets handle paradox. Chashaw wrings "sophisticated" paradox out of simple, mundane events and situations.

> Gloomy night embrac't the Place
>   Where the Noble Infant lay.
> The Babe look't up and shew'd his Face;
>   In spite of Darknes, it was Day.
> It was Thy day, Sweet! and did rise
> Not from the East, but from thine Eyes.   [17–22]

It was a natural night and the babe looked up as natural babes are wont to do. The fourth line transforms that natural event into an alliterated and obvious paradox which any loving and proud parent, pagan or Christian, might experience. The final two lines elaborate the paradox in the direction of a specifically Christian mystery which is finally summarized and capped in the paradox-laden thirteenth stanza:

> *Wellcome, all* Wonders in one Sight!
>   Aeternity shutt in a span.
> Summer in Winter. Day in Night.
>   Heaven in earth, and God in Man.   [79–82]

This fully sophisticated batch of paradoxes, coming in rapid succession, has been prepared for and generated by preceding stanzas.

Milton, in contrast, hits us, at the outset, with a pair of fully digested paradoxes for which he does not prepare us: "Trinal Unity" and "wedded Maid, and Virgin Mother" (ll. 3, 11). They are, of course, fully conventional and commonplace for all Christians; they do not deter us as we read. But Milton would probably have agreed with Crashaw that the rude shepherds from their time-bound perspective might not understand them, yet he does

not, as Crashaw does, employ their vision nor "prepare" his paradoxical
statements over reader-time for such untutored observers. After such initial formulations, I might add, Milton uses noticeably little of the tautly
paradoxical language which Crashaw favors. And while alliteration binds
together the logically disparate elements of Crashaw's paradoxes, it rather
fuses "sympathetic" parts of Milton's poem to evoke a harmonious and
unified vision. Nature "sympathizes" with divine impulse by doffing her
gaudy trim, and an elevated, poetic impulse descends to fuse together the
parts of Milton's ode.

Technically, Crashaw seems to have worked stanza by stanza, building
up a mosaic of interchangeable parts. His revisions tighten up a stanza or
clarify the relationship of stanza to stanza, while his habit of tinkering and
its results imply that sequence and development of the whole were not
fixed in his mind. His revisions generally work well here as they do not
always in other poems. Yet, one might argue that when Crashaw inserted
two stanzas, one addressed to the "Poor World" and the next to the "Proud
world" which became stanzas seven and eight in the final version, he broke
the movement of the poem slightly and thus had to refocus on the manger
before widening his scope in the final lines. The point, however, is not
whether he succeeded in his revision or not; rather, the point is that he re-
vised by manipulating stanzas. In the third stanza from the end, Crashaw
contrasts the simplicity of the shepherds to the worldliness of

> those gay flyes,
> Guilded ith' Beames of earthly kings;
> Slippery soules in smiling eyes.

In the first version, he speaks of

> poore Shepherds, simple things,
> That use no varnish, no oyl'd Arts,
> But lift clean hands full of cleare hearts.

In the revision, the last two lines read:

> Whose Wealth's their flock; whose witt, to be
> Well read in their simplicity.

Varnish and "oyl'd Arts" followed logically neither from his brief comment
on the "gay flyes" nor from his portrait of the shepherds, while talk about
their "Wealth" does extend the previously established portrait, and puts
their virtues positively rather than negatively as well. Crashaw also changed
the gifts which the angels offer the babe. In what was finally stanza nine,
the world offers snow. In the first version of the following stanza, the
angels offer "The downe that their soft brests did strow," which Crashaw
changed to "rosy fleece of fire." The white and cold of the one stanza thus

contrast to the red and heat of the next, and set up the capping paradox of the stanza following that, focused on the Virgin's breast, in which the babe is commended for choosing "Not to ly cold, yet sleep in snow." Here, modification of one single line alters and tightens the relationship between three stanzas. Again, the unit of composition is the stanza rather than the line.

Milton's formal arrangements are paradoxically more flexible or fluid and yet more tightly integrated than Crashaw's. While one might delete a stanza of Crashaw's without damaging the effect and the whole very much, one cannot do so with Milton. Instead of tinkering with bits of a mosaic, he weaves a web of associations, motifs, images, and themes, whose countless filaments radiate out from any single stanza to bind it firmly to the rest. Formally, Milton was more regular here than in his mature poetry, selecting a fixed stanza form rather than the freely flowing verse paragraphs of *Paradise Lost*. With a single exception, the stanzas are end-stopped so that metrical, syntactical, and intellectual units coincide. Perhaps the exception will best illustrate the rule and indicate something of the weblike quality of Milton's verse. Stanza XVI is not end-stopped; thought and syntax flow smoothly into the next stanza and it is clear that Barker, when he divided the poem into three parts or movements, had to adjust his division to accommodate this two-stanza sentence. Barker was (quite sensibly) making his division in terms of images, themes, and motifs rather than logic, progression, or clear-cut steps. The middle section, he urged, was dominated by images of harmony, song, and joy, while the final section is much more judgmental and destructive, "full of discordant sounds, distorted forms, and shadows."[18] Stanza XVI fits in smoothly with his conception of the middle section:

> But wisest Fate says no,
> This must not yet be so,
>   The Babe lies yet in smiling Infancy,
> That on the bitter cross
> Must redeem our loss;
>   So both himself and us to glorifie:
> Yet first to those ychain'd in sleep,
> The wakefull trump of doom must thunder through the deep.
>
> [149–56]

Milton is making a gradual transition from the hopes inspired by the angelic hymn and the "smiling Infancy" to his reservations about the "bitter cross" and the "wakefull trump"; it makes sense to see this verse as concluding the middle section. Unfortunately, it is syntactically bound to the next:

> With such a horrid clang
> As on mount *Sinai* rang

> While the red fire, and smouldring clouds out brake:
> The aged Earth agast
> With terrour of that blast,
>   Shall from the surface to the center shake;
> When at the worlds last session,
> The dreadfull Judge in middle Air shall spread his throne.   [157-64]

That stanza surely belongs squarely in the third section, discordant and distorted as the things it represents are. Yet Barker put it in the second section because it was so firmly tied syntactically to stanza XVI.

My point is not to quarrel with Barker's division; he is suggestive when he looks at the kinds of pattern (sounds, images, associational links) rather than logic, "message," or intellectual structure, and his divisions make sense—particularly if we add "give or take a stanza" to each. The divisions are much more fuzzy than they are in Crashaw's poem, and derive not from the form of the stanza (despite the fact that all but one are end-stopped and therefore syntactically self-contained) but from the flow of motifs, images, and emotions. Such a romantically organic texture embodied in "organ tones" appropriately expresses an achronologic view of history. Music binds the nativity to the creation and the millennium, not causally or through chronological concatenation, but thematically through implications of ascent. When time can "run back" as Milton says it can in this poem, then events are bound together through some sort of eternal significance which lies outside of the matrix of human time. The elevated voice and diction are requisite for a speaker who sees essentially as God does. His vision is not composed of discrete units as was Crashaw's but is unified or interwoven. Like the speaker in *Paradise Lost,* the voice here is more than human, his vision cosmic, his vantage point above the world. It is the poetic counterpart to the tone awkwardly established by a systematic treatise on divinity, a tone which seems to deny literary process of speech, human involvement in the things of this world, the tonality and color of human utterance.

Milton's use of the word "now" is a good index of his handling of time and eternity. The first of the five "now's", like "this" in the first line, points two ways. The speaker queries the Muse,

> Hast thou no verse, no hymn, or solemn strein,
> To welcome him to this his new abode,
> Now while the Heav'n by the Suns team untrod,
> Hath took no print of the approaching light.   [17-20]

Given the tradition, touched by Crashaw as well, that the sun rose late on the day of Christ's birth, this "now" could refer to "then" as well as to the predawn of a seventeenth-century Christmas day. It is precisely the interconnection between the two events, the eternal present which significantly binds them, which this poem works out. It does not do so by focusing on "this minute" and wringing an eternal vision from it, as Crashaw does, but rather through ambiguous reference frontally assaulting conventional, human notions of time much as Milton's paradoxes assault us directly with sophisticated theological lore.

If the first "now" points two ways in time, subsequent "now's" point more clearly to "then." That time when the ocean "now hath quite forgot to rave" (l. 67) is presumably the same time when Nature "Now was almost won/To think her part was done" (ll. 104–5), when our bliss "now begins" (l. 167), and when Astaroth "now sits not girt with Tapers holy shine" (l. 202). "Now" locates us at the day of the literal birth and is used three times with present tenses; one "now" occurs with a past tense verb, however, and one with a present perfect which is pivotal in a typical swirl of tenses. In stanza V, Milton begins in the past; "peaceful *was* the night," the "Prince of Light/His reign . . . *began*," "the Winds . . . *whist*" and "*kist*" the waters. Then, the ocean "*now hath* quite *forgot* to rave" and in the next line, the "Birds of Calm *sit*" in the present tense (emphasis mine). Milton continues the present tense into the following stanza, then reverses direction and drops back into the past. It were too long to record all of these shifts of tense;[19] this one, centered upon the word "now," must suffice as a single yet typical example. The tenses of the verbs and the ambiguity of the use of "now" embody syntactically and semantically the achronological texture of Milton's vision.

All of the moments to which "now" refers prefigure future events as well. Nature would have been wrong "to think her part was done" on that past day, but it will have "its last fulfilling" at the apocalypse. If in one sense "our bliss" merely begins with the birth and can begin for each of us at any moment in our lives, it will be "full and perfet" only "then" when the false gods like Astaroth are finally silenced and the Dragon finally trampled underground. The destructive and punitive aspects of Judgment Day are related not to the fall, as we might expect, but to Sinai and the Law; the joyous aspects are connected to the creation "when of old the sons of morning sung." Milton was a long way yet from arguing against a rigorous Sabbath and the confining strictures about marriage, polygamy, and divorce. That phase would come much later. Yet it is noteworthy that even so early he locates the effect of sin on Sinai rather than in Eden; his mature portrait of paradise would culminate on the note of glorious redemption as much as sinful loss. Here, the closest we come to paradise is the creation, a locus of joy, song, and harmony. Milton seems instinctively to have associated the middle, fallen, sinful phase of his tripartite historical scheme with the Law rather than the apple, even in this youthful venture.

The tone is matched by theological configurations, as we might imagine. Crashaw's baby "lifts earth to heaven, stoopes heav'n to earth" (l. 84) in a

reciprocal, two-way arrangement essential to the mediator. Milton's babe
is noticeably muscular, to the distress of some critics, and "Can in his
swadling bands controul the damned crew." He exercises dominion and
power while his advent is rendered glorious. From such a babe one can only
expect that eschatological figure of Puritan thought and controversy to
emerge, and the millennial references in the poem are indeed judgmental in
tone and remind us of how all knees shall perforce bow to him on the great
day. Rosemond Tuve argued that the poem is about "the Incarnation not
the Nativity" while Martz stated it is about the redemption rather than the
incarnation.[20] Both critics make their point in relatively abstract language
(as befits the cosmic implications so obviously evoked throughout) and
both seem to be remarking in different terms about the same quality of
the poem—a tendency to de-emphasize the love which one accords a baby.
Crashaw positively wallows in that sort of "sweet" emotion; Milton's vision,
despite the fact that he was much younger when he wrote, is far more adult
and serious. His muscular Christ will be exalted above us all, just as his
speaker is exalted by holy vision above our normal ken; the cosmic hero
matches the stance adopted by the poet.

   The central movement in Barker's scheme, evoking song, light, harmony,
and unity, resonates around a timeless chord, sounded first at creation and
to be resoundingly struck in the millennium. Here Milton shuttles through
the tense system most grandly, here he juxtaposes "then" to "now" (in
precisely that inverted order—ll. 165, 167) so that they move against chronological flow, backwards rather than forwards from "now" to "then."
Beginning and ending are bound by peaceful, joyous "concords" for they
are both outside time, which entered with the fall and will be shut up at
the apocalypse. The "age of gold," which time runs explicitly backwards
to reach (while our vision is simultaneously being carried forward to the
millennium), is at once the paradise we lost and the paradise we shall regain.
There is no chronological connection between event and event; Milton's
version of an eternal vision overarches time. There is similarly no mediatorial connection between earth and heaven, for God's might overarches
all, and descends throughout the poem to control events here. Milton's
speaker approximates the stance of Milton's God, in a quasi-antinomian
way, and with the chord of eternal harmony and the clang of final victory
ringing in his ears, descends into time and down to the manger. The vision
gives meaning to the manger and must proceed it as "doctrine" preceeded
"use" in the Puritan sermon; poetic process does not, here, as it does in
Crashaw's poem, wrest a vision out of the manger. The central section, in
Barker's analysis, unfolds the "final vision," and the poem balances in an
unprogressive way upon that middle section. The process of speech in this
poem is deployed to deny process in history and as our vision is swirled
back and forth through time, the effect is that time stands fixed.

Milton no doubt felt that his religious thought had developed well beyond what he articulated in the Nativity Ode, when he wrote *Paradise Lost,* and there can be little doubt that the energetic and fearless Milton did undergo considerable development throughout his life. But the ways in which the Nativity Ode both is and is not a Puritan poem suggest something quintessentially Miltonic which would not change over all those years.

Section Three: The Hope for Israel

All Israel shall be saved. —Romans 11:26

Chapter 8: PURITAN TYPOLOGY: FIGURATIVE LITERALISM

"Even the most rigid believers in 'engaged' literature will allow that poetry directly inspired by passing events derives much of its vitality from emotions which, however violent at the time, are usually ephemeral; it therefore rarely rises to very great heights. A poem concerned with the temporary and the topical, however wittily ingenious it may be, however tense with the moment's passion, is never so strong a candidate for immortality as one inspired by a perennial theme."[1] Unlike the majority of students of seventeenth-century poetry, C. V. Wedgwood followed those remarks, typical of and fair to the predilections of literary historians, with an analysis of poetry and politics in seventeenth-century England. Her admission is therefore doubly forceful because it comes from a student of political poetry. The emphasis upon transcendence, the aspiration to "great heights" and "immortality" are characteristic. Literary criticism conventionally involves working into the "system" of a poet or poem and explicating from within a world radiating out from that center. Since poets habitually make pretensions of "elevation" and "immortality," particularly in times of social crisis, we expect the literary critic to follow his masters and recapitulate those aspirations. All poetry and that part of literary criticism which molds itself to its subject is an attempt to transcend, extricate oneself from, or escape time's winged chariot.

The desire to transcend time, achieve great heights, and become immortal is, obviously, impossible to achieve. Moreover, cultivating a perennial theme probably resembles, in as many ways as it differs from, publishing an occasional, political tract, for if one chooses *not* to express the parochial and temporally local emotions which political events arouse, one has chosen to suppress, refine, or rise above them; the emotions remain constant, as do the pressures they inevitably exert. Poetic transcendence, both as a literary aim and a critical norm, probably should be regarded with a mixture of sympathy and skepticism—sympathy because it is human activity, occurs often in concert with psychological or social pressure or tension, and is something we all desire to achieve; skepticism because, pursued without self-consciousness, humility, and a sense of humor, it may become dictatorial and potentially dangerous. At the least, poetic transcendence ought per se to become an object of intellectual curiosity, for it is peculiar (being a wish impossible to fulfill) and not to be swallowed entirely whole. In this chapter, I wish to consider various modes of transcendence, varieties of pattern which emerge from men's attempts to soar above the sorrows of this sphere, and to distinguish them as they fit together with the distinct political parties of seventeenth-century England. One can only do so, however, by first beginning to regard poetic transcendence as an object of some critical scrutiny.

It is worth noticing, at the outset, that the poetry of Donne, Herbert, Crashaw, Vaughan, Herrick, Lovelace, and Suckling appears only minimally in Wedgwood's discussion, largely because those poets were relatively apolitical in focus. In addition, although Jonson was implicitly almost always political when flattering the nobility with masque or ode or lambasting dissidents on the stage, yet his lyric poetry often seems equally apolitical. Lovelace ascends to greatness, according to Wedgwood, "because the theme of love and absence is common to all generations"; out of political passions and ephemeral moments he erected an immortal lament. In contrasting these men to Milton, who wrote voluminous political prose and produced political verse as long as his politics were publicly viable, we might of course accuse these poets, inclined to established conservatism, of being politically escapist; however, to do so means we run the risk of psychological or socioeconomic determinism, which I am not willing to do. To say a man was psychologically so constituted that he became an "escapist" is to imply strongly that he has no choice; to say politics drives him there carries us into the more rigid areas of Marxist analysis. Still, if that sort of talk is unfair to the human situation, so too is that approach to literature in which "perennial themes" and "literary traditions" propagate in some mysterious, immaculate conception above this darkling plain. Poetry is human behavior. Men write it. Because, as Wedgwood's remarks brilliantly demonstrate, literary critics are more inclined to err toward the transcendent rather than the reductive extreme, I shall by way of partial antidote lean toward the latter where I lean at all. I wish to explore how the "moment's passions" were expressed, in comment and through silence, in a variety of seventeenth-century writing, and how the essential patterns of Puritan and Anglican verbal art express in miniature the political analysis, history, and development of the two parties.

Joan Webber, who has had the daring to label her subjects politically as "radical Puritans" and "conservative Anglicans," argues that conservative Anglicans ascend from the contemplation of the things of this world to attain to an eternal vision perceived by an hydropic "I" which gathers all the cosmos into itself. "Radical Puritans," on the other hand, are for her time-bound pragmatists.[2] Her thesis accurately accounts for the final vision which these two sorts of writers attain, at least in a general way, but does not take into account the manner and method, the mental *route* by which these men arrive at their final vision. All Christian theologians, as I have previously remarked, must perforce account in some way for both time and eternity; differences between the political parties emerge most clearly when one examines the *sequence* in which various men move from one to the other. Puritans immediately jet up into eternity, then descend to reform the times; Anglicans initially work within the times, then gradually transcend them. Both manifest a certain disinclination to be where they presently are and a preference for being somewhere else in a purified, peaceful, time-free rest; both are in a sense unhappy with this world, as all Christians should be. But the Puritans are first of all unhappy with it and in a transcendent frame of mind, then through a curious paradox, become optimistically able to return down to reform. Anglicans, on the other hand, begin generously enough with a liberal and humane assessment of man, somewhat more optimistic than the Puritans, but get forced out of this world just as their politics of absolute monarchism were. Historically, the Puritans undertook a theologizing and systematizing extravaganza before they settled down to reform and were free for revolution. Historically, the spokesmen of the establishment seemed at first more flexible and secure, until their world came crashing down; they then completed an essentially meditative movement and redirected their attention upward from the things of this world to an *O altitudo!* outside of and (they hoped) beyond political passions. The history of these developments is implicit in the historiographic theories of the two groups, since men describe their past in the same style in which they cope with their present.

When Stephen Marshall preached to explain what was "a right understanding of the times," he simultaneously embodied Puritan historiography and a revolutionary appeal to action of a particular sort. Three sorts of "understanding" Marshall dismissed out of hand—"astrological," "diabolical," and "prophetical"—and while "historical" understanding was "extremely and deservedly cried up by learned men" and pursued by "choicest wits, . . . yet my text hath nothing to do with it, and truly though it be an excellent thing, men may have it and yet die fools."[3] Historical understanding focused on a "continued series, a chronology of all the years," whereas a "theological" or right understanding concerned itself with "*some particle of that time which is the opportunity of the duty*, the season of the duty." Marshall contrasted the two orders of time, "the one of them, the length, the duration of time which the Greek calls χρόνος," and the other, "the season, the opportunity is called καιρός, which is the *tempus commodum*, the tempestivity of time, the ripeness of time." "*There is the space of time*" which "is nothing but the continuation and succession of so many minutes and moments one of another," and "there is the season *of time*" which "is time apted and fitted to do a business" (p. 17). If one has aban-

doned the chronological process of history, as Marshall does here, and if
one finds oneself in a civil war (and is, indeed, winning) in an effort to
reform and deliver an elected English nation, one experiences an extraordinary number of these special, pregnant moments or seasons. Severed
from chronological continuity and causally independent of each other,
they are open to all good men in all times.

Marshall then applied this historiographic doctrine pragmatically, noting
optimistically "our times are times of deliverances" when "the Lord, as in
other parts of the world so especially amongst us, seems to be laying out
the platform of his Temple and to set out a new edition of his Church,
fairer and more beautiful than ever" (p. 38). His sermon is a striking, revolutionary *carpe diem*, exhorting the English to acquire a "gracious and a
practical knowledge of the times, which is so to know the times as to
understand the moment and exigence of all affairs which fall within the
times in reference to their own duty" so that they "may improve all
occurrences which fall out to the right end." Full of enthusiasm (both
literal and rhetorical) Marshall felt he knew both "the times" and "the
right end"; John Milton seems to have also, for he portrayed his Jesus in
Paradise Regain'd and his Samson confronting precisely this problem.
Neither, he could serenely show, must act too soon, too quickly, too inde-
pendently, or out of private promptings; both must await the *"tempus
commodum"* and then they could infallibly do their "duty."

That sort of time scheme permits one to move backward or forward,
yet always away from the passions of one's particular movement, to find
"pure" primitive models for the future purified state; recurrence and
repetition rather than continuity and progress dominate such a vision and
hence the stories about one's heroes are deeply dyed with cyclic recurrence
and improgressive repetition as well. And as the Puritans so ranged backward and forward through time, they fused a literal with a wildly figurative
reading of the Bible, drew their models of conduct from an ancient, literal
Israel while they sought to erect an eschatologically typical Israel; the latter
had, through the peculiar process of Puritan theologizing, been reduced
from a type to a mere analogue of the English Church and nation. To put
it another way, the Puritans followed the old, traditional practice of going
beyond a literal reading of the Old Testament to analyze the figures of the
Christian Church found therein; these had been apparently confirmed by
past ecclesiastical history and therefore seemed objectively "real" rather
than subjectively imaginative. But because, in their view, everything, in all
times, had ever been the same, the Puritans showed a marked tendency
simultaneously to reduce ecclesiastic types to literal statements and to extend their sense of security about the phenomenal basis of ecclesiastic
typology to speculations about the apocalypse. Eschatological projection,
which can never per se be "confirmed," came, through this curious process,

to seem literally true; the hope for God's English Israel, therefore, seemed to be at once a hope for ancient Israel and a hope for the New Israel of the millennium; the Christian Church of "our times," allied as that notion seemed to be with the establishment, dropped out of sight in their analysis. The enthusiasm of revolutionary preachers like Marshall could only flow freely after this process had locked past and future in an adamantine embrace sufficient to crush and kill the present. It could only flow, in short, when men had been taught not to concern themselves with "the continuation and succession of so many minutes and moments one of another." Then the proposition that "all Israel shall be saved" became a statement of political ideology. Then the revolution could begin.

In making this point I both agree with William Madsen's argument that Puritans could be as wildly figurative as any of the Roman Catholic expositors they so rudely pummeled for indulging "their own fancies,"[4] and disagree with his conclusion that it is impossible to distinguish between the typological practices of Puritans and Anglicans.[5] If we attend to the distinction which Eric Voegelin and Norman Cohn have both made between Christocentric, ecclesiastic typology and eschatological typology,[6] we can, Madsen's quite valid point notwithstanding, make distinctions in typological analysis. Father Danielou is making a statement of faith rather than of fact when he says that typology lends itself to and can "only be expressed in" a theology of progress and development over time.[7] Men who believe that (and they are many, particularly in the Established Church of seventeenth-century England) propose a basically dualistic historical frame: historical phenomena before the advent of Christ prefigure spiritual phenomena after Christ. Typology becomes "phenomenal prophecy," in Eric Auerbach's phrase,[8] and as such has a certain solidity or reliability which other figurative readings of the Bible do not. First of all, as Samuel Mather put it, "there is some *outward* or *sensible* thing that represents an higher, spiritual thing" (p. 52); the outwardness and sensibility, the physical and historical reality of the type, reassured men like Calvin that they were not pursuing "mere human invention" when they examined types. No man can eschew figurative language if he writes anything more interesting than a telephone directory; H. R. MacCallum has shown lucidly how the "phenomenal" basis of typological analysis appealed to Calvin and reassured those of his disciples who were devoted to the "plain style" by providing a large stock of seemingly nonmetaphoric metaphors.[9] Secondly, types of this Christocentric, ecclesiastic sort may be checked against the historical data of the New Testament to see that they have been actually fulfilled. Mather gave three rules, for example, by which one could "know when a thing is a type, and that the Lord did ordain and design it to that end and use" (p. 53). These rules were important because "men must not indulge their own *fancies*, as the Popish writers use to do, with their allegorical

senses" (p. 55). Some types are explicitly so named in Scripture, "as Adam
. . . is called *a type of him that was to come*" in Romans 5.14. Sometimes, "there is a *permutation of names* between the *type* and the *antitype*
. . . as for instance, Christ is called *David*" (p. 53). Thirdly, "when by
comparing several scriptures together there doth appear an *evident and
manifest* analogy and *parallel between things under the Law and things
under the Gospel*, we may conclude" that the former is a type of the latter
(p. 54). Whether or not these rules would do what Mather claims for them
is beside the point; for they illustrate that Puritanic need to avoid rhetoric,
metaphor, and "fancy," or as Calvin put it, the "audacity" with which
"many of the ancient" of the Roman Church had "recklessly played with
the sacred word of God as if it had been a ball to be tossed to and fro."[10]
Phenomenal prophecies were safe because they were objectively real, historical events, and they had been fulfilled by Christ and his Church.

Eschatological typology, as distinct from ecclesiastic or Christocentric
typology, adds a third, spirited age of the Holy Ghost to the dualistic conception of an age of the Father and an age of the Son. The prophet or
adept often thinks he is displacing or abrogating the Christian dispensation,
much as Puritan controversialists displaced Jesus from the center of the
theological world, and turns his attention to the future when the types
which concern him will be brilliantly fulfilled. Of course, these types cannot be "checked" or their fulfillment and prophetic accuracy ascertained,
but they often seem to acquire the solid status of ecclesiastic types through
simple mental extension.[11] Once Calvin had sanctioned typological analysis
in general, his disciples were free to escape the passions of their world by
peering backward and forward into the future, and with the Old Testament
opened wide as a source of metaphor, they could enunciate a literally figurative reading of a new, bipolar worldview. For having squeezed Christ out
of what was originally a Christocentric typology (in much the same way as
they removed Jesus from the flux of human history) the Puritans had a
unique medium for expressing a newfound, revolutionary optimism that
God's English Israel should be saved in the future as it had in the past.

Puritan typology, then was the vehicle by which revolutionaries raised
the events of their time above history; it provided a way to equate their
struggle with that of Israel, and thereby served to rationalize their revolution as the work of God wrought through his agents on earth. The Puritans
came to believe that they lived in moments "apted and fitted" for the
doing not of mayhem, destruction, or the fragmentation of society, but
rather of a "duty." The conservative establishment, in contrast, practiced
Christocentric typology as a way of fitting their own moment and struggle
into the process of history, of defusing the Parliamentary rhetoric, of
checking the enthusiasm which swept the elect nation. Restricting oneself
to ecclesiastic typology can, in troubled times, check what a member of

the establishment takes to be fantasies or dreams of the future; it also means that, when past and present seem to betray one, when one's *fidei defensor* has died without his head, the transcendental pressure to look to the future will be more explosively articulated, since a smooth vehicle for expressing that pressure does not lie ready to hand. If, as Madsen argued, we cannot distinguish parties on the basis of whether they do literal or figurative interpretation, we can distinguish them on the basis of the scheme of history and sense of time which they embody in their handling of the types.

From at least apostolic times, typology had clearly been a polemical strategy, first of all for legitimizing the claims of Jesus to fulfill prophecy (in the Gospels), then for the practices, particularly sacramental, of the Church. Irenaeus, for example, found himself in much the same situation as establishment Anglican conservatives of the seventeenth century when he combated the Gnostic dualism. Danielou's remarks show that situation clearly: if it is true that God's plan involves historical diversity in providential unity, how is this paradox "to be explained? It is just at this point that the Gnostics offer their solution, with their theory of different worlds and different gods. To deny the difference [between the Old and New Testament] only leads to underestimating the newness of the Gospel. Such a charge could be brought up against those, as for instance, the pseudo-Barnabas and even St. Justin, for whom all had already been given to the Patriarchs." With their patriarchal obsession, the Puritans also argued that the patriarchs had had a full, gospel-like revelation; hence when Danielou goes on to summarize Irenaeus's thinking, he might equally refer to the strategies of a seventeenth-century conservative: "'If everything had been foretold, wherein lies the newness?' But, if the differences are accentuated, do we not destroy the unity of God's plan?" (p. 33). Irenaeus replied in terms of that pedagogic theory of history so dear to Anglican conservative hearts. Not only were the Israelites, the patriarchs and prophets, infantile and in need of raising, but even Christian knowledge was partial: "our Lord in these last times when he had summed up all things into himself, came to us not as he might have come, but as we were capable of beholding."[12] Despite his having "summed up all things into himself" and therefore completed certain historical patterns, even these were not fully articulated. Irenaeus thus holds Christians in a somewhat problematic state, checking claims to assurance and a full knowledge of all of God's future plan.

Augustine, with a sensibility much more akin to that of the Puritans, emphasized the eternal truth which the types embody—the unity—at the expense of the historical diversity manifested through historical progress. His "theology of grace"—part of his attack upon the Pelagians—converged with his aims in refuting the dualistic Manicheans. The former believed that man can save himself by fulfilling legal prescriptions and therefore argued "that even the old law, according to the Apostle, is holy and just and good, and that this could confer eternal life on those that kept its commandments, and lived righteously by faith, like the prophets and patriarchs, and all the saints." Although their emphasis on "works" and the way they praised "the law in opposition to grace"[13] clearly suggest Laudian "Arminianism," the Pelagians also resembled the Puritans of the seventeenth century by accusing theologians like Augustine of teaching that "the Holy Spirit was not the assister of virtue in the Old Testament" or in other words of arguing that the patriarchs were saved through a different economy of salvation from Christians (iii, 6; *NPNF*, 5:404). Sensitized by his controversy with the Manicheans over much the same ground, Augustine incorporated that Puritanic aspect of the Pelagian attack into his own thought by pointing out that the promise of salvation was eternal and thus in no way related to the temporal chronology of progressive history. All men, in all times, may be divided into two classes: those men who experience grace, essential to the New Testament, and are saved, and those who, even when they try to live virtuously, do so in the spirit of selfish legalism, the spirit of Sinai which genders to bondage. The distinction is not historical but generic or sociological; the terms "new" and "old" get stripped of temporal meaning. "Far be it from us to deny that righteous Noah and the righteous men of the earlier times . . . belong to the Jerusalem which is above" Augustine exclaimed, in tones owing to the Pelagian argument and in phrases which seventeenth-century Puritans could revel in, for "the New Testament is more ancient than the Old" (iii, 7–8; *NPNF*, 5:405). With the temporal relationship between the two testaments thus dissolved, Augustine could focus on the eternal significance inhering in the type. The type came to imply for him the whole, eternal theology of grace.

These were not Augustine's only words on the subject;[14] he could point to historical differences. The patriarchs believed in a Christ of the future: "Of the faith whereby we live, of one and the same they lived, believing the incarnation, passion and resurrection of Christ in future, which we believe as already accomplished" (iii, 11; *NPNF*, 5:406–7). My first point is that these were words uttered in controversy, for strategic purposes; my second, that, even when pointing to the difference between the patriarchs and us, Augustine never lost sight of that eternal significance which was "one and the same" as that whereby we live. Controversy, in short, pressed Irenaeus to stress developmental progress over time and pushed Augustine to stress the eternal and timeless significance.

Intellectual, systematic, lawyerly, with clear abilities to organize affairs here on earth, Calvin confronted intellectual adversaries who appealed to historical tradition as the mainstay of their authority. The basis of the priestly function lay in a chronological matrix, initiated by a clear-cut

historical gesture to Peter and extending down in timely succession to
sanction sacramentally transmuting acts. With such adversaries, it is not
surprising that Calvin chose to lay emphasis upon the eternal meaning of
events rather than their chronological significance, quoting with approval
and elaborating upon Augustine's remarks. "The children of the promise
. . . have belonged to the New Covenant since the world began," he wrote,
completely destroying the temporal meaning of "new" as he did so. These
promising children "believed especially in the Mediator, . . . not in hope
of carnal, earthly, and temporal things, but in hope of spiritual, heavenly,
and eternal things."[15] Their aspirations transcended time, in precisely the
way Calvin's analysis of sacred history did. Immediately after these phrases,
Calvin quoted with approbation Augustine against the Pelagians, differentiating his own view which "distinguishes between the clarity of the gospel
and the obscurer dispensation of the Word that had preceded it" from his
predecessor's which "simply separates the weakness of the law from the
firmness of the gospel" (III, xi, 10; McNeill ed., pp. 459–60). Calvin so
completely agreed with Augustine he could term the latter's views "simple"; his addition, based on the difference between "obscurity" and
"clarity," focused on man's perception of Christ and thus located important elements of the transaction within men. It jibed completely with the
Puritan emphasis upon the subjective perception of Christ rather than
some objective, sacramental, or liturgical presence or practice and meant
that the validity of the patriarchs' religious experience was to be measured
by the degree to which they apprehended an unchanging truth. Change
occurred not in the world but in men's heads.

Typology offered an apparently stable way of embodying this historiography; one of the principal differences "between the Old and New Testament consists in figures," Calvin stated. The Old Testament, "in the
absence of the reality . . . showed but an image and shadow in place of
the substance; the New Testament reveals the very substance of truth as
present" (II, ix, 4; McNeill ed., p. 453). Reality being preferable to "the
absence of reality," the Christian dispensation is superior to the patriarchs,
presumably because of the process of history. On the other hand, that
image or shadow was tinted with specifically Christian color and content,
a notion which English Puritans would embroider upon in most bizarre
ways. According to Calvin, the Old Testament is a book open to all Christians rather than closed by Christ's "*consummatum est*," and the phenomena recorded there, substantial because historical fact, provide a solid
base for (admittedly retrospective) interpretation.

Such an intellectual formulation fused with the British desire to identify
with Israel as God's peculiars and nourished that manner of reading the
Old Testament which Dryden parodied and exploited in *Absalom and
Achitophel*. When Thomas Taylor, in 1635, titled his catalogue of types

Christ revealed, or the Old Testament explained, he emphasized the clarity and Christian color of the Old Testament dispensation. This habit of mind led to some odd phrasing, as when he called circumcision "a distinguishing sign of the Jews from all other people who were without God, *without Christ*."[16] Samuel Mather, for all the conservative rules of validation which he provided, argued that "either the Gospel," which he defined as "the glad tidings of man's recovery by Jesus Christ," was "preached unto [the patriarchs] of old, or else it will follow that they were all *damned*, or else that they were saved *without Christ*." This solicitude for the patriarchs, echoed by Milton in his defense of polygamy, Mather hammered on hard: "if the Old Testament saints were *saved*, it was by *Christ*, and if by Christ, they had the *Gospel* preached to them as well as we" (p. 7). Milton simply radicalized this view when he argued that "a lot of Jews, and Gentiles too, . . . are saved although they believed or believe in God alone, either because they lived before Christ or because even though they have lived after him, he has not been revealed to them." For, he contended in a way which would unload much of the specific content of Christian doctrine and move remarkably close to a Puritanic sort of deism, salvation comes "by means of Christ, for he was given and sacrificed from the beginning of the world," yet "the ultimate object of faith is not Christ, the Mediator, but God the Father" (*De Doctrina Christiana*, book 1, chapter XX; Yale ed., p. 475). Subordination, patriarchalism, ahistorical sociology, and a curiously flattened typology underlie these notions.

Stephen Marshall, preaching on infant baptism, said the ancient Jews "were under the same misery by nature, had the same Christ, the Lamb slain from the beginning of the world, the same condition of faith and repentance" as his English audience had.[17] Thomas Cooper wrote early in the century that Noah bestowed a blessing on his son Shem "that he might continue in the worship of JESUS CHRIST (his God) and Savior."[18] Thomas Wadsworth, late in the century, provided what is probably the most strange verbal representation of Christ in the Old Testament, however, when he explained that "with respect to the Old World [i.e., that sinful time before Noah's flood], above two thousand years before he came in the flesh, Jesus Christ the Eternal Son of God was alive then."[19] What these men meant by Christ and Jesus, in such statements, is anyone's guess. If pressed, they no doubt would have explained that they didn't mean that Jesus was literally alive, or that the Jews were literally Christians, or that the patriarchs actually professed a faith in Christ. It took a man of Milton's boldness to follow where these verbal inadvertencies led.

The consequence of such writing is to open the Old Testament wide to all Christians, rather than to close it, and to support the notion that all of the elect, in all times, were under the same covenant with God. Insofar as these Puritans suggested that the patriarchs and prophets had specific knowledge of Christ, they minimized the progress often associated with Christian history; the Jews may have been children, but to the Puritans they differed little from "mature" Christians. Dod casually remarked, at one point, that "if it were well tried, many of these that brag of their strength above the Jews would be found inferior to many of the Jews."[20] It was a fine jibe at the "secure sinners" among the established ecclesiasts who clung most tenaciously to a progressive, pedagogic theory of sacred history. And, finally, such a curious manner of exploiting typology reinforces and/or elaborates the Puritan habit of de-emphasizing the importance of the historical advent of Christ.

The Puritans' curious way with typology provided fluent release for a newly emergent optimism, which I shall consider a bit later. In addition, however, it easily degenerated into analogy and fused with the increasingly overt millennial note of Puritan thought. Millennialism always involves, when radically pursued, a similar stopping of chronological time, while confusion between ecclesiastical and eschatological types may provide a seemingly respectable basis for the projection (and in extreme cases, the acting out) of one's fantasies. It will be well to detach these various strands for individual scrutiny before showing how they were woven together into the texture of Puritan thought.

Once English Puritans had identified themselves with Israel and the Israelites with Christians, the typical relationships between the two groups easily collapsed into simple analogy. "Scripture may be analogically applied," asserted the radical millenarian William Aspinwall;[21] given the propaganda war with Rome over "mere human invention" and the careless way the Church Fathers had kicked Scripture about like a football, the remark is at first shocking from the mouth of a thoroughly advanced and radical Protestant. Yet even Mather spoke about "a manifest analogy and parallel" between two events (p. 54), conservative Puritan as he was; perhaps it is not entirely surprising that Aspinwall believed that when Isaiah prophesies concerning a "land," he was really talking about an "island," and where the Authorized Version translates "hosts," Isaiah really referred to "militia." Attacking Cromwell from his left flank, accusing him covertly of betraying the revolution, Aspinwall shows how Isaiah's warnings about "the most high one" refer to Cromwell's recent assumption of the protectorship. Similarly, Lewes Hughes explicated Revelation and Isaiah in *A looking-glasse for all true hearted Christians* (1642). England is an "Armageddon" or "a mountain of delights"—a place of particular godliness—and can await hopefully "for the judgment of God's Sion in this land."[22] Elaborating upon the paranoid vision of a worldwide Papist conspiracy against the English, Hughes notes that in Isaiah 63.1 the prophet speaks of Edom and Bezra, "the metropolitan city of the Edomites and a type of *Rome*, the metropolitan city of the Papists,

of whom the Edomites were a type." Just as the Edomites "did profess
themselves to be Jews . . . and did profess the same religion," yet "did
(notwithstanding) hate the Jews . . . so the Papists, professing themselves
to be the people of God, . . . are the greatest enemies that Christ and his
church hath in all the world" (pp. 2-3).

Aspinwall and Hughes were neither untypical nor very subtle Puritan
theologians. They did less adroitly and more overtly what countless Puritan
preachers tended to do covertly and more subtly. That both read Isaiah is
simply fortuitous; that Hughes handles Isaiah exactly as he does Revelation
is quite noteworthy, for looking backward in search of a timeless vision
rooted among the patriarchs, in Eden, or at creation, is an effort to transcend present time very like looking forward to the second coming, the
new Eden, the recreation of a "new Heav'n and Earth" beyond the final
shutting up of time. The old peace, Sabbath rest, and paradise lost will then
be regained; the eternal redemption which the "lamb slain from the beginning" initiated then will be concluded in the last days. Christ is displaced
out of time, the manger, typology, and history, just as surely by a millennialist as by a student of Genesis. Most commonly, the same man makes
both gestures, both forward and backward, as Hughes does in turning to
Isaiah and to Revelation. That double vision was always central to Milton's
grand style.

Chapter 9: THE CALLING AND CONVERSION OF THE JEWS

The Puritans used this literal yet figurative, retrospective yet millennial way of reading the Bible to interpret Paul's remark that "all Israel shall be saved." The statement seemed to be literal in several ways yet, at the same time, prefigured the apocalypse. It was the cornerstone of their political analysis since it projected England's future. But before we turn to the transcendental politics which developed out of this text, let us first consider a unique literal reading which the Puritans developed almost entirely by themselves. According to this view, "Israel" was not a metaphorically Christianized fulfillment of an old type. Rather, Paul's statement, referring only to Jews, meant that in the final days there would be a calling of them home and final conversion of them to the faith.

Paul titillated the English; he introduced this prophecy by saying: "I would not, brethren, that ye should be ignorant of this mystery, lest ye should be wise in your own conceits." Mystery, mystery, who could solve the mystery? It was hard to keep one's theological pen off this one, given that attractive hint; a surprising number of theologians devoted whole tracts to explicating it alone. When Marvell's amorist referred to the "conversion of the Jews," he was not loading his argument with obscure theological bric-a-brac. His contemporaries would almost certainly have heard of it and, the more is the wonder, many would have developed distinct opinions about it.

The longer Englishmen thought and wrote about this mystery, the more thoroughly they demystified it. Indeed, in a little over a century, they turned one mystery—predestinate election—into a rational certainty, uncovered a second—the calling and conversion of the Jews—and turned that into a self-apparent certainty as well. The first mystery was celebrated by Calvin. It was inconceivable to him, given the abject, sinful nature of man, that God should deign to save him, yet incredibly he did. Following the majority of the Roman fathers, he read "Israel" typologically to mean "all the peoples of God," the "elect," or the Church of Jew and Gentile converted.[1] The text, in other words, was not about a Jewish question; Israel was no longer peculiar to God. Circumcision had once been a sign of "outward calling," but that is "ineffectual without faith." In crucifying Christ and refusing the gospel, Israel lost its peculiar status through lack of faith, for "the honour which the unbelieving refuse when offered, is justly taken from them." Circumcision was no longer "a common symbol of God's favor to all the Jews, so that they ought to have been all counted his people" (pp. 409–10), and as a result Calvin, a solid ecclesiast disinclined to speculate about the millennium, posited a decisive historical change in the status of the literal Israel and, on the basis of Paul's talk about "mystery," figuratively metamorphosed ancient Israel into the Christian Church through types.

For all his cool intellectualism, Calvin celebrated the mystery of salvation through faith throughout his works in an awed and inspiring way. Calvinists meant it when they said that they preached a "comfortable doctrine," for to emphasize man's sinfulness was simply a part of celebrating God's unimaginable mercy. From that strain developed the Puritan feeling for the "awful sovereignty of God" which John New has commented upon (see Introduction, n. 25), and the means for "giving God the glory." But if Puritans followed Calvin in that way, they departed from him as their battles with the established ecclesiasts grew protracted. Matthew Poole, deeply steeped in Puritan theology, writing in retrospect after its flowering, and no strident partisan, provides an excellent index to the immense changes which occurred in the interpretation of this small phrase in England. When, a century after Calvin, Poole asked himself what mystery it was to which Paul referred, he arrived at an entirely different answer. Paul, he thought, could not possibly mean by this "mystery" that the elect are saved by God; that was "no mystery at all."[2] Rather, Poole concluded, Paul must be referring to the final calling and conversion of the Jews.

Poole wrote at the end of a long period of Puritan speculation. Surprisingly early, Puritans seemed to become particularly fascinated by the conversion of the Jews, developed clear-cut theories about it, and forced them on the attention of the English nation at large. Admittedly, there had always from time to time been some speculation about the future of the Jews in Christian theology, but the Christocentric Anglicans came much closer than the Puritans to the general tone and shape of Christian thought when they used terms like "Jewish" and "Judaical" reproachfully. In contrast to the Puritans, they were inclined to remember the old charges of deicide leveled against the Jews, to distinguish sharply between the Old and the New Testaments, and to regard Jews as a sort of anti-Christian. Thus the *Book of Common Prayer* urged God to "have mercy upon all Jewes, Turkes, Infidels, and heretikes" (which is to place the Jews in a clearly anti-Christian category) and to "fetche them home, blessed Lorde, to thy flocke, that they maye bee saved among the remnant of the true Israelites."[3] Obviously, in Cranmer's view, as in Calvin's, the Jews were not now "the true Israelites" of a specifically Christian Church. To much the same effect, John Stockwood in 1585 preached on the "heavy judgments

of God, executed upon that people for their sin and disobedience" and
held them up as hideous examples of "rebellion and unrepentance."[4]
Thomas Lushington (whose witty sermon centered upon the Gospel
account of the resurrection as an historical event) decried the violent theological controversies of his age, complaining that there was "no point con-
troverted, but the opposite tenet may be reconciled, be they distant as
heaven and hell, as incompatible as Jews and Christians."[5] Examples of
this sort could be multiplied manyfold.

Even advanced or radical Protestants of the Elizabethan period took a
dim view of the Jews as a group. Francis Tayler maintained in 1583 that
"the Jews were wicked and rebellious, despisers of God and his word, and
therefore justly cast off."[6] John Foxe the martyrologist, excited in 1578
as he was by the "conversion of a certain Jew," was yet horror-struck by
the Jews' "unbelief" which was so hideous that God "must needs avenge
him upon the whole nation and root out the remnant of the whole race
altogether."[7] These early Puritans shared Calvin's amazement that God
would pardon any sinful man; since, in the traditional view, the Jews were
particularly wicked, they were therefore extravagant examples of his
mercy. To make that point, Tayler went beyond merely castigating the
Jews to concede that "God hath still reserved unto himself a number
according to the election of grace" (sig. c4^r), echoing the language of
Romans concerning election. Foxe also pointed out that God, being merciful, did not do what one might rationally expect—root out the remnant;
rather he "reserved to himself a covenable number of all the remnant of
that seed" (sig. A[8]^v).

Their remarks, reined in by the tradition of despising Jews, were yet the
entering wedge of a new optimism concerning Israel's future, literally conceived; Tayler and Foxe were really saying that "*not* every particular man"
of the Jews was "cast off" (Tayler, sig. c4^r, emphasis mine). After this
hope for Israel flowered, sending John Eliot in search of the ten lost tribes
among the Amerindians and leading Sir Edward Spencer to exult that "we
are the likeliest nation under heaven to" convert them,[8] conservative Puritans like Sutton, Prynne, and Lightfoot sought vainly to reimpose the reins
and challenge the proposition that "every one of that nation" would be
saved—a proposition which, Sutton added, "I dare not say."[9] One of the
things this controversy shows is the way in which a position, once the
province of such advanced or radical Protestants as Calvin and Cranmer,
could ossify into a conservative stance while progressive Puritans marched
right past it into new fields and dreams.

Several reasons why Puritans were especially attracted to this notion
suggest themselves. First, Paul's Epistle to the Romans provided the central proof-texts for this as well as the doctrine of predestinate election.
Puritan commentators were nothing if they were not thorough; once peer-

ing into Romans to find out about election, they shredded the whole book equally fine—including texts on the future of the Jews. Second, the calling of the Jews provided an excellent outlet for rising millennialism, and optimism about the Jews soared into overt eschatology. Third, the notion that England was an elect nation settled into confidence, and Israel's peculiar relationship with God in the Old Testament furnished an attractive parallel for the nation's destiny. Finally, patriarchalism and concern for the Father flowed smoothly into special interest in the affairs of Israel as well as England.

When, in 1621, Sir Henry Finch published the first chiliastic exposition of our text, he filled his margins with citations from two places in the Bible—Romans and Revelation. His book was pivotal in the development of Puritan thought, owing much to the traditional ecclesiastic interpretation of "Israel" yet going beyond, and his use of proof-texts was also pivotal.[10] As the millennial strain latent in Puritanism surfaced openly, both in this context and more generally, writers stopped citing Paul and turned to John's vision.

Romans pleased early and/or more conservative writers because of the restrained hope which Paul's use of the term "remnant" implied. Paul quoted Isaiah's prophecy that a remnant would escape and be saved (Rom. 11.1-6) yet he also used "remnant" to describe how many Jews had been cut off or lost—so many that only a small remnant would remain in the final days (Rom. 9-10). Consequently, the term "remnant" suggested to early Puritans (and their later, more conservative descendants) that some Jews would be saved but that many more would perish; they typically spoke of a "remnant" or "seed" or "little flock" of Jews being finally converted.

Andrew Willet, distinguished commentator on Romans and author of a small Latin tract, *De Judaeorum vocatione*, accepted this view, faithful to the more pessimistic side of Calvin's theology, yet he disagreed with Calvin about the meaning of the term "Israel." More optimistic than Calvin, he believed there would be a "national calling" foretold by Paul, a calling of a true "remnant" or rectified "nation" picked out from all Jews and specially chosen by God.[11] On the one hand, then, he did not think that many Jews would be saved. On the other hand, however, his notion of a "national calling" came to imply, for later expositors, quite a general, wide-ranging conversion. In short, he took a centrist position which looked back to Calvin, yet he opened a verbal gate through which more advanced thinkers would drive great numbers of Jews. "All Israel" could be understood only in a qualified sense, he believed, but still must be read literally. His views were restated or echoed by Thomas Draxe in 1608, Thomas Cooper in 1615, Elnathan Parr in 1618, Thomas Sutton in 1632, and William Prynne in 1655.[12] Sutton captured the essence of this initially

liberal yet finally conservative view when he wrote: "the Jewish nation
shall be converted, yet every one of that nation I dare not say" (p. 384).

Once "all Israel" had been so literalized, even in this qualified way faithful to the spirit of Calvin, expositors working from Revelation simply expanded the boundaries of the "nation." To the generation which followed
Willet, Draxe, Cooper, and Parr, the notion of a "national calling" seemed
axiomatic, presumably because so much talk about it had turned it into
Puritan orthodoxy, and in their growing optimism they simply dissolved
the limitations and theological restraint of their predecessors. Thomas
Thorowgood in 1650 dismissed the topic casually: "the Jews before the
end of the world shall be converted to Christianity." His additional comment is more telling: "this truth is to be found in the Old and New Testament, and hath been the constant belief of the faithful of every age."[13]
He may have been right about the faithful in every age; in Protestant polemic the faithful are often highly invisible. Yet certainly many quite
visible and seemingly faithful Protestants, like Willet or Calvin, had obviously disagreed with his views. At any rate, the "mystery" had become
for Thorowgood a "truth"; assurance had produced oversimplification.
Robert Maton, in *Israel's redemption* . . . (1642) assumed there would
be a full terrestrial reign of Christ over the converted Jews and that many
more than a mere remnant would be saved.[14] Others who asserted or tacitly
assumed (out of increasing casualness) these opinions were Thomas Collier
(1656) and Moses Wall (1652).[15] Edward Nicholas opened up even further
vistas when he asserted that not the two visible but also the ten lost tribes
would be saved. Hope for Israel boomed indeed.

Time had passed for the remnant. The term does not appear in Revelation. By the late 40's and 50's, only conservative Puritan theologians who
doubted that absolutely all Jews would be converted—Sutton, Prynne, and
Lightfoot are the most conspicuous examples—remembered the remnant.
Indeed, when in 1655 Prynne argued that "Israel" in our text "meant only
. . . the elect and *true Israel* of God, both *Jews* and *Gentiles*," he urged a
different interpretation from most of the contemporary "learned orthodox
divines and writers" whom he footnoted in an attempt to bolster his position; even he had to admit that they "are much divided" (p. 65). While
there was some division, they were less divided than Prynne would have
one believe; as a matter of fact, most of the contemporary divines disagreed
with him, interpreting Israel literally to refer to Jews alone. For Prynne,
however, the Jews "were the greatest haters, revilers, persecutors, blasphe-
mers, betrayers and the only murders [*sic*], crucifiers of our Lord Jesus
Christ himself, and his Apostles . . . as the evangelists, Acts and other
Scriptures testify." They had been "judicially and penally given up to a
blind, obdurate, obstinate, impenitent, stupid heart and spirit, a reprobate
sense, a cauterized conscience, and divorced, rejected, reprobated, broken

off, cast off by God himself," while the Gentiles had been "engrafted, called and taken into special covenant in their stead" (p. 65). Prynne was a bit hysterical on the subject because he was fighting a petition by Manasseh ben Israel to readmit Jews legally into England, a proposition which apparently frightened him badly. What is more interesting about his remarks, however, is the manner in which he argues from a progressive view of history and, despite his disinclination to venerate the cross and the crucified Jesus, invokes both here. Hysteria and what seems to have been a perennial bad temper renders the tone of his remarks anti-Semitic in a way which Calvin's do not, on the surface at least, seem to be; but his interpretation of "Israel" and of the general theological patterns involved is almost exactly Calvin's. By 1650, however, these views were antique, a century old, and were no longer a part of advanced or radical Protestant thinking. They had, during the years, become in fact a bit reactionary.

The process of Puritan theologizing, then, reduced the typological metaphor of Israel to a literal statement. At the same time, the new hope for the future of the nation was based on a sort of eschatological typology, embodied in such common, metaphoric phrases as the New Jerusalem. The two fused to produce a mode of thought and talk profoundly upsetting and mystifying to the ecclesiastic establishment. An excellent example of the resultant confrontation occurred in 1621 when Henry Finch published *The world's great restauration, or the calling of the Jewes* and Laud commented upon his eschatological notions. Finch argued that "the Jews refusal of Christ" led to their rejection (a traditional enough belief), "notwithstanding which, a small remnant, a hole [sic] seed, shall be left *Rom.* 11.5." However, "in the last days . . . not a few singled out . . . but . . . the nation in general" shall be saved.[16] Here we can see what talking about a "national calling" produced, for if Finch in some part qualifies his optimism by recalling that there will be "refractories" on that last glorious day who will not heed the call, still he manages to suggest that something more numerous than "a little flock" shall be saved, escape, and "dwell in their own country."

Laud was frankly appalled. Preaching before Charles on the royal birthday and taking as his text "pray for the peace of Jerusalem," Laud generally flattered the king that such prayers would operate on his behalf, then in a few paragraphs, scornfully animadverted on Finch's book: "I had now done with *rogate pacem* . . . but that Jerusalem is come again in my way" as a result of Finch's book. "But it is a strange Jerusalem. Not the old one, which is literal in my text, for which David would have prayers: nor that which succeeded it, Jerusalem of Jew and Gentile converted, for which we must pray. 'But Jerusalem of gold and precious stones . . .' And this Jerusalem upon earth, is that which is called the Heavenly Jerusalem . . . and the new Jerusalem."[17] Laud's criticism is firmly anchored in a bipartite, progressive view of history and Christocentric, ecclesiastic typology. The "old" Jerusalem, the type, is literal and has been replaced by the "new," spiritual antitype—the Christian Church "of Jew and Gentile converted"—instituted by Christ at a definite point in time. To Laud, Finch makes up or hallucinates a "strange" eschatological antitype, located in the future, unverifiable, upsetting to ecclesiastic order, the product of his "own fancy." From Laud's historical, Christocentric point of view, the "old" Jerusalem is quite different from the Christian Church. He is baffled by Finch because, in his view, Finch does not straighten out his chronology or locate his ideas within the process of history. Jerusalem "upon earth" is, as Finch handles it, "the Heavenly Jerusalem" of the future; that is, Finch reads "all Israel shall be saved" literally, yet appears to Laud to use eschatological metaphors. When the Puritans removed the process of history and the matrix of chronology from life on earth, they in effect implied that everything is always the same; Israel of the past equals Israel of the present equals Israel of the future; a literal reading thereby becomes simultaneously metaphorical, and a prophecy can point to the past, the present or the future, or all three, at once.

The Puritans were anxious to demystify not only religion but also language. Epistemological Baconians,[18] they advocated the plain style and methodized their thoughts under the categories of abstract nouns as a way of escaping the shape-shifting effects of human language. However, it is impossible to evade the problems of language. As the Puritans reduced the polysemous words "Israel" and "Jerusalem" to what they hoped would be literal, stable meanings, they created terms semantically more ambiguous and unreliable than anything which more highly figurative writers had ever produced. Laud, for example, precisely because he was relatively at home with and tolerant of the imprecise and polysemous nature of human, corrupt speech, could handle the multiplicity of meanings clearly and firmly, label the "literal" and the "new" easily, and guide his auditors through the process of metaphoric language at the same time he implied the process of history. But when any part of the Bible could be taken by the Puritans equally well to point in any direction in time, their preaching acquired a whole host of ambiguities which they could optimistically exploit in any way they chose. That could only happen after they were well drilled in certain theological presuppositions and came to believe that all men in all times had believed just exactly as they believed. Given their belief in intellectual progress, they finally decided, after accepting the further light of succeeding generations, that all men agreed with them regardless of history, just as they believed that all men had been saved on their own terms of salvation. This confidence was doubly dangerous because even Laud linked "Israel" and "Jerusalem" with the English nation; there was widespread agreement that England was an "elect nation," as William Haller has demonstrated, even among the establishment.[19] Once the drilling on Puritan orthodoxy had been completed, the hope for an elect, peculiar nation, a new English Israel, could fully blossom.

The pressures at work transforming the meaning and significance of the term "Israel" were at work transforming the whole of Puritan theology. Just as the Puritans demystified "Israel" and opened the gates of the millennium to most if not all Jews, so what Perry Miller has called the "federal school"[20] came to believe that the mystery of the "covenant" was also "no mystery at all." Miller has showed how these federal theologians began imperceptibly to maneuver God toward a legalistic corner. A covenant is binding upon both parties, they asserted. As Bunyan put it, "God might chuse whether he would give me comfort now, or at the hour of death"; "I might not therefore chuse whether I would hold my profession or no: I was bound, but he was free."[21] However, if God was initially free to enter the covenant, he was not free once he had done so; then he was bound to perform his part. As a result, even the unstable Bunyan achieved a kind of assurance, despite his view that God "was free." Firmly "covenanted" churches, in England and America, achieved a greater degree of assurance than Bunyan. More radical speculators embroidered on the notion. The Ranters placed a negative construction on the inflexibility of predestinate election. George Fox, the Quaker, put the opposite, highly positive interpretation; he denied that man was sinful by nature, asserting that he knew himself to be sanctified. John Goodwin and John Milton radicalized this thrust intellectually, denying the doctrine of predestinate election, attacking the view that men could be damned beforehand, and asserting that grace was offered to all.[22] Edward Lane, schoolfellow to Milton, wrote a book to confute the theory that "not one man in a million will be saved," and he appended some remarks about the conversion of the Jews to it, remarks which opened salvation to Jews equally wide.[23]

If those men were quite advanced or radical Protestants, more sedate Puritans made much the same point, albeit in a more restrained way. Thomas Manton, whom Wood dubbed "the prelate of the Protectorate" and *DNB* describes as "the most popular of the Presbyterians," insisted in sermon after sermon that "the great design which the scriptures travail with is, to set forth a grant of pardon upon gracious and commodious terms, if sinners will but accept of it."[24] He believed that the Christian religion was superior to all others, because "this privilege is discovered to us in all its glory, and that upon very commodious terms, fit to gain the heart of man, and reduce him to God" (2:187). And he believed that man may "accept" this pardon for himself, that is, that man may act positively in the matter of his salvation. In yet another sermon, Manton used striking adjectives when he remarked that "in the Christian religion all things are provided for which are necessary to establish a regular hope of pardon . . .

there is a full satisfaction given to divine justice, and the foundation laid for pardon in the death of Christ, . . . we have privileges offered to us by a sure covenant in Christ's name." And that pardon "is dispensed upon rational terms, such as faith and repentance" (15:444). "Regular," "full," "sure," and "rational"—all deny the sense of mystery Calvin had labored to assert at the same time they hold out an optimistic future to fallen man.

No doubt after the federal theologians rested their case, the hope of pardon did seem regular, full, sure and above all else rational. The map of God's mind had been drawn with immense and systematic precision; it is not surprising, therefore, that as solid a Presbyterian writer as Manton would arrive at such seemingly Arminian views. However desperate and compulsive we may think the federal theologians were to have labored so long and hard over their summas, the effect of their work must have been truly liberating. How could a divinity student at Cambridge or at Harvard look at those polished masterpieces, notice the immense coherence of their assertions, follow the clear "method" of their schemata, and not believe that he could learn to know the mind of God from them? If a half-century of discussion formalized the language one used to speak of the name above all names, and the process of threshing out the Sabbatarian position hardened men's convictions that they knew the right answer to the fourth commandment, much the same sort of activity, applied to the mysterious mercy of God in pardoning sinners, transmuted that pardon into a firmly covenanted hope and a rational pattern. To see just how far Puritan optimism had progressed, one has only to remember New's point, that both Elizabethan Puritans and Anglicans were unanimously agreed that man could not act positively for his salvation (*Anglican and Puritan*, ch. 1). The more "liberal" Elizabethan Anglicans at most admitted a sort of negative free will—that man could reject the means of grace. Puritans like Manton, Goodwin, and Milton suggested that man could not only reject but even positively accept the means of grace offered by God.

The elaboration of Calvinism in England was, as a result, curiously self-destructive; the more completely God's English worked out the theology of predestinate election, the more certain they were of their own rational powers and of the hope held out to them. The more the Puritans gave God the glory by mapping out the glories of his power and plan, the more they conceived of his plan as truly a "comfortable doctrine," until ultimately that human sinfulness which for Calvin had both differentiated man from God and defined God's awful sovereignty and mercy, began to disappear from their thought. Simultaneously, they began to quote Revelation rather than Romans, to advance nontheological rather than theological arguments, and to focus on the promise of the apocalypse rather than the human limitations affected by predestinate election. Always inclined to be charitable to Israel, the Puritans simply extended their own commodious pardon to the Jews. They had demythologized predestinate election and were well on the way to demystifying the conversion of the Jews; they had also literalized a typological metaphor while creating a profound verbal ambiguity about the term "Israel" which pointed both backward and forward in time as a literally figurative reading of the text.

Chapter 10: HUMANE OPTIMISM AND PURITAN DEMYSTIFICATION

If the process whereby Puritans extended salvation ever more widely to both Christians and Jews turned Calvinism inside out doctrinally, a similar reversal occurred in the kinds of examples the Puritans brought to support their reasoning. Puritanism was at first rigorous and systematic Bibliolatry; as the century progressed, however, Puritans came to argue not from theological considerations, but from humane reasons. The change in their concern may most economically be presented by contrasting Theodore Beza's daily prayer for the conversion of the Jews as rendered by Thomas Thorowgood with a "query" raised roughly a century after Beza prayed by Thomas Collier. Beza prayed:

> Lord Jesus, thou dost justly avenge the contempt of thyself, and that ingrateful people is worthy of thy most severe indignation; but, Lord, remember thy covenant and for thy name's sake be favorable to those miserable wretches and to us, the most unworthy of all men, unto whom thou hast vouchsafed thy mercy, bestow this goodness also, that we may grow in thy grace, that we be not instruments of thy wrath against them but rather, both by the knowledge of thy word and by the example of holy life, we may by the assistance and virtue of thy holy spirit reduce them into the right way, that thou mayest be glorified of all nations and people forever.[1]

Collier, arguing on behalf of readmitting Jews legally into England, asked,

> Whether those men that say they love the Jews and pray for their conversion yet will not willingly afford them a being in the nation where they might enjoy the means of conversion, do not therein declare that their love and desire to them doth flow either from rational conviction from the letter of Scripture, or from custom and tradition, or else at the best mixed with much ignorance, not knowing that true love doth not only desire but also useth all means for the promotion of the party beloved.[2]

Beza traces all of his points back to "thy covenant," "thy name's sake," "the knowledge of thy word," "the example of holy life," and "the assistance and virtue of thy holy spirit." All testify to Beza's sense that there are God-given patterns outside man which he should look upon and follow. Collier does not feel he must fit his theories to some external and/or prior set of considerations, patterns, or examples. He argues that we follow not scriptural examples but human nature and the quality of true love. He can sneer at men who write "from rational conviction from the letter of Scripture."

Thomas Calvert shows something like Collier's concern in the way he made use of a series of old horror stories about the Jews. Whereas Stockwood, Tayler, and Foxe, before 1600, had stressed the "heavy judgments" visited by God upon the Jews in order to emphasize God's mercy in saving some of them, Calvert, and even Prynne in a curiously perverse way, recalled these stories fifty years later to comment upon the Jews as people. Prynne rattled off a lengthy list of old wives' tales, crucifixions of Christian children, riots and pogroms, and other horrors in his not short *A short demurrer to the Jewes long discontinued remitter into England*; his point was that as men and neighbors the Jews were troublemakers and that no right-thinking community would wish to have such amongst them. That some anti-Semites ran amuck and made pogroms was less a comment upon them, to Prynne's view, than it was upon the Jews' unsettling influences upon a community. Prynne was following a very old strategy, when, as one D. L. put it, he "raked together all the rabble of Popish authors, and filled men's brains with strange stories, and [his] late printed books with marginal notes of friars', and monks' and abbots' relations."[3] While I do not accept his implication that the Catholic Church was as a body anti-Semitic, D. L. was right that Prynne's sources were old-fashioned. But it was Thomas Calvert who turned the old ad hominem strategy inside out. In his "Large Diatribe" prefixed to his translation of *A demonstration of the true Messias* he recounted much the same stories Prynne had in order, as he put it, to "provoke Christians to be . . . pitiful to the Jews about the misery that lies upon them."[4] That is, he tells these stories not to show how wicked the Jews are, but to wring a tear on their behalf by showing how other men have been wicked to them. Similarly, Collier turned the old charge that the Jews were deicides to a new use when he argued that "in crucifying the Lord they did no more than was the counsel and determination of the Lord . . . though it was their sin yet it was God's counsel; yea it is by Christ crucified that we have life" (p. 4). His adroit use of the *felix culpa* to subvert the old charge of deicide was in the same spirit as Moses Wall's remark that "we ought much to mind their conversion . . . and that . . . first, because they have the same human nature with us" (p. 49).

Not all men accepted "that charitable opinion of most Christians that there shall once be a calling of them home" as John Lightfoot put it. Indeed, Lightfoot himself, unflinching Calvinist in a newly liberal age, dissented from "that supposal of the universal call of the whole nation as of one man."[5] He seems to have done so not from the hysterical reason which moved Prynne, but rather out of intellectual and theological rigor and acuity. A precise mind, he retained that old dedication to "thy covenant" and "the knowledge of thy word" which underlay Beza's prayer. Yet the pressure exerted by humane optimists like Calvert, Collier, and Wall told on his prose. Puritanically, he moved the source of the Jews having "been rejected and blinded" back in time and away from the crucifixion. "I know well enough that the casting off of that nation is commonly assigned to that horrid wickedness of theirs in murdering the Lord Christ," he explained, but because the cross was not central to his world view, he dated their rejection from "before such time as our savior manifested himself in the flesh."[6] Thereby Lightfoot indirectly disentangled the Jews from the old charge of deicide. Most important, however, Lightfoot appreciated "that charitable opinion of most Christians" and the loving tones it involved; he said he was "unwilling to recede" from such a view, yet it could not be "digested without some allay and mitigation" (*Harmony*, p. 195). The problem is, as he saw it, that God will simply not save very many of us. Lightfoot's admissions show how outdated systematic Calvinism had become while they record just how secular and optimistic were the arguments contemporary preachers by then advanced.

I find it difficult, when writing about this topic, to be equally fair to the claims of reason and of emotion, of logic and of love. On the one hand, theological reason and logic, when applied to this Jewish question can sound like superrationalized anti-Semitism, perhaps even totalitarianism. Yet, while Prynne was an anti-Semite of a particularly unlovely nature, and while logic can justify killing, on the other hand it seems to me a bit facile to dismiss men like Beza and Lightfoot as we welcome the liberal and humane views of Collier, Calvert, Wall, and what Lightfoot perceived to be "most Christians" of the mid- or late seventeenth century. A change occurred in the way Puritans thought and argued and wrote, and like all changes it probably involved at once losses and gains, some attractive and repulsive elements. On the one hand, the Puritans lost theological acuity and logical precision; at the same time, they gained a more loving tone which had been markedly and lamentably lacking in their early writers. On the other hand, they lost an objective standard against which to measure and if need be check their own worst impulses and gained the freedom to follow what Bishop Hickes later called "illuminations, prophecies, visions, dreams, raptures, inspirations, voices from without, irresistible impulses within," be they for good or for ill.[7] Even were we able to claim that Beza hated Jews (an unlikely proposition, since among other things he wrote a separate tract about their conversion), we would have to admit that his devotion to God as the principle of reality could function to rationalize hostility; yet it could also check any hateful impulse he might

have to "be . . . instruments of thy wrath against them." And unfortunately, history did not allow us to see just how loving a Collier, Calvert, or
Wall would in practice be to the Jew next door; yet it is true that it is easier
to be loving toward an abstract and, at that time, legally distant and long
absent group than it is to cope with the reality of individual, live men. History abounds with too many examples of liberals who have concerned
themselves for the underdog from what are psychologically self-serving
reasons.

Furthermore, it would be foolish to forget that there were severe limits
to what change did occur and blithely to glorify the Puritans for having
developed full-blown religious toleration as well as modern democracy and
physical science while they struck the first decisive blow leading to the
death of God. Leo Solt's reservations concerning their toleration, democratic leanings, and scientific spirit are well founded.[8] The Puritans seldom
tolerated atheists and Catholics, they most frequently feared democracy,
and they almost always set their scientific pursuits within the old hierarchy,
subordinate to theology. Carrying Solt's analysis to our immediate topic,
we can see clearly that to the Puritans the only good Jew was a converted
Jew, and, however much they may have demystified religion, they always
devoted themselves to answering that key question: what shall a man do to
be saved. In this they were of their age, and with perhaps a handful of exceptions, they always assumed that only God saved men and that he was
supremely, absolutely greater and other than man.

Yet within these limits a change did begin to occur, however partially—a
change always implicit in the very bipartite structure of the sermons they
had always preached. Roughly speaking, over the course of a century Puritan preachers turned from abstract doctrines to earthly applications. After
the Puritans had elevated God and defined him out of this world and its
chronos, after ascending to the study of pure doctrine in their summas in
what amounted to a systematizing binge, after giving him the glory by
stressing his great authority and distance above fallen man, after exorcising
a loving, suffering Christ from this world and after turning him into Truth,
fixed forever firm and sure, after tracing out how the community of the
saints extended back in time to the very beginning, built on the rock of the
Law and the eternal covenant to all good men, after hammering out a
plain style and rocklike prose to fix God and that community, a prose
freighted with conceptual diction to match their pursuit of Truth, assertive
to match their authoritarian God, unornamented as a proper vehicle for
stripping away externals, and abstract as a way of distancing God, they
descended to this world. They set about to reform it and cope with men,
assured that they knew all the important answers. If at first they demanded
a closer walk with God and approximated that feat with the dry pages of
their summas, they ultimately obtained a kind of assurance from that exer-

cise which permitted them to walk amazingly securely and at times, it almost seems from their pages, alone. Filled with God's power, they did not entirely forget him, but perhaps they did begin to turn their backs. They could allow certain tendencies of their thought and art to go to completion. Setting God at a great distance from man, both intellectually in theological formulae and stylistically through abstract diction, made it harder to see him, just as taking Christ out of this world had. The danger was, that once he was thus moved out of sight, he might go out of mind. It may be significant that Bunyan's fiercest temptation was to "let him go."[9] It seems that some Puritans succumbed. Perry Miller remarked upon how the Puritans ultimately turned from theological argument, reasoning "not from theology and revelation, but from law, from the study of nature, from the principles of reason and common sense."[10] Basil Willey and Don Cameron Allen would urge that this was the effect of a wider, newly emergent renaissance rationalism, serving new emotional demands;[11] yet the Puritans were innovators in their age, busy forging just such changes rather than being blown about helplessly by the winds of some new "spirit." When Willey and Allen would suggest that the Puritans were not alone in taking these new steps, they are helpful; but the story of the development of Puritan thought provides us a concrete example of how the practical efforts of men created that spirit, and allows us to see where the new winds came from. As they turned from the "doctrinal" to the practical stage of their mental, emotional, and stylistic development, they allowed a vanishing God to more openly disappear from their thoughts.

With so much in mind, we can now make sense of the basically mixed character of the Puritan sensibility. The Puritans exhibited, as I have been at pains to show, a sense of disease in this world and an unhappiness with the things of this world; at the same time, they demonstrated signs of a marvelous ability to function in this world. If, on the one hand, the Reformation was a profoundly frightening experience, dislocating men, severing old and long established ties of authority and commerce, inducing a sort of mass insecurity, as Zevedei Barbu presents it,[12] it was, on the other hand, also a liberating gesture freeing men for new kinds of commerce, relocating them and rehabilitating them with a "comfortable doctrine." A protestor protests out of anger and fear and frustration, but he also protests because down deep he thinks that something can and should be done "about it" and that raising his voice will count. The reformers of the Renaissance and the Reformation needed more room—be it social, economic, intellectual, physical, or spiritual—and they set out to make it for themselves. They were men of zest and innovation, men able to take a chance and break with the old ways. If for John Donne the new philosophy called all in doubt by making men puny, unimportant, casting them adrift in huge, uncharted spaces, the new developments provided Milton with the necessary space and poetic elbow room within which to pan his cosmic, zooming, movie camera; he could not have penned his soaring lines in anything but an apparently limitless universe. The zest with which Milton exploited that space marked him out as a quintessential advanced or radical Protestant, fully prepared cheerfully to pursue things unattempted yet in politics or theology, prose, or rhyme.

There is plenty of evidence to support Barbu's notion that at least the English Puritans (if not, as he claims, the whole English nation) were compulsive because frightened by a changing universe. Puritan theology became monumental in a whole host of ways, noisily shouting in form and content that there was indeed order in this universe. The length of their sermons and summas, the way they repeated the same doctrinal points, the improgressive way they made intellectual progress by elaborating rather than forging anew—all that noise was difficult to ignore and the Puritans seem to have begun to believe what they so insistently chanted and heard.

And once convinced by their own pleading, their fears dissolved in a new optimism, their compulsive fascination with God relaxed, they could descend from afar from the sphere of our sorrow to set things right here below and await the glorious, triumphant "new Heav'n and Earth, wherein the just shall dwell." Having speculated upon "the just" for so long, they thought (as Milton clearly did) they knew who they were.

The ability successfully to cope with changing patterns in this world must count as something important in our assessment of the history of advanced or radical Protestantism. For the Puritans won the civil wars (even if they lost at the Restoration) and they won convincingly on the intellectual and political level; never again would feudal theology and political science function as they had. There was a certain joy manifest among the Puritans, if we may judge by the revolutionary sermons delivered to them, as they marched into battle.

This new optimism about the future of Israel—whether that term referred to Jews, the covenanted Church, or God's Englishmen—which so surprisingly wrecked Calvinism, was accompanied by another astonishing development. Jesus, exorcised from the world of Puritan divinity as an object of humiliation and suffering, came again into that world. As we might expect, he was a new Jesus, "King Christ" or "Lord Jesus," a sort of *"deus in monte"* as Calamy put it,[13] who would battle the Assyrians and rule men in the kingdom of the saints. Still eternal and outside time, kept firmly away from the "center" or pivotal point of human history, he would yet come, as Nayler indicated when he acted out his reentry. The new Puritans were no longer primarily backward looking but faced the future with hope; whereas they had initially looked back to God's mercies to ancient Israel in order to be reassured by the extreme power exercised by Jehovah-Jireh,[14] they now projected that authority confidently into the future and a new *"deus in monte"* who would indeed take care of them. George Fox focused throughout on the love of Christ while Bunyan cast himself upon "Lord Jesus" in *Grace Abounding*. John Milton devoted a minor epic to him. But again, lest these examples seem exceptional, we can see this process at work in the preaching before Parliament during the civil wars, which John Wilson has analyzed.[15] Turning to his "Calendar of Printed Sermons Preached to Members of the Long Parliament," and picking out from the short titles those which, even in such shortened form, make reference to points of sacred history, we note that initially Old Testament references predominate heavily, but that beginning in roughly 1646, the titles refer at least as often, if not more often, to topics in the New Testament, to Christ, and to the apocalypse (see Appendix). The preachers selected to address Parliament were never, even in the most free-wheeling times, the most radical spokesmen of the period, and Wilson's well-focused sample is particularly revealing about developments in more than the tiniest vanguard of the Puritan movement. By 1646 the fortunes of war were beginning to run in the Puritans' direction and at that point a great many men must have felt confident enough to look forward to "King Christ."

Looking forward to the future is in one way exactly like looking back to the past, to Eden, the patriarchs, the *locus* and *tempus amoenus*. In both cases, one is looking away from the distasteful present, transcending time. But looking forward is a much more helpful business than looking backward. It is significant not only that the Puritans finally found a Christ of the future with whom they could identify, but equally significant that they thought he would come into the world again. For they were entering into the world, politically, themselves and achieving a success. That hopeful prospect had always been latent in Puritan thought and Puritan art. For the Puritans had always concluded their sermons with "uses" in this world. And, self-consistent people, they organized their sermons in precisely the same style in which they organized their theology and their revolution.

Edward Lane's *Look unto Jesus or an ascent to the holy mount to see Jesus Christ in his glory* (London, 1663) exemplifies how these changes converged. As an antidote to the view that not one man in a million would be saved, he looked to Christ's mercy; but that mercy will be dispensed in "the Holy Mount" and in "his glory" at the apocalypse. In an *Appendix shewing the certainty of the calling of the Jevvs*, Lane argued that the old "remnant" referred to Judah or the two visible tribes; "all Israel" was obviously more extensive and embraced all twelve. The calling of the Jews was a "certainty" by the time Lane wrote, hardly more mysterious than predestinate election had become. The return of the new Puritan Christ, the new, humanistic optimism of Puritan theology, the extension of salvation to more and more men as well as more Jews, the demystification of theology into certainty and "no mystery at all," and the increasingly overt millennial note of advanced or radical Protestantism all came together in a book like Lane's.

Chapter 11: ANGLICAN ASCENT

The Puritans, those proto British Israelites, forged a transcendental politics out of their hope for Israel. The conservative Anglicans, in contrast, ultimately had to transcend the world of politics. "What are all these *wars and tumults,* but the *world's outcry* to us? What are those *defects and imperfections* in the creature, but their *broken language* whereby they do *beseech* us to *depart* from them and *seek* after our *eternal patrimony* of the creator?" queried Richard Harwood in 1644.[1] The Puritans fused transcendence with political action; the Anglicans proved incapable of keeping them together and had to seek sanctuary. As a result, Anglican religious writing often seems apolitical and concerned with Wedgwood's "perennial themes" (see chapter 8) as it rises above or escapes from the "passions of the moment."

The pattern informing the development of Anglican responses to political crisis is precisely the pattern which informs their most typical utterances. Like the Puritans, the style in which they preached was the style in which they tried to come to terms with the world around them. Joan Webber has described for us how the "conservative Anglican" style at work in spiritual autobiography allows the writer to work himself up from and out of situations in this world to an *O altitudo!*; he begins with a local, time-bound focus and ascends through meditation to a cosmic view and "I" which sees and subsumes all within it.[2] That is roughly the pattern which informs several other kinds of basically conservative writing—the poetry of meditation, the masque, and spiritual exercises which are formed by a "psychology of ascent."[3] When we turn to the lessons which Royalist preachers brought to their auditors during the civil wars, we can see how manner and matter coincided perfectly and we can then confidently talk about an Anglican life style. Moreover, we learn how a pattern, which produced some of the finest spiritual meditations we have from that religious age, could also degenerate into escapism and maudlin sentimentality. Throughout, it will be well to remember that during the civil wars, the cause of Royalism suffered greatly and perhaps finally, despite the last flicker of the Restoration. Conservative Anglicans were fighting what turned out to be a losing battle, as conservatives may, perhaps, always do; the force of political events told sharply upon their utterance and in some cases debased it. The apolitical texture of Anglican prose could be both elevating and whining depending upon the author, but even the less lovely results can be understood as the product of political and social crisis.

154

Let me begin, then, with a handful of sermons preached before the king at Oxford during the wars. At least two objections might be raised to this practice: first, that English religious expression was in many ways homogeneous during the century and second that political polarities did not necessarily coincide with religious polarities. Concerning the first, it is true that many of the sermons which Falconer Madan lists in *Oxford Books* and which were preached during the wars seem indistinguishable from the Parliamentary fare delivered in London at the same time. William Stampe's *A sermon preached before His Majestie at Christ-Church in Oxford, on the 18. of April, 1643* (Oxford, 1643) used Isaiah's situation in the fifty-ninth verse to explicate the process by which God withdraws himself from his people, as he was always doing in Puritan sermons. William Stroude preached *A sermon concerning swearing* (Oxford, 1644) against blasphemous soldiers, a topic which received frequent attention from both Oxford and London pulpits. Richard Spinkes's *A sermon preached in Oxford before the King's Majesty, April 19, 1643* (London, 1643), which urged further reformation of the clergy, was so much like the Parliamentary fare, that according to the title page, Spinkes was "imprisoned there for the said Sermon," and Madan argues that it was something of a hoax.[4] Somewhat nasty, *A sermon preached before the King's most excellent Majesty at Oxford, by H. K. D.D.* ([London?], 1643) on Psalm 101 (variously attributed to Henry King and Henry Killigrew)[5] removed from Old to New Testament examples indiscriminately and extolled the virtues of punishing God's enemies at great and somewhat grisly length. It forewent utterly the Christocentric typology (very popular with Royalists) which linked David in the Psalms with Christ and thence with the king and can be distinguished from those preached at London only by political point of view. Henry Leslie, in *A sermon preached at the publique fast the ninth of Feb. in St Marie's Oxford . . .* (Oxford, 1643), applying Jeremiah's warning to Israel to all the people of England, preached a providential sermon rooted in Old Testament examples, which simply turned inside out the usual practice of equating and thereby extolling England with Israel; Jeremiah condemned Israel, and Leslie condemned England; but the manner of arguing from the Old Testament, the form, and the style are indistinguishable from Puritan sermons being preached by the opposition in London.

Moreover, even if not all "Puritans" were Parliament's men and not all "Anglicans" were Royalists, in an explication of general tendencies that problem should not detain us. Since religious writing was the most fundamental and emotionally charged of all writing in the seventeenth century, it should reflect and coincide with such *major* political divisions as those which arose during a civil war. Allowing for the fact that religious expression was in important ways homogeneous and that innovative Puritan modes of thought and analysis were picked up and used by establishment men, for the fact that the coincidence between Anglican and Royalist, or Puritan and Parliament man was by no means perfect, and for the fact that the fortunes of the Royalists were on the wane, we can still say that these court sermons work within a progressive view of Christian history, employ slightly different typological schemata, trace out human causes at work over time, avoid or seek to avoid controversy and finally the affairs of this world altogether, and are written in a style, noticeably different from Puritan sermons, which matches their intellectual point of view.[6]

Of the sermons preached by Richard Harwood, Jasper Mayne,[6] George Wilde,[7] and Walter Curle,[8] three exalted "peace" above the virtues of "truth" and "holiness" which the Puritans so loved, while Harwood advised turning our backs on "all these *wars and tumults.*" Since the Puritans always pursued religious controversy in the name of "truth" and "holiness," we can see how the Anglicans resisted Puritan pressure by attacking the virtue of controversy and conflict itself; that strategy coincided neatly with a markedly conciliatory tone in their preaching, quite different from the manner of the Parliamentarians. In addition, these sermons focus upon the acts of men disrupting peace rather than upon eternal, cosmic, Satanic conspiracies, upon historical acts in chronos rather than sociological patterns through all time, upon men's pursuit of peace rather than God's providing it.

Jasper Mayne took I Cor. 1.10 as his text, much as he and his fellows used exempla from the New Testament with noticeably greater frequency than the Parliament preachers did. Attempting like Paul to be all things to all men as he preached "concerning unity and agreement," Mayne certainly bent over backwards to state fairly his opponents' arguments as well as he could. His example was the Corinthian Church, rather than Zion or Jerusalem, he used classical as well as scriptural examples to illustrate his points, and he traced out the chronological and human, rather than eternal and divine steps by which division of opinion arose. His first paragraph announced the problem:

> Though truth, from what mouth soever it be spoken or in what shape or dress soever it appear, be but one and the same, and where it is rightly understood carries this uniting, peaceful quality with it, that it makes all its followers of one consent and mind too; yet I know not from what mist or impotence lodged in our nature, with whom errors and mistakes do for the most part prevail more than arguments or demonstrations and with whom our own misconceits (conveyed into us from such whom we think too holy to deceive us or too learned to deceive themselves) do for the most part stick so deeply and take such root and impression in us, that 'tis not in the power of truth itself to remove them. This one, uniting, peaceful bond of minds, this ray of our souls, according to the several teachers of it and according to the

several forms and shapes into which they have cast it, hath always been
looked on as so many several truths, and, to the discredit and disadvan-
tage of it, hath in all ages been as severally entertained and followed.
[Pp. 1-2]

Mayne will freely admit that truth is unitary, as the Puritans insisted, but
he focuses upon how it appears to be diverse *in this world*. John Sprint
briefly captured the Puritan spirit when he insisted that "between an
affirmative and negative of the selfsame thing there can be but one truth
(which we are commanded diligently to try and follow),"[9] but Mayne did
not revere quite that form of diligence so highly. Willing to pause with the
fact of diversity in this world, he explains it at length in terms of sublunary
human passion, error, and self-interest, drawing his opening example from
"the heathen philosophers," among whom "we find the number of sects to
be much greater than the number of sciences. Every new famous teacher
who professed severity in his looks and austerity in his manners had the
power to draw a cloud of disciples after him, and to erect a new truth with
a new school" (p. 2). Even "in the very Church of God itself" founded by
Christ, "the Gospel no sooner began to be preached to the world, but it
began to have its sects and schisms and sidings too. The apostles taught but
one faith, one baptism, one Christ, one plain, open way of salvation to
men; yet they were misunderstood by some as if they had preached many.
Or as if . . . they had (every one where he went) scattered a several gospel" (p. 2). The chronological steps are clearly laid out: "This diversity of
minds proceeded at length to diversity of language and speech." Controversy next inflamed rhetoric "as if none had been in the right but they
only who most vehemently could charge others with being in the wrong"
(p. 3). Trouble built up over time.

Walter Curle took the breathtaking step of suggesting that if men wanted
"peace" and Mayne's "unity and agreement," they should not worry so
acutely as the Puritans did about the "truth" of theology. "It were better
for the Church to want some truth than to have no *peace*. And I doubt not
but a man may be saved though he never read or study controversies"
(p. 12). That is about as far from Sprint's dictum as one can get, and would
have been anathema to those Puritanic Calvinists who followed Truth
through the thick pages of folio commentaries and the thinner pages of an
hour-and-a-half sermon. The notion also strikes at the vitals of the queen
of the sciences. Like Mayne, Curle had a very human explanation for the
love of controversy: fallen men most often write "rather for contention
than for truth's sake" since "such being the love of men to themselves, *ut
nemo patiatur se vindei, licet sciat vere esse quae audit*, that no man will
suffer himself to be overcome, though he know it to be true that is said
against him" (pp. 12-14). The fault lies in human nature, self-love, shared
presumably by both sides (although the Puritans were more contentious),

rather than anti-Christian forces or impulses which Puritans often attacked in only some men—their enemies.

Curle and Mayne also expressed misgivings about the Puritan emphasis upon holiness. Of course, Mayne's conciliatory stance led him to apologize that he had "no design or purpose to bring holiness into contempt"; he did not wish to lend "encouragement to the lives of vicious teachers . . . the shame of their mother" since he was "so far from disliking holiness either in preacher or people, that I wish we all made but one united kingdom of priests" (p. 55). Yet he counseled that we "be not too credulous; do not presently believe every man that says he hath the spirit." Do not "mistake zeal and [the] strict life of [the] preacher for his sufficiency" (p. 54). Curle invoked the example of "Christ himself" who "seems to give *peace* the precedency" over holiness in Matthew 5.24, "where he sends us from his own altar and will not accept our oblation till we have sought peace and reconciliation with our brother, thereby preferring an act of peace before an act of piety, and showing that even the holiest of our actions are not acceptable to God when our affections are not peaceable towards men" (p. 3). The New Testament example inverted the Puritans' preference for holiness even at the expense of peace.

The antidote was, as Harwood put it, to fly "the *world's outcry* to us" and "to *depart* from them and seek after our *eternal patrimony* of the creator" (p. 24). Peace is to Curle "the best of all earthly blessings, the blessing of blessings, a mother-blessing, as I may say, as that which blesseth all other blessings, and without which they are no blessings. *Tam bonum, ut sine ea nihil bonum,* so good, that there is nothing good without it" (p. 7). Wilde felt that "the blessings of peace are beyond both *Greek* and *Latin* oratory; the *Gospel* and *Christ's* most precious blood must come in to rate them. Our peace, *Pax nostra Christum valet,* it cost God no less than an incarnation, and a crucifixion too: whereby he achieved the title and honor, not only of being the author of peace, *I Thes.* 5.25. but is the prince of it, *Esa.* 9. prince of that peace which is itself a princess" (p. 7). For all their attempt to transcend and escape time and this sphere of our sorrows, the Puritans were finally unwilling to stop combating Satan here below. They could not ultimately follow an otherworldly peace. And for all that the Royalists traced out the human actions and temporal causes of events in this world, they were willing and sometimes eager finally to turn their backs on the world in search of the peaceful, "eternal patrimony."

In the foregoing examples we find these Royalists not only advocating a lifestyle utterly different from the Puritans', but also tracing out how men act and what the consequences of those acts are, citing examples from pagan and New Testament sources, and referring to heathen as well as the Hebrew languages. Curle and Wilde mention Christ's suffering explicitly.

Furthermore, they were conscious of and at home with rhetoric. Mayne makes much the same kind of analysis I have been making, tracing out how "this diversity of minds proceeded at length to diversity of language and speech." Harwood makes witty use of alliteration, paradox, and parallelism when he writes "a *kingdom prepared* for *us*, and we not yet prepared for the *kingdom*" or "we *love* not *God* at *all*, if he hath not *all our love*" (p. 24), constructions which depend as much on verbs as upon nouns. Wilde plays on "prince," "peace," and "princess" and translates *valet* strikingly as "rate" and "it cost" rather than something more passive like "is worth." These active verbs add point and force to his references to "Christ's most precious blood" and "an incarnation, and a crucifixion too." The syntactical patterns of the wit in both cases coincide with the more active way these preachers represent men, their motives, passions, and causes.

To the same effect Curle, in extolling peace, joined two theological virtues together just as peace would join men, then focused upon "an act, and an object whereupon this act is to be executed" by men rather than God. Explicating his text, Hebrews 12.14, "follow peace with all men, and holiness without which no man shall see the Lord" in a way obviously reminiscent of Andrewes, he pointed "first" to the syntactical "combination and conjunction of these two: not *peace* alone, or *holiness* alone, but *peace* and *holiness* both together. Secondly, the order and disposition of them: first *peace*, then *holiness*" (p. 1). Scriptural syntax and word order are to Curle signs of important truths and prescriptions for acting. Concerning the "combination and conjunction" Curle urges us "as we find them tied together in the text, so let them be knit together in our hearts and meet and kiss each other in our lives" (p. 2). We must perform "an act" upon "an object"; the act is "to follow," and Curle shows how vehement it must be. He dwells at length on the transitive effect of his central point, this human act, upon something else. "Doctrine" (if so we may call it) and the force of his wit both depend upon or derive from action-packed syntax rather than such static concepts as salvation and damnation. His point is not "pacification" but our urgently following peace.

Of the three remaining Royalist tracts the most obvious point to make is how heavily they were influenced by military and political defeat. The turmoil of the wars upset all Englishmen both on the Parliamentary and on the Royalist side; yet the Parliamentary preachers lamented the bloodshed and division as signs of national sinfulness and saw their defeats as visitations and perfecting trials from God. These things would, through further reformation and praying, right themselves. The Royalists were, in contrast, a bit more melancholy. They were able to trace out more acutely than the Puritans how human, Machiavellian motives influenced men, but they had no ready solution for the troubles which resulted. They proved incapable of turning the text "a house divided against itself" into an appeal for political action, as Calamy had done. This strain intensified as the course of the wars progressed toward their defeat and the death of their king, as their world more obviously crashed down around them.

The clearest example was Henry Ferne's sermon "preached before his Majesty at Newport in the Isle of Wight, November the 29, 1648," which, a note to the reader informs us, "had the fate to be the last that was preached before his late Majesty."[10] Ferne took the plight of the prophet in Habakkuk 2.3, as his example to console the King: "The prophet, in the former chapter, had a foresight of what the *Chaldeans* would do to God's people . . . and here he would fain have a sight of their deliverance. We find him there sore troubled to see all go contrary not only to his desire but as he then thought to the course of divine providence and rule of justice" (p. 1). Given, as Harwood had put it, that "we have been thy Eden," and given the successes of the parliamentary forces, the course of the wars must, when Ferne preached, have appeared to "go contrary . . . to the course of divine providence and rule of justice." The world must have seemed upside down indeed to a Royalist at that time, and it is no wonder that they wished to transcend or escape it. In such circumstances, the Prophet

> raises himself above the pitch of sense or carnal reason, . . . gets up to his *watch tower*. . . . There he sets himself (ver. 1), looking upward and harkening what token for good, what answer for instruction and comfort that he might have wherewith to satisfy himself and those that argued with him. . . .
>
> Thus waiting and expecting, he is not long without an answer; it comes in the next verse. . . . Wait yet, though it tarry, . . . and till it come, the just man shall live by his faith, . . . shall live, outlive the evil day, or be taken from it and have the shortness of this life lengthened out with eternity. [Pp. 1-2]

The sermon that follows applies the case of Habakkuk to the king, explaining the loss of the holy cause as still directed by the providence of God. Climbing above the smoke into that tower seems to succeed for Ferne and right his world, although one can only speculate about the king's feelings. Ferne points away from the conflict which has nearly concluded, because only by rising above the sublunary disaster can one console oneself. Unfortunately, the king had to face the block.

After the defeat, all the Royalists had to confront the beheading of their king; no watchtower was tall enough to raise them above that horror. That fact may explain why succeeding Royalists began to talk extravagantly about the "crucifixion" of Charles. The anonymous piece, *The devilish conspiracy, hellish treason, heathenish condemnation, and damnable murder, committed, and executed by the Jevves, against the anointed of the Lord,*

Christ their King (London, 1648), was followed by Henry Leslie's *The martyrdome of King Charles, or his conformity with Christ in his sufferings* . . . (The Hague, 1649). The anonymous writer of the first, perhaps John Warner, showed the king's conformity to Christ by pointing out how "anointed of the Lord" could refer to the Christian magistrate as well as Christ, and by speaking throughout his tract of "Ch . . . the King." Both painted the Puritans as Jews and deicides, as the title of the first tract shows. It seems that in doing so, these two men were attacking the Puritan habit of linking themselves with Israel; the parallels, in their hands, now show to the discredit of both Jews and Puritans, rather than emphasizing the sanctity of the English Israelites. Bishop George Hickes and Simon Patrick, among others, would develop that line during and after the Restoration. Hickes would admit that "indeed, God by being temporal head of the Jews had frequent occasions to raise up certain extraordinary persons, by the powerful impulse of his spirit, to work miraculous deliverances for his people and execute supralegal commissions in certain cases of special exigence where it would not be convenient to wait for the ordering process of law." However, he insisted, "our Savior, who put an end to the Jewish state and his Father's temporal reign, put an end thereby to all future pretensions of supralegal impulses and zeal, and both by his doctrine and example hath forbidden such unwarrantable proceedings to Christians, as unbecoming their meekness and sobriety, inconsistent with evangelical peace and obedience, and destructive of that authority and power . . . [of] the civil magistrate."[11] Christ came "into the world . . . to destroy the church of the *Jews* and seal up *vision and prophecy*," but the Puritans "have vainly imagined that God would still be making new discoveries and raising up new prophets and heroical zealots to the world, and upon this supposition have pretended, like the prophets and heroes of the Old Testament, to illuminations, prophecies, visions, dreams, raptures, inspirations, voices from without, irresistable impulses within . . . as if the glorious majesty of God did dwell among Christians, as it did in the midst of the Jews, to make and interpret their laws, model their religion, conduct their armies, fight their battles, and constantly sit at the helm of government to order affairs both in church and state" (p. 3). In these remarks lay the possibilities for satiric parody of the Puritans' Old Testament bias which Dryden exploited in *Absalom and Achitophel*.

Hickes touched on more than the Puritans' fascination with Israel in these remarks. He represents them as breaking that peace which became so important to Royalists, and he shows them deluding others or deluded themselves, but in either case as acting on very human, but not quite Satanic or anti-Christian impulses. He portrays Christ, the center of history, ending one epoch and beginning another. And when he spoke of the Puritans as having "made the common people of *Great Britain* consider them-

selves as the people of *Israel* and . . . act like enthusiasts and follow their
leaders, like the Jews of latter times, to commit such execrable treasons as
ought not to be mentioned without horror and tears" (p. 22), he seems to
have had the crucifixion in mind. Henry Leslie had played extravagantly
with that theme when he condemned the Puritans for the "Jewish" way
they "have lately murdered, if not the Lord of glory, yet I am sure a glorious Lord: though not Christ the Lord, yet the Lord's Christ, God's anointed. This is a parricide so heinous, so horrible, that it cannot be paralleled
by all the murders that ever were committed since the world began but
only in the murder of Christ."[12] Perhaps mere historical accident (the fact
that Charles was beheaded) combined with the fact that Christians often
think of the crucifixion as a parallel for personal disaster, explain these
expressions, extravagant because of the recent sorrow. Yet, talking about
Charles's crucifixion certainly fitted in with other tendencies in Anglican
prose. When the Puritans met such setbacks, they did not talk about a
crucifixion; they found Old Testament parallels for these visitations and
trials and controversies between God and his people. Moreover, the
Anglicans had a long history of calling the Puritans Judaical and of making
jokes of the sort embodied in Jonson's "Rabbi" Zeal-of-the-Land Busy.
Combining this tendency to equate Puritans and Jews (through aversion to
both) with their love for bowing to the humiliated Christ and their veneration of the holidays which were anniversaries of his nativity and exaltation,
we can say that this tactic, certainly open to all Christians and therefore
telling only a limited amount about the Royalists, was still congenial to
their general religious temperament.

But whether we decide that the Anglican veneration of Christ had anything to do with the Royalist tactic of comparing the king's death to a
crucifixion or not, we can see in these Anglican sermons the ecclesiast's
loyalty to the Church of Christ and a decided interest in humanly com-
prehensible actions—Christ's suffering, the true Christian's imitation of
him, the sinful man's pursuit of self-interest, the faithful man's pursuit of
peace—set within a progressive view of sacred history centered upon Christ
and the changes he wrought. I have argued in chapter 1 that the Puritans,
obsessed with the eternal Son of God, had difficulty imitating Christ. The
more ecclesiastically centered Royalists thought of themselves and their
heroes as following the suffering Christ, in his Church, in history, in battle,
and in their personal lives.

Even the otherworldly quality of many of these sermons derives from,
and is rendered particularly poignant by, this interest in the human actions
of Christ and his martyrs. These men turned their backs upon the sphere
of our sorrows because they had been forced to experience how sorrowful
that sphere really is. After all, as members of the establishment, they had
been initially at home with the things of this world, and the wrench must

have been doubly painful. The arm of the Lord had not extricated them
from their difficulties by some wonder-working, almost magical mercy. All
they could see was the murderous, fallen nature of man about them now.
Thus *Eikon Basilike*, published in 1649, and at once an apology for the
king's various acts and a religious meditation which seeks to transcend the
ill consequences of those acts, is an excellent example of Royalist prose.
The two-part structure of the book—each section contains an historical
account of what the king had done and why he had done it and then a
prayer based upon but ultimately turning away from those acts in the face
of death—shows the mechanics of this religious sensibility in action. One
begins with the mundane in order to go beyond. The sublunary events are
ultimately shown to be unimportant; but the reader is carried to that conclusion only through a minute analysis of those events.

The contrast between what I have called Puritan and Anglican prose,
between the Parliamentary and the Royalist sermons, finally yields a paradox. The Puritans, devotees of the doctrine of original sin, ultimately suggest man can be a hero by seizing that providential moment; they produce
books of worthies and divine champions, who will erect Christ's kingdom
in England. The Anglican ultimately suggests, in the bitterness of defeat,
that God's English are greedy, ignorant, perversely emotional, or criminally
hypocritical and that heroism is next to impossible in this world. But the
Puritan arrives at his conclusion only after having initially denied, in
theology and in syntax, that man can act to any purpose. And the Anglican
forsakes this world only after having acted, both physically and stylistically,
within it. The Royalist finally throws himself upon the transcendental mercies of a Christ who suffered in time on this earth; in his final humiliation
he bows timelessly to that Jesus to whom he had bowed in the liturgy
every time he went to church. In renouncing this world, he follows Christ
actively out of action. The Puritan, on the other hand, riding the crest of
God's mercies, models his basically anti-ecclesiastic views of the world
upon the marvelous heroes of the Old Testament whom history cannot
separate from him. He submerges his individuality in the force of God's
providence, which will carry him to victory, then marches steadfastly into
battle. He bows in victory to Christ the King who will judge the quick and
the dead in all his majesty and power after human history has ceased and
he has successfully reformed the times.

Some of this Royalist prose becomes sentimental and even a bit gro-
tesque under the pressure of events. The implicit claim of *Eikon Basilike*,
for example, that the king was tender-hearted to his subjects, a good man
who never wittingly hurt anybody, and a profoundly religious man who
concluded his thoughts in prayer and an *O altitudo!*, was after all a political strategy developed for a pragmatic purpose. We may lament that
Charles had nowhere to go except Habakkuk's tower, yet we may reason-

ably ask why he had not more successfully and more vigilantly spied out
the shape of his times from a better outlook. My point is not to explicate
the strengths and weaknesses of Royalist political thought, however; rather
I wish to observe how nearly the development of Royalist thinking paralleled the aesthetic patterns inherent in "conservative Anglican" prose as
Webber describes it. Supporters of the establishment initially laid claim to
the things of this world and finally felt themselves pressed out of this
world, since all that remained in the end for them was an *O altitudo!*
Meditators, adepts with a "psychology of ascent," kept a kind of internal
anniversary with an emblem or sign, located themselves initially in chronos,
either literally or through imaginative reconstruction delved into transitive
acts here below, then spun up into kairos. Whether specifically derived
from the manuals to which Martz has called our attention or not, a great
deal of nonpolitical, spiritualized poetry on themes which were indeed
perennial and timeless did emerge from poets we call "metaphysical."

Moreover, the court masque, as Barber and Fletcher analyze it (see n. 3
above) was likewise "transcendental" in the way it opened vistas of meaning inhering in the situation on stage and in the theatre. The masque was
an attempt to turn the court into Olympus and assert the permanence of
monarchy; the king was the focal point of act and speech, indeed he even
fueled them with solar power, and after he had been aesthetically trans-
mogrified, masquers and audience united in an effort to assert that illusion
was reality. It was illusion, monarchy was dying, and the antimasquers,
those representatives of dissident outside influence, persistently reinvaded
the closed-circuit system of the masque.[13] At the heart of this bit of desperate, political magic was the same "psychology of ascent," which Ben
Jonson beautifully captured when he exhorted himself to "Leave things
so prostitute" in order that "curious fooles, and envious" might

> heare thee sing
> The glories of thy King;
> His zeale to God, and his just awe of men,
> They may be blood-shaken, then
> Feele such a flesh-quake to possesse their powers,
> That no tun'd Harpe like ours,
> In sound of Peace or Warres,
> Shall truely hit the Starres
> When they shall read the Acts of *Charles* his Reigne,
> And see his Chariot triumph 'bove his Waine.[14]

Ever a realist, Jonson puns, at last, on "wane," yet despite that, he exalted
Charles in an *O altitudo!* in masque after masque through patterns very
like those of other conservative art. Hill has called the conceited metaphysical verse "lyric of conflict,"[15] and it is true that that poetry does

recognize polarities, opposites, tensions; but they are, first of all, studiously not political tensions and the effort of the poetry is, as Dr. Johnson said long ago, to yoke them together by violence. A mismatched team will not plow a straight furrow, as Johnson no doubt knew; for all its conciliation, peace, and love, for all its checking of individual and parochial passion, this poetry did not provide a smooth way for dealing with affairs of state. Herbert, to cite only the most obvious example, turns explicitly away from political passion for place, fame, and influence; apolitical in intent, his poetry is therefore potentially bad politics (even if profoundly moving piety) just as the escapist motives of the masque were. These poets were "apolitical" because they chose to be apolitical; they were, after all, partially free agents at least, even if they found themselves in a society of conflict. Students of poetry who rank "perennial themes" above "transitory passions" are no more determined by predestinating canons of good taste; they too exercise their choice in following their heroes.

Let me be clear on one point. To argue as I have been doing that Royalists responded politically in the same style in which they wrote sermons and poems is not to make any extraordinary claims, such as Fletcher advances, that aesthetics determined politics.[16] The notion seems to me ludicrous. Rather I am arguing that political activity resembled poetic activity because the same kinds of men, with much the same sort of life style, were acting in these two spheres. That there would emerge a coherence between these two sorts of behavior should not be surprising, unless we believe that human beings are actually random and basically disorderly creatures. Aesthetics determined politics no more than politics determine the aesthetics of any particular man. But a man who could and would enter the establishment would perform any number of tasks in a way consistent with that gesture, would behave in writing a poem (if he set himself that task) much as he would behave politically (if he set himself that task). The conservative impulse is always to hold things together here below, join and conjoin opposites in poetry and among parties as well as in theology or political theory. And if that impulse cannot function, the habit of justifying things here below through a transcendental gesture turns into escapism. If we enjoy the harmonious vision generated by metaphysical poetry, which often joins the concrete and worldly with the abstract and spiritual, we ought also to remember the potentially dangerous implications of Johnson's description of that poetic act. The metaphysicals "yoked by violence" and for all their talk of peace and harmony, the Royalists were capable of violence also. Perhaps political controversy was thrust upon them by the Puritans; the Puritans clearly loved controversy dearly while the Anglicans often seem to engage in it simply because they had been attacked. Both sides were innovative, but the Anglicans seemed to innovate in reaction to the Puritans and hence in a reactionary way. But, even if they did not look for a fight or positively seek to change things until forced to (a point which could be disputed), the Anglicans as a group were neither better nor worse than any other group of men. They did, however, act in particular ways, whatever they were doing. Poetry and prose, politics and piety all offered varying spheres of activity, but the behavior of any man was and still is remarkably self-consistent.

Part II: USES

Section Four: Soldiers and Selves

Chapter 12: PURITAN SOLDIERS IN PARADISE LOST

Michael Walzer has applied Puritan doctrines to military uses in a way which shows how exciting the airy speculations of theologians could be. Puritan military tactics, he shows, mirrored Puritan notions about the gathered Church which in turn derived from their conception of God. The Puritan God marched out of the pages of the summas and onto Naseby field.[1] This is not a matter of peripheral behavior—chance singing of hymns as the soldiers straggled into battle, chaplains in the ranks, a tendency to cut hair close, etc. Protestantism spawned a new theory of massed troop deployment, perfected by the Protestant hero Gustavus Adolphus on the continent; his tactics were published in England and were explicitly connected to theories of the gathered Church by English writers. The important fact here is not that the New Model was a gathered Church; the important thing is that it *fought* like a gathered Church. The Puritans who fought with guns acted in precisely the same style as the Puritans who spun out theological doctrines, each functioning in a different sphere yet functioning in the same way.

I would like here to trace out a military campaign or battle and analyze the different military styles; I would equally enjoy pursuing a comparative analysis of the biographies of several men of differing political and religious views. Both would give a certain rough validity to my ideas about social styles. But, for the first, I am a literary critic, not a military historian, and much of that analysis has already been made. For the second, there would be a monumental problem of selecting representative men and a severe problem of getting minute enough data. Both would lengthen out this book too far. So I shall content myself, in this section, by looking at two different yet related sorts of activity—the act of portraying a military hero and the act of shaping one's life, not on the streets, but by writing a spiritual autobiography. Both are literary approximations of the more concrete kinds of behavior, but they will have to suggest just how far we might press out from theological doctrine-making into physical action. Particularly the act of writing a spiritual autobiography (but also the penciling in of one's own version of the *miles christi*) are of profound interest and importance to the man doing them. They will, then, confirm how directly Puritans and

Anglicans applied their theological doctrines and predispositions to uses in this world.

The central paradox of Puritan political analysis, typical of revolutionary ideologies, derived from the tension in their thought between God's overarching, predestinate providence and man's ability to act and commit a revolution. Like Marxists who ride the paradigms of dialectical materialism yet feel they must press forward as the vanguard of the proletariat, the Puritans simultaneously thought that God's English were ultimately elect and therefore that the future of the nation (defined in terms of the millennium) was assured and yet felt they were called to strike a blow on behalf of God's plan. We often think of Puritans as devotees of predestination, incapable of preaching works and deeds. Nothing could be farther from the case, as we can see in Stephen Marshall's wildly extreme (and, in his time, notorious) exhortation to bloody deeds, which if far from typical in tone, does show the possibilities of Puritan commitment to action: *"Cursed is every one that withholds his hands from shedding of blood."* The right thinking should "go and *imbrue* his hands in the *blood of men"*; "He is a *blessed man that takes and dashes the little ones against the stones."*[2] The sermons before Parliament are full of similar, if less spectacular pleas. The sense of divine destiny was most fully articulated in terms of the notion that England was God's elect and peculiar Israel; the tension between that view and the urge to act developed fully in Puritan military sermons and the portrait of the *miles christi* which the preachers drew there.

The surprising thing about seventeenth-century political rhetoric is not that the Puritans turned Israel into England (and vice versa) but rather that the establishment Anglicans and apologists for the king did so little of it in comparison to the Puritans. The rhetorical topos was so easy, obvious, and alluring. For that topos provided an electrifying way for a Bible-reading Christian to articulate a sense of optimism concerning the future of his nation.[3] All Israel shall be saved" came to mean "England will be saved" to a surprising number of men because they basically and instinctively agreed with Milton (although they did not all put it so bluntly or even formulate it for themselves at all) that God reveals "himself to his servants, and as his manner is, first to his English-men."[4]

Confidence in the future of the English nation blossomed surprisingly early. "Could the gunpowder treason take effect?" queried Thomas Cooper no more than ten years after the event. "Shall not Antichrist be confounded? . . . Hath not the Lord begun to enlarge us far and near to *Virginia* and *Ireland*? And are not their hopes in vain that seek to root God's church out of England?"[5] He did so in a book "proving the gathering in of the Gentiles, and final conversion of the Jews." When one remembers that the Armada was less than twenty-seven years behind Cooper as he wrote, his faith seems sudden and "Israelitish" indeed.

By mid-century, such confidence had settled firmly into place in the English mind. In 1642, Lewes Hughes held up *A looking-glasse for all trve hearted Christians, vvherein they may see the goodnesse of God in giving deliverance unto them from their Popish, cruell, and bloodie enemies . . .* (London, 1642). His glass, first silvered by Foxe, reveals that "the greatest and cruelest enemies that true Christians have in all the world are the Papists" (p. 1), and Hughes records his intellectual debts openly: "The names of, and places where these good Christians suffered martyrdom are written in the book of Martyrs" (p. 1). Hughes's central thesis elaborates his remark that "there is great hope that this year will be a year of recompense for the judgment of God's Sion in this land" (p. 3); and he develops it first by applying Revelation 16.12–16 (Hughes mistakenly cites "*Rev.* 16.3"), and particularly the word "Armageddon" which "doth signify the hill of the Gospel" or "a mountain of delights"—a place of particular godliness to England (pp. 3–4). Hence, "the true professors of the Gospel in this Land may observe for their comfort that God hath made this Land an *Armageddon*"; his proof comes from the defeat of the Armada, a second Spanish flotilla in 1639, and the Gunpowder Plot—the first and the last being the prime examples during the century of God's special care of his Englishmen.

Stephen Marshall, preaching before the Commons in the spring of 1645, exhorted that body that the "work" of building up Sion "is upon the wheels," and Parliament should, through praying, get busy about it. All good men in "*all the Christian world*" pray "in our behalf; our cause is God's."[6] When he preached, later that year, at the public thanksgiving for the victory at Naseby, he asked that a "sacred record . . . of God's mercies to Zion" be kept. Since "not only the managing of a kingdom of men but of the kingdom of our Lord and Savior Christ Jesus seems now to be in the hands of the two honorable Houses of Parliament,"[7] such a history would resemble the Bible, "since the whole Book of God is nothing but a chronicle, a Book of Acts and Monuments of the Lord's wonderful works" in preserving "his Church" (p. 22). The Parliamentary historian would be like Noah, who kept "a copy of all" in the Ark, to be "reprinted and spread over all the world." Marshall was profoundly moved when he contemplated such a work: "Truly I have often thought that were all the copies in the world lost of God's admirable dealing with an unworthy people (except only those mentioned in the Scripture) there might be a reimpression of them out of the admirable things that God hath done for us since these public calamities came upon us; and all the world might learn sufficient out of our story what a God our God is, and learn to know, and trust, and fear him for ever" (p. 32). That is to attribute considerable religious importance to the history of elected England. Yet it seemed to Marshall that English history merited that sort of attention, for in the next year he exclaimed that "our times are times of deliverances, the greatest deliverances that I think the Lord hath wrought since he brought *Israel* out of *Egypt*."[8] Of course, Christian theologians had often maintained that the greatest deliverance in all of sacred history intervened between these two events. Puritanically, Marshall skips over Christ's advent as he demonstrates why he wanted a sacred record kept of his extraordinary times.

The "true" English, then, were fighting the last battle in a cosmic war; the fall occurred only to be fulfilled in English history when the millennial paradigm which William Haller has shown to lie at the heart of this view of the elect nation would be completed. Since the onset of the millennium would be accompanied by the conversion of the Jews, an optimist needed some Jews about to convert. Sir Edward Spencer pointed out that the English nation prayed annually, in the collect for Good Friday, for the conversion of the Jews "and indeed I believe we are the likeliest nation under heaven to do it."[9] John Foxe, who articulated the notion of the elect nation in a way which his countrymen never forgot, preached one of the earliest extant sermons "at the christening of a certain Jew" and expected the same outcome. The most obvious biblical metaphor for articulating such a notion was the "peculiarity" of ancient Israel; Elizabeth became a "Deborah" to her people while monarchs were clothed in Davidic robes by admiring preachers. With rising revolutionary optimism, however, the monarchical function came to seem less important. Typological metaphor then converged with the new, literal reading of "all Israel shall be saved," and to many Puritans the Jews took on a special function as a sort of catalyst for the apocalypse, which required that they be readmitted legally into England. Financial motives may well have impelled the interest of men like Cromwell in Manasseh ben Israel's petition for legal entry, yet the apocalyptic and "Judaical" theology must surely have played a part. For the emigrés in America set about industriously transmuting American Indians into the ten lost tribes, and produced, by the way, a colorful literature about the question. Given all the things which the colonists must have had to think about, it will seem at first surprising that they fastened on this one, until we recall it was a.i apparently logical, optimistic, millennial expectation about their plantations on this new potential Eden.

The wonder is not that a sense of national "peculiarity" fused with that analogic way of reading Scripture into which Puritan typology degenerated so that "Israel," "Jerusalem," and "Sion" became the dominant metaphors for England during the mid-century; rather, the wonder is that it didn't happen sooner and that Anglican-Royalists did not make as great use of the rhetorical strategy. Bishop Hickes and Simon Patrick insisted that the Puritans were noticeably more interested in Israel than their opponents, and Dryden's *Absalom and Achitophel* attacks the descendants of the

Puritans from within the framework of that Puritanic mode of analysis to suggest much the same point. This blossoming British Israelitism was so obviously potent as a political rallying cry that it was difficult to control, and the excesses which occurred were to be expected. A man named William Phineh delivered "The Law read June 10, 1656, unto the people Israel belonging to the returning from captivity, at the Tent of Judah"; a note indicates that the "Tent of Judah" was pitched opposite the Blue Boar tavern. Seventh-day Sabbatarianism, obviously, edged strongly toward something like Phineh's extreme literalism. Arise Evans, however, provides a better example of the complex of verbal strains and how they fused into odd configurations. He worked out from the Puritan optimism about the calling of the Jews, spiced his thought with a heavy dose of nationalism and eschatology, and picked up the motif of the Puritan "King Christ" of the fifth monarchy. But he converted all this, through some delightful alchemy which we cannot recover, into what appears to be political mon-archism and a plea for restoration, modeled, it would seem, on reverence for King Christ. Just as John Stennet's seventh-day Sabbatarian tract im-plied monarchism in its title—*The royal law contended for*—so Evans argued that Charles II would be restored, fight the proud Dutch, march triumphant-ly through Europe while Jews flocked to his army, enter and conquer Jeru-salem, and establish there his rightful kingdom, a visible manifestation of the second coming.[10]

Such drolleries need not detain us farther, since they simply establish how extensive and explosive this sort of thought and talk could be. Super-literalistic acting out of millennial expectations became extraordinarily common during the 1650's; the knowledge that large groups of men were gathering on hilltops to await the Son must have appalled and chastened a man like Milton; perhaps their example spiritualized his millennial utter-ances. As men made the antinomian leap of announcing the third dispen-sation and superseding Christ, the Puritan impulse to dress the English in patriarchal garb went to completion. Typological analysis always involves the anachronistic costuming of sacred characters, but insofar as the cycle plays are representative of medieval thinking, the older tradition was to dress them like one's contemporaries. The Puritans handled anachronism in quite the opposite way by dressing England in the habits of the patri-archs. If, as Kermode argues, a certain sort of thinker becomes engrossed with the "concords" between beginnings and endings,[11] and if millennial thought involves projecting a "pure" beginning forward in time so it be-comes a pure ending, then the patriarchal cast of Puritan thought strength-ened the tripartite symmetry of their vision. The patriarchs lived out the first age of human history and they re-emerged through this sort of talk to usher in the last stage. Patriarchalism cemented the concords between the Puritan beginning and ending.

From at least St. Paul onward, the soldier of Christ had been a Christian commonplace; and theologians as different from Puritan exegetes as Erasmus and Loyola had devoted much comment to the figure.[12] The soldier was a hero, and it is in shaping the lives and conduct of their heroes that men often most fully express the convergence of intellectually held ideology and personal yearning. In literary terms, the English soldier of Christ from Guthlac to Red Crosse Knight had led a very positive, active, and decisive life slaying dragons and acting out the proposition that evil (embodied in whatever literary form) might in important ways be finally overcome by an individual and heroic act. But when he rode into the troubled years of Tudor politics and the ever more partisan bickerings of seventeenth-century England, he found it harder to win clear-cut victories. Spenser, who seems to look both ways, back to the older Catholic traditions and forward to certain emphases of militant Protestantism (to which Milton presumably responded) can serve to focus the distinction I am making. His centrist sensibility produced a typical epic hero who does achieve a full vision of the celestial city and then goes out and slays his dragon, much as his literary forebears had, but he cannot either sustain that vision (he must descend from the mount of contemplation into this world of action) nor consummate his marriage with Una. Continued adventures face him on his wayfaring and warfaring. This latter tendency, to hold the Christian hero in a sort of suspended animation beneath the awful sovereignty of God, was seized upon, refined, and elaborated at great length by Puritan preachers during the seventeenth century.

In the process of outlining the revolutionary ideology of Puritan thought, Michael Walzer has rightly pointed out that the Puritan military sermon did not emphasize winning individual battles nor even, necessarily, fighting at all.[13] Rather, the Puritans prized military drill and the ordered deployment of massed troops. True, many of the sermons Walzer quotes were preached before the London Artillery Company in peacetime, and no doubt the preachers, in order to allure recruits, had to tackle the problem that noncombatant drill is drudgery. Still, Richard Sibbes articulated an important strain of Puritan thought when he compared the Church to an army. "The people of God themselves are beautiful, for order is beautiful. Now it is an orderly thing to see many together to submit themselves to the ordinances of God. . . . An army is a beautiful thing because of the order and of the well-disposed ranks that are in it. In this regard, the church is beautiful."[14] Sibbes did not address these remarks specifically to soldiers, but other Puritan preachers such as John Davenport explicitly exhorted them to develop harmony within their ranks;[15] the massed military formations, developed by Gustavus Adolphus, passed smoothly from the cohorts of that Protestant champion to the ultra-Protestant ranks of the New Model, which concretely acted out Sibbes's analogy between Church and Army by forming itself into what amounted to gathered churches (Walzer, pp. 275-77). Davenport suggested that soldiers should practice both in times of peace and "in a time of *fears* (as the case now stands) wherein man should be like ants, providing for that winter which they foresee not" (p. 14). Military historians have noted that, during the civil wars, the antlike orientation of the iron-sided troops broke the more individualistically disciplined assaults of cavalier forces. Puritans saw soldiering as directed toward the good of the group as much as the good of the individual; Davenport began with individual achievements but concluded with communal values when he noted, "since every man will have recreation, if that be best which is freest from sin, that best that most strengtheneth a man, that which enables a man most to be of use for the public good be best, then abandon your *carding, dicing, chambering, wantonness, dalliance,* scurrilous discoursing, and vain raveling out of time, to frequent these exercises which are special helps fitting you to be serviceable and instruments of public welfare" (p. 18). Theoretical theology and practical military concerns are matched even by syntax; Davenport would have the soldiers "fitted to be serviceable"; they do not actively "serve." They are instruments; they are not quite individuated actors.

Puritan preachers began to integrate divine providence and individual acts through a sense of divine instrumentality. Josiah Ricraft extolled Cromwell in utterly commonplace, Puritan language: "As a valiant, faithful commander, brave Cromwell deserves perpetual honor, who for his gallant actions the Cavaliers have (Anabaptist-like) rebaptized him (if I may properly so say) and given him a new name, called *Old Iron sides,* and very well they might call him so, for oftentimes he did prove to them as an iron rod to break them in pieces; God hath used him as one of the great instruments to rescue our religion, laws and liberties."[16] Apart from the matter of his nickname, these lines might be about any Parliamentary worthy, as befits a description of an "iron rod" and "instrument." More, Cromwell's achievement is as impersonal as his "heroic" role, being defined communally in terms of "religion, laws and liberties." Much the same heroic pattern, combining anonymous agency with group orientation, emerges from a fine "fiction" related by Thomas Adams during a military sermon: "A boy was molested with a dog; the *Friar* taught him to say a gospel by heart and warranted this to allay the dog's fury. The mastiff spying the boy, flies at him; he begins (as it were) to conjure him with his *gospel.* The dog (not capable of religion) approacheth more violently. A neighbor passing by bids the boy take up a stone; he did so, and throwing at the dog, escaped. The *Friar* demands of the lad how he sped with his charm: 'Sir,' quoth he, 'your *gospel* was good, but a stone with the *gospel* did the deed.'"[17] If the Roman Catholic priest wants to know how the boy did, the boy himself speaks not about himself but about two agents—the "gospel" and the "stone"—in describing a victorious, freely willed act.

Adams' little "fiction" (which as a Puritan he must apologize for: "Fables are not without their useful morals") with its clear antipapal overtones, leads us to a second point. The dog was "not capable of religion," nor, alas, are many in this world. Hence the battles of the Puritan soldier of Christ are interminable and his foes without number. "If you be the soldiers of Christ, you shall never want *Canaanites* to fight against. . . . If you could cut down sin like Hydra's head, it grows again; banish sin, like the ill spirit that haunted Saul, it returns again" warned Thomas Sutton.[18] "We are all soldiers as we are Christians" announced Adams at the outset of his dedication, and life is war; "Now to this war every *Christian* is a professed *soldier*, not only for a spurt, for sport, as young gentlemen use for a time to see the fashion of the wars, but our vow runs thus in baptism: that every man undertakes to fight manfully under Christ's banner against sin, the world, and the devil, and to continue his faithful soldier and servant to his life's end" (sig. A3r and v). After civil war had broken out, Simeon Ashe derided those who "by reason of cowardliness soon grow discouraged in sad and weighty undertakings, because they find the way to heaven craggy, the duties difficult, and services something hard."[19] Since the Puritans had preached for a half century on duty and never-ending strife, both in military sermons and in the more usual, spiritual Sunday-fare, they had prepared a group of men to enter the civil wars weaned from such "cowardliness" and willing to follow their duty not "for a spurt, for sport" but rather steadfastly to the end of their lives, like Bunyan's less bellicose Christian.

To evoke this challenging vision of the world, with innumerable hosts arrayed against the destitute and lowly faithful, fitted in with the Puritans' emphasis upon God's omnipotence. Preaching just before Naseby, Marshall in *The strong helper* celebrated with some joy the doctrine that the more destitute the faithful are, the more God will hearken to their prayers. Preaching in *A sacred record* immediately after Naseby, which he clearly reckoned a Parliamentary victory whatever military historians conclude, Marshall was, if anything, more grim, calling on his auditors to rededicate and continually to repent in order that they might merit further mercies.[20] If he was joyous and celebratory where others might be sad, stern and demanding where others might be lighthearted and celebratory, Marshall thereby articulated in a striking way the Puritan emphasis upon divine control. On the other hand, stressing rededication, or in such a fiery sermon as his notorious *Meroz cursed*, Marshall illustrated how, for all his devotion to divine intervention and overriding control, he and his Puritan brethren could call men into stirring acts of effort or revolution. One simply became agent to that overarching source of power.

When John Vicars penned that "sacred record . . . of God's mercies to

Sion," he produced just the sort of Puritan providential history Marshall had in mind. Both his title, *Jehovah-Jireh*, and the form in which he cast it emphasized God's glorious control of events in this world. Because battles illustrate God's providence rather than testifying to the independent heroism of a commander or soldier, Vicars severed event from event, snipped the chronological and causal cords we normally think might bind a military strategy together, and capped each narrative episode or battle with "*Jehovah-Jireh*" or "God in his Mount" dispensing mercies to the faithful. He got rid of human, causal chronology another way by tracing the causes of the war not to politics but to Eden, not to history but to the sociology of a timeless struggle between Christ and Satan.[21]

Placing such an emphasis upon divine providence lessens one's interest in military strategy, the development over time of a campaign, acts of bravery, or the fame which derives from these. Sutton pointed out that military metaphors, when applied to the Christian life, did not entirely cover the issue; spiritual warfare was far more important than human combat: "When you have done most honorable and worthy service in the one [sublunar] kind of war, you can have no more but a smoke of honor, a shadow of wealth, and blast of fame, a wreath and coronet of palm and laurel, a monument of brass and marble, a memory preserved from oblivion by thin paper walls; but when you have served in the other [spiritual], you shall be crowned with a crown of life . . . receive an eternal weight of glory . . . live forever with your leader and captain" (pp. 3–4). "Beware of carnal confidence in your *arms*" counseled John Davenport succinctly (p. 19). The Puritan God almost usurped or absorbed into himself the fame of his faithful, as well as all their activity, for "God himself is a man of war. Divine oracles call him *Dominum Exercituum*, the Lord of Hosts," Sutton added (p. 9).

Yet the role of anonymous agent could still appear, in its own special way, heroic; "above all creatures, he loves soldiers" (Sutton, p. 7) not simply because he was a bellicose God, but also because soldiering both required the expenditure of a great deal of energy and could express an inner, spiritual state of faithfulness and almost realism. Military drilling particularly attracted Puritans because it provided such an excellent way to keep busy and thereby foil the Devil. "It is good to be doing, that when Satan comes, *inveniat occupatum*, he may find thee honestly busied. . . . So long as we are well exercised, the devil hath not so fair a mark of us" (Adams, pp. 18–19). In short, for all their passive instrumentality, their antlike place in a massed formation, their subordination to divine providence, Puritan soldiers of Christ were and must be active. They exercised both body and will within a Puritanically constrained frame.

They did so willingly, in both the theological and nontheological senses. Faithful military drilling never occurred "by constraint, but of a ready

mind" thought Davenport (p. 15). *"Nam complacet Deo famulatus coactus.*
God could never endure forced service. Do all then with a willing heart"
counseled Adams (p. 29). Moreover, such acts of will testified to an inner
faith. God's cause was always just, and therefore, to express true faith, the
Puritan soldier must fight only a "just war." It was for that reason that
Puritan apologists spent so much time and ink resolving cases of military
conscience and proving that the Parliamentary cause was a "just war." But
once the right answer emerged from these disputations, the "iron rods"
and "instruments" could beat down their opponents as a way of directly
keeping the faith. Moreover, since God was, in his glory, always victorious,
and since he had historically displayed a fondness for fighting for his "true"
Englishmen, such an active commitment became political realism of the
highest order. Stephen Marshall was moved by the spirit when he explained
that all good men in "all the Christian world" pray "in our behalf; our
cause is God's" and hence, he exclaimed, "there is not a good man in the
world, no not at Oxford, who prays *Thy Kingdom come* but prays for us"
(*Strong helper*, pp. 22-23). To fight on these terms was to participate in
the inexorable unfolding of truth; the "Kingdom" Marshall expected in
England was apocalyptic. The rewards were internal rather than external;
the heroism involved a leap of faith before he could hope to act well. But
to be a member of the Church Militant which would bring in the Church
Triumphant and the kingdom of the saints was a glorious work. One could
with joy give God the glory, look forward to his millennial presence, beat
down Antichrist, yet still be politically prudent. The civil wars were, in
many ways, the best of all possible Puritan worlds.

It is this specifically Puritanic conception of the *miles christi* which
accounts most successfully for what Michael Wilding has recently described
as the pacifist criticism of military heroism in *Paradise Lost*.[22] Conflating
Paradise Lost with *Hudibras* and arguing that a cynical or world-weary loss
of commitment informs both, Wilding implies that the Puritan epic is a
deeply cutting criticism of Puritanism as well as militarism. Rather, however, it seems that Milton always remained faithful to the revolution and
that his God is the arch-Puritan in the way he repeatedly sends his creatures
on missions which are strategically impossible and eventuate in no conclusion. Wilding's analysis has one advantage over the work of some of the
Satanic critics: it assumes neither that the Father is arbitrary nor that Milton was being purely whimsical as he wrote; that is, Wilding assumes that
there is a coherence even to the most anomalous-seeming vision and looks
steadily at the patterns and configurations which emerge through these
confrontations. But, writing in an age when militarism has been massively
discredited, particularly among intellectuals, he misses the curiously unheroic militarism that the Puritans developed (and that *Hudibras* was designed to discredit), which lay behind Milton's literary scenes. Raphael

describes one such impossible mission when he welcomes Adam's offer to narrate the first day of human life. The angel explains why he has not heard the story which Adam is so obviously bursting to tell:

> For I that Day was absent, as befell,
> Bound on a voyage uncouth and obscure,
> Farr on excursion toward the Gates of Hell;
> Squar'd in full Legion (such command we had)
> To see that none thence issu'd forth a spie,
> Or enemie, while God was in his work,
> Least hee incenst at such eruption bold,
> Destruction with Creation might have mixt.
> Not that they durst without his leave attempt,
> But us he sends upon his high behests
> For state, as Sovran King, and to enure
> Our prompt obedience. Fast we found, fast shut
> The dismal Gates, and barricado'd strong;
> But long ere our approaching heard within
> Noise, other then the sound of Dance or Song,
> Torment, and loud lament, and furious rage.
> Glad we return'd up to the coasts of Light
> Ere Sabbath Eev'ning: so we had in charge.   [8:229-46]

In contrast to Satan, who is forever posturing that he craves "Warr then, Warr/Open or understood" (1:661-62), Raphael frankly admits that nothing much more than practice or drill occupied him. The threat that some might issue "forth a spie,/Or enemie" is verbally checked by a dialectical movement; Raphael first posits a reaction ("Destruction"), then a synthesis ("his leave"). God's permissive providence allows his creatures free choice and reason, yet retains overarching control. Having progressed through this dialectic, Raphael can then sketch the results of God's peculiar "leave"; sending these angels on this mission permits them affirmatively to testify to their faith in God's supreme rule. There is a good deal of joy in such a mission. Raphael recalls the "Song and Dance" of the creation, narrated just before in book seven, as a contrast to the "Noise" of hell; the passage closes as the angels reascend to heaven "Ere Sabbath Eev'ning" and, presumably, to the hymn of praise which concludes that day of rest and book seven so magnificently. God's "State, as Sovran King" allows us to share the Puritan love of giving God the glory. Old Testament elements —God's wrath (which, although mentioned, does not function here) and Sabbath regulations—recall important Puritan concerns. Most important, however, these angels are drilling, both physically as they are "Squar'd in full Legion" and spiritually as God *enures* their "prompt obedience." The "use" of this exercise, which the Puritans seem to have enjoyed so much,

is not to inspire "carnal confidence" in arms or win hand to hand combats.
Rather it provides a vehicle whereby the angels can respond affirmatively
to the ultimate reality—God's providence—while functioning within it, and
a way for us to participate in the Puritans' joy in unceasing commitment.

Similarly, virtuous angels guard Eden from book three to the beginning
of book ten; during the immense amount of time the reader spends on this
section, he hears a few stories about faithful angels winning partial successes in books four and six, but notices that the lengthy campaign on the
perimeters of Eden is a strategic failure. After the dire event of the fall,
the angels ascend to heaven and report to God:

> Up into Heav'n from Paradise in haste
> Th' Angelic Guards ascended, mute and sad
> For Man, for of his state by this they knew,
> Much wondring how the suttle Fiend had stoln
> Entrance unseen. Soon as th' unwelcome news
> From Earth arriv'd at Heaven Gate, displeas'd
> All were who heard, dim sadness did not spare
> That time Celestial visages, yet mixt
> With pitie, violated not thir bliss.
> About the new-arriv'd, in multitudes
> Th' ethereal People ran, to hear and know
> How all befell: they towards the Throne Supream
> Accountable made haste to make appear
> With righteous plea, thir utmost vigilance,
> And easily approv'd; when the most High
> Eternal Father from his secret Cloud,
> Amidst in Thunder utter'd thus his voice.   [10:17-33]

There are a number of secondary things of an appealing nature in this
passage. The angels are sympathetic and concerned about man; as good
soldiers they have followed orders and reported back promptly. They
trust their commander in chief and are not "abasht,"

>   as when men wont to watch
> On duty, sleeping found by whom they dread,
> Rouse and bestir themselves ere well awake.   [1:332-34]

Still Milton is primarily at pains to show that these angels have both failed
to exclude Satan and momentarily forgotten that the mission was always
impossible. Angels rush out (as we gather at the scene of an automobile
accident) to get "news" which is really not news at all. The first seven lines
of book ten have reminded us of that:

> Meanwhile the hainous and despightfull act

Of *Satan* done in Paradise, and how
Hee in the Serpent had perverted *Eve*,
Her Husband shee, to taste the fatall fruit,
Was known in Heav'n; for what can scape the Eye
Of God All-seeing, or deceave his Heart
Omniscient.   [10:1-7]

God looks down on earth, just as he had at the beginning of book three
when Satan first approached, and as he receives the angels' report, he recalls that earlier interview:

be not dismaid,
Nor troubl'd at these tidings from the Earth,
Which your sincerest care could not prevent,
Foretold so lately what would come to pass,
When first this Tempter cross'd the Gulf from Hell.   [10:35-39]

By verbally joining book ten with book three in structural symmetry,
Milton incarnates formally God's prevenient grace, enunciated in the first
scene and now about to operate when he sends "Mercie collegue with Justice" (10:59). Simultaneously, Milton shows that the angels' concern, the
whole strategy of guarding Eden, is beside the point; even before they left,
the angels had been told it wouldn't work. Moreover, he weaves a typically
Puritan pattern, giving us the "truth" or "doctrine" of the situation from
a "school divine" in book three, then descending to uses here and at the
end of the poem generally. The angels, although they do momentarily
make a mistake and forget what they have heard, still basically understand
what is expected of them. They "made haste to make appear/With righteous plea, thir utmost vigilance." Their inner, spiritual state, their faith
and attentiveness, will justify them; when they make that plea they are
"easily approv'd." Milton's God expects no more but he does require faith
and realism. We may not like his attitude; we may thirst for brilliant personal victories, clear-cut and decisive, but that is not the sort of life the
creatures lead in *Paradise Lost*.

Similarly, book six is the providential history of a divine mercy much in
the spirit of Vicars's *Jehovah-Jireh*. God intervenes to conclude a war which
he has so organized (by pitting numerically equal forces against each other)
that neither creaturely side can win alone. By the time "Warr wearied hath
perform'd what Warr can do," neither it nor the combatants have accomplished anything. This seems more than a matter of mere poetic "faking."[23]
Certainly, Milton must reserve Satan from this battle to tempt Adam and
Eve, but given the way in which this sort of episode recurs in the poem, it
would seem that Milton did *not* drag epic combat in where it was inappropriate to his overall strategy merely to follow convention, but rather set
out positively to show that epic combat and "carnal confidence in arms"

are inappropriate in his Puritan universe. On the second day, the armor of both sides "help'd thir harm" (6:656; cf. 595-97). On the first, each faithful angel fought "As onely in his arm the moment lay/Of victorie." "As" tells the story. Abdiel, Michael, and Satan approached single combat expecting, wrongly, a quick and decisive outcome. Abdiel taunts Satan before they square off:

> nor is it aught but just,
> That he who in debate of Truth hath won,
> Should win in Arms, in both disputes alike
> Victor.   [6:121-24]

Reasonable or not from a human point of view, Abdiel does not overcome Satan, although he makes him bow. When Michael and Satan later encounter,

> Together both with next to Almightie Arme,
> Uplifted imminent one stroke they aim'd
> That might determine, and not need repeate,
> As not of power, at once.   [6:316-19]

"Next to Almightie," they are *not* almighty nor do they finally determine the outcome.

Single, just creatures become emblems of this problem. Abdiel debates magnificently with Satan at the conclusion of book five, yet all he can ultimately make is a physical "retort" as he walks out of the meeting. Returning, in the first few lines of book six, to the camp of the faithful, he perceives that he can't even bring back news of the revolt; God's omniscience costs him this minimal moment of heroism. Both Enoch and Noah preach to their sinful societies, to no avail; they don't even have a faithful company to fall back upon, as Abdiel does.

The strategic "failures" of the virtuous angels best reveal the dynamics of Milton's universe because, in a somewhat Manichean story like *Paradise Lost*, we expect the "good guys" to win. Yet the divinely inspired Raphael impartially awards few wreaths "of Palm and Laurell" and explicitly comments on how thin and weak the "paper walls" of epic fame are. Persistently shifting his focus away from the combatants, he dissolves the fight between Gabriel and Satan into a long disquisition on the healing properties of angels and comments, as he turns from Abdiel and Satan,

> Mean while in other parts like deeds deservd
> Memorial.   [6:354-55]

He does briefly relate a few of these, but concludes the list:

> I might relate of thousands, and thir names
> Eternize here on Earth; but those elect

> Angels contented with thir fame in Heav'n
> Seek not the praise of men: the other sort
> In might though wondrous and in Acts of Warr,
> Nor of Renown less eager, yet by doome
> Canceld from Heav'n and sacred memorie,
> Nameless in dark oblivion let them dwell.   [6:373-79]

He draws precisely Sutton's contrast; the faithful pursue an eternal fame, the fallen the fame of mundane warfare. He begins, in book six, the process of redefining heroism, turning away from military might, strategy, and fame which Milton's narrator concludes at the beginning of book nine. Epic combat in *Paradise Lost* renders weapons "trivial" and "Arms ridiculous," a notion Milton reiterated in *Samson Agonistes* (lines 131, 142, 263). The form of Raphael's story, particularly the way he shifts his focus, enforces the point aesthetically.

In short, both fallen and unfallen angels live under the same constraints. Milton's Puritanic God is infinitely different from his creatures and at an immense distance from both faithful and Satanic. There seems no need to retell Satan's ill-success; God simply brings greater good out of his evil endeavors. But if both groups live in the same world, they respond to it differently. The fallen angels have all the wrong attitudes outlined in the Puritan military sermons. Satan has such "carnal confidence" in his own arm that he goes to war with omnipotence and finally argues that he is self-created. The paradoxical reflex of this attitude is that he and his followers fight in a "spurt, for sport," act like dilettantes or Adams's "young gentlemen," grow "discouraged in sad and weighty undertakings," become restless when they don't immediately win, and get frustrated and angry as they learn that they cannot completely shape their own destinies. Perhaps Ashe's term, "cowardliness," does not penetrate to the essence of their attitude; perhaps "unrealistic" is more acute. They don't take either God or the wars seriously. Delusion or self-delusion infects even their use of language; what, after all, can it mean to "defie th' Omnipotent to Arms"? Satan either does not know what words mean or he consciously perverts them. In a verbal medium, either act warps reality. That reality is that Milton's is a Puritan God, above all omnipotent.

The faithful angels, in contrast, constantly rejoice in their limited situation, gladly join in (as Abdiel does at the beginning of book six), continually sing God's marvelous omnipotence. Thereby, they exercise reason and choice and achieve merit. "Freely they stood who stood, and fell who fell" (3:102), applies to both angels and men.

> Not free, what proof could they have givn sincere
> Of true allegiance, constant Faith or Love,
> Where onely what they needs must do, appeard,
> Not what they would?   [3:103-6]

Here Adams and Davenport re-echo in Milton's lines, insisting that God
does not constrain men or enjoy "forced service." It is more than an echo.
Milton was indeed an "advanced or radical Protestant" and he pressed the
optimistic claims of revolutionary preachers like Marshall so far as to employ the word "merit" frequently and centrally in his poem. Divine agents
had become, for him, capable of meritorious action.

Still, the actions are circumscribed. The creatures do act to shape their
ultimate destinies but they do not act transitively and decisively upon an
external reality. They testify to their commitment, accept reality, and, as
the Son says when he rides out to victory on the third day, "stand still."

Stand still in bright array ye Saints, here stand
Ye Angels arm'd, this day from Battel rest.   [6:801-2]

Standing is the perfect verb to represent this Puritan mode of heroism.
Beginning at least with the sonnet on his blindness, it became a crucial
verb in Milton's poetry. Standing is an act, a gesture; particularly as it contrasts to sitting, which Satan favors, it requires effort. But it is an intransitive act. The double sense of the Son's words, underlined by the repetition
of the verb, fuses physical and spiritual activity: the faithful must and they
do rejoice to maintain an erect physical posture, to rest, to witness God's
glorious triumph, and to keep the faith.

Neither Puritans nor Anglicans spent all their time preaching sermons, although the Puritans might have been willing to try. So let me turn from
that literature to three books which celebrated the heroes of the civil wars
after the fact. Since one of the three extolled celebrated Royalist heroes,
it provides a directly contrastive counterexample to the two Puritan pro-
ductions. The three allow us to see men shaping not ideal projections of
their fantasies of heroic effort but rather concretely shaping the prior
facts of men's lives; thus they provide us with a second kind of approach
to the subject of militarism. More important, however, they show Puritan
optimism in sharp contrast to Royalist world-weariness, account for Milton's strident sense of "merit," and illuminate the difference between
Hudibras's anti-Puritanic pacificism and *Paradise Lost*'s faithful rendering
of the spirit which moved the revolution.

England's worthies under whom all the civill and bloudy warres since
Anno *1642, to* Anno *1647, are related* . . . (London, 1647), which has
been attributed to John Vicars, and *A survey of England's champions and
truth's faithful patriots* . . . (London, 1647) by Josiah Ricraft, differ
from James Heath's *A new book of loyal English martyrs and confessors,
who have endured the pains and terrours of death, arraignment, banish-
ment, and imprisonment, for the maintanance of the just and legal government of these kingdoms, both in Church and state* (London, [1665?]),

from the titles onward. Although the Royalist Heath obviously hopes to continue Foxe's *Book of Martyrs*, beginning as he does with the "Marian persecution" and the time when "the flames thereof [were] extinguished . . . by the most happy and auspicious assumption of *Queen Elizabeth*," he is out of touch with the most telling extensions of Foxe's historiography. For his book concerns "martyrs and confessors," while Vicars and Ricraft focus upon "worthies," "champions," and "patriots." Heath's book, in short, is a collection of tales about earthly losers; in contrast the Parliamentary heroes are represented (like the Puritan God) as above all triumphant. Without doubt, the historical accidents of the time of composition and the individual temperament of the compilers influenced the tone and shaping of these books, yet neither singly nor taken together will they explain these books. Vicars and Ricraft celebrated the Puritan victors in 1647, before the final triumphs had been achieved and solidified. Heath wrote after the Restoration, which he had celebrated three years previously in *The glories and magnificent triumphs of the blessed restitution of King Charles II* . . . (1662), so he did have a triumphant model to meditate upon and take courage from if he wanted it. In spite of that, he focused on loss. Moreover, all three authors depended heavily upon newsletters and pamphlets in compiling their books, so that the views expressed were generally held rather than purely idiosyncratic.

Just as the new, Puritan optimism emerged in talk about champions and patriots while that sense of loss which drove the Royalist finally into spiritual transcendence loomed in Heath's martyrs, so the titles set the tone for the tomes. Providential historiography informs all three, yet when Heath set out, in a different work, to trace the causes of the civil wars, he dismissed, from the very first sentence onward, providential guidance from consideration; in sharp contrast to Vicars, he wrote: "No higher or greater cause can be assigned for the war (setting aside the sins of all times and nations, to which the justice of heaven is seldom long a debtor) but the fate and catastrophe of kingdoms and monarchies, which do at certain periods of time taste of that vicissitude and mutability to which all other sublunary things are more frequently subjected."[24] "Kingdoms and monarchies," then, are often a sort of rock against the vicissitudes of time, but even these fail as the gap between providential guidance and the apparent course of human affairs seems to widen. God seemed to have abandoned the Royalists, even when they wrote after the Restoration; all that remained was temporal and sublunary vicissitude or Habakkuk's visionary tower. If the rock of monarchy was crumbling for Heath, the iron rod, God's instrument, was happily overwhelming enemies for Ricraft.

Ricraft's introductory praise of Cromwell as an "iron rod," which preceded the lists of his military accomplishments, was, with the possible exception of the business about his name, almost equally impersonal.

Heath, in contrast, described his Royalist martyrs in much more personal terms, setting the context for the tale which follows, reporting a man's ancestry and early life. The outcome of each story is tied directly to some human cause. Money, for example, killed Sir Henry Slingsby; Heath begins the story by observing that "Cromwell never . . . stirred a *plot*, but money stuck at the bottom." He had "an army of *Janizaries* which without constant pay could never be kept at his beck and obedience, and all the design he practiced could not raise him money without the tricks of jealousies and fears . . . and this was the original of this horrid plot" (p. 220, i.e., 420). If the motive was money, the "original" is tied in the telling securely to the outcome.

An establishment apologist, Heath anchors his tales securely in the chronological causality of time and this world. After the flames of Smithfield had been extinguished by the accession of Elizabeth, he reports, a "strange and a new kind of fire, like a subterraneous conflagration" was kindled and spread through "secret whisperings and murmurings against the government" until, having gained strength, it burst out visibly. Heath's step by step account is well stocked with Machiavellian motives. The first open sign of the "subterraneous conflagration" was the war with Scotland, in which

> The Scotch rebels fought for that they had sacrilegiously got, and the English rebel for what sacrilegiously he should get. The event of that unlucky war, or rather preparations to it, soon inflated and puffed up the Nonconformist in England, the quarrel, as the grave lecturers deceived and imposed on the people, being thought to be the same: against bishops, against the liturgy, against ceremonies, and such like; but it was clearly against the bishops' lands, against loyalty and obedience, and against the indispensable duties of a good conscience, things more indifferent to these strict disciplinarians than a reverend decency in holy performances. [P. 6]

Vicars and Ricraft, in contrast, were busy giving God the glory in static, repetitious, and cosmic terms. For example, General Skippon was such a scourge that when he fell wounded at Naseby Charles was said to have exclaimed *"That though he had lost the victory at* Naseby, *yet* Skippon *was slain.* But praised be God it proved otherwise." Skippon was loaded on a horse litter to be brought to London, Vicars continued, and "coming to Islington . . . it pleased the Lord that it should so fall out (to the greater setting forth of his power and providence) that . . . a great mastiff-dog on a sudden ran most fiercely out of a house, fell furiously upon one of the horses that carried the litter, got the horse by the stones, behind, made the horse thereby fling and fly about and beat and shake the litter up and down, to and fro, in a most dangerous manner shaking the good gentleman's sorely wounded body thereby, and ready continually to overthrow the litter and greatly endanger the noble gentleman's life; all which while there being no possible means to beat off the dog or make him leave his hold of the horse, till they ran him through with a sword and killed him; which as soon as they could they did, and so brought this noble gentleman to his house in *Bartholmews* the Great, where notwithstanding all this (the Lord had so admirably enabled him to bear this terrible brunt) being laid to rest in his bed, prayers sent up to God for him in all the churches in *London*, and special care had to the cure of his wound, by God's blessing on the industry and fidelity of the honest and religious chirurgeon Mr. *Trapham*, who at length by God's mercy got out a great piece of rag of his waistcoat, which had been beaten into his body by his armor through the force of the bullet and lay festering in the wound; but thus got out, in God's good time a perfect cure was made of it" (Vicars, pp. 55–57). As a brute beast, the horse probably neither could apprehend nor appreciate God's merciful hand in all this, but clearly Vicars does. A marvelous story well told through the attack by the mastiff, Vicars' narrative loses steam precisely when we expect the climax. We hope to see the finger of God but instead we get "which as soon as they could they did," a clause which crashes into bathos. God's intervention, on the other hand, so cumbers the rest of the narrative as to snarl the syntax irreparably; who, we might ask, "got out" the bit of rag, given the massive subordination and paren-thesis-building which Vicars indulges in here? Was it Mr. Trapham, his "industry and fidelity," or God? All three are equally possible and theo-logically sensible, and the second particularly focuses upon the good doc-tor's divine instrumentality rather than upon his own personal skill and action. We may, from a literary point of view, initially suspect that Vicars' narrative talents did not match his story here and that he fell into inco-herence. But when we think about it, that incoherence and anticlimactic quality expresses admirably and exactly the theological patterns of Puritan thought. Giving God the glory entailed, quite logically, diminishing the force of human acts and of turning men into divine agents.

Because the cyclic nature of Puritan typology coincides with their peculiarly strong sense of providential history, Vicars's and Ricraft's tales are, in a certain sense, profoundly dull. They give no sense of the progres-sion of events, of how any particular worthy got from one battle to the next, of how military strategy developed from engagement to engagement. One of the most extreme forms of this narrative technique occurs at the end of Vicars's account of Fairfax's campaign. Fairfax was in so many battles that Vicars tired early of devoting more than one sentence to each victory (and hence he could record little more than a series of triumphs) and degenerated to making mere lists: "104. *Dorcester*. 105. *Lichfield Close*. 106. *Wallingford* Castle; August 1646, *Gotbridge* Castle. 107. *Ruth-*

ian Castle. 108. *Ragland* Castle. 109. *Pendennis* Castle. 110. *Flint* Castle"
(p. 45). Since the simple fact of winning was all that was important (testifying to God's providence and glory as it did) there really was little more
to record. We can see this pattern clearly in Vicars's *Jehovah-Jireh* as well.
Battle is separated from battle, cause from effect; the civil wars, we recall,
were for Vicars the final act of the play pitting Christ against Satan. In
such a view, all human history solidifies—an interminable and never-ending
struggle between the two teams, to be concluded only at the millennium—
and everything is always the same. Thus Vicars pauses at the end of the
narrative of each episode to comment upon *Jehovah-Jireh* or "God in his
Mount" dispensing his mercies to his Parliamentary Englishmen. Once one
has settled into the rhythm of the book, one need almost read no farther
to get the point.

Heath sees his and his cause's adversaries not as faceless agents of a cosmic, Satanic conspiracy but with sharply etched, individual and idiosyncratic motives which derive not from eternal verities but from the immediate affairs of this world. Parliament, in Heath's narrative, "proceeded step
by step" in stripping Laud of his rights and prerogatives, benefices, power,
and authority. Cromwell's motives were financial. The flames of that "subterraneous conflagration" spread gradually and Heath recounts them as
they occurred, in a chronological matrix, step by step. His adversaries,
therefore, seem a batch of low-minded criminals, and if they are not so
terrifying as the Puritans' enemies, still they cannot be stopped. Human
nature takes a real pummeling, in Heath's pages, because he keeps his focus
firmly on affairs here below. Reading him, one can understand the Royalists' desperation when the monarchy crashed about them, the pressures
behind their transcendental escapism, and the dilemma faced by Restoration apologists for the establishment when they contemplated the wars
and the death of Charles. For these criminals and enthusiasts, deluded or
self-hypnotized by their own theology, were also holy men. When they
forced the establishment to choose between "peace" and "holiness," they
ground them between a rock and a hard place. "Holiness" was difficult to
object to, yet peace alone seemed to guarantee the continuation of the
monarchy and the religious establishment. When Dryden concluded his
Religio Laici by appealing to peace, he clearly turned his back on theology
and arguments from religiosity and truth. We must, in formulating our
belief, try to follow truth as diligently as possible, consulting the Bible,
Church, and authorities. However,

> If still our Reason runs another way,
> That private Reason 't is more just to curb,
> Than by disputes the public peace disturb.
> For points obscure are of small use to learn;
> But common quiet is mankind's concern.   [446–50]

Such a position would, of course, give a Puritan apoplexy. But it is a slender position in its own right. Individual men have proved to be monstrous, the pursuit of theology has turned out to be upsetting, rational analysis had finally eventuated in revolutionary rhetoric. There was, from the establishment point of view, almost nowhere to turn, except to a thin, quasi-rational, political prudence, difficult at best to enforce, or else to an *O altitudo!*

If that spirit produced the attack upon military glory in *Hudibras*, something quite different informs *Paradise Lost*. Obviously, Milton was not in a position, as Restoration approached and passed, to pen a paean to truth's famous champions in England, and he deliberately chose not to write a national epic. The English were not, finally, a noble and puissant nation, but rather "basely and besottedly" ran "their necks into the yoke" of an intolerable tyranny;[25] Milton was at work on the poem before that happened and he must have seen it coming. Still, like his angels, Milton could not step out of the world totally; William Riley Parker remarked tellingly that he loved controversy not wisely but too well.[26] If the Puritans taught that life was a treadmill existence, that teaching could sustain them after the collapse of the Commonwealth. Milton's angels do not win military victories any more than the characters of *Hudibras* do, but on the other hand, they do not give up. One achieved merit by rejoicing in the treadmill, for the treadmill was there, ineluctably, and one could hardly blame it for its very existence. While the patterns of military action in *Paradise Lost* in some ways resemble the patterns in *Hudibras*, they derive from different world views and testify to quite different levels of political commitment to the controversies of this world. Defeat simply required rededication, more wayfaring and warfaring. An ideology which focuses on group movements teaches its revolutionaries how to regroup after defeat; it does not produce the sort of world-weariness Wilding posits in *Paradise Lost*.

Chapter 13: TWO
SPIRITUAL AUTOBIOGRAPHIES

When a man orders his personal life he expresses in the most intimate terms his world view, or life style. There he reveals the marrow of his ideology, his bone-deep attitudes toward, approaches to, and means of coping with the world in which he lives. Each man is privately his own hero and it therefore comes as no great surprise that many of the same patterns I have been examining in theological speculation and the *miles christi* emerge in spiritual autobiographies as well. From considerations of space I shall select only two, John Donne's *Devotions upon Emergent Occasions* and John Bunyan's *Grace Abounding to the Chief of Sinners*. I select these two, in some ways untypical men, partially because of their very atypicality—which will test most severely the terms of my analysis— and partially because Joan Webber has already juxtaposed them while anchoring her analysis in the political differences between the two.[1] I wish to extend her analysis and modify it somewhat, but her work provides an excellent point of departure. While the theologian (shaping doctrines), the biographer (shaping lives), the historian (shaping events) and the preacher (shaping champions and utopias) seem to address themselves to objective facts or external verities, the spiritual autobiographer (shaping his life) engages in a nakedly subjective undertaking. Dealing with "externals" may distract us from the subjective pressures at work in the shaping; reading autobiographies leads us to focus on those subjective pressures immediately. In the process of this book, such an analysis prepares us directly to confront Milton's shaping of *Paradise Lost*.

Both John Donne and John Bunyan were unusual men. Donne turned to the English Church only after secular preferment was denied him, but then he manifested an extremely intense (some might say overintense) religious sensibility. He was preoccupied, in both his secular and his religious verse, with the union of the many in one; his cynical amatory poetry, for example, seems to be a reaction to confronting sexually the many. Death and suicide were perennial motifs, regardless of this subject, and fused naturally with a marked interest in the apocalypse when, as Milton's angels sang, God should be all in all. The three constellate together in the love poems, where Donne seeks a blindingly intense and revelatory sexual confrontation. He might be called a Puritan in these respects; indeed, the radical Baptist Bunyan shared many of these concerns; the apparent resolution of his spiritual crisis is a sort of private apocalypse with suicidal overtones. The desire to gather the many into one informed what Henri

Talon spoke of as Bunyan's "desire to survey his whole life in one glance
. . . to recapture all the threads of his past at one go, and knot them to a
present that was always slipping through his fingers."[2] As a Baptist and
storyteller, Bunyan cannot really be regarded as an orthodox Puritan any
more than Donne can be regarded as a simple Anglican.

   Grace Abounding to the Chief of Sinners and *Devotions upon Emergent
Occasions* are, from a literary point of view, as unusual as their authors.
Although Donne had his imitators, no one ever produced a work precisely
on the model of his devotions. Bunyan, as Roger Sharrock has shown,
traveled a well-trodden artistic path—the Puritan *vita*; "but the uniqueness
of Bunyan's treatment lies in its psychological penetration and freedom
from rationalization into stock Calvinist formulae."[3] The idiosyncracies of
these men, of their spiritual development, and of their works, which prevent us from labeling them Puritan or Anglican in neatly partisan terms,
will remind us that the terms Puritan and Anglican here refer not to a tightly grouped set of doctrines, a fully realized ideology or world view, but to
tendencies and directions toward which writers in this controversial age
more or less strongly inclined.

   Donne articulated the problem to which both he and Bunyan address
themselves in the opening to his first prayer: "O Eternall, and most gracious God, who, considered in thy selfe, art a *Circle*, first and last, and
altogether; but considered in thy working upon us, art a *direct line*, and
leadest us from our *beginning*, through all our wayes, to our end, enable
me by thy grace, to looke forward to mine end, and to looke backward to,
to the considerations of thy mercies afforded mee from my beginning, that
so by that practise of considering thy mercy, in my beginning in this world,
when thou plantedst me in the *Christian Church*, and thy mercy in the beginning of the other world, when thou writest me in the *Booke of life* in
my *Election*, I may come to a holy consideration of thy *mercy*, in the beginning of all my actions here: that in all the beginnings, in all the accesses,
and approaches of spirituall sicknesses of *Sinn*, I may heare and hearken to
that voice, *O thou Man of God, there is death in the pot*, and so refraine
from that, which I was so hungerly, so greedily flying to."[4] He opens by
stating the old Augustinian paradox centering on the difference between
the divine and the human perception of time and space, using one of his
favorite conceits—the line and the circle.[5] He draws a line in human life
"from our *beginning*, through all our wayes, to our end" and then shows
how that line "in this world" gets repeated in "the other world." The
straight line, which involves no repetition, generates cycles and circles.
The whole pressure of Donne's thought and art is directed toward precisely
this goal; transmuting the transitory things of this world (even the act of
love) into the circle of eternity, of elaborating upon the "sign" to elucidate

"the thing signified," of rising from "here" and "now" to "then" and
"there."

Each of the twenty-three devotions is a self-contained, tripartite unit,
yet the whole progresses linearly through the chronological stages of
Donne's sickness and the Latin poem which serves as a table of contents
and which the *Devotions* explicate at length. While one can imagine that
individual devotions might be omitted, one cannot imagine reordering the
sequence in any way nor can one imagine a devotion which might precede
the first, with its examination of "this minute" when Donne first experiences the onset of the disease, or follow the last, when he had recovered.
The *Devotions* are so completely rooted in the progress of the fever over
time that the linear quality could never be eradicated.

While Bunyan was as concerned with eternal circularity as Donne, he
was in contrast not nearly as committed to the lines of human life and
time. Roger Sharrock sees a four-part arrangement, conventionally Calvinist: "before conversion," "conversion," "calling," and "ministry" (p. xxx).
James Thorpe sees, equally plausibly, a bipartite arrangement followed by
three "anticlimaxes": "before the Fall," and "after the Fall."[6] That two
good critics divide the work so differently suggests that the parts are not
nearly so clear as the parts in Donne's *Devotions* because a pattern of
progress and development over time is not so strong. Indeed, one might
argue that there is almost no progress at all and the form is loose and addi-
tive because nothing is ever finally resolved.[7] The last episode in "A brief
Account of the Authors Imprisonment," for example, seems to be theologically crucial, for it centers on the right apprehension of the covenant
between God and the elect. Bunyan reflects "that God might chuse whether he would give me comfort now, or at the hour of death; but I might not
therefore chuse whether I would hold my profession or no: I was bound,
but he was free." In terms of Sharrock's division, that understanding would
seem essential to a full conversion; in terms of Thorpe's division, it is hard
to see how such a fundamental point of covenantal theology can really be
anticlimactic. The point is not whether Sharrock or Thorpe are wrong but
that both are right and that other patterns might equally be deduced. Gain-
ing comfort, which he finally wins, seems to have concerned Bunyan from
his childhood onward; the problem was constant. He added bits to the
piece and other pens did too, because his search was never-ending and in
important ways circular.

In the third expostulation, Donne contrasts his situation, his "*Station*"
or "*prostration*" to that of Christ "thy *Sonne*, who first lay upon the
earth, and praid, and then had his *Exaltation*, as himselfe calls his *Crucifying*, and first *descended into hell*, and then had his *Ascension*." "To
morrow" Donne may, in contrast, "be laid one Story lower, upon the

Floore, the face of the earth, and next day another Story, in the *grave*, the wombe of the Earth: As yet God suspends mee betweene *Heaven* and *Earth*, as a *Meteor*; and I am not in Heaven, because an earthly bodie clogges me, and I am not in the Earth, because a Heavenly *Soule* sustaines mee" (p. 13). In the midst of Bunyan's spiritual afflictions, after he had heard a voice saying "*Didst ever refuse to be justified by the Blood of Christ?*" he falls back again into his troubles. "Wherefore still my life hung in doubt before me, *not knowing which way I should tip*; only this I found my Soul desire, even to cast itself at the foot of Grace by Prayer and Supplication" (pp. 53–54). Both men are caught between two things, Donne between heaven and earth, Bunyan between tipping into damnation or into salvation. If the way they locate themselves "in the middle" is similar, the differences in the two formulations are representative of their differing sensibilities and styles.

Donne is between heaven and earth, between the linear progression of events in his earthly life and the circular structure which culminates in heaven. On earth, he can only move in straight lines, e.g., here, downward from "one Story lower" to "another Story" while in heaven he will participate in the great circle which is God and his plan. Bunyan, on the other hand, ignores the difference between "here" and "there" or "now" and "then"; he wants to be there and then now. When he finally does tip, he tips forever, and that is his problem and fear as well as the source of his joy and final consolation. Both are, in a sense, dissatisfied with "here" and "now" and want to be "there" and "then." But Donne is willing to follow out his straight lines in the hope that they may finally generate or be exalted into circles. Bunyan, on the other hand, pictures his world in essentially circular terms, with the repetition of temptations (the circle of despair in which for much of the book he represents himself as languishing) and repetition of God's mercies. It is worth remembering, in this connection, that Bunyan's title derives from and participates in the theory of providential history, with its catalogue of repeated mercies. In the absence of any linear movements in *Grace Abounding*, we may well conclude that Bunyan somehow desired to run in circles; certainly we may have compassion for a man caught, as Bunyan seems to have been, in the cycles of despair or anxiety, yet still make note of the pattern. At the same time, Bunyan wants and seems to feel he gets his final assurance, his place in the circle of eternity, while Donne remains ever conscious of the difference between our limited perception here and the final perception then; he is content to follow the lines of his life since that is all a man really can do.

Donne refers, in the same passage, to Christ's humiliation and exaltation. Linear movement upwards, from a position lying "upon the *earth*" to "his *Exaltation*," is repeated to form part of a circular pattern *after Christ's death* when Christ "*descended into hell*, and then had his *Ascension*." The

pattern is precisely what Donne hopes will happen with him, that his beginning and ending here on earth will be repeated by beginnings and endings after death. Donne's position in the controversy over bowing at the
name of Jesus is hard to make out here and elsewhere, but it seems clear
that he first and explicitly identifies Christ's exaltation with the crucifixion
and not with the millennium (although there is implicit a second eschatological exaltation). Bunyan, on the other hand, speaks of refusing "to be
justified by the Blood of Christ." He treats the entire experience of the
voice with care since that voice is extrascriptural. One is hard pressed to
know what Bunyan is thinking about when he speaks of the "blood of
Christ," but since Bunyan nowhere, either here or in his other works,
dwells on the scene of the crucifixion, one must assume that he is not
meditating upon the blood and wounds. Far more likely, although admittedly impossible to prove, is the view that Bunyan has the apocalyptic
blood of the lamb on his mind. Whatever we conclude about Bunyan's
reference, the fact remains that, here as elsewhere, Donne is far more inclined explicitly to evoke the end of Christ's linear movement, on the
cross, than is Bunyan;[8] Bunyan is far more inclined to think first about
the final exaltation and how he shall fare there, rather than about how he
must fare until then, than is Donne.

Let me pick out a single, illustrative metaphor, common to both, from
among many to show how verbal patterns express and embody intellectual
and spiritual patterns. Both men use ladders, Bunyan more spectacularly
at the end of the final section as he unravels his covenanted relationship
with God. Bunyan is bound, but God is free. "Wherefore, thought I, the
point being thus, I am for going on, and venturing my eternal state with
Christ, whether I have comfort here or no; if God doth not come in,
thought I, I will leap off the Ladder even blindfold into Eternitie, sink or
swim, come heaven, come hell; Lord Jesus, if thou wilt catch me, do; if
not, I will venture for thy Name." The sense of isolation is existential, the
gesture a gripping leap of faith; that the overtones are suicidal (although,
of course, inspired by the fear of the gallows which was the objective point
of departure for the whole section) merely contributes to the intensity of
the moment, the pressure Bunyan was under, the imperative desires which
moved him. They eventuate in timeless assurance, binding past, present
and future in a bittersweet mixture, drawing triumph out of defeat, affirmation out of self-destruction: "Now was my heart full of comfort, for I
hoped it *was* sincere; I would not have been without this trial for much; I
am comforted everie time I *think* of it, and I hope I *shall bless* God for
ever for the teaching I have had by it" (p. 101, emphasis mine). The tenses
of the verbs flow from past to future, as the assurance he receives transcends time. He has attained an eternal state, finally tipped one way and
not the other, and he can now operate within the world with security,

since mentally through his leap of faith he has already gone to heaven.

Bunyan leaps from the top of his visionary ladder, and his gesture, carrying him out of the world, paradoxically permits him to descend into and act within that world he has left. In general, the radical can only operate effectively in this world after he has completed his analysis of the nature of the world to be reformed. That depends upon securing an overriding vision of utopia, of the way things ought to be, against which this world is to be measured. Bunyan, a religious radical, can only secure that vision of utopia by leaping off the ladder, peering blindfold into eternity, escaping time and place, entering heaven, before he can set affairs right in this world. He must then descend from the heights of his visionary ladder, in comfort.

Donne's two ladders do not figure nearly as prominently as Bunyan's yet reveal a good deal about the kinds of action and option Donne sees open to him. Given that Donne sees himself suspended between heaven and earth, it is not surprising that they are Jacob's ladders. In the seventh expostulation, reflecting upon the help which his doctor gains through group consultation, Donne recounts the many helps we have provided us in this world in order to get to the next. He concludes by rejecting "schismatical singularities" and joining himself to "thy *Catholique Church*" where he is able to "associate thy *Word*, with thy *Sacrament*, thy Seale, with thy Patent" and "associate *the signe* with the *thing signified*" (p. 40). All of this joining together, and the helps which association provides, he elaborates upon by showing how the many angels help us also. "In *Jacobs* ladder, they which *ascended* and *descended*, and maintained the trade between *Heaven* and *Earth*, between thee and us, they who have the Commission, and charge, to guide us in all our wayes . . . all these, who administer to thy servants, from the first, to their last, are *Angels, Angels* in the plurall, in every service, *Angels* associated with Angells" (p. 39). Donne is confident that there is an "association" and "trade" between heaven and earth, God and man, "signe" and "thing signified," "word" and deed. In contrast to Bunyan's ladder, which expresses his existential crisis and terrible sense of isolation—which Donne would label "schismatical singularities" —Donne's ladder here expresses the conservative's confidence in things of this world, the liturgist's confidence in physical "signes and sacraments," the rhetorician's confidence in human speech, and the ecclesiast's confidence that the Church does provide the means of "trade" between heaven and earth.

Donne's other ladder, in the second meditation, recalls how Anglicans wrote human history. Donne remarks upon how "Earth is the center of my *Bodie, Heaven* is the *center* of my *Soule*; these two are the naturall places of those two; but those goe not to these two in an equall pace. . . . *Ascension* is my *Soules* pace and measure, but *precipitation* my *bodies*:

And, even *Angells*, whose home is *Heaven*, and who are winged too, yet had a *Ladder* to goe to *Heaven*, by steps" (p. 6). Bunyan tries to get to heaven by "precipitation," all in one leap; Donne is apparently willing (there seems no other recourse) to go to heaven by steps, one after the other, just as he recounts the steps of his sickness and the steps of his recovery. While each step is transformed, through meditation, into an emblem of the entire pilgrimage, yet each is also a part of a linear progress through time and of the history of a tightly focused temporal event with beginning, middle, end, and steps.

Bunyan's psychology seems to have remained constant through his life. He, like Donne, was a spiritual hypochondriac: "even in my childhood [God] did scare and affright me with fearful dreams, and did terrifie me with dreadful visions. For often, after I had spent this or the other day in sin, I have in my bed been greatly afflicted, while asleep, with the apprehension of Devils, and wicked spirits, who still, as I then thought, laboured to draw me away with them; of which I could never be rid" (p. 6). Bunyan here points out a difference between past and present; he "then thought" one thing, the implication being that he thinks differently now (although one is far from certain precisely what the difference could be). On the other hand, the phrase "this or the other day" indicates a recurrent situation; locating it precisely in time does not even matter. While Bunyan can distinguish between what he labels "then" and what he labels "now," still there are numerous instances when "then" and "now" refer indiscriminately to either past, present, or future, or all together. Certainly, the act of joining "then" and "now" in an eternal present is not unusual in narrative or in religious writing. Yet Donne always clearly distinguishes between his use of "then" and "now," between "this minute" when he "was well" and "this minute" in which he is ill (p. 1). Just as for Calvin the word "new" has a less distinct temporal reference than for Luther, so do Bunyan's "then" and "now" when contrasted to Donne's.

This is not to deny that Donne creates a kind of eternal present; one of the most immediately striking and commonly noticed traits in the poetry is Donne's ability to create a sense of temporal immediacy and a voice which seems to speak while it acts. The *Devotions* give exactly the same impression of having been written down minute by minute while the disease advanced. In this way Donne freezes an amatory conversation or a bad night in the sickbed in timeless words. The direct address in his secular poetry, a reaction to distant, Petrarchan analyses of life, as it were, after the act, is matched in the religious poetry by a meditative process which so effectively bridges past and present and future that his speakers can say "Spit in my face, you Jewes" or "At the round earths imagin'd corners, blow/Your trumpets, Angells." But throughout his writing, Donne either carefully distinguishes between "then" and "now" or clashes them with witty dissonance together to achieve surprise or temporary confusion. In the seventh of the Holy Sonnets he does both, clashing present and future in the first lines only to separate them later by stressing "there" and "here":

> For, if above all these, my sinnes abound,
> 'Tis late to aske abundance of thy grace,
> When wee are there; here on this lowly ground,
> Teach me how to repent.   [10–13]

He would like to have the divine vision, would like, one feels, to have it here and now; but finally he is sufficiently rooted in this world to realize that he cannot have it until then and there and that he can only try to progress toward it "by steps."[9]

Both Donne and Bunyan suggest the circularity of divine vision by repeating linear movements, citing Scripture and constructing miniature biblical histories which trace out a problem from beginning to end. But Bunyan more obviously repeats himself and his constant problem. In the midst of five pages of his greatest turmoil, regression, and despair, he thrice constructs lists (each progressing from Old Testament legalism to New Testament grace) of other sinners to whom he compares himself. In the first list, he moves from "*David's* Adultery and Murder" which "were . . . against the Law of *Moses*," through Peter's denial of Christ, finally coming "nearer to *Judas*, than either to *David* or *Peter*" (p. 47). His second list also progresses from sins against the law to self-conscious sins against Christ as he considers "*David, Hezekiah, Soloman, Peter*" and again finally compares "my sin with the sin of *Judas*" (pp. 47–48). The third list is identical to the second, except that Manasseh substitutes for Hezekiah. He concludes that David's "were but sins against the Law . . . but [Bunyan's] is a sin against the Saviour," Solomon's were "but sins against the Law . . . *but I have sold my Saviour*," Manasseh's were "great sins, sins of a bloody colour . . . [but] *you have sold your Saviour* (p. 51). It is precisely the conclusion he arrived at when first contemplating David's sin six pages before. Bunyan's arrangement here brilliantly records the motions of a mind going around in the circles of despair.

Donne also constructs such miniature histories, but he never articulates them in identical language, he does not construct essentially identical lists of names, and while he may eventually be making the same point with each, does so in varied terms and verbal motifs. When the physicians apply pigeons to draw out vapors, Donne constructs a prayer each sentence of which runs through sacred history. In the first he prays, "O Eternall and most gracious God, who though thou have suffred us to destroy ourselves, and hast not given us the power of reparation in ourselves, hast yet afforded us such meanes of reparation as may easily, and familiarly be compassed by us, prosper I humbly beseech thee, this means of bodily assistance in this thy ordinary *creature*, and prosper thy meanes of spirituall assistance in thy holy *Ordinances*" (pp. 72–73). Here he moves simultaneously through history from fall and Law to redemption and from physical to spiritual. The movement is even clearer in the second sentence: "And as thou hast caried this thy *creature*, the *Dove*, through all thy wayes, through *Nature*, and made it naturally proper to conduce medicinally to our *bodily health*, through the *Law*, and made it a *sacrifice* for *sinne* there, and through the *Gospel*, and made it, and thy spirit in it, a witnes of thy *Sonns baptisme* there, so carry it, and the qualities of it home to my *Soule*, and imprint there that *simplicity*, that *mildness*, that *harmelessnesse*, which thou hast imprinted by *Nature* in this *Creature*." Here we move, in much the same pattern as the first sentence, from Law to gospel, type to truth, nature to grace, while the repetitions begin to generate circular motion, beginning and ending with nature. Pleading that he might appropriate the stance of Christ victorious over death, that "I may, in the power and triumph of thy Son, tread victoriously upon my grave, and trample upon the *Lyon*, and *Dragon*," he evokes the second coming, before he finally replaces the sacrifice of the dove with "the blood of thy Sonne *Christ Jesus*" shed on the cross (p. 73).

In one of the more obviously "hydroptic" devotions, the seventeenth, Donne absorbs a number of voices into himself, at the same time tracing out another miniature biblical history from Jacob to Moses to Isaiah to Paul to Christ:

Thy *voice*, thy *hand* is in this *sound*, and in this *one sound*, I heare this *whole consort*. I heare thy *Jaacob* call unto his *sonnes*, and say; *Gather your selves together, that I may tell you what shall befall you in the last daies*: He saies, *That which I am now, you must bee then*. I hear thy *Moses* telling mee, and all within the *compasse* of this *sound, This is the blessing wherewith I blesse you before my death*; This, that before your death, you would consider your owne in mine. I heare thy *Prophet* saying to *Ezechias, Set thy house in order, for thou shalt die, and not live*; Hee makes us of his *familie*, and calls this a setting of *his* house in order, to compose *us* to the *meditation* of *death*. I heare thy *Apostle* saying, *I thinke it meet to put you in remembrance, knowing that shortly I must goe out of this Tabernacle*. This is the *publishing* of his *will*, and this *Bell* is our *legacie*, the applying of his *present condition* to our use. I heare that which makes al sounds *musique*, and all *musique* perfit; I heare thy *Sonne* himselfe saying, *Let not your hearts be troubled*; Only I heare this *change*, that whereas thy *Sonne* saies there, *I goe to prepare a place for you*, this man in this *sound* saies, *I send to prepare you for a place, for a grave*. [P. 99]

There is only one deviation in this chronological progress through history; the Apostle precedes Christ, probably for the simple reason that all testimony should lead to, be perfected by, and culminate in him.

I have argued that Bunyan does not progress and that therefore analyses of the book into developmentally defined sections will always encounter some difficulties. Let me turn briefly to what Sharrock describes as the section about "conversion," "the most important part of his life-story" which takes up "almost two-thirds of the book" (p. xxxi). Just before it, Bunyan had progressed fairly steadily through acquaintance with the Baptists and experience of the love of God. As he moved into this section, comprising roughly the center third of the whole (pp. 41–78 in Sharrock's edition, which runs to 103 pages in all), he seemed fairly and firmly "converted," in moderately solid spiritual shape, so that he could summarize his situation thus: "For after the Lord had in this manner thus graciously delivered me from this great and sore temptation, and had set me down so sweetly in the Faith of his holy gospel, and had given me such strong consolation and blessed evidence from heaven touching my interest in his love through Christ; the Tempter came upon me again, and that with a more grievous and dreadful temptation then before" (p. 41). With such assurance, faith and evidence, another man might be reckoned "converted," and certainly to have progressed far beyond a period "Before the Fall." Bunyan, however, regresses and relapses, or perhaps we might combine Sharrock and Thorpe and say he falls out of conversion. He dithers for thirty-seven pages over the possibility of "selling Christ," a metaphor which, if it clearly articulates his fascination with Judas, does not very clearly suggest precisely what Bunyan wanted and feared to do. At the end of the second he remarks: "Now I shall go forward to give you a relation of other of the Lord's leadings with me, of his dealings with me" (pp. 78–79). He is right; for all these pages he has not gone forward at all. He has teetered. Occupying such a substantial portion of the middle of the book, this section blunts our sense of Bunyan's progress monumentally, blurs his conversion much as Calvin's had been blurred, and the resultant inconclusiveness eddies out into the whole of his work.

At the conclusion of his illness and his devotions, Donne faces that threat of relapse, that perverse circularity of despair, which was central to Bunyan's work. Something has happened to Donne during the course of book and illness, and after it has happened, he begins to worry that it may happen again. He sees "that nothing can come neerer a *violating* of [God's] *honor*, neerer to the *nature* of a *scorne* of thee, then to sue out thy *Pardon*, and receive the Seales of *Reconciliation* to thee, and then *returne* to that sinne, for which I *needed*, and *had* thy pardon before" (p. 146). Hence, he prays not to relapse. "But because, by too lamentable *Experience*, I know how slippery my *customs* of sinne, have made my *wayes* of *sinne*, I presume to add this *petition* too, That if my *infirmitie* overtake mee, thou

forsake mee not." He is on dangerous ground, as he himself knows, because to relapse is horrible, but to assert that he will never again is probably an expression of pride. Yet despite his spiritual hypochondria, Donne
does not succumb to despair, apparently because he has just recovered
from his illness. God's "*Correction* hath brought mee to such a *participation* of thy selfe . . . to such an *intire possession* of thee, as that I durst
deliver my selfe over to thee this *minute*, if this *minute* thou wouldst accept my *dissolution.*" In this minute, he feels assured enough to die—so
assured his phrase "dissolution" seems almost negligible beside Bunyan's
powerful gallows imagery. But *God* must accept his dissolution; Donne is
not standing on top of a ladder from which *he* can pitch himself.

Donne concludes his prayer by wishing he might never again "*relapse*
into those *sinnes*, which I have *truely repented*, and thou hast *fully pardoned*" (p. 147). What is done is done, repented of, pardoned, just as it
will ever be repented of and pardoned. He faces the prospect of relapse
only after he has recovered from his disease. Recovering is but one of a
series of steps; this is the last. And he steps out into the future with a
sense of having completed something, even if it is not final. The pun in
the refrain of "Hymne to God the Father" illustrates the process by which
Donne transmutes a finite historical event with beginning, middle, and end
into a symbol of his and mankind's eternal estate.

Donne ends with relapsing; Bunyan, for all his relapsing, ends with certainty. Bunyan's personal apocalypse provides him with a sort of escape
from uncertainty and circularity. The conclusion of Donne's disease leads
him to the uncertainty of his next step and the threat of relapsing. Bunyan's assurance, spreading over all time because it reflects his eternal state
in heaven, is a function of the new Puritan optimism which permits the
radical and the reformist to set about ordering this world aright. Donne's
seemingly time-bound journey through a disease eventuates in circular
movement and a lesser degree of assurance that, for all that has irrecover-
ably happened, he will remain spiritually well.

N. J. C. Andreasen sees the dominant pattern of the *Devotions*, informing both individual, tripartite sections and the process of the whole, as the
expression of a "psychology of ascent."[10] Webber makes a similar point
less sharply as she traces how "conservative Anglicans" were drawn to
contemplate eternity, to transcend or try to escape from time. At the
heart of both theses is the conservative sense that things of and acts in and
upon this world do have a larger meaning, do count in and of themselves
as well as beyond themselves. Milton's God, on the other hand, *seems* to
have sent his angels on a series of meaningless missions. What distinguishes
the spiritual autobiography of a radical Puritan from that of a conservative
Anglican is not time in one and eternity in the other, but the patterns that
each weaves out of the two and the sense of human act and human potential that flows therefrom.

Section Five:
Paradise Lost

Chapter 14: CHOOSING HEROES: THE SATANIC NEGATION

Paradise Lost makes us want to choose a hero from among its characters, yet in important ways that choice is nearly impossible to make.* Another way of putting that proposition is to say that the poem both does and does not seem an act of political commitment. In this chapter I want to explore those two, basically Puritanic paradoxes. I shall, in the process, show that on its surface, the text of the poem asks us clearly and consistently to reject Satan as hero, yet also briefly suggest how he converges with all of the other characters in a heroic "core" or deep structure of antinomian and ultimately self-deifying aspiration that he shares with all the other nominees for hero who have been proposed in the history of comment on the poem. Let me begin with the political "feel" of this, in many ways private poem.

When, during the Democratic Party's Convention in Chicago in 1968, the poet Allen Ginsberg began to chant "om" in a city park, his song "felt" like a political act of radical commitment even though it is difficult to work out the ideology of it. Something like that must have occurred to its readers when *Paradise Lost* was published. Perhaps slightly out of date since the revolutionary moment had passed, some sort of revolutionary fervor must still have been apparent to readers attuned to the nuances of Christian language when they read it. There are, of course, important differences between Ginsberg's verbal chant and Milton's immensely crafted, written document. Ginsberg purported to be making a gesture of reconciliation, while Milton's song was from first to last immensely assertive. No poem that I know adopts the stance that it will give its readers the truth whole

---

*As I turn my attention primarily to *Paradise Lost*, I wish to signal a slight shift in analytic approach by recognizing the importance for my thinking of Joseph Summers's *The Muse's Method* (London, 1962) and Stanley Fish's *Surprised by Sin* (London, 1967). I mention these two works for two reasons. Were I to name all the fine studies of the poem which have affected me, I should probably inadvertently forget some, they are so many. Secondly, Summers and Fish seem to me to have been extremely valuable because they have spent relatively little time ostensibly on background, ideas, and precisely the sort of subjects I have hitherto focused upon and they riveted our attention upon the words of the text. Insofar as I am able here to pivot from a consideration of dogma to art, prose to poetry, theological doctrines to poetical uses, I rest in large part on the formalist analysis they have provided, a kind of concern for the texture of the verse which historically had not, it seems to me, informed criticism of Milton.

and complete quite so absolutely as does *Paradise Lost*; no poem I know
has a narrator so cosmically omniscient.[1] Preoccupied with the oedipal
problem of what relationship sons ought to establish with father, showing
its villain as a "bad son" and the virtuous characters as good sons, the
poem aggressively explores the central questions of Puritan theology. The
aggressive assertiveness in itself does much to force us to the belief that
we ought to choose sides and heroes, and it is that pressure upon the reader which expresses political commitment.

It is probably fair to say that the majority of commentators on *Paradise
Lost* have focused upon attaining the "paradise within" rather than upon
erecting the commonwealth among men. There are several strains in the
poem which evoke such an apolitical response, traits expressive of certain
apolitical elements in Puritanism itself. The poem posits an almost
Manichean struggle, a totally polarized confrontation, and that effect does
make us feel we ought to choose sides and heroes. But the confrontation
is so handled that in the end creaturely strategy plays little part. In a whole
host of ways the verse exerts an intense, transcendental pressure, forcing
the reader to rise above mundane conceptions of heroism. Just how intense
that pressure is may be seen by the relatively depressurized effect of the
final books, which in contrast descend to apply spiritual lessons to events
in this world. The struggle is to rise, the descent is easy, marking out plainly where Milton's energies are directed—toward a "higher heroism." Finally,
the poem articulates an elitist strain which always ran through the Puritan
theology of the "elect," particularly as it emphasizes splendid isolates. This
elitism is held in tension with a communitarian drift as well. Although not
unique to Puritan ideology, the traits of Manicheanism, transcendence, and
elitist-communalism do cohere there and help to account for some of the
limitations of Puritan political analysis. These limitations were radically
articulated in *Paradise Lost*.

Quite clearly, the Puritan preachers thundered with great success to
assess and direct the passions of their moment; from their early insistence
upon extempore preaching, tailored to seize the spiritual present in their
congregations, they had shown themselves capable of dealing directly with
events and men before them. They did not need the buffer of ritual between themselves and their present and their contemporaries. Yet, if such
an ability to act directly at any time is one of the principle ingredients of
successful political activity, there were limitations to the Puritans' political
vision. Elitism ran rampant when their revolution culminated in the sort of
consolidation of power which might, in its final stages, almost have satisfied the wishes even of Hobbes. Theologians of the elect could too easily
press the quest for a closer walk with God until it produced *milites christi*
who thought of themselves as the agents and instruments of God. The next
step was antinomianism, the notion that the sanctified adept is freed from

the moral law of God and can rise above all other men to do as he feels
divinely impelled. Based upon the polarization of nature and grace, antinomianism could turn a closer walk with God ever closer, until the adept
thought he had fused with the Father. Mistress Hutchinson in Massachusetts, George Fox and the Quakers, and (negatively inverted) the strange
doctrines of the Ranters all attest to this development at the cutting edge
of Puritan radicalism. Fox's many inquisitors were intensely sensitive to
the possibility of self-deification inherent in Puritan theology, for they
always asked Fox whether he thought himself to be Christ.[2]

From the exalted position of an agent or semideity, it is easy to believe
that all men in the world, even one's enemies, pray for one's inevitable
triumph. A man with that view may well find it difficult to deal pragmatically with political problems. Elitist pride can make him intractable, alien-
ating potential allies; setbacks and opposition may seem foolish annoyances,
hindering the Lord's work, not to be dealt with carefully; if his efforts as
agent seem ineffectual or not decisively important, inhumane treatment of
his enemies is too easy a next step. Seizing kairos by the forelock in revolutionary activity means, apparently, participating fully in the moment,
which is only a step or two away from sentimental surrender to the now.
Allowing typology to degenerate into analogy, hunting answers for the
future in Revelation, trumpeting the hope of Israel on the basis of God's
former care of his peculiars, concentrating on the eternal enmity between
the hosts of Satan and of Christ: none of these really allowed a man to
assess steadfastly his situation here and now, to gauge the temper of the
chronological times, to evolve strategy and avoid needlessly antagonizing
allies. The Puritan's first impulse had always been to get on top of events
through systematic analysis, and having so withdrawn from the hurly-burly,
it often proved too easy not to return to it successfully. Transcendental
distancing, antinomian elitism, and Manichean polarization of the issues
could make it difficult to deal with one's fellow men. The result was that
some Puritans came to espouse, oxymoronically, a politics of antinomianism.

To put it another way, there had always been a potentially incoherent
core to Puritan thought, deriving from the tension between extreme individualism and Puritan communalism; dreams of a single walk with God
danced in polarized and polarizing heads with visions of a massed army in
good order. The individualistic pressure broke down churches into sects,
sects into churches of one; the communal drive gathered militant parishes,
in peace or war, and spawned what we might call the cells or communes of
the Quakers and other, overtly millennial groups as well as the New Model.
Any single Puritan might react to this strain in an infinite variety of ways,
and when Puritanism was radicalized, men often moved toward the extremes of the spectrum. Bunyan records the individualism in his intensely

personal, some might say egoistic concern for God's abounding grace to a single sinner; George Fox records the second in the *Journal*, the tale of organizing the Society of Friends.

Milton's version of the Puritan vision seems to have been closer to the individualism of Bunyan than the communalism of George Fox, for he increasingly concerned himself, over the years, with splendid isolates. We can see this development in the poetry. In *Comus*, a domestic "society" seemed to be viable, even if the larger world was dominated by Comus and his rout; similarly in *Paradise Lost*, Adam and Eve leave paradise "handed" in that same kind of "little commonwealth" or "society ordained by God" which the Puritans praised so much in their marriage manuals and treatises of domestic economy.[3] In *Paradise Regain'd*, Milton instinctively focused upon those of Jesus' efforts to regain paradise which occurred outside society; critics have often mused why he chose the temptation, essentially an internal exercise of the isolated individual, rather than the gesture on the cross, which occurred in a highly social setting with even some political overtones. As he returns to men, in the last lines of the poem, Milton's Jesus does not enter a society but goes to his mother's house, "private." Milton might, in contrast, have used the final lines to evoke his public ministry among men, for that too lay between him and the dire cross. Finally, Milton cast Samson in a drama which destroys societies; his hero is denied even the minimal society of the marriage bed.

Within *Paradise Lost* itself we can see mounting emphasis on individual isolation. Abdiel, a type of the "one just man," has a society of angels to which he can return in book six; later, in book eleven, two other exemplars of the "one just man"—Enoch and Noah—do not have that resource to fall back on; they must remove their "Tents farr off" in isolation (11:727), signaled also by the adjective "one." In *Paradise Regain'd*, the only society we *see* Jesus achieve is again angelic, during the fleeting moment when the choir of angels bear him from the spire. Milton so defined the action of *Samson Agonistes* that angels could not enter it. The only sense of community articulated for Samson is grisly indeed; he is "conjoined" and "inmixt" (*SA*, ll. 1657, 1666) with his enemies in death and destruction. God says in *Paradise Lost* that if man had not fallen he would have merged upward with the angels. Unfortunately, he fell, canceling the opportunity for that sort of community, and as Milton explored that lapse in his three mature poems, he increasingly stressed the radically disruptive impact of the dire event upon human society.

We can also see these apolitical tendencies developing in the prose, particularly if we consider Milton's situation as he wrote the later tracts. In *The Readie and Easie Way* . . . he commented bitterly upon the way in which a noble and puissant nation, "so valorous and courageous to winn thir liberty in the field," might still "be so heartless and unwise in thir counsels" as "after ten or twelve years prosperous warr and contestation with tyrannie, basely and besottedly to run their necks again into the yoke which they have broken, and prostrate all the fruits of thir victorie for naught at the feet of the vanquished" (CE, 6:123). Milton here applied the Puritan tendency to focus on kairos and discredit the corruption and folly of unredeemed human history to the sacred record of God's mercies even to his English Sion. He did so another way in his *History of Britain*, finding there a record of folly in the whole historical fabric of the nation; he did so another way by working out *De Doctrina* so meticulously with energy which might have been directed here below; he did so yet another way by almost inventing for himself Salmasius as an opponent worthy of being addressed not in English but in Latin, at a distance from England, and calling forth all his talents and energies to crush in defeat. Particularly the second round of that battle gave Milton the feeling (long after the reality had disappeared) of striking a higher blow on behalf of a transcendentally puissant nation which he could no longer see physically and could hardly imagine intellectually.[4] Then, in *The Readie and Easie Way* . . . , as even his syntax began to show signs of disintegration, he made one last, desperate, angry, betrayed attack, not even on his Royalist enemies but on his countrymen and upon his potential allies on the Rota.

The internal pressures upon Milton leading to this radical outburst are easy to understand. Milton had suffered, in the preceding twenty years, a series of almost intolerable frustrations and disappointments. His marriage, his blindness, and the impending collapse of the revolution come immediately to mind, followed quickly by the disaster of his divorce tracts, his forced weaning from the main stream of liberal Puritan reformism, his increasing perception that "*New Presbyter* is but *Old Priest* writ large." There were others, of course, ramifying from these, but just that list would suffice to crush an ordinary man. That they did not is extraordinary; that they did not crush this radicalized Puritan, temperamentally responsive to the paranoia and elitism which could complement each other so neatly in the Puritan vision, is if anything more surprising.

Externally, the revolutionary fervor had fragmented itself into sects and ultimately, as the individualist strain in that analysis came to the fore, into churches of one. As Milton wrote *The Readie and Easie Way* . . . , Charles II practically had his foot in the boat, an invitation to return in hand. Given both these internal and external pressures, it is not really very important that Milton showed evident signs of paranoia during these years, that the figure of "the detractor" to whom Joan Webber has called our attention should loom ever larger in his prose,[5] that in a single, short, much-quoted passage from the *Second Defense*, Milton had already moved from a minute, painful rebuttal of the charge that he was physically ugly (a charge even he knew he should ignore) to a prayerful query whether his sin "could have called down" blindness "upon me above others"; having first showed himself oversensitive, then having stated what must have been real and wracking self-doubts, he finally overcompensated, preposterously asserting that "the divine law, the divine favour, has made us not merely secure, but, as it were, sacred, from the injuries of men" (CE, 8:67, 73). The emotional strain evident in the way in which his attention swung, in *The Readie and Easie Way* . . . , between attacks upon the Rota, who after all opposed Restoration as stoutly as he, and the sins of the nation, without coming in any way to terms with the emerging political reality of Charles, is equally obvious and unimportant. True enough, a hard-boiled politico might keep his guns trained at Charles rather than swinging them to potential allies and that very nation he had sought to serve and reform. But revolutions and their collapse produce just such transcendental, elitist politics in many men—in many men who do not carry the additional private burdens which Milton bore. And, however misdirected and shrill, the pamphlet's very existence, like the battle with Salmasius, the examination of the history of his nation, the working out of his personal beliefs systematically, did testify to a sort of intense political energy and commitment. It was a mix of bravado and bravery. Perhaps the saddest sentence Milton ever penned was that which he began the third paragraph from the end of *The Readie and Easie Way* . . . : "I have no more to say at present." Typically long-winded like his Puritan brethren, never quite able to relinquish the battle, Milton found it in himself to say three more, long, essentially repetitious paragraphs after that devastating clause. What is important to notice is how, as those most understandable pressures told on Milton to disorder even the logic and flow of his prose, he continued to fight. If Puritan other-worldliness, under fire, drove him to profess silence about politics here below, the commitment remained. A good Puritan soldier, he kept on marching, even if out of the political arena.

Particularly the final books of *Paradise Lost* resonate to the betrayed revolutionary zeal of Milton's late pamphlets. They are arranged in "loops of time" or "movements of unredeemed human history" which MacCallum and Summers have outlined. The movement "from peace and corruption to war and violence to the new peace and the new corruption" obviously springs from the Puritanic concern for kairos.[6] It is so pervasive as an organizing principle that although I shall be explicating cycle after cycle in what follows, I shall hardly pause to comment each time on the Puritanic aesthetic being expressed and shaping the presentation of events. What I wish to focus on here is the way in which these repeated loops, which underlay even Puritan military strategy, make it difficult to distinguish the Satanic negation from the faithful affirmation.

The clearest description of what these loops of history are like occurs in book eleven when Michael comments upon the values of martial con-

quest in terms echoing *The Readie and Easie Way*. . . . Victors, men of
"high renown," flourish in an age when

> Might onely shall be admir'd,
> And Valour and Heroic Vertu call'd;
> To overcome in Battle, and subdue
> Nations, and bring home spoils with infinite
> Man-slaughter, shall be held the highest pitch
> Of human Glorie, and for Glorie done
> Of triumph, to be styl'd great Conquerours,
> Patrons of Mankind, Gods, and Sons of Gods,
> Destroyers rightlier call'd and Plagues of men.
> Thus Fame shall be atchiev'd, renown on Earth,
> And what most merits fame in silence hid.   [11:689–99]

The world of the victors, in which men are blasphemously and inaccurately
hyperbolized into godhead and in which things are homicidally destroyed,
attends only to "Glorie" and a false kind of "Fame." What most merits
fame, however, lies hidden and demands an apocalyptic uncovering. Like
all such revelations, this one drives us transcendentally upward toward a
higher heroism out of this world. Milton rationalizes that ascent; mundane
fame and victory are nearly impossible to distinguish from infamy and defeat. Both can become self-defeating, even self-destructive, because the
victors are

> of true vertu void;
> Who having spilt much blood, and don much waste
> Subduing Nations, and achievd thereby
> Fame in the World, high titles, and rich prey,
> Shall change thir course to pleasure, ease, and sloth,
> Surfet, and lust, till wantonness and pride
> Raise out of friendship hostil deeds in Peace.

The vanquished, however, are in much the same boat:

> The conquerd also, and enslav'd by Warr
> Shall with thir freedom lost all vertu loose
> And fear of God, from whom thir pietie feign'd
> In sharp contest of Battel found no aide
> Against invaders; therefore coold in zeale
> Thenceforth shall practice how to live secure,
> Worldlie or dissolute, on what thir Lords
> Shall leave them to enjoy; for th' Earth shall bear
> More then anough, that temperance may be tri'd.   [11:790–805]

Surely, when Milton writes about the vanquished, he has England in mind;

the echoes of *The Readie and Easie Way* . . . are too obvious to miss. More important here, however, is the force of a dialectical movement, in which the thesis of military fame is canceled by its antithesis, defeat, the two collapsing to "inmix" and "conjoin" victors and vanquished, much as Milton "inmixes" and "conjoins" Samson physically with the Philistines in *Samson Agonistes* (ll. 1657, 1666) so that both suffer "the same destruction."

> So all shall turn degenerate, all deprav'd,
> Justice and Temperance, Truth and Faith forgot;
> One Man except, the onely Son of light
> In a dark Age, against example good,
> Against allurement, custom, and a World
> Offended.   [11:806-11]

In this absolute passage, at least, victors and vanquished alike lose all "vertu" and "all" turn degenerate. Not only is it impossible to distinguish one group from the other (which makes any concern for mundane military or political opposition pointless) and difficult to pursue an unredeemed, humane strategy of any sort with success; in addition, we feel ourselves as well as the "One Man" excepted from this world and driven toward that higher heroism which the narrator enunciates at the beginning of book nine, and thereby toward antinomianism.

Paradise Lost opens in the midst of one of those movements of unredeemed history, following a war, building through two books toward a sort of phony and corrupt peace (the claims of which were most strikingly articulated by Belial), and eventuating in Satan's exhortations to further "Warr, then Warr/Open or understood" (2:661-62). The process of cycling through that movement reveals the poverty of Satan's strategies, although as with so many matters in the poem, the issues involved emerge ever more sharply and concretely later, as the poem proceeds.

Satan apparently believes he has two strategic options open to him: open war or covert guile. Both are intelligible only in human terms. The second, sneaky way would win few admirers. The first might gain him that "Fame" which, Milton believes, we too much admire but God ignores. But Satan does not pursue either option; rather he shuffles them together, conjoins them through a series of stagy verbal magic tricks so that they fuse in a strategy which is disgusting from both an unredeemed and a more elevated point of view. For example, he plays a marvelous shell game with the words "force" and "guile" in the first two books. After the narrator has characterized his *modus operandi* correctly as "guile" (1:34), Satan collapses "force or guile" (1:121) to "fraud or guile" (1:646), which does sound similar but isn't. He returns to "open Warr or covert guile" (2:41), but Belial again explodes the fake duality:

> for what can force or guile
> With him, or who deceive his mind, whose eye
> Views all things at one view?   [2:188-90]

Satan seems to understand the first part of the proposition, since he comments that "who overcomes/By force, hath overcome but half his foe"
(1:648-49) and he seems to opt for guile when he speaks of going "Thither, if but to pry" (1:655). Magic enters his speech, however, and he cries
out in conclusion:

> Warr then, Warr
> Open or understood must be resolv'd.   [1:661-62]

"Understood" seems to be the key term, for Adam and Eve do not understand. "First on mee th' assault shall light" struts Adam (9:305), assuming
glibly that Eve is right that "A Foe so proud" would never "first the weaker seek" (9:383). Satan proves to be quite the opposite of "Proud," as
oozing charm from every pore he oils his way around first Sin and Death,
then Gabriel, and finally Eve. All three scenes offer Satan the chance to
strike a blow in open war; he never does. The farcical scene with Sin and
Death sinks the seeming grandeur of Satan's opening rhetorical flourishes
in acts of bathos. Satan and Death face off in the language of epic or
romance, two apparently proud warriors disputing territorial right of way.
The martial flytings are of a piece with all of Satan's *public* speeches in
the first two books; there he consistently seems to assert his opposition to
something, his difference from it (while his private musings reveal the
"covert guile"). When they turn from words which seem to distinguish
one from the other to deeds, however, Satan and Death are syntactically
conjoined in a single, common expectation—"thir fatall hands/No second
stroke intend" (2:712-13)—and

> now great deeds
> Had been achiev'd, whereof all Hell had rung,
> Had not the Snakie Sorceress
> .   .   .   .
> Ris'n, and with hideous outcry rush'd between.   [2:722-26]

It is the first of a whole series of such scenes. Satan confronts Gabriel at
the end of book four, blows himself up grandly like a beach ball (or
Pandaemonium itself) until he "dilated stood." Again

> now dreadful deeds
> Might have ensu'd, nor onely Paradise
> In this commotion, but the Starrie Cope
> Of Heav'n perhaps, or all the Elements
> At least had gon to rack, . . .

> . . . had not soon
> Th' Eternal to prevent such horrid fray
> Hung forth in Heav'n his golden Scales.   [4:990-97]

Michael and Satan share the same expectations as "one stroke they aim'd," and there are verbal similarities between their stroke "Uplifted imminent" (6:317) and "a noble stroke" which Abdiel "lifted high,/Which hung not, but so swift with tempest fell" (6:189-90). Raphael's summary of the military situation includes yet another instance when "great deeds" get checked, interrupted, and disappear as the result of external intervention —this time by God:

> all Heav'n
> Resounded, and had Earth bin then, all Earth
> Had to her Center shook. What wonder? when
> Millions of fierce encountring Angels fought
> On either side, the least of whom could weild
> These Elements, and arm him with the force
> Of all thir Regions: how much more of Power
> Armie against Armie numberless to raise
> Dreadful combustion warring, and disturb,
> Though not destroy, thir happie Native seat;
> Had not th' Eternal King Omnipotent
> From his strong hold of Heav'n high over-rul'd
> And limited thir might.   [6:217-29]

Yet another example occurs when the Father intervenes in the war in heaven at the end of the second day:

> and now all Heav'n
> Had gon to wrack, with ruin overspred,
> Had not th' Almightie Father where he sits
> Shrin'd in his Sanctuarie of Heav'n secure,
> Consulting on the sum of things, foreseen
> This tumult, and permitted all, advis'd.   [6:669-74]

The farcical quality of Satan's encounter with Sin and Death, although not so obvious in other places, infects almost all of his military confrontations.

Obviously, the same thing keeps happening over and over, even to the syntax of sentences. Milton whips up a bit of cosmic, melodramatic froth, then reminds us that his Puritanical God permits all from his throne fixed forever firm and sure. Chaos cannot break out because this fictive world is not melodramatic. The Puritanic sense of repetition may underlie the feeling some readers have that the longer they read about Satan the more

bored they get with him; certainly it is true that few of his apologists draw
their argument from the second half of the poem. It is equally true that
Satan's deeds match the narrator's words; that is, we cannot argue that
Milton simply turns on the voice of the establishment, brings in the narrator to deny these bits of melodrama as part of a divine propaganda campaign. Satan and the angels repeatedly demonstrate, through their *acts,*
that he is correct. Facing Death "the suttle Fiend his lore/Soon learnd,
now milder, and thus answerd smooth" (2:815-16); after God hangs out
his mysterious scales, Satan flees "murmuring." As soon as Eve bites, he
slinks into the bushes. His final appearance dissolves in hisses. He always
instinctively attacks the seeming weaker, his own baby boy, lesser, "unknown" angels, and Eve. He always uses guile rather than the force he
would like us to focus on.

In short, the very constraints which define the sphere of action for a
Puritan soldier of Christ obtain for Satan as well, and the Puritan view of
creaturely action which underlies *Paradise Lost* makes it difficult to tell
the fallen from the unfallen. Neither can win a big, clear-cut victory,
although both expect to. In profound ways the Puritan world view pre-
vents us from choosing heroes, even as it generates a Manichean feeling
that we ought to. Yet, on the surface at least, the process of speech in
Paradise Lost does allow us to make that distinction we are being always
impelled to make. We can distinguish, in very Puritanic ways, between the
motives of faithful joy and Satanic rage. Rage is a Satanic emotion, associated with or attributed to God only through Satanic influence. Of the thirty-
two instances of the word "rage" in *Paradise Lost,* four refer to battle
(1:277; 6:211, 217, 696) and four to the fires of hell (2:171, 213, 581,
600); Turnus (9:16), Cain (11:444), the builders of Babel (12:58), and
Pharoah (12:194) rage. Four times the Satanic crew project the emotion
on God (1:95, 175; 2:144, 268) although admittedly Abdiel, when sur-
rounded by them, also does so once (5:891). These are the only instances
in the poem where God is described as raging. Twelve times the Satanists
feel rage or expect to feel it, far and away the most common use of the
word, which seems to be one effect of hellfire, the wars which the Satanists
provoke, pagan epic, or obvious Biblical sin. After Satan bows to Abdiel's
"stroke" at the beginning of the war in heaven,

> Amazement seis'd
> The Rebel Thrones, but greater rage to see
> Thus foil'd thir mightiest, ours joy filld, and shout,
> Presage of Victorie and fierce desire
> Of Battel.   [6:198-202]

While we might be tempted to explain the joy of the faithful here simply
by noting that they are winning, that cheering "Presage of Victorie" is

fallacious; moreover, other passages show that the two responses are symptomatic of a profound difference between the faithful and fallen troops. For example, in a contrasting situation, where Satan seems momentarily to be winning, he scoffed, "make a scorn," and "derided" God and the faithful angels in what is essentially a joyless humor (6:568, 629, 632–33). He approaches earth and paradise in a rage violent enough to provoke the narrator's plea for some "warning voice" (4:1-10). When Gabriel's sword cleaves him, he leaves the field

> Gnashing for anguish and despite and shame
> To find himself not matchless, and his pride
> Humbl'd by such rebuke, so farr beneath
> His confidence to equal God in power.   [6:340-43]

That is essentially his response: to rage in frustration when his overweening pride smashes into the brick wall of reality—God is omnipotent. The self-destructive attitude matches the suicidal strategy of making war with omnipotence, both articulated in semantically destructive phrases.

In contrast, only at that fleeting moment, after the first salvo from the cannon, when Satan feels "Presage of victory," do the virtuous angels ever experience rage; "thir armour help'd thir harm," and the faithful pause

> A while in trouble; but they stood not long,
> Rage prompted them at length, and found them arms
> Against such hellish mischief fit to oppose.
> Forthwith (behold the excellence, the power
> Which God hath in his mighty Angels plac'd)
> Thir Arms away they threw, and to the Hills
> (For Earth hath this variety from Heav'n
> Of pleasure situate in Hill and Dale)
> Light as the Lightning glimps they ran, they flew   [6:634-42]

to pick up the mountains. The faithful have been doing their best and the situation must be frustrating. Their rage is real. But the two parentheses have a curious effect on the passage as a whole. The first, a providential historian's intrusion giving God the glory in Puritan formulae, discusses "power" and may lead us momentarily to expect some new superweapon. Not so. This is non-military power; "Thir Arms away they threw" in the next line. The second seems to suggest that the earthly pleasures of topographic variety (a sort of physical "grateful vicissitude,"[7] I suppose) derives from heaven. It is an odd point to make just here, but it does associate pleasure (even quite innocent pleasure) rather than rage with the faithful's subsequent acts. A few lines earlier, Satan had been scoffing at God's "Thunder," yet in these lines the pagan conception of the wrathful Jove is lightened with such words as "Lightning glimps," "Light" and the

airy sprightliness of "they ran, they flew." The most important thing about
this passage is the way it shows how the virtuous angels accept the fact that
war makes arms ridiculous in the universe they inhabit; the ease with which
they adapt to this constraint is an index of faithful realism acknowledging
the Puritan constraints on their "Fame." It portrays their act of faithful
recognition by transmuting "rage" into "pleasure," jovial dance, and a
game of throwing mountains. When the Satanic crew "in imitation" of the
faithful "to like Armes/Betook them," they turn that game into "jacula-
tion dire," "dismal shade," and "infernal noise; Warr seem'd a civil Game/
To this uproar" (6:662–63, 665–68). They have mastered only the art of
sinking—here turning a game into a horrid muddle.

A single, small and then a large, general example will clinch the point.
When, on the third day, the Son rides dazzlingly forth in a burst of visual
effects and optical metaphors, he recreates the order of heaven easily and
smilingly, in both senses of recreation. He arrives mounted on a chariot
which is one of the most memorable eyefulls in the poem; "farr off his
coming shon," his chariots "were seen," indeed were "First seen" by "his
own." During his approach he is "Illustrious farr and wide" and attended
by "his Sign in Heav'n" (6:768–76). Under his direction,

> Heav'n his wonted *face* renewd,
> And with fresh Flourets Hill and Valley *smil'd*.
> This *saw* his hapless Foes but stood obdur'd,
> And to rebellious fight rallied thir Powers
> Insensate, hope conceiving from despair.
> In heav'nly Spirits could such perverseness dwell?
> But to convince the proud what *Signs* availe,
> Or Wonders move th' obdurate to relent?
> They hard'nd more by what might most reclame,
> Grieving to *see* his Glorie, at the *sight*
> Took envie, and aspiring to his highth,
> Stood reimbattell'd fierce, by *force or fraud*
> Weening to prosper, and at length prevaile
> . . . or to fall
> In universal ruin last.   [6:783–97, emphases mine]

The visual nature of their response contrasts with the smiling face of
heaven. The Son's "Glory" is expressed in a smiling "Sign"; "force or
fraud" as a *modus operandi* meshes with a despairing, all-or-nothing
militarism which, given the impossibility of the first term, is self-destructive. The passage beautifully portrays a sensibility which cannot stand a
smile, which ignores the sign it contains (that war with omnipotence is
vain since the Son so easily cancels and erases what little the Satanists
have "accomplished"), as well as the self-deceiving and self-destructive

options which pervade the revolt. It accounts for the whole of Satan's enterprise in miniature. God moved, according to his plan, and Satan could not stand that fact; scorn of the reality of the Son leads him to scorn the "puny habitants" of earth, his followers, and ultimately himself.

Furthermore, these ventures always involve a variety of magical tricks. Satan is almost vaudevillian in book ten as he turns invisible, then magically appears stage center cracking sick jokes. Similar is the way he blows himself up like a balloon near the end of book four. He also transmutes situations and words, turning Sin's appalling domestic romance into smooth "lore," the process of "winning cheap the high repute" into "hazard huge" (2:472–73) and "peril great" into a venture "without our hazard" (10:469, 491). Perhaps his most magical verbal trick is to wage war with omnipotence. He is so deeply dyed in this sleight of hand that he seems almost to be taken in by it himself at times. Consider those golden scales which God hangs out at the end of book four. It is, syntactically speaking, impossible to tell precisely what the Father weighs in the two pans:

> Wherein all things created first he weighd,
> The pendulous round Earth with ballanc't Aire
> In counterpoise, now ponders all events,
> Battels and Realms: in these he put two weights
> The sequel each of parting and of fight;
> The latter quick up flew, and kickt the beam. [4:999–1004]

Is Earth balanced against Air, or the two together poised against some other thing? Does the Father make one measurement, or two, or perhaps three if we read "ponders" literally? If more than one, which is the crucial measurement? Finally, God does balance the outcome of battle against the outcome of disengagement. The sequel "of fight" is lighter, but who is to tell whether a light event is better or worse in the eyes of God than a heavy one? Here the magical syntax conjoins Satan with God, both doing sleight of hand, but the most interesting effect is achieved by Gabriel, who tells Satan that he has been weighed and found wanting; whatever else we can say about God's measurements, we certainly never saw him do that. Yet, Satan "knew/His mounted scale aloft" (4:1013–14)—which is much more (but quite possibly also less than) we know.

I have, in effect, been arguing against variations upon the Satanic interpretation of *Paradise Lost,* even though the state of the scholarship in the last decade or so would suggest that these views are not being hotly debated,[8] because the controversy concerning the hero of *Paradise Lost,* simply by virtue of its long-during acrimony, is the single most telling bit of evidence of the commitment which went into the writing of the poem. Michael Wilding has recently argued, by conflating *Paradise Lost* with

Hudibras, that the antimilitaristic sentiments in both attest to a common
world-weariness and loss of commitment.[9] True, Wilding can only make
his case by conflating men of widely different political sentiments; that
very juxtaposition makes his analysis apolitical, and it is not surprising
that he arrived at the view that Butler and Milton were similarly apolitical.
But more important, Wilding's arguments are merely a recent expression
of a long tendency among many of Milton's readers to suggest that *Paradise
Lost* represents some sort of *recovery from* the period of political commitment. Generally, that view has been most advocated by the more insistent
apologists for Milton's God, that is, by men whose impulse has been to
deny the persistence of Satanic analysis.[10] Yet, nothing in the history of
comment upon the poem suggests that a Satanic interpretation will permanently disappear. Everything about the history of criticism, the shifts
in taste we see there, and the persistence of this one debate, suggests that
Satan will find his future apologists again.

When he does, we shall rejoin a discussion inspired by Milton's com-
mittedness and the curious effects it wrought in his verse. A comparison
with the other great "secondary epic"—the *Aeneid*—will clarify this matter.
The hero of that poem is forcibly submerged, as an individual, in much
larger, national issues. But, even if Aeneas is as anonymous as any character in *Paradise Lost,* even if the point of his actions lies as far outside himself as it does for them, we have not, historically, worried very much as
critics about who is the center of that poem. When Aeneas finally strikes
Turnus, he says he does so as agent of Pallas, much as the Puritan soldiers
do in God's name during the war in heaven, yet finally, *"hoc dicens ferrum
adverso sub pectore condit fervidus."*[11] It is Aeneas who strikes openly in
the syntax as well as in the sense, in marked contrast to the fact that only
eleven offhand lines in *Paradise Lost* name any angels who committed the
military verbs (6:362–72). In every *major* bellicose encounter where a
blow falls, Milton consistently and exclusively employed metonomy and
through that circumlocution made his military heroes even more anonymous than Aeneas, who does, after all, win what ironic glory attaches to
"condit." Similarly, critics of the *Aeneid* have never generated anything
like the debate concerning the ideology of *Paradise Lost;* there is no
question of whether Virgil was secretly of the anti-imperial party, for
instance, despite the fact that we may feel Virgil understood some of the
limits of empire. Something, or perhaps a lack of something at the center
of *Paradise Lost* keeps that kind of question boiling. The Puritan epic puts
us on an aesthetic merry-go-round in pursuit of a hero and an ideology we
can never quite reach and hold on to. Consider all the possible heroes
critics have nominated—Satan, God, the Son, Adam, the "epic voice," the
reader. There seem to be so many possible heroes because Milton is redefining heroism. He is attempting to raise us above mere mortal concep-

tions and carnal confidence in arms, much as a Puritan divine would wish. That is, the difficulty we have working out the ideology of the poem (and by implication its hero) derives from its consummate expression of the incoherence at the heart of Puritan political analysis.

So far I have, as the explicator of process of speech, been working at the surface. The deeper psychological structure seems to me another matter, and its nature is suggested by the variety of heroes which have been proposed. For the fact is that in a profound way, all of these nominees converge into a single figure—the Father. It is the self-consuming convergence which is essential. There are pre-eminently two splendid isolates—the Father and Satan. Locked into his own conniving in such a way that he cannot truly share his thoughts even with his followers, Satan is obviously and profoundly alone, a would-be intelligence agent in Eden. On the other hand, Adam and the Father agree between them, when discussing the creation of Eve, that the central thing which distinguishes God from all his creatures is his solitariness (8:403–33). William Riggs has recently returned to the point, which needed restating, that the narrator and Satan share a number of common traits.[12] The narrator purports to know more than any mortal can, as Anne Ferry made abundantly clear in passing;[13] it is a wise child who knows its own begetting, Telemachus remarked acutely, and the Goddess of Wisdom commended him, in case we have any doubts about his sagacity. Yet this narrator says he knows about the beginnings not only of himself but of the whole universe, knowledge which, coolly considered, we can only attribute to the begetter himself. Adam's whole history in this poem is focused on trying things unattempted yet; we weep for the most obvious of those things, yet we rejoice, at the end, when he commends an angel for measuring the whole "Race of time" (12:554). Whether or not Milton's readers are few, the poem tacitly assumes they share this prodigious ability with Michael, Adam, and Milton. Indeed, it is the readers who are probably most exalted of all, since they are expected not only to measure the race of time but to appreciate (which first implies literally comprehending) God's just ways. The deep core, which contributes to our confusion about the ideology of this poem, is self-deification, the extreme toward which antinomianism tends, the ultimate expression of that transcendent pressure in Puritan thinking, the last, great attempt to distance oneself from politics by rising above one's fellow men. As all these heroes aim to merge themselves (and their abilities) with God, they participate in a Puritan experience of the sort which clothed the Son, in discussions about bowing at the name of Jesus, in the language and attributes of the Father.

The case for Satan might have been more forcibly made, had it not been argued in defiance and opposition to the Father but rather in conjunction with him and all the other characters. I shall not pursue the point that Satan resembles those other characters in more, and more important ways than he differs from them, but were such an argument advanced, it might provide an explosive picture of the deep structure and the emotional core of the poem, and in addition give us a more humane view of the author. It seems to me that Milton was not secretly of the devil's party because that is not the way human beings behave. It seems prodigious to assume that Milton stated he was justifying the ways of God, spun out a poem of such considerable length, and did all that so that secretly he could show just the opposite; such a position deals very nearly in secret codes and crucial "keys." No more does it seem to me likely that Milton was simply of God's party, since his poem provokes more debate than almost any religious utterance one can name. Both positions suffer from absolutism, admittedly not surprising in responses to this poem. Rather, it seems to me more likely that Milton was of two minds about the issues of individualism and authority which raged about him, that a conflict within was the source of an apparent if ultimately somewhat hazy polarity on the surface, that the tension he experienced led him, if anything, to try to overpolarize the issues in his fable, but that the fact that his was basically a unified rather than split personality accounts for the haziness which still troubles us.

Still, I cannot let this matter of choosing heroes go, because consensus on this matter seems to be impossible to establish. Men choose heroes, or label a character a hero, for many different reasons. That is, of course, true of any literary work. Dryden chose Satan for structural reasons; the action of an epic was to begin with the hero *in medias res.* Yet, of course, that and a whole host of other structural approaches run into trouble when, for example, we ask what the action being imitated here is, who completes the action, etc. No character in the poem is clearly and unequivocally the hero because Milton devotes most lines to him; Satan disappears totally in books seven, eight, eleven, and twelve, Adam does not appear until book four, God may be implicit in every line but does not show explicitly in enough to give him, or for that matter the Son, a clear edge. When we ask which character most fascinated Milton, we are probably also in part asking which character most fascinates us, and clearly the personal values of the critic have a great deal to do with defining the hero. In *Paradise Lost and Its Critics,* A. J. A. Waldock scoffed at the received wisdom concerning Milton—that he was a consummate artist—and relished the sneering Satan as his hero. The more straightforward and self-possessed critics, like Empson, have candidly admitted to personal bias.[14] Further, the dance of scholarly controversy has become formalized over the years; we know fairly well, by now, what the implications of one position or another will be. And that too, even though it may have nothing to do with this particular poem, makes the choosing of heroes feel arbitrary.

All of these factors, some admittedly not specific to *Paradise Lost,* must enter into and perplex the thinking of any self-possessed critic. But there are other, more crucial matters affecting this decision as well. On the one hand, we judge Satan only within the context of the universe Milton has articulated. That world view is so forcibly stated that we often forget it is a fiction, as when C. S. Lewis argued that Satan degenerated physically when in fact it is the language, particularly the similies and metaphors, used to *talk about* Satan which degenerates. Take away the Puritan universe of overarching permissiveness, and Satan might appear quite different; perhaps, again, that is true of all fictions and their characters, yet when we condemn Satan, we often fall into the same absolute language which Milton seems to use. Few of us really accept all the features of the universe which Milton drew, yet the condemnations of Satan often read as though we did.

Most important, however, the question of choosing heroes seems to me essential to the experience of most readers of the poem, and perhaps reflects something of the dialectic of the poem itself. It is hard not to begin reading the poem for the first time without feeling, in the first hundred lines, that we must make choices. Few sensitive readers of the poem have not, at some moment in their lives, been attracted to Satan. Yet the pressure to choose God, the faithful, and Adam or else Satan persists, the search for ways to distinguish the two groups persists, and ultimately, as I have tried to show, the surface asks us to choose to reject Satan, because he has no fun in his life, because he cannot see or tolerate the reality within which he exists, because he is suicidally bent on a self-defeating mission, because he destroys the meaning of words themselves with his verbal tricks and his war on omnipotence.

One of the anomalies of Ginsberg's chant in Chicago in 1968 was that it was a song of reconciliation in a setting of polarized conflict. Both elements seem to me to be contained within *Paradise Lost,* for its ostensible subject and its aggressive tone embody a sense of polarization and contention while its deity, his mercy, the regeneration of Adam, and the ways in which all of the characters tend to merge point toward reconciliation. Reconciliation *seems* to be embodied particularly in the Son, defiance and lack of submission in Satan, yet Satan persistently caves in, slinks off, disappears, while the Son and Adam can successfully pose challenging questions to the Father and work out problems. We are not reading either a political or a theological tract when we read this poem, although certain theologizing critics have seemed to deny the latter part of that statement. The diversity of the interpretations offered reminds us that the poem does succeed as a poem, polysemously, and that means that we cannot absolutely dismiss Satan from our thinking. At the same time, this polysemous poeticalness dampens the sense of clear-cut ideology; Ginsberg's chant was not politically efficacious since the strife about him continued, and perhaps no poetry can be, simply because it is profoundly ambivalent in order that it succeed as poetry. Still, it seems wise not to forget the sense of strife at work here, telling upon the reader, informing the acrimony of the criticism written about the poem. That is the expression of commitment, and when yoked with themes of reconciliation it produces a heightened version of the Puritan political analysis, with all its attractions and its limitations.

Chapter 15: THE SON: THE HERO AS EXPRESSIVE DEFINITION

The Son is an obviously Puritanic candidate for hero in this poem. His subordination to the Father logically extends the way Puritans deemphasized the second person of the Trinity; his mediatorial action in book three occurs before time. His mode of speaking, featuring "me" rather than "I," places him as syntactic object within a larger, circumscribing framework—paternal control. Rendered both before time and before the reader has read about the fall, his act is motiveless and points beyond intervening human history to the new heaven and earth. There are, in addition, two other ways in which he functions Puritanically: precisely in his role as expressive agent of the Father he serves to define the deity, and he does so in the Puritan mode of elaborating controversy;[1] secondly, insofar as even he does not exert transitive, decisive, syntactical control over his enemies, he resembles the creaturely heroes in the epic. In effect, that second fact elevates the faithful creatures in an antinomian way; if the Son is like them, then they are themselves godlike. The Son is, as a result, an exemplar of the "one just man."

His victory expresses, as does his merit, the new optimism which sprang out of Puritan polemic. Checking "His Thunder in mid Volie" (6:854) as he routs the damned, he rides

O're Shields and Helmes, and helmed heads . . .
Of Thrones and mighty Seraphim *prostrate*. [6:840–41, emphasis mine]

They are indeed prostrate; he does not knock them down, for immediately before, the enemy "all resistance lost,/All courage; down thir idle weapons drop'd" (6:838–39). The almost self-conscious reining in and checking of transitive power persists right to the end of the battle. As the walls of heaven open wide to disclose "the wastful Deep; the monstrous sight/Strook" the Satanic crew "with horror backward, but far worse/ Urg'd them behind" (6:862–64). The most obvious antecedent for "worse" is "sight," and while it is true that the sight of the Son (who has "into terrour chang'd/His count'nance" [6:824–25]) and that chariot of blazing eyeballs and lightning would indeed be terrifying, it seems to exert a visual rather than visceral sort of force upon the damned:

                                    headlong themselves they threw
Down from the verge of Heav'n, Eternal wrauth
Burnt after them to the bottomless pit.   [6:864-66]

Presumably if they had lingered, "Eternal wrauth" would have forcibly
impelled them; my point is that the Son, even on the day of his victory,
does not exert ultimately compelling force upon his enemies. He is cast
in the mold of the Puritan hero, even though he is, quite clearly, not an
earthly hero.

   Paradise Lost unfolds in much the manner of Puritan theology. Both
are processes of self-revelation, self-analysis, and self-elaboration. The first
five lines of the poem articulate the whole theme much as early, short
statements of Puritan belief had; they form part of a slightly larger unit of
twenty-six lines which does the same thing at greater length. And the poem
eddies out from this central, thematic statement, unfolding the implications
of five lines in larger and larger cycles, moving gradually toward that point
where the "doctrines" developed in the first part may be applied pragmatically by characters and the reader to events in this world. To put it another
way, the poem unfolds and displays the nature of the divine impulse, a
movement of release outward into creative multiplicity and then a movement back toward God who shall again in the last days be "all in all."

   The theological formulae of the doctrine of subordination are *dramatically expressed* by the Son in one of the most important phases of that
self-elucidating rhythm. The Son makes visible "what by Deitie" the
Father is (6:682). The visual metaphors which cluster around his military
victory are only one example of the way he functions as "Effulgence" of
God's glory. There are repeated "transfusions" of power and might outward from the Father or his speeches through the Word into creative acts.
In short, the Son is subordinated to the Father in a sort of Platonic scheme
of Idea and physical reality while at the same time he unfolds and justifies
(in the absolute sense of expressing outwardly the essential justness of the
informing Idea) the Father. That is, presumably, part of what Milton
planned for his poem as a whole. Clearly it captures the essence of the
central, Puritanic mode of expression at work in controversial prose as
well.

   In further illustrating that point, I do not wish to involve myself in the
debate over Milton's trinitarianism and his Christology. It is not to my
purpose to trace his views back to some single source nor to split hairs
concerning the nature and degree of his subordinationism. Popular sermon
fare of his own age offered plenty of examples of a loose, casual tendency
to disregard the equality of Father and Son. That orthodox Puritan habit
of mind was not, therefore, idiosyncratic to Milton nor did he have to dig
back in dusty tomes to find models for what he thought. Moreover, it
seems unlikely that a man of Milton's independence would concern him-

self very much with models; he certainly did not when arguing his ideas about divorce, for it was only after he had published his views that he uncovered Bucer's remarks on the subject. Highly articulate, he was capable of stating his views for himself; it is not to my purpose whether Milton read Arminius or any other single theologian. Nor do I wish to pursue the question of how firmly and thoroughly he subordinated Son to Father; the wonderfully fluid medium of his verse is, first of all, ambiguous and seems designed to frustrate all attempts to extract its doctrinal marrow. While the urge may be strong to treat this poem Puritanically, it seems wise to realize that attempting to extract precise doctrine from a poem is, in this case, primarily a response (accurate indeed) to the Puritanic sensibility at work; that is no reason to dig the mine, however. There is abundant evidence that some sort of subordination occurs, but that comes not from the few abstract formulations of what look like "doctrine" in the poem (generally mined by critics at work extracting the *medulla theologiciae* of Milton's subordination) but rather from scenes which dramatize the Son's expressive and revelatory or apocalyptic function. The Son acts out his role as "Bright Essence" in perfect harmony with the cyclically apocalyptic movement of the poem as a whole, and it is that latter, basic process, which I wish to elucidate here.

In at least four central, symmetrically arranged places in the poem, the Father "transfuses" his power to or through the Son. In doing so, the Father speaks of his plans and the Word becomes manifest in the Son, who elaborates upon it both verbally and in action as he extends the Father's meaning. In the process the Son as medium becomes the acting message. The most sustained of these transfusions occupies most of book seven and balances against a more sharply militaristic example at the end of book six. I shall work outward from these two examples at the center of the poem.

At the end of book seven, the angelic choir calls our attention to the way in which books six and seven embody the essence of the divine plan— bringing good out of evil.

> Great are thy works, *Jehovah,* infinite
> Thy power; what thought can measure thee or tongue
> Relate thee; greater now in thy return
> Then from the Giant Angels; thee that day
> Thy Thunders magnifi'd; but to create
> Is greater then created to destroy.   [7:602-7]

We see the beginnings of this creative or recreative process even during the martial exploits of book six, when the Son rides forth to rescue us and the universe from impending chaos. The Satanists have muddled both heaven and even the game of war. What connects that moment when "all Heav'n/

Had gon to wrack" with the Son's victory on the "third sacred Morn" is neither strategy nor time. God does not call a ceasefire nor does Raphael mention the passing of the night between. Instead, the Father assesses the situation and begins to transfuse his power to the Son. Having "foreseen/ This tumult, and permitted all" (6:673–74), the Father speaks; as he describes the nature of the Son he simultaneously tells us precisely what he will do:

> Effulgence of my Glorie, Son belov'd,
> Son in whose face invisible is beheld
> Visibly, what by Deitie I am,
> And in whose hand what by Decree I doe,
> Second Omnipotence.   [6:680–84]

In so few words he has initiated the process whereby the Son will realize, visually, verbally, and in act, the mysterious tautology of the name Jehovah or "what by Deitie I am." Then he tells the Son:

> Into thee such Vertue and Grace
> Immense I have transfus'd, that all may know
> In Heav'n and Hell thy Power above compare,
> And this perverse Commotion governd thus,
> To manifest thee worthiest to be Heir
> Of all things, to be Heir and to be King
> By Sacred Unction, thy deserved right.
> Go then thou Mightiest in thy Fathers might,
> Ascend my Chariot, guide the rapid Wheeles
> That shake Heav'ns basis, bring forth all my Warr,
> My Bow and Thunder, my Almightie Arms
> Gird on, and Sword upon thy puissant Thigh;
> Pursue these sons of Darkness, drive them out
> From all Heav'ns bounds into the utter Deep.   [6:703–16]

The transition between this speech of the Father and the Son's response dramatizes the transfer of power:

> He said, and on his Son with Rayes direct
> Shon full, he all his Father full expresst
> Ineffably into his face receiv'd,
> And thus the filial Godhead answering spake.   [6:719–22]

The most fascinating words here are "expresst" and "answering." As we first read the lines, "expresst" seems to be predicated to the Son; however, as so often happens in Milton's verse, once we turn the corner at the end of the line and read on into the next, we realize that it may be predicated to the Father, modifying "all." Wavering syntactically in this way at the end of the line in a manner beloved by Milton, the word suggests that somehow the Son received the Father's speech (which is, of course, what he has most immediately expressed in context) into his face and made it visual. The partial redundancy of "answering spake" may further suggest that the Son's face and voice "answer" to what the Father has said. In the speech which follows this dramatic transition, the Son accepts the Father's "Scepter and Power" until he shall resign them "when in the end/Thou shalt be All in All" (6:731-32). The flow of power out from the Father will be completed when that power returns to him.

Something like this happens with the diction. As the Father describes how he is transfusing power to the Son, his verbs and nouns become more concretely military. He instructs the Son to "go," "ascend," "guide," "bring forth," "gird on," "pursue," and "drive." He mentions his "might," "Chariot," "Wheeles," "Warr," then breaks the latter vague term down into "Bow and Thunder," "Almightie Arms," and "Sword." When the Son ascends "Triumphant through mid Heav'n" (6:889) at the end of battle, the trip is only briefly described. But as he reascends after creation in book seven to the

> holy mount
> Of Heav'ns high-seated top, th' Impereal Throne
> Of Godhead, fixt for ever firm and sure,   [7:584-86]

action and diction grow progressively more blurred, vague, ethereal:

> Up he rode
> Followd with acclamation and the sound,
> Symphonious of ten thousand Harpes that tun'd
> Angelic harmonies: the Earth, the Aire
> Resounded, (thou remember'st, for thou heardst)
> The Heav'ns and all the Constellations rung,
> The Planets in thir station list'ning stood,
> While the bright Pomp ascended jubilant.   [7:557-64]

First the "Harpes," then "Earth," "Aire," "Heav'ns," and "Constellations," and finally the most nebulous "Pomp" act in their clauses, while the verbs become increasingly less vivid—"tun'd," "Resounded," "rung," "stood" (which together with "station" is almost redundantly static), and "ascended."

The same sort of transfer or transfusion is handled fairly briefly and pointedly in book seven. The Father announces his plan to create "Another World," and tells the Son:

> And thou my Word, begotten Son, by thee
> This I perform, speak thou, and be it don:

My overshadowing Spirit and might with thee
I send along.   [7:163–66]

The narrator again restates the transfer:

So spake th' Almightie, and to what he spake
His Word, the Filial Godhead, gave effect.   [7:174–75]

The words beautifully realize John's Gospel, for the "Word" functions momentarily both as object of "spake" and as subject of "gave." The Son as "Word" is uttered here and then he gives effect to that utterance, his expressive role condensed into a single word. A few lines later the narrator again summarizes: "all his Father in him shon" (l. 196). The rest of the book merely acts the transfer out at length.

Just as the transfer in book seven is more brief and pointed than that in six, so generally the further we proceed through the poem, the more baldly the lines articulate this transfer as the truth of the matter emerges through repetition and elaboration. The most diffuse example occurs in book three, the most pointed in book ten. In book three, the Son, "the radiant image of His Glory," serves as expressive catalyst not only for action but also for speech, drawing out and clarifying "that word which clos'd/Thy sovran sentence, that Man should find grace" (3:144–45). The Father's first speech is, in tone and diction, primarily judgmental; the short, harsh term "ingrate" sets the mood for much of it. It seems impossible to argue, as Fish has tried to do, that the Father speaks the truth tonelessly, and Fish not only must shift his critical grounds but further belie the experience of countless readers when he argues the point (pp. 81–87). But Fish astutely noticed how the scene expands through progressive definition in a typically Puritanic schema. The first speech begins with judgment but *ends* on "grace" as it narrows the discussion from "Mercy and Justice both" to "Mercy first and last" which "shall brightest shine" (3:132–34). The speech is a microcosm of the whole scene, which moves from Old Testament justice to the new mercy in a loose but clear way, and embodies in diction and motif the proposition that God brings good out of evil by bringing mercy out of justice. "Ingrate" is far from the last word on the subject, and if it colors our response to the rest of the scene as we read (coming first as it does), it is nevertheless clearly balanced by the merciful thrust of the Son's expressive function. Twice the Son prompts the Father that "thy word is past, man shall find grace" (3:227), the second time as he volunteers to descend on man's behalf. The scene as a whole (particularly the Son's act of obedient volunteering) unfolds and clarifies the issues raised by this first word on the subject; it defines through elaboration just as Puritan controversy had done.

Book three is probably the most Puritanic moment of the poem for the reader, not because Milton's God calls him "ingrate," but because Milton

risks poetic disaster by bringing in the Truth speaking. It enunciates the
simple, "comfortable" proposition that mercy flows from or flowers
together with justice, and book ten will dramatize that "doctrine" pragmatically. God speaks here like a school divine in the "plain style" because
Puritan school divines, by all odds the most systematic men of their time,
desired to see like God and speak in a verbal medium as close to his as
possible.[2] Systematic divinity as a literary form seems directed, first and
foremost, to dissolving our sense of "process of speech." Only a certain
type of highly abstractive, transcendental mind reads such stuff to be
"moved." Like the narrator, this scene and its "plain style" suggests that
there is a kernel of truth to be extracted here; Fish has indirectly made
the point that we respond to this scene in a Puritan manner, suggesting
that the reader accepts the Father and Son as authority figures here; the
first two books have in a host of ways been so disorienting that the confused reader is looking and pleading for "the answer to it all" and welcomes the forceful, accurate plain talk. The argument may be a bit
ingenious since it will not explain the fact that readers have persistently
been put off by the scene, yet it seems to address itself to something
essential to the poem. Insofar as this "plain speaking" does reassure us,
it demonstrates that the Puritan mode might indeed be moving.

   Just as book three follows and is colored by our response to the first
two books, so book ten follows "the hainous and despightfull act" (10:1).
If we are not entirely certain, as we read book three, that we merit the
term "ingrate," we probably vicariously participate in Adam's sense of
guilt as we turn to ten; Milton does nothing to alleviate our feeling that
something terrible has happened and something terrible must occur in
reaction. The Father harps on "Justice," on "the mortal Sentence,"
"Judgement," and judging (10:47-55), but between them, he and the
Son turn that language around to mercy. Characteristically, the Father
first announces the doctrine and his plan:

> Easie it might be seen that I intend
> Mercie collegue with Justice, sending thee
> Mans Friend, his Mediator, his design'd
> Both Ransom and Redeemer voluntarie,
> And destin'd Man himself to judge Man fall'n.   [10:58-62]

A brief transition again transfuses power to the Son, albeit more vividly
than ever before:

> So spake the Father, and unfoulding bright
> Toward the right hand his Glorie, on the Son
> Blaz'd forth unclouded Deitie; he full
> Resplendent all his Father manifest
> Express'd, and thus divinely answer'd milde.   [10:63-67]

"Blaz'd" is the most vigorous verb to describe this process in the poem, violently suggesting the judgmental fire of Sinai; moreover, as it is followed by "unclouded Deitie," it can be transitive as well as intransitive. Again Milton stacks participles in such a way as to make their actors uncertain and to suggest that the Son expressed all that the Father had made manifest in his opening speech. The Son amplifies the Father's remarks by elaborating on his own motives. The Father knows (because he has always planned it that way) that

> Whoever judg'd, the worst on mee must light,
> When time shall be, for so I undertook
> Before thee; and not repenting, this obtaine
> Of right, that I may mitigate thir doom
> On me deriv'd, yet I shall temper so
> Justice with Mercie, as may illustrate most
> Them fully satisfied, and thee appease.   [10:73-79]

It is indeed "easie" to see what is happening here. The Son's speech redefines "judging" by tempering and mitigating it.

Building on our vicarious sense of guilt, Milton baldly turns a "blaze" into something "milde," directly confronts our fearful expectations with the divine sense of mercy, establishes motives for Father and Son which come closest to making their love anthropomorphically understandable of any of these scenes, and by referring again to book three (when the Son "undertook" this merciful mission), glosses the issues of that earlier, somewhat diffuse and abstract exchange with a pragmatic, concrete, easily seen and realized act. When we understand that "justice" will light on the Son, we perceive a motive impelling him to mitigate that justice, which he obviously does. Moreover, the transfer of power occurs here in a construction, centering on "blaze," at once vivid and more nearly transitive than any other transfusion. The process of unfolding the definition of God's plan enters, with the beginning of book ten, a phase of application and "uses." The last three, redemptive books, portraying as a whole the process of Christian regeneration which concludes the poem, manage to turn many readers around, mentally, in their attitude toward God and the fall. Few of Satan's apologists draw their arguments from his last appearance; conversely, the apologists for God thrive on the later books. The latter argue most easily from such a scene as this and occasionally lament God's first appearance in the poem. Indeed, readers who find the last two books feeble or lax may do so precisely because they easily can see what the Father intends. Mercy began quite clearly to temper justice in the first lines of the poem, we can see if we read retrospectively, but repetition and elaboration are required to set forth this essential divine program as we first read because at first we simply don't believe it. We begin most com-

pletely to believe it when we can see it applied concretely to another man
and, by extension, to us. Then we are prepared to read retrospectively—by
the concrete "uses" of the last three books.

Milton's God is always doing the same thing in a self-revealing way. The
apocalyptic urge, so much a part of having Truth speak God's mind directly to us, creates the contrast between two key pauses—in book two and in
book three. In the former, the Satanic debaters have gotten off the subject
—"open Warr or covert guile"—and Beelzebub and Satan have the task of
reversing the flow of debate and snuffing out "popular vote" (2:313) in
order to consolidate Satan's emotionally based political power. They have
to stage that dramatic moment when Satan can step forward to volunteer.
Drama derives from a pause in the conversation, and Milton pumps in
added suspense with words like "expectation," "suspence," and "awaiting"
(2:417-18). No such inflation seems necessary for the pause in book three
when "all the Heav'nly Quire stood mute." This pause flows directly out
of the conversation between Father and Son, particularly out of the joyous
tendencies of the Son's prompting the Father to reveal his merciful plan.
Events proceed naturally through divine transfusion in the way they inevitably must. The narrator is almost Satanic in book two, calling our
attention to the fear which the damned felt but *not* to the fear which we
should feel. In contrast, he speaks the plain truth in book three, matching
the style of the Father:

> on mans behalf
> Patron or Intercessor none appeerd,
>
> .   .   .   .
>
> And now without redemption all mankind
> Must have bin lost, adjudg'd to Death and Hell
> By doom severe.   [3:218-24]

Both scenes occur before the fall, before the poem has really provided us
with any compelling reason to notice the implications of the action *for us.*
Yet, because of the narrator's plain style in book three, we may fear a
threat to us at precisely the moment when that threat is being theologically lifted from us by the Son; paradoxically, as Satan formulates what is
the real threat to us, in book two, we may not even notice, our attention
directed to the fear of the fallen. Repetition of a situation—here a "pause"
—and an act—divine transfusion—uncovers and makes clearer for us the
issues, even so early in the poem. If painful at first reading, the narrator's
honesty and openness in book three appears, in retrospect, ultimately
merciful as well.

As the Son, in his subordinated yet definitively expressive role, acts
out the nature of the Father and his plan, he resembles a Puritan soldier.
My point is not simply that he checks his thunder in mid-volley or employs

the "me" of divine agent rather than "I" of individual heroism. Rather, I am thinking of the paradox at the heart of Puritan revolutionary preaching—that God will prevail yet his earthly Saints must fight the battles of the Lord. The Son shows us how men could resolve for themselves the dilemma of that paradox; their acts simply make manifest God's loving plan. Infused with the mana of their triumphant Father, quite literally enthusiasts, these sons of God apocalyptically uncovered and revealed God's overarching glory in the act of marching resolutely out to battle. As they struck a blow at Antichrist, they too became the effulgence of God's glory.

Chapter 16: THE FATHER: THE HERO AS PERMISSIVE PARENT

Perhaps the most incredible of all the paradoxes generated by *Paradise Lost* derives from Milton's portrayal of the Father. He is, on the one hand, unbelievably different from all his creatures, yet in a most curious way he is like them. He exerts overarching control of his universe yet at the same time checks that control and permits all. He is the source and center of all power yet in myriad ways he refrains from using it. Above all creatures, he is nonetheless a distinctly Puritan hero as he operates in this strange poem.

We may uncover this paradox in several ways. One derives from the Son's role as definitive agent, a role which strongly implies that the Father is more nearly invisible than the Son. When Milton cast the Son as definitive agent to the Father, something very like the secularization of Puritan thought seems to have been at least partially at work. For example, on the verbal level Seymour Chatman is right that God imperceptibly exerts his control over the creation through past participles;[1] yet on the surface, he gets elided and does not appear as actor. Theoretically, the Son's subordinated role suggests a similar paradox, that God is radically other than his creatures and must be accommodated to them by the "Effulgence" of his "Glorie" (6:680), and on the other hand, that without that expressive agent, the Father would in effect be held incommunicado by his own nature. The problem with a God who has been elevated so far above us as the Puritan God had been is that he may simply disappear; out of sight, out of mind. In short, the role of the Son distills for us one of the essential tensions of Puritan thought. Just at that moment when one has succeeded in elevating and glorifying God one may become so confident about this world that one will at least partially begin to forget him. *Paradise Lost* asserts with probably greater force than any contemporary poem that God is just, and simultaneously has raised graver doubts about his justice than any of its time, at least for some of its readers. The next logical step in the case of the disappearing God would seem to be *Samson Agonistes*. Although God has completely disappeared from the action of that poem, we can scarcely bear to question whether he justly controls the events and draws his champion back to him. If Samson and God do not act in concert, then Samson is merely a socially disruptive suicide and the madness of Swift's age reigns.

Returning to *Paradise Lost,* we may again notice that, if the Son truly expresses and defines the Father (the source of all power), and if the Son habitually checks "His Thunder in mid Volie," then even the overarching power of the Father must be equally self-checking and in the mode of Puritan heroism. In actual fact, this line of reasoning is borne out by the drama of the poem. Theologically speaking, the Father checks or limits his control of events when he asserts so very strongly that man is free. All his rational creatures, both angels and men, who have that power of choice, are sufficient to have stood, yet free to fall:

> Freely they stood who stood, and fell who fell.
> Not free, what proof could they have givn sincere
> Of true allegiance, constant Faith or Love,
> Where onely what they needs must do, appeard,
> Not what they would? what praise could they receive?
> What pleasure I from such obedience paid,
> When Will and Reason (Reason also is choice)
> Useless and vain, of freedom both despoild,
> Made passive both, had servd necessitie,
> Not mee.   [3:102–11]

The calculus of pleasure which the Father employs here may seem niggling and defensive, a way of worming out of the question of his responsibility for the fall which this radical poem keeps raising in its very effort to rebut it. But in the same breath, God permissively surrenders a great deal to his creatures here. He articulates the very basis of the newly emergent, Puritan optimism and he explains why the word "merit" is so often repeated and so theologically central to *Paradise Lost.* If not his thunder, God does here clearly check his control of the creatures in "mid Volie" and at the same time he damns them as ingrates, releases them to Christian liberty.

This self-limiting, permissive stance flowers in book seven. Milton's most magnificent lines there delineate not what God did but what his creatures did, of themselves, in response to the initial divine creative impulse. We can see this most clearly when we consider what Milton added to Genesis. In Genesis God controls as subject the action of every sentence but one in the entire story of creation. The single exception, Genesis 1.12 ("And the earth brought forth grass, and herb yielding seed after his kind, and the tree yielding fruit, whose seed was in itself, after his kind.") restates verbatim a command which God has just given explicitly in Genesis 1.11; there, of course, he does exercise overarching syntactic control. Milton added to Genesis whole passages in which God does not figure verbally at all. The profusion of verbs which Milton's muse employs in book seven and the cosmic dance they spell out enable the creatures to follow the divine lead, to respond to his gestures on their own. Book seven is a cosmic dance, but it is far more than a rehash of Sir John Davies's *Orchestra*, for it embodies syntactically a *mutuality* of effort in a circular movement. The creator begins, the creation responds, and the creator completes as action returns to him, both within the individual days and through the story as a whole.

The simplest way to account for the liveliness of the creation in Raphael's narrative is to trace out, in a representative list of verbs, the pattern Milton weaves in assigning subjects and thus naming actors. During the first two days, the creator alone figures as the actor in the sentences. But, beginning with the third day, the creation begins to act in response. At 7:279, the waters "Fermented the great Mother to conceave." The mountains "appeer Emergent," and "thir broad bare backs upheave"; the waters "Hasted" and "uprowld," and "found thir way"; the rivers "stream," and "draw thir humid traine." God calls them good, resuming briefly his role as actor. Then the earth "Brought forth the tender Grass," and vegetation "clad" earth, "sudden flour'd," "made gay," "forth flourish't," "forth crept," and "up stood." Finally the trees "Rose as in Dance," "spred," and "gemm'd thir blossoms." A dew "Went up" to conclude creaturely activity in 7:334. On the fourth day, God again acts—he "made," "set," "fram'd," "form'd," "sowd," "took," and "plac'd" the heavenly bodies or lights, in 7:346-63. But then, from 7:370 to 7:386, he again relinquishes control. The "Dawn and the *Pleiades* before him danc'd/ Shedding sweet influence," the moon, "borrowing her light," "keepes," "shines," and "holds," stars "appeer'd/Spangling," and "bright Luminaries . . . Set and Rose."

On the fifth and sixth days, the creation is even more active. First "God created the great Whales, and each/Soul living, each that crept, which plenteously/The waters generated by thir kindes" (7:391-93). With the verb "generate" activity passes from creator to creature, each kind emerging, showing itself, frolicking in an incredible array of verbs and participles. The sense of emerging upward, prevailing in previous descriptions, culminates as the earth gives birth:

> out of the gound up rose
> As from his Laire the wilde Beast where he wonns.　　　[7:456-57]

Animals "rose, they walk'd," they "upsprung," while "Clods now Calv'd," and the lion "half appeer'd . . . pawing to get free/His hinder parts, then springs." This sort of activity concludes as

> Aire, Water, Earth,
> By Fowl, Fish, Beast, was flown, was swum, was walkt
> Frequent.　　　[7:502-4]

This odd passive construction draws our attention to the activity of the creatures and emphasizes it first by parallellism and then by syntactic inversion.

As his final gesture of making, God "formd," "breath'd," "created," and "bless'd" man into being and "brought" him into and "gave" him Eden (7:524–30). Having initiated the creation, God concludes it by forming its capstone. But if a cycle ends here, the dance and the cycles go on. For example, we have already learned, in book three, that God released man to choose on his own. As a result, God here simultaneously closes one cycle by resuming control and initiates a second in which his rational creature will again begin to act on his own. This second cycle, of course, will culminate at the apocalypse when power will again return to the center and God shall be all in all in the "New Heav'n and Earth."

The Father, then, is an extraordinary kind of permissive parent. With four exceptions, only God "permits" in *Paradise Lost,* and three of those exceptions, at least, seem to prove the rule that only God can be so supremely confident of his creation and its goodness as to allow it to proceed unchecked. Eve wrongly speculates about what "fate" permits in a line of reasoning that is fallacious throughout (9:885). In book nine, she makes it a point to say that Adam permits her to leave (9:378) and then throws his "permission" back in his face as they quarrel after the fall (9:1159). In book twelve, Michael states that when man

> permits
> Within himself unworthie Powers to reign
> Over free Reason, God in Judgement just
> Subjects him from without to violent Lords.   [12:90–93]

It is dangerous for man to permit; Adam's dilemma at the end of his quarrel with Eve shows how the permissive shoe can pinch. He feels uneasy as he allows her to leave because he is only a partial, limited creature. But on the other hand, he can only keep her with him, at that late stage of the spat, by force, and force will only alienate her farther. If there is a kind of surrender when man permits passions to usurp reason's throne, there is a similar kind of surrender when Adam allows her to go; yet given the heat which their discussion has generated, the way he has already dangerously alienated her, and the much more terrible loss of confidence he has experienced, he unwillingly gives his partial permission.

In contrast, God serenely "permitted all" (6:674): "hypocrisy" (3:683), the strength of Gabriel and Satan (4:1009), "freedom" for Adam to question his wisdom (8:435), the war in heaven (6:674), and "venial discourse" (9:4). Some of these things are horrid; the Satanic angels receive his permission to arise from the burning lake (1:212), to regain their lost shapes (10:574), and to have a sort of semiglory (10:451). After the fall,

God no longer permits Adam and Eve to live in the Garden. Yet at the same time, the way in which he releases the creation to fulfill itself in book seven and the way he releases his moral creatures to stand or fall for themselves testify to his lofty certitude. He enjoys a challenge, permitting not only Satan but also Adam and the Son to query him; he approves when Adam "embold'nd spake, and freedom us'd/Permissive" (8:434-35) to enquire about a mate, and he approves when the Son adopts much the same role and challenges the terms of his providence in book three. The Father assumes much the same stance, in these interviews, as Milton does vis-à-vis his readers: initially a bit chilly and neutral in tone so as not to give the whole lovely show away. The respondent—be it Adam, any other creature in the poem, the Son, or the reader—must work out his choices for himself without much emotional reinforcement. Only later do joy and mercy emerge. The perfectly permissive parent permits his creatures moral as well as generative exercise, because, as he himself queries:

> What pleasure I from such obedience paid,
> When Will and Reason . . .
> Useless and vain, of freedom both despoild,
> Made passive both, had servd necessitie,
> Not mee.   [3:107-11]

They must first stand for themselves and only then will he or Milton reassure them. Thus God derives a kind of pleasure from permitting his creatures to exercise their ability to choose and watching the toughminded function properly—but it is a pleasure only the omniscient can have, free from nagging doubts and uncertainties. A poet is, of course, omniscient about his poem.

That supreme confidence about permitting is only one of a whole host of ways in which the Deity is segregated from his creatures, his Puritanically overarching power and control asserted. And it is that vast distance between creator and creatures which explains why Satan can use antimonarchial slogans in attacking God while at the same time his right-hand man, Beelzebub has "*Atlantean* shoulders fit to bear/The weight of mightiest Monarchies" (2:306-7). Explaining his defeat, Satan argues:

> But he who reigns
> Monarch in Heav'n, till then as one secure
> Sat on his Throne, upheld by old repute,
> Consent or custome, and his Regal State
> Put forth at full, but still his strength conceal'd,
> Which tempted our attempt, and wrought our fall.   [1:637-42]

God, according to this version, is a shifty monarch maintained by "old repute," "custome," and "consent," and Satan seems to be arguing, almost perversely against his own case, that his revolution (actually an attempted coup d'état) had the beneficial result of revealing God's "strength." He is right in a way. His confrontation does have the effect of drawing God's nature more fully out into view for us, and one of the things we notice is that he is no earthly monarch. Who can have "consented" to his rule? The antimonarchic rhetoric here does not fit the case because God is not a creature. Conversely, as Satan vainly tries to bridge that immense gap between creator and creature and pull God down, he argues in a quasi-democratic way on behalf of what must have seemed to Milton clearly monarchical impulses. Satan is like Nimrod,

>   who not content
> With fair equalitie, fraternal state,
> Will arrogate Dominion undeserv'd
> Over his brethren,   [12:25–28]

and he warrants Adam's curse:

> O execrable Son so to aspire
> Above his Brethren, to himself assuming
> Authoritie usurpt, from God not giv'n:
> He gave us onely over Beast, Fish, Fowl
> Dominion absolute; that right we hold
> By his donation; but Man over men
> He made not Lord; *such title to himself*
> *Reserving*, human left from human free.   [12:64–71, emphasis mine]

The politics of regicide mesh beautifully here with the Puritanic elevation of God above his creatures. Milton did not discredit the Puritan revolution when he put "revolutionary" arguments in Satan's mouth; rather he showed thereby how confused Satan is about the order of the universe, for he anthropomorphizes the Deity in an unacceptable way, implying that what one may say about a human king may be equally well said about God.

   Divine permissiveness is represented in sexual metaphors. God's parenthood comes metaphorically most clear during creation when

>   on the watrie calme
> His brooding wings the Spirit of God outspred,
> And vital vertue infus'd, and vital warmth
> Throughout the fluid Mass.   [7:234–37]

Milton liked the metaphor sufficiently well to use it in the preambulatory twenty-six lines, and it does catch neatly the rhythm of outflowing power which will reverse only at the end of time. This serene release seems to characterize God and distinguish him from the creation, much as Adam's

discussion of God's nature does when he discusses his need for a meet
help. God says that he, God, is the supreme isolate,

> alone
> From all Eternitie, for none I know
> Second to me or like, equal much less.   [8:405-7]

Whether or not this line proves that Milton was this or that kind of sub-
ordinationist, Adam elaborates upon it in terms of the difference between
God and man:

> Thou in thy self art perfet, and in thee
> Is no deficience found; not so is Man,
> But in degree, the cause of his desire
> By conversation with his like to help,
> Or solace his defects. No need that thou
> Shouldst propagat, already infinite;
> And through all numbers absolute, though One;
> But Man by number is to manifest
> His single imperfection, and beget
> Like of his like, his Image multipli'd,
> In unitie defective, which requires
> Collateral love, and deerest amitie.   [8:415-26]

Here is another paradox. If, on the one hand, man manifests his imper-
fection by propagating, yet, by propagating man elaborates God's
creative impulse. Permission to speak has flowed from Father to human
son; Adam's speech leads him to consider marriage and an outpouring of
progeny. A sort of sexual transfusion occurs here, roughly parallel to the
transfusion of power to the Son, flowing out from God permissively
through Adam's rib.

In short, when God and Adam seem to be differentiating God from man,
their remarks link and conjoin them. There are other links as well. For
example, when Eve talks about how Adam permits her to leave in book
nine, she raises issues which inform the whole, vast literature of Puritan
marriage manuals. Thomas Carter articulated the central thrust of that
voluminous outpouring when he argued that the Puritan father should act
much as Milton's God does here. "God gave unto man the rule of the whole
earth and the domination of all the creatures therein contained,"[2] and man
must exercise this domination, perhaps not so extensive as that of Milton's
God, yet clearly sufficient so that the wife "must be obedient and dutiful
and under the subjection and government of him" (p. 47). Yet for all the
difference of "degree" which obtains (just as, Adam reminds his heavenly
Father, it does between God and man), Eve had a certain equality with her
husband. She was made "not from the head of man . . . lest she should

claim to rule . . . nor of the foot, lest she should be disdained and despised . . . but from the very body" to mark her equality. From the pinnacle of Puritanic male chauvinism, Carter could yet attack those men who "to show their authority, will hold their wives (in stead of fellowship) in such subjection and servitude, that no servant will perform the like" (p. 16). Much the same situation obtains between man and God. Adam reminds God, in the process of asking for a wife, that God is different from man; yet at the same time, God does not hold man in utter subjection and servitude either, as he takes pains to explain in book three.

Carter was defining the "society ordained by God," and the paradox embedded in his remarks has sexual, social, and theological implications. Sexually, it accounts for the radical tension in the attitudes toward women which we find in *Paradise Lost*. Adam implies, in his remarks upon "degree," that he desires an equal: "Among unequals what societie/Can sort, what harmonie or true delight?" (8:383-84). Similarly, the Father predicts that Eve will be

> Thy likeness, thy fit help, thy other self,
> Thy wish exactly to thy hearts desire.   [8:450-51]

Against these, however, we can range arguments from degree which emphasize sexual inequality: "Hee for God only, shee for God in him" (4:299). At the same time, Carter's "commonwealth" implies both the communal and leveling values of Puritan thought and the authoritarian individualism which went hand in hand with it, surfacing openly in the Protectorship. Theologically, the resemblance between Carter's husband and Milton's God reminds us that Puritan speculation on marriage was basically antinomian. The Puritan male thought of himself as aspiring to a position of lesser deity in the family, a position which was openly modeled on and drawn by analogy from his conception of God. William Gouge unflinchingly asked the key question; he had drawn the parallel between Christ and the Church (his spouse) and husband and wife, and when he came to Ephesians 5.24, "the Church is subject unto Christ in all things," he put the query: "Is mortal and sinful man to be obeyed as the Lord Christ the eternal Son of God?"[3] In his answer, he qualified twice, *but did not say no!* That was indeed antinomianism, coming from a Puritan divine dedicated to exalting God far above man. Whether or not Milton had ever read Carter or Gouge does not matter, for Johnson has shown the similarities between Milton's views and standard Puritan attitudes toward marriage and divorce;[4] the spirit was the same, the hope of divine husbandry, the Edenic underpinnings, the analogic method. The Puritan male first analogized his way up to a position of supreme isolation and mastery, then sought a merging mutuality with his wife. The same solitariness obtains for Milton's God, the husband's supremacy, and the retreating one just man. Yet through the Son, God appears to us; the husband must above all love and cherish his wife, and the one just man must somehow press unrelentingly on in this world. God is paradoxically like us "fit" readers and different from us. We get into trouble when we permit things to happen to us laxly, yet in important ways we ought so the elevate ourselves that we can be permissive as well.

Chapter 17: ADAM AND EVE: THE HERO AS GARDENING SOLDIER

Adam and Eve are pastorally defined soldiers of a Puritan Christ, wayfaring and warfaring among flowers rather than wars. They are in many ways like angels, both before and *after* the fall. That they resemble angels before the fall seems clear; that they must cope with a Puritanically constraining world after it is equally clear, though less noticed. Furthermore, they may be tempted at any moment in Eden, just as we may be; they must exercise reason just as we must choose wisely. Their garden, ever "tending to wild," provides them a vocation which like us they may not disregard and a format for standing still just as Puritan soldiers and angels do. Like both the militant angels and us, their work or calling testifies primarily to their faith; the aim is not necessarily to accomplish something over time. They are not only like angels, but they are the first Christians in an anachronism-laden poem; tempted, they sin, convict themselves of it, and are spiritually regenerated through loops of spiritual calling and repentance.

However, if angels, Adam and Eve, and we are in these ways conflated, Adam and Eve are slightly more like us than like angels. They lack a sustaining social context, which faithful angels have—an arena for public acts which will nourish good deeds, promote the virtuous impulses from whence they flow, and support the claims of reason. Like Milton's audience, they eventually prove to be "fit" but they are saddeningly few. The society of the faithful angels, then, provides a utopian vision against which the realities of human existence may be contrasted. Insofar as Adam and Eve approach the angels after the fall, they testify to Milton's hope, that newly emergent and clarified Puritan optimism in which he was as a young man nourished. Insofar as they differ from angels, they simultaneously confirm how fallen and irreparable is the fabric of human life on this earth and demonstrate an elitist, antinomian, utopian claim for exemption from human society. Through striking use of anachronism Milton achieves a cyclic vision of history (within which decisive gestures become impossible). Milton exploits Puritan aesthetic structures and tones to articulate a sense of fallen, elitist optimism.

It is a curious fact that although scholars have been at pains to delineate the differences between angels and men, they talk most often and force-

242

fully about the similarities. Angels are pure intellect, intuitively understanding what we must painfully learn, and in talking about their bodies we must
use a lot of oxymoron. On the other hand, Milton's angels really digest,
they blush (and therefore must have sexual feelings), they can be tempted
into ungrateful disobedience, they can be fooled by hypocrites, and most
importantly they are exemplars of the one just man. This poem applies a
lot of pressure to readers, forcibly inducing them to extract norms of conduct in ways which I have linked to the Puritan sensibility. What is most
revealing is the way critics behave under that pressure, easily conflating
angels with men even after they have discussed all the differences. Partly
this may be due to the very odd world which *Paradise Lost* portrays. Like
science fiction, it has an unusual cast of characters. After all of the talk
about God, hell, Satan, chaos, and unlapsed Adam and Eve, angels seem
quite the natural thing, much as Martians do in science fiction. That is not
true of all literature, of course, for when angels obtrude into the "realistic"
world of a Dickens novel, to mention just one example, we find them out
of place. But, although few of us have Blake's familiarity with angels, we
feel so at home with them in this poem that we naturally think they might
furnish models of conduct; there are not, after all, so many humans to
imitate.

Another and equally curious problem concerns Adam and Eve in paradise. They do look a lot like us, even though few critics agree with Millicent
Bell that no fall occurs to distance them from us.[1] If Bell had it her way,
we would be forced to argue that absolutely nothing happens in *Paradise
Lost* and that the poem is reductively ordered by a madcap Puritan mind.
Quite obviously Milton thought that something decisive had happened,
since unlike Blake, he did not spend afternoons in the backyard naked
with his wife: to Milton Paradise was lost and we can't go back home quite
so casually as the Blakes pretended. Few critics accept Bell's way of
phrasing things, including me. Her argument is super-Puritanic, articulated
in rigid and absolute terms, and ought to be qualified by such a distinction
as Ogden proposed between intention and act, between (in psychological
terms), inner fantasy and public behavior.[2] Yet before we laugh Professor
Bell entirely away from the lectern and off stage, we ought to reflect upon
a few questions which she raises. How *are* we to respond to Eve's unlapsed,
bad dream? Does it teach us what Ogden says it does, that

> Evil into the mind of God or Man
> May come and go, so unapprov'd, and leave
> No spot or blame behind.   [5:117-19]

If it does support his distinction between intention and act, and thereby
qualifies Bell's absolute argument, doesn't Ogden's interpretation tacitly
assume that a comment about prelapsarian behavior applies to us after

the fall as well? Is there anything which makes us want to qualify that
term "Man" with "unlapsed"? Milton did not. Don't we feel that Adam
and Eve's spontaneous hymn in book five is a good model for seventeenth-
century Puritan worship? Or, how are we to take Raphael's strictures about
uxoriousness and Adam's statements which provoke them in book eight?
Whether or not we accept the view of marriage which they suggest, do we
not feel that these remarks embody something like Milton's belief about
postlapsarian sexual relations? What are we to make of the brief episode
at the beginning of book eight in which Eve departs as Adam struts his
"studious thoughts abstruse" and neglects even to notice her loving beauty?
Is only an unlapsed man capable of ignoring a vibrant human relationship
in pursuit of scholarship or can professors of the humanities profit from
this scene as well as the first dwellers in *alma mater?* What of the quarrel in
book nine? Is it merely a prelude to the fall or can it show us something
about how a basically loving couple can fall out? If we judge from the way
in which the many critics of *Paradise Lost* tacitly answer these questions,
we conclude that even before it was lost Milton's paradise furnished models
of conduct for all of us living after the dire event. Granting, then, that
Professor Bell would have astonished Milton, that the theological status of
the couple does change during the course of the poem, we yet see that she
indirectly put her finger on something important about the poem; the
change from pre- to postlapsarian life is neither radical, dramatic, nor con-
clusive. Important ties still bind us to that blessed state. Milton challenges
the reader to figure out which elements of his millennial pastoralism apply
to this world in which we live and which apply only to the future. Insofar
as paradise really was lost, finally and for all, *Paradise Lost* is utopian or
escapist fantasy; it does not talk about this world but about a world
radically different from it. But, insofar as the Puritan ordering suggests
that paradise was never entirely lost, the poem implies that talk about
Eden is really talk about our condition; to that extent the poem is utopian
in the way it blunts the distinction between fictive and external reality
while suggesting that the former should determine and shape the latter.
The questions I have posed about events before the fall do not have a
simple answer. Adam and Eve both resemble us and are different from us;
a change did occur yet certain things remain constant. It is the double
quality of our answers to these questions, the tension between change and
lack of change, which creates the distinctive veiling of utopian impulses in
Paradise Lost.

   We are never quite sure how to take More's *Utopia* because of his wit;
we are never quite sure how to take *Paradise Lost* because of the Puritan
aesthetic at work. Obviously, Milton did not have More's wit; he could
not laugh at his own creation in the way More did with his pun on *utopia-
eutopia.* The humanistic mode of witty, verbal child's play was foreign to

his sensibility, so much closer to the aggressive, oedipal confrontation of the Puritans. Thus, he *challenges* us with these questions rather than pulling our sleeve as More does. But if the modes are different, and Milton's is Puritanic, the curiously ambivalent poise between the urge to reform and the pangs of despair is quite similar. Like More, Milton talks about a world we ought to emulate and at the same time suggests it is so radically different from our world that we cannot.

Milton so ordered *Paradise Lost* that we are thrown into the middle of a movement of unredeemed history and shown how the claims of open war and covert guile, scrambled together, conjoin faithless victors with faithless vanquished. It then proposes, while moving us further along through such cycles in the plot of Satan's adventures, an alternative (yet unearthly) society and history of the faithful angels, with different modes of conduct. To the society of heaven in book three and the company of the faithful angels in books six and seven, Milton adds another such society—Eden. To notice that this society is a flowered treadmill does not demean it or lessen its attractions. A Puritan would positively have loved to tend such a garden ever tending to wild, just as he would positively have responded to God's "State, as Sovran King" (8:239). Such a garden provides the perfect format for constantly imposing order on one's existence and surroundings. It is as though Milton here pastoralized Puritan theology, captured in plants and trees the stuff of Puritan summas and military sermons. We recall the obvious relish with which such theoreticians as Bownd and Dod threshed out the kernels of Sabbatarian doctrine and elaborated on their implications, and we recall that in the process both stated that like them Adam had a "calling" or "work" in Eden so potentially absorbing as to remove his mind even from God.[3] I have suggested how the Puritans' rage for systematic and logical order did in some ways ultimately remove their minds from God; hence when we see Adam and Eve on this lovely treadmill, we can, from this perspective, come fully to realize how immensely attractive that state might have been. And we can further realize how readers, judging the effect of *Paradise Lost* when it was first published and their ears were still attuned to the controversies of the age, might well have detected a Puritan hand at work shaping this particular state of bliss.

Then too, we can begin to appreciate the implications of the quarrel which separates Adam and Eve in book nine. Eve seems to begin it when she tentatively suggests that the two of them are not getting enough done; exchanging looks and smiles

intermits

Our dayes work brought to little, though begun
Early, and th' hour of Supper comes unearn'd.   [9:223-25]

Earlier in the poem, however, supper flowers naturally from God's creative
impulse in Eden, just as everything else does there. Milton has been at
pains to make that clear when he sketched the menu Eve offered to
Raphael and Adam in book five. The "Mother of Mankind" (5:388) simply
culls "Whatever Earth all-bearing Mother yields" (5:338). Adam remarks
that "Nature multiplies/Her fertil growth, and by disburd'ning grows/More
fruitful," and Eve adds that "earths hallowd mould" is "of God inspir'd"
(5:318-22). Supper is the fruit of one of these outpourings of divine
creativity, flowering through earth and Eve's teeming hand. So much makes
it clear that no one can *earn* either supper or its hour in Eden. Yet in book
nine, Eve is predicating a kind of exchange over time—"dayes work" for
"hour of Supper"—and everything about this poem, including the notion
of creative outflow from the Father, insists that the assumption is false.

Eve's suggestion is only tentative ("hear what to my minde first thoughts
present," she says in qualification of her suggestion [9:213]), but it is set in
a foreboding context of division and change. The narrator has initially
lamented that he "must change/These notes to Tragic."[4] The permissive
conjunction of "God or Angel Guest/With Man" is about to be broken; no
longer will there be such joint "rural" repasts; no longer will God permit
man "Venial discourse." Whatever he means by "Tragic," the narrator contrasts his new subject to the matter of epic or heroic romance, to

> the wrauth
> Of stern *Achilles* on his Foe pursu'd
> Thrice fugitive about *Troy* Wall; or ráge
> Of *Turnus* for *Lavinia* disespous'd,
> Or *Neptun's* ire or *Juno's,* that so long
> Perplex'd the *Greek* and *Cytherea's* Son.   [9:14-19]

Rage and heroic modes of conduct perplex; the narrator sings a higher
heroism which embodies Raphael's aesthetic assumptions, his disinclination, in relating the war in heaven,

> to indite
> Warrs, hitherto the onely Argument
> Heroic deem'd.   [9:27-29]

Throughout the passage, the narrator provides his own "warning voice" in
answer to the plea he had made at the outset of book four, for he traces
out the first and at the same time the longest loop of unredeemed history.
He recalls how God and man were once truly conjoined by permission,
conversation, and supper, how that union broke down into the false distinctions of victor and vanquished, rage, and military heroism with its code
of decisive action. This cycle will only conclude when God and man are
rejoined.

Satan provides a second warning voice when he apostrophizes earth and comments at length on change. Earth, he rationalizes, must be better than heaven, "For what God after better worse would build?" (9:102). After suggesting causal sequence and chronological improvements, he then argues that by seducing man he will not only augment his legions (progressively improve, perhaps even in time perfect his position) but also draw "all this" with him, since it is "to him linkt in weal or woe" (9:132-33). "All this" seems to indicate a cosmic sweep of Satan's hand; the universe is bound, in some obscure causal connection, to man and will consequently change when Satan changes man. Such a victory will be impressive, Satan thinks, because thereby he will

> have marr'd
> What he *Almightie* styl'd, six Nights and Days
> Continu'd making, and who knows how long
> Before had bin contriving, though perhaps
> Not longer then since I in one Night freed
> From servitude inglorious welnigh half
> Th' Angelic Name.   [9:136-42]

One can only speak of rhetorical strategies here since the thought is so radically inconsistent. Satan wants to reduce God to a creature whose actions may be measured in time. He wants to add luster to his exploit by suggesting that what he is about to ruin instantly God took a long time to build and longer to plan. He wants to contrast God's efforts to his own splendid gesture, which took only one night. To do so, he undercuts his own suggestion that God took a long time to create the universe; perhaps he took less than one night to do it. Satan is giving his own version of Raphael's quandary about the relationship between "immediate acts" and the duration of "process of speech." He seems at first to believe that the duration of the verbal process matches the period of the deed, then seems to reverse himself and agree with Raphael, not for theological but for strategic, rhetorical reasons.

As Satan "feels around" rhetorically for that formulation which will dress up his acts most impressively, he involves himself in self-contradiction more obviously than he has before. His arithmetic has gone bad when he mentions "welnigh half," while the words "though perhaps" explicitly signal the way he shifts from pose to pose. We are near the end of the explication of Satan's character, near the end of the process of Puritan clarification and definition of what it means to be Satanic, and the contradictions and poses not only have become familiar but (like the Father's transfusions of power to the Son) more open and obvious. The change is not in Satan but rather in the clarity with which he is portrayed.[5]

With the narrator's voice in our ear telling us he must change his tune, and Satan's suggesting that God changed his plan and shuffled up a new creation after Satan wrecked heaven, we read Eve's first thoughts fore-

warned. As she speaks she creates a new distinction, speaking first of how
"we labour" (9:205), then suggesting that she and Adam "divide our
labours." As she turns the word "labour" from a verb into a noun, she
destroys the communal endeavor of "we"; it is no longer "our labour"
but "our labours," as though each had his own. As she argues that they
split up physically, she further fragments "our labours" into "our taske"
(l. 221) and "our dayes work" (l. 224) which, she implies, are different
from "looks" and "smiles." Thus she distinguishes the pleasures of "our
labours" from the work. Adam valiantly attempts to put all these things
back together again; work, he points out, is not there before them to be
gotten *done* (implying some sort of *terminus ad quem*) at all:

> Yet not so strictly hath our Lord impos'd
> Labour, as to debarr us when we need
> Refreshment, whether food, or talk between,
> Food of the mind, or this sweet intercourse
> Of looks and smiles, for smiles from Reason flow
> To brute deni'd, and are of Love the food,
> Love not the lowest end of human life.
> For not to irksom toile, but to delight
> He made us, and delight to Reason joyn'd.
> These paths & Bowers doubt not but our joynt hands
> Will keep from Wilderness with ease, as wide
> As we need walk, till younger hands ere long
> Assist us.   [9:235-47]

"Refreshment" embraces more than mere "food" or "th' hour of Supper,"
including, in addition, "talk between," "looks and smiles." God made
"our joynt hands" and "delight to Reason joyn'd," and these conjunctions
will keep the "Wilderness" sufficiently in check. Labor, then, as Adam
describes it, is an active if uneventful emblem of their condition, their
"handed" relationship, and their love. If standing still in the manner of
Puritan soldiers or military angels seems an unnecessarily athletic sort of
Christianity, this very similar conception of labor, so deeply involved as
it is with love, may suggest something of the attractions of the former,
which is equally a labor of a slightly different love. Eden seemed "fallen"
to Professor Bell; it seems more accurate to say that Milton instinctively
framed the Puritan ideal of work in flowers there.

It is impossible to say what caused Eve suddenly to make her suggestion
or what caused Adam, after twenty-one lines of fairly successful explanation, suddenly to reverse himself with a "but" and egoistically imply that
Eve may be getting tired of him (9:247-48). A second "but" in his third
and final speech (9:370) advances the downward movement one step
farther toward something very like quarreling. It seems to take two to

tangle and wrangle in Eden, but why they wrangle is unclear. Just as we never see Satan fall (in books five and six he is fallen, and Sin's narration of past events in book three details only the effects of the lapse, never the change), so we do not see here the *causes* of the argument but rather a couple arguing. In the Puritan mode, the poem is detailing states of mind, not causes of action. Adam and Eve's plight changes during the course of the quarrel; they get in deeper, make more obviously unkind remarks. Finally things so far degenerate that it is impossible to say that Adam should have done one thing rather than another; if it is unwise to send Eve off, she cannot be restrained by force. But again, these are matters of degree; "quarreling" remains constant.

As the society ordained by God comes apart, Satan bombards us (and Eve) with a whole barrage of "changes." Eve furnishes him the clue to this strategy, completely ignoring his guileful, groveling flattery in her amazement over a simple novelty—a talking snake:

> What may this mean? Language of Man pronounc't
> By Tongue of Brute,
>
> .   .   .   .
>
> such wonder claims attention due.   [9:553–66]

Satan seizes on the idea that he has suddenly changed and praises the fruit for radically altering him. He fables how he was *"at first* as other Beasts . . . *Till on a day"* (9:571, 575) he spotted the fruit, climbed the tree, and

>   to pluck and eat my fill
> I spar'd not, for such pleasure *till that hour*
> At Feed or Fountain *never* had I found.
> Sated *at length, ere long* I might perceave
> Strange *alteration* in me, to degree
> Of Reason in my inward Powers, and Speech
> Wanted not *long.*   [9:595–601, emphases mine]

The change occurs, obviously, in a chronological matrix; only after hearing about it does Eve comment (adversely) on Satan's flattery: "thy over-praising leaves in doubt/The vertue of that Fruit" (9:615–16). We all wish she had pursued that "doubt" farther. She is still concentrating on the change while she too feebly queries Satan's fiction. She is hooked, and Satan can proceed to suggest that she alter herself as well.

Apostrophizing the tree itself, in the second round of the temptation, Satan pretends that the virtue of the tree allows him to trace out "Things in thir Causes" and "the wayes/Of highest Agents" (9:682–83). He concludes in an equally causal vein by applying "these, these and many more/ Causes" so as to prove Eve's "need of this fair Fruit" (9:730–31). He represents himself as agent of historical progress, striving higher than "Fate/Meant mee" (9:689-90), speculates on the effects of eating the fruit, considers God's response, and outlines God's motives, again in a historical frame:

> he knows that in the day
> Ye Eate thereof, your Eyes that seem so cleere,
> Yet are but dim, shall perfetly be then
> Op'nd and cleerd, and ye shall be as Gods.   [9:705-8]

Causality, temporal sequence, and drastic change all coalesce in his temptation. "Here grows the Cure of all" (9:776), dreams Eve as she bites.

In contrast to all Satan's talk about cause and change, the two most dramatically placed verbs in the poem do not, syntactically, affect an object:

> So saying, her rash hand in evil hour
> Forth reaching to the Fruit, she pluck'd, she eat.   [9:780-81]

The fruit is there in the sentence, of course, and we are no doubt thankful that Milton didn't write "she plucked the apple and eat it." Stripped, on the surface at least, of their objects, short and crisp in sound, the verbs are vivid and memorable, the action forceful with the furtive haste of greed. Still, the actions represented are discontinuous, not moving smoothly over time but proceeding by a sort of quantum jump. The hand (rather than Eve) reaches forth, held in our gaze a moment longer than necessary by "in evil hour," then the focus widens from metonomy to take in Eve as she bolts the fruit. The Son had darted his "Thunders" during the war in heaven in much the same manner:

> in his right hand
> Grasping ten thousand Thunders, which he sent
> Before him, such as in thir Soules infix'd
> Plagues.   [6:835-38]

Here again quantum jumps separate the phrases and parts of the action, intervene between grasping the thunders, sending them before him, and their infixing themselves in the damned. Again, the focus is changed at each leap, while the transitive verbs predicated to the Son do not operate on the objects of his ire—although, of course, his thunders ultimately do.

The verbs to pluck, to taste, and to eat form a Puritanically recurrent pattern which shows that in and of themselves the acts are morally neutral. Four times these verbs constellate together and three are morally dangerous. Satan fables about how:

> Amid the Tree now got, where plenty hung
> Tempting so nigh, to pluck and eat my fill

I spar'd not. [9:594-96]

And Eve, recounting her bad dream, recalls how her "guide"

> paus'd not, but with ventrous Arme
> He pluckt, he tasted; mee damp horror chil'd. [5:64-65]

Both instances forshadow Eve's fateful act, yet the fourth occurrence seems clearly to be a valid dream of good. It transports Adam into Eden after his creation:

> Each Tree
> Load'n with fairest Fruit that hung to the Eye
> Tempting, stirr'd in me sudden appetite
> To pluck and eate; whereat I wak'd, and found
> Before mine Eyes all real. [8:306-10]

The acts of plucking and eating, even when they are "tempting," need not be evil. Nor do the external trappings of the acts count for much. For example, "guides" figure in three of these recurrent scenes. Satan guides Eve in book five (l. 91) and book nine (l. 646), yet in contrast an agent of the divine "guides" Adam during his dream in book eight (ll. 298, 312). One can no more count on a guide than one can determine the moral force of plucking and eating, uncover hypocrisy, or be certain that the island one moors one's "night-founder'd Skiff" to is not a whale. There is nothing one can *do* about these ambiguities of one's existence. The key verbs of the poem are not only severed from their objects, but the acts which they represent are not in themselves morally significant.

Clearly, it is the inner motive rather than the external gesture which counts in this Puritan universe. Another recurrent pattern in eating scenes shows this fact another way. Adam's lunch, recounted even more briefly than Eve's, provides a crystal clear example of how Milton shifts the focus from the act immediately to a longer discussion of the motive or emotion:

> She gave him of that fair enticing Fruit
> With liberal hand: he scrupl'd not to eat
> Against his better knowledge, not deceav'd,
> But fondly overcome with Femal charm. [9:996-99]

To much the same effect, when Eve recounts her bad dream she turns just as quickly from the act to her guilty emotions: "mee damp horror chil'd" (5:65). So, indeed, does Satan during his lying temptation when he recalls "such pleasure" (9:596). After Eve takes her fatal bite,

> Earth felt the wound, and Nature from her seat
> Sighing through all her Works gave signs of woe,
> That all was lost. Back to the Thicket slunk

The guiltie Serpent, and well might, for *Eve*
Intent now wholly on her taste, naught else
Regarded.   [9:782-87]

Here our attention is swung more slowly from Eve's act to her narcissistic
concentration on nothing but "her taste." In the process, the narrator
makes a number of important observations, showing, for example, how
unheroic Satan is even by fallen standards at his moment of "triumph."
When he talks about how "Earth felt the wound" and "all was lost," he
establishes another, inconclusive pattern of recurrence. We cannot, for one
thing, take the statement "all was lost" seriously, unless we are prepared
to deny Adam freedom of choice for his subsequent act. And if that fact
qualifies the decisiveness of the one phrase, subsequent events qualify the
finality of earth's wound. "A second groan" awaits her when Adam tastes,
"compleating . . . the moral Sin/Original" (9:1001-4), and while the sin
may be complete here, it is not until book ten that "These changes in the
Heav'ns [and Earth], though slow" go to completion (10:692). As usual,
Milton at first represents process in such a way that it seems immediately
decisive, then backs off to show that, through recurrence, it is only very
gradual; we recall how he pumps phony melodrama into martial flytings.
It is therefore highly significant that Milton begins to talk about the
"wound" of Earth here as though completed (only to show later that it
was not), as a way of moving from the act of eating to the much more
revealing and morally important matter of Eve's inner feelings and motives.
The entire transition serves to undercut, fuzz, or blunt the force of seemingly decisive acts.

Examples of repetition and "foreshadowing," leading up to the fall,
embody that Puritan notion that one confronts an endless series of
temptations. "The great events in *Paradise Lost* should be read . . . as
a discontinuous series of crises in each of which . . . the important factor
is not the consequences of previous actions, but the confrontation, across
a vast apocalyptic gulf, with the source of deliverance," writes Frye.[6]
"Discontinuous" may belie our sense of unity generated in the poem, but
there is a good deal to the remark, for it emphasizes the freedom of will
essential to Milton's conception of Adam and Eve and suggests how Puritan
aesthetic structures are deployed to assert that freedom. Adam and Eve's
characters or personalities remain constant, the situations they confront
recur, and the syntax of their gestures repeats itself; their moral status
changes because all of a sudden they respond in a different way to one of
those temptations. The causes of their acts are not traced out in terms of
temporal concatenation or second causes. We cannot say why Eve feels
horror one evening, curiosity one noon when considering the fruit. We
cannot say why she remains handed with Adam up until book eight and
goes her separate way thereafter.[7] We cannot say why Adam can answer

Eve concerning "disproportion" in the universe one evening, but must pursue "studious thoughts abstruse" about the same problem the next day, or why, having answered Eve concerning separation at the beginning of book nine, he inserts his "but" and errs into egoism. The answer to the question "what cause/Mov'd our Grand Parents . . . to fall off," posed by the narrator at the outset of the poem, is not necessarily the answer to the question "Who first seduc'd them," which immediately follows it (1:28–30, 33). The process of answering the second question, we should remember, carries the narrator (and us) down to hell. However, Satan is not the answer to the first question—and we don't really ever get an answer.[8] Surely we must be suspicious when Satan tries to con us into thinking he caused the fall. If there is a cause, it must lie within the individual characters, in those states of mind and soul we are persistently asked to focus on in lieu of external acts. But we do not even see Adam and Eve change their minds. We only see them, just as we only see Satan, with *changed* minds.

Chapter 18: ADAM AND EVE: THE HERO REGENERATE

After the fall there remains salvation, a process which for Adam takes three circular books paralleling much of the form and format of *De Doctrina*. As early as book three, the Son had drawn his Father from talk about justice wreaked on an ingrate to talk of mercy and salvation:

> Man shall not quite be lost, but sav'd who will,
> Yet not of will in him, but grace in me
> Freely voutsaft; once more I will renew
> His lapsed powers, though forfeit and enthrall'd
> By sin to foul exorbitant desires;
> Upheld by me, yet once more he shall stand
> On even ground against his mortal foe,
> By me upheld, that he may know how frail
> His fall'n condition is, and to me ow
> All his deliv'rance, and to none but me.
> Some I have chosen of peculiar grace
> Elect above the rest; so is my will:
> The rest shall hear me call, and oft be warnd
> Thir sinful state, and to appease betimes
> Th' incensed Deitie, while offerd grace
> Invites; for I will cleer thir senses dark,
> What may suffice, and soft'n stonie hearts
> To pray, repent, and bring obedience due.
> To Prayer, repentance, and obedience due,
> Though but endevord with sincere intent,
> Mine ear shall not be slow, mine eye not shut.
> And I will place within them as a guide
> My Umpire *Conscience,* whom if they will hear,
> Light after light well us'd they shall attain,
> And to the end persisting, safe arrive.
> This my long sufferance and my day of grace
> They who neglect and scorn, shall never taste;
> But hard be hard'nd, blind be blinded more,
> That they may stumble on, and deeper fall;
> And none but such from mercy I exclude.   [3:173–202]

Here, if anywhere, is an excellent example of why it is unwise to treat even the "plain style" of the Father as though it were clear and unambiguous, for the passage is full of mysteries. The Father seems to be stating that there are three groups of men, those who are "elect," those who are saved through repentance and regeneration, and those who deny the offered means of grace; but "seems" is all one can securely say. From the pun on "will" in ll. 173–74, a pun which raises the very doubts it is apparently "intended" to resolve, ambiguity pervades this passage. The first ten lines present the situation of mankind, renewed, on "even ground," and "upheld"; again Milton's participial style moves God out of the syntactic role of subject-actor. Briefly, Milton seems to be arguing, much as for example the Independent, John Goodwin, did when he attacked what he took to be Calvin's doctrine of predestinate election in his commentary on Romans,[1] that God extends election to all men. Some, however, are more elect than others. "The rest" are described in various states of spiritual weakness or well-being. Presumably some of them "safe arrive," by the end of the passage, but, since not all of the spiritual states attributed syntactically to "the rest," "thir" inner lives, or "them" would lead so far, not all of "the rest" make it. Initially, for example, "the rest" seem to be "penitent," a fearful, self-seeking state in which they must be "warnd" and act in response to "Th' incensed Deitie" rather than to a perception of divine mercy, a state the limitations of which I shall explain shortly. Further, when the Father speaks of offering men "What may suffice," we may take him to mean "what may suffice" for men to "safe arrive," but we may also take him to mean "what may suffice" to convict men justly of willful hardheartedness for rejecting "offerd grace." The Father proposes another choice which will separate those who safe arrive from those whom he excludes when he refers to "*Conscience,* whom if they will hear,/Light after light well us'd they shall attain." In short, the Father here takes us through a series of situations in which man must exercise choice, and he evokes those situations in an order of spiritual progression away from justice and toward the perception of mercy. The last five lines make it clear that not all men make the right choices and progress, yet in a sense the impact of all that precedes these lines suggests, simply because Milton focuses on "the rest" rather than the two groups of men who make up "the rest," that all *will* "safe arrive."

My point is that this passage works, as do all of the lines in *Paradise Lost,* as poetry. It is not unambiguous statement of clear kernels of truth or doctrine. The *feeling* we get from this passage is optimistic, as we seem to see "the rest . . . safe arrive." And similarly, Milton's argument in *De Doctrina* was, in its time, optimistic. Like Goodwin and many other advanced Puritans, he was turning his back on Calvin, whom establishment writers were now quoting against the Puritans. There he argued that God bestows on all men "sufficient" grace for "salvation," but "not equally upon each" (I, iv; Yale ed., p. 192). With the exception of the superelect,

we are in the same boat, all start on "even ground," and certain elitist feelings associated with Calvin's theology have been leveled. This new, optimistic development in Puritan theology accounts for the importance of "merit"
in *Paradise Lost,* for if we are, in important ways, on "even ground,"
merit is what distinguishes one from the other. The old urge to make such
distinctions, which underlay Calvin's theology, had not disappeared. Rather, it flowered in Milton's notion of a "superelect," a category with
antinomian potential whether or not Milton realized it. Milton's God is
articulating an optimistic development in Puritan thinking away from
Calvin, yet the ranking and notions of prestige, which might flower in
antinomianism, were still there, both in the impact of the poem and the
ordering of *De Doctrina.*

De Doctrina is one of the most Puritanic things Milton ever did. Simply
sitting down to systematize one's beliefs is of itself characteristic. The
argument begins abstractly, focusing on God, and works out toward more
practical concerns—the effect of God's providence for man, by the close
of Book I, and pragmatic virtues, rules for worship, etc. in Book II.[2] After
defining God and articulating his views on the Trinity, Milton settled
down, for the rest of Book I to outline the dual nature of "The PROVI-
DENCE of God with regard to the fall of man," focusing first on sin and
the fall, then on the restoration of man (I, xi; p. 382). It applies the initial
discussion of the nature of God to the whole of human history from the
creation to the millennium. *Paradise Lost,* then, particularly dramatizes
the subject matter of the first book. The quickest way to give some concrete sense of the manner in which Milton's presentation unfolds is to outline it briefly, using chapter titles where they illuminate the issues being
discussed and the order of the topics.

Subject matter	*Chapter title*
I. Sin	Of the fall of our first parents, and of sin (ch. xi)
A. cause	
B. effects	Of the punishment of sin (ch. xii)
	Of the death of the body (ch. xiii)
II. Restoration	Of man's restoration and of Christ the redeemer (ch. xiv)
A. cause	[Redemption]
1. office	Of the mediatorial office and its threefold function (ch. xv)
2. ministry	Of the administration of redemp- tion (ch. xvi)
B. effect	Of renovation and also of vocation (ch. xvii)

Subject matter	Chapter title
1. mode	
a) natural	
(1) calling	
(2) faith	
b) supernatural	Of regeneration (ch. xviii)
(1) repentance	Of repentance (ch. xix)
(2) saving faith	Of saving faith (ch. xx)
2. manifestation of mode	Of ingrafting in Christ and its effects (ch. xxi)
a) newness of life	
b) increase	
(1) absolute	
(2) relative to	
(a) Father	Of justification (ch. xxii)
(b) Father and Son	Of union and communion with Christ and his members; also of the mystic or invisible church (ch. xxiv)
i) union	
ii) glorification	
aa) imperfect	Of incomplete glorification (chs. xxv–xxvi)
bb) perfect	Of complete glorification, also of Christ's second coming, the resurrection of the dead, and the conflagration of this world (ch. xxxiii)

This section not only covers the whole history of the human race but also suggests the shape of an ideal spiritual biography. Each chapter would, from the latter point of view, describe a step toward spiritual growth. The trouble is that each chapter is a self-contained essay. A thin tissue of logical outline minimally connects them, but nowhere does Milton explain how a man might pass from one phase to the next, and one must assume that some sort of quantum leap is necessary. Indeed, Milton implies more than once that a man might experience two phases together or vacillate between them. For example, "natural renovation" (attended by a "natural" sort of "penitence" and natural "faith") is selfish and motivated by merely human considerations; in this partial condition, "a man stops sinning because he is afraid of punishment, and turns to God when he calls merely for the sake of his own salvation" (I, xvii; p. 458). It is transitory, for when it occurs, men "undergo a change for the better, at any rate for the time being" (I, xvii; p. 457). "Supernatural renovation," in contrast, and true "repentance" focus on God, the adept "seeing with sorrow that he has offended God, by his sins, detests and avoids them and through a sense of the divine mercy, turns to God with all humility, and is eager in his heart to follow what is right" (I, xix; p. 466). Although Milton distinguished verbally between "penitence" and "repentance" (or *"poenitentia"* and *"resipiscentia"*) the distinction is not ironclad, since "penitence is common to the regenerate and the unregenerate" and Milton freely stated that he distinguished "between penitence and repentance for the sake of precision, though I admit that in common usage the two terms are often interchangeable" (I, xvii; p. 458). This verbal ambiguity suggests an ambiguity in the spiritual life of the individual as well. Penitence/repentance and faith "may well be a real beginning, but also each may be either merely natural or altogether false" (I, xvii; p. 458). The entire passage wavers between "precision" or hair-splitting and tentativeness or fuzziness for a whole host of Puritan reasons.[3]

Such terms as penitence, repentance, and regeneration are so important to any Christian thinker that, when we see Milton laboring so carefully to distinguish them, we can assume, I think safely, that he will use them in his poetry with much the sort of precision which he uses in his prose. Given so much, we can say that "penitence" and "regeneration" are clear-cut terms, the first referring to natural renovation and the second to supernatural renovation and true saving faith; "repentance" is also probably unambiguous, referring to the supernatural rather than the natural variety, but may hover slightly ambiguously between the two categories. As a result, we can say that book ten concerns natural renovation and "penitence," book eleven supernatural "repentance" and "regeneration," and book twelve, saving faith. Each of these books is a loop, ending on the same note with which it began, within the larger cycle of the three books as a whole. During each loop, Adam or the reader regresses, then regains ground and forges ahead. The process by which he advances is obscure, nonlinear, slightly discontinuous, and the conclusiveness of each change is as a result muted, as the structure of *De Doctrina* would imply. Indeed, if anything, the poem is less clear-cut than *De Doctrina,* for there the poet systematized abstractions while here he dramatizes the ebb and flow of human consciousness in moving lines.

The ways in which these three books are organized and fitted together may most shortly be illustrated by considering the quantum leap of faith which occurs between the end of book ten and the beginning of book eleven.[4] At the end of book ten Adam summons Eve to "penitent" prayer, and the adjective signals the limitations of what they are doing. His motives are starkly "natural" at the end of book ten. Eve had suggested that they commit suicide, and Adam responds:

> Death
> So snatcht will not exempt us from the paine
> We are by doom to pay; rather such acts

> Of contumacie will provoke the highest
> To make death in us live: Then let us seek
> Some safer resolution, which methinks
> I have in view, calling to minde with heed
> Part of our Sentence, that thy Seed shall bruise
> The Serpents head.   [10:1024-32]

He begins with pain and paying, fears provoking God, looks for a "safer" plan, and remembers the promise of the seed. He goes on to discuss techniques of subsistence and hopes they may live "commodiously" (10:1083). His interests are, in short, self-seeking—"he is afraid of punishment" and prays "merely for the sake of his own salvation"; *De Doctrina* glosses Adam's motives well here.

Given these quite mixed, not to say positively self-seeking motives, it is no wonder that in 10:1097 the narrator calls Adam "penitent." Whether the word "repentant" in the first line of book eleven teeters ambiguously, referring both "to the regenerate and the unregenerate," or whether it refers unambiguously only to a regenerate soul, it is certain that five lines later the unambiguous term "regenerat" signals that some sort of quantum leap has occurred between the "penitent" end of book ten and the beginning of book eleven:

> Thus they in lowliest plight repentant stood
> Praying, for from the Mercie-seat above
> Prevenient Grace descending had remov'd
> The stonie from thir hearts, & made new flesh
> Regenerate grow instead.   [11:1-5]⁵

Just as, in book three, the Father seems to signal one of those amazing spiritual great leaps forward through repetition of phrases, so Adam and Eve's prayer (which may be vehicle or cause of this leap) involves one of the two or three most extensive, concentrated passages of verbal recapitulation in the entire poem.

> What better can we do, then to the place
> Repairing where he judg'd us, prostrate fall
> Before him reverent, and there confess
> Humbly our faults, and pardon beg, with tears
> Watering the ground, and with our sighs the Air
> Frequenting, sent from hearts contrite, in sign
> Of sorrow unfeign'd, and humiliation meek.
> Undoubtedly he will relent and turn
> From his displeasure; in whose look serene,
> When angry most he seem'd and most severe,
> What else but favor, grace, and mercie shon?

> So spake our Father penitent, nor *Eve*
> Felt less remorse: they forthwith to the place
> Repairing where he judg'd them prostrate fell
> Before him reverent, and both confess'd
> Humbly thir faults, and pardon beg'd, with tears
> Watering the ground, and with thir sighs the Air
> Frequenting, sent from hearts contrite, in sign
> Of sorrow unfeign'd, and humiliation meek.   [10:1086-1104]⁶

Now, however, repeating does not change verbs to nouns; here the main shifts are between "us" and "they" and in the tense of the verbs. On the one hand, this passage, precisely because it recapitulates itself so extensively, seems just a bit formal, the opposite of "unpremeditated," and one wonders whether that is not a sign of the natural, limited nature of Adam's and Eve's state at the end of book ten; on the other hand, perhaps this sort of repetition, in some obscure way, fitted together in Milton's mind with that mysterious moment in which true regeneration begins. At any rate, the metaphor of the "stonie" heart, taken from Ezekiel, figures in Milton's discussion of regeneration in *De Doctrina* as well as the key passage in book three, and reinforces our sense that, although Adam and Eve have not done anything truly regenerate to date, they are indeed being unambiguously termed regenerate. The quantum leap, it would seem is really the release of energy from "Prevenient Grace" and the equally "prevenient" understanding of the narrator, for it is only at the very end of book eleven, when he reinterprets the story of Noah, that Adam begins unmistakably to show signs of that "regenerate" behavior which the narrator attributes to him at the beginning of the book. To put it another way, the narrator and God jump from "penitence" to "regeneration" at the beginning of this looping book while Adam can only follow and catch up at the end of the book. Between beginning and end, moreover, Adam behaves in ways which are pretty clearly neither regenerate nor even very penitent. Thus, the reader is exposed, during the course of book eleven, first to motifs of regeneration, then to behavior much less lovely, and finally to regenerate behavior again; the quality of spiritual life, after an initial leap forward, regresses, as it were, then moves forward again. Crucial to the final advance, as I pointed out in chapter 5, is Adam's speech assessing the story of Noah:

> Farr less I now lament for one whole World
> Of wicked Sons destroyd, then I rejoyce
> For one Man found so perfet and so just,
> That God voutsafes to raise another World
> From him, and all his anger to forget.   [11:874-78]

Book ten presents us with much the same looping motion. It opens, as
I have remarked, with terrific emphasis upon justice, which is then divinely
linked to mercy. The punitive tones and talk of sentencing involve us
readers in precisely that fear of punishment which triggers natural penitence, while the emergent mercy (insofar as we can respond to it) begins
to mitigate our fears. However, it is not until the very end of the book
that Adam shows signs even of a minimal "penitence." In the sentencing
scene, he shifts the blame to Eve; Milton seems to be at some pains to
point up his shabby treatment, for the contrast between Adam's shuffling
answer and Eve's short, direct response is vivid. Adam then convicts himself of sin in an egoistic, despairing way, concluding:

> all my evasions vain,
> And reasonings, though through Mazes, lead me still
> But to my own conviction: first and last
> On mee, mee onely, as the sourse and spring
> Of all corruption, all the blame lights due.   [10:829-33]

He has made some real progress, taken the blame, convicted himself of
sin. Yet the passage is one of those delicately complex utterances, difficult
simply to categorize in terms of the schema of *De Doctrina,* for despite his
progress, Adam focuses narcissistically only upon his own act rather than
Eve's or God's response; he is in a maze of despair, he hasn't begun to
think about the judicial consequences (much less the merciful ones) of his
doings, and he hates Eve, "that bad Woman." There is no hint of the promise of the seed, no love (either human or divine), no concern for the
outer world or the future of mankind. However beautifully mixed, the
passage does show how Adam attains at the very end of the book to that
spiritual state which was evoked in us readers with the opening lines. Thus,
this speech closes the loop of "penitence" which informs book ten.

Book twelve also ends where it began. The narrator speaks of "the world
destroy'd and world restor'd" (12:3), and Michael summarizes, remarking
how Adam has "seen one World begin and end;/And Man as from a second
stock proceed" (12:6-7). These are literal statements with a spiritual,
metaphoric meaning. Adam seems to understand them literally while we,
capable of the knowledge requisite to saving faith, see the metaphoric implications. It is that metaphoric understanding which Adam must acquire,
and the issue emerges most startlingly in his penultimate question. There
he makes it clear that he thinks of the battle between Satan and Christ
literally. Michael then relates the crucifixion briefly, moving out to the
apocalypse before he stops talking, and Adam can then exclaim:

> O goodness infinite, goodness immense!

> That all this good of evil shall produce,
> And evil turn to good; more wonderful
> Then that which by creation first brought forth
> Light out of darkness! full of doubt I stand,
> Whether I should repent me now of sin
> By mee done and occasiond, or rejoyce
> Much more, that much more good thereof shall spring.   [12:469-76]

In short, the basic schemes and patterns of these last three books are circular and biographically discontinuous. Indeed, I may even have over-schematized them in so brief a summary. Perhaps it is better to say that these books wonderfully catch the ebb and flow of human consciousness and everyday spirituality; that in constrast to a systematic, Puritan treatment of spiritual growth, with its neat categories and implicit sense of steady progress, this drama records the real vicissitudes of human existence with its emotional ups and downs. By weaving together the Son's mediatorial descent, Sin and Death's pontifical triumph, and Satan's last magic show, Milton intensifies the emotional drift of the reader in book ten, as a parallel experience to what Adam is feeling. Visions of death, sin, sex, and war affect us (as well as Adam) in book eleven in much the same way, while in book twelve the cyclic history of Israel, so perfectly adapted to this sort of pattern, accomplishes the same thing another way. All three books feel to the reader like the movements of unredeemed history, initially proposing a kind of peace, swirling our attention back into corruption of various sorts, then moving finally (if inconclusively) toward a new peace. Like the Son's chariot, these cycles have wheels within wheels.

The discontinuities between books ten, eleven, and twelve, the result of not tracing out chronological concatenation and causal connection but rather of focusing on such eternal matters as "Prevenient Grace," emerges also in the structure of book eleven. Four times Adam "looked and saw"; once "the face of things" is explicitly "quite chang'd" (11:712), and in each of the other three instances we realize that his point of view, understanding, and response to the vision is "quite chang'd" as well (11:556, 638, 840). To repeat, we see Adam's mind "chang'd" but we do not see the moment when the "things" he looks at *or* his understanding of them *changes*. Similarly, Adam does progress through these three books, but that sense of process is confused and made more complex by the way he spiritually ebbs and flows, even down to this last, by then surprisingly literalistic question about the combat of Christ and Satan. True, he does achieve a kind of equilibrium in his final speech to Michael; there the ebb and flow ceases, because he has "Measur'd this transient World, the Race of time." Yet, if we judge Adam's future by what we know of his personality in the twelve books, we expect further vacillations after he is moved out of Eden.

Just as the operation of divine mercy is more completely uncovered and revealed to us the farther we read, so the claims of mortal existence are fully exhausted in these last few books. The transcendent pressure mounts. Adam and Michael take their place physically above the plane of human existence in book eleven. Below them lies the slough of victors and vanquished, the plight of man comfortless "as when a Father mourns/His Children" (11:760-61), the inescapable imbalance which occurs when "upstart Passions catch the Government/From Reason" (12:88-89). Political "Government" deteriorates to the point where "Tyrannie must be" (12:95). It is a dim view of the human condition indeed when tyranny ineluctably prevails, a vision dimmed further by Adam's failing eyesight and the shift in Michael's mode from literal to spiritual instruction.

                              so shall the World goe on,
To good malignant, to bad men benigne,
Under her own waight groaning, till the day
Appeer of respiration to the just,
And vengeance to the wicked, at return
Of him so lately promis'd to thy aid
The Womans seed, obscurely then foretold,
Now amplier known thy Saviour and thy Lord,
Last in the Clouds from Heav'n to be reveald
In glory of the Father, to dissolve
Satan with his perverted World, then raise
From the conflagrant mass, purg'd and refin'd,
New Heav'ns, new Earth, Ages of endless date
Founded in righteousness and peace and love
To bring forth fruits Joy and eternal Bliss.   [12:537-51]

Like so many passages, this contains the poem as a whole. It recounts how the process of speech has made mercy "now amplier known" and reminds us of the way the verse is doubly apocalyptic, Puritanically uncovering its own assumptions and implications as it drives toward the glory of the millennium. It caps the political analysis, conjoining "*Satan* with his perverted World" and destroying both. "World" occurs with great frequency in these final books, universalizing evil and destruction. There is no place to run in this world, for it is Satan's. Politics is dead.

Yet—and here we return to a basic element of the Puritan sensibility which shaped this poem—there is something to be done; Adam must continue to learn (and he is eager to do so) and be regenerated. Transcendental activism is still essential, just as the faithful angels must fight on. In a Christian poem, it is not of course unusual to experience *contemptus mundi*. Christian doctrine rests upon a transcendent aspiration above and beyond the sphere of our sorrows. What happens in the final books of *Paradise Lost,* is, it seems to me, a great deal more complex than simply resigning the world over to Satan, however. On the one hand, we can see the radical controversialist's mind splitting earth from heaven, rearticulating the basic grounds of Calvinistic divinity. If the world and Satan are one, the other must be radically different. Meanwhile, Adam attains to specifically Christian knowledge and salvation through the working of Puritan anachronism. Historical distance is crushed, for the poem so defines and shapes *our* knowledge that by the end Adam knows precisely what we know, and we know no more. Furthermore, as Adam unites with us historically and intellectually, we all unite with God, not only imaginatively because of the constant eschatological note but also intellectually, in the mode of Puritan theologians, through comprehension. We take it all in, which means that not only the eternal Son of God but also the Father is in a sense "indwelling" in us. Rightly or wrongly we feel not only that Adam knows about God but that we do also. This feeling is our response to an antinomian poem. Given that it is impossible for fallen men either to know God aright or unite with him, to feel this way is to feel superhuman. The poem tricks us into thinking that we can become one with, even be as God. And finally, as the distance between heaven and earth, God and man's understanding is paradoxically crushed, as well as being polarized and increased, so transcendental aspirations away from this world are redirected toward this world. Adam walks out of the enclosed garden of Eden into the active life of the Puritan soldier, and as he comes straight at us, he brings us imaginatively with him, away from retreat and toward action.

The final step in Adam's ascent toward saving faith begins when he asks about the combat between Christ and Satan. Michael replies by telling of the crucifixion, but characteristically spends only a few lines on the drama of the cross (out of the many thousands in this poem); we expect that in a poem shaped by a Puritan. His speech does not even end on that historical "climax" (Fish, *Surprised by Sin,* p. 324) although, as Summers astutely remarked, "another poet would have ended the narrative here" (*Muse's Method,* p. 218). Rather, he swings his, Adam's, and our attention out to the apocalypse, and he will do so again before the poem ends as the millennial pressure builds. In talking briefly about the cross Michael focuses on a noun—a "God-like act" or "this act"—rather than a verb.

> For this he shall live hated, be blasphem'd,
> Seis'd on by force, judg'd, and to death condemnd
> A shameful and accurst, naild to the Cross
> By his own Nation, slaine for bringing Life;
> But to the Cross he nailes thy Enemies,
> The Law that is against thee, and the sins
> Of all mankinde, with him there crucifi'd,
> Never to hurt them more who rightly trust
> In this his satisfaction; so he dies,

But soon revives, Death over him no power
Shall long usurp; ere the third dawning light
Returne, the Starres of Morn shall see him rise
Out of his grave, fresh as the dawning light,
Thy ransom paid, which Man from death redeems,
His death for Man, as many as offerd Life
Neglect not, and the benefit imbrace
By Faith not void of workes: this God-like act
Annuls thy doom, the death thou shouldst have dy'd,
In sin for ever lost from life; this act
Shall bruise the head of *Satan,* crush his strength
Defeating Sin and Death, his two maine armes,
And fix farr deeper in his head thir stings
Then temporal death shall bruise the Victors heel,
Or theirs whom he redeems, a death like sleep,
A gentle wafting to immortal Life.   [12:411-35]

Of the seven verbs predicated to Christ in the first four lines, only one is active: Christ acts only six in all—"to the Cross he nailes," "so he dies,/But soon revives," "rise," and "redeems." The only transitive verb, vigorous and definite, is the metaphoric "nailes," part of Michael's explanation that the combat between Christ and Satan is not literal. True his "act" is busy, annulling, bruising, crushing, and fixing, but like the acts of angelic war, these verbs are not syntactically performed by a hero. Christ's act is mysterious because metaphoric and because it produces further actions of itself. It is also not the dramatic act of a mundane hero.

I have already quoted Adam's response to Michael's narrative of the crucifixion and apocalypse; as he articulates the paradox of the *felix culpa,* Adam attains specifically Christian knowledge. True, Milton was more careful than Thomas Hayne, whose Adam knows that Abel is a "figure of him who by dying, shall overcome the power of the Serpent," or Du Bartas, whose Noah employed much the same, self-consciously prevenient knowledge to rebut Cham.[7] Milton puts most of that sort of talk in the mouth of Michael. But Adam does appear to understand Michael, he is sufficiently "fit" as an audience that he can "stand" full of doubt whether he should repent his act of disobedience or rejoice in the loving possibilities it will allow to flower forth. The verb "to stand" is central to this speech, as we might expect, and the joy is not unmixed; perhaps the most toughminded aspect of *Paradise Lost* is that even here Adam is "full of doubt," that as the line ends, there is a moment when Adam's position remains precarious: "full of doubt I stand." Perhaps, if we ever see Adam's situation change, it is here, as he goes beyond doubtful standing in the next line. Yet even there, Adam proposes one of those "whether . . . or" conundrums which, while they often seem to bear the weight of positive assertion, yet ultimately remain tentative. Clearly, if we count words in this speech, we conclude that it is more important for Adam to "rejoice" than to "repent." Yet never is repentance denied. Something awful has happened, and the poem never lets us entirely forget it, even in its greatest moment of joy.

Moreover, just as Michael does not conclude his speech by fastening on the cross, so there is a final exchange between Michael and Adam. The speech about the crucifixion does not end Adam's education any more than the speech itself could conclude (in such a Puritan poem) upon the scene of suffering and humiliation. Michael rushed forward to the apocalypse, then in his final speech makes another rush at that goal to which so much of this poem has tended. He recounts the Christian era, the time between the cross and us readers, then again throws our attention out beyond the end of time in a rhythm essential to the poem as a whole; the final lines will throw us out beyond the time span of the epic (if one can indeed talk about the time span of a poem which has throughout focused on so much nontime). Adam's ultimate response to this vision "now amplier known" amounts to a Puritanic internal discovery; it culminates his education, quietly and steadfastly fuses time and eternity in a Puritan way, recapitulates the motifs of cyclic degeneracy, the promise of the seed and the millennium, and clarfies and elaborates the parts which have gone before. Adam also recapitulates God's plan and nature—bringing good out of evil— and suggests that the Redeemer is an instructive example, subordinated to, yet carrying man to faith and love in the only God. His is a speech of Puritan perseverance, striking, especially when contrasted to his more exuberant, penultimate response to the crucifixion which precedes it, for its quiet note of acceptance and determination. It dismisses the human concerns of time and history and the exploits of men, resting rather on the absolute, immutable, eternal will of God. Yet it is a speech of steadfastness and perseverance, facing the future with commitment. Just because it is so quiet, so much less flashy than the penultimate speech, and voices so many strands of the Puritan aesthetic, even in its tone, it may not attract attention to itself. In this so very Puritan poem, that fact leads me to feel it is Adam speaking at his most educated:

> How soon hath thy prediction, Seer blest,
> Measur'd this transient World, the Race of time,
> Till time stand fixt: beyond is all abyss,
> Eternitie, whose end no eye can reach.
> Greatly instructed I shall hence depart,
> Greatly in peace of thought, and have my fill
> Of knowledge, what this Vessel can containe;
> Beyond which was my folly to aspire.
> Henceforth I learne, that to obey is best,

And love with fear the onely God, to walk
As in his presence, ever to observe
His providence, and on him sole depend,
Mercifull over all his works, with good
Still overcoming evil, and by small
Accomplishing great things, by things deemd weak
Subverting worldly strong, and worldly wise
By simply meek; that suffering for Truths sake
Is fortitude to highest victorie,
And to the faithful Death the Gate of Life;
Taught this by his example whom I now
Acknowledge my Redeemer ever blest.   [12:553-73]

The antinomian quest has succeeded; Adam sounds more than human, yet at the same time like us. He has completed the Puritan leap of faith and is ready to move out into the world. Sturdy, Puritan soldier of Christ, he is about to march through time in pursuit of the only victory this radical poem can propose—the victory beyond time and the human condition. By stopping his story at this point, Milton simultaneously implies that it and the quest it records are never ending and demonstrates how essentially apolitical Puritan analysis really was. The poem reveals everything about itself as well as a great many things about the mechanisms of Puritan thought.

Afterword

George Fox tells a story in *The Journal* which reveals to me as much as any single episode in all the writing of the period about the texture of religious life in the mid-seventeenth century. Fox had recently converted a man named James Lancaster, and the two had been preaching on an island. As they returned to land, a great crowd of men attacked them "with staves, clubs, and fishing poles and fell upon me with them beating and punching and thrust me backward to the sea. And when they had thrust me almost into the sea, I saw they would have knocked me down there in the sea and thought to have sunk me down into the water. So I stood up and thrust up into the middle of them again. But they all laid at me again and knocked me down and mazed me. And when I was down and came to myself I looked up and I saw James Lancaster's wife throwing stones at my face and James Lancaster her husband was lying over my shoulders to save the blows and stones."[1]

I read that story in the late 1960's, at a time when, among other things, I was advising students who had been arrested for sitting in on various activities of which they disapproved, had often been jailed, and in some few cases had been disowned by parents. What I saw, instantly, was that religious commitment could sunder a family in those days much as political commitments can now. The men who attacked Fox were almost certainly centrist Puritans, Presbyterian or even Independent worshipers in what Fox called "steeple houses," and they had told Lancaster's wife that Fox, in converting him, "had bewitched her husband." Many of the parents who so anguished over the doings of their activist children were similarly reformist-liberal and were often violently nonplussed by the radical forms the reformist impulse their children had been raised in could take. One of those centrist Puritans struck Fox with a Bible during a melee in a church, during service, when Fox sat in and wished to speak. The beatings and jailings he suffered, as he nonviolently pursued his organizing mission, not only struck a responsive chord in anyone familiar with and sympathetic to young activists of the late 1960's, but showed that Mark Twain was probably mostly wrong when he ridiculed the beginning of *Pilgrim's Progress.*[2] The figure of Christian, running through the fields, away from his wife and children, with his fingers in his ears to block out their cries is, at first encounter, comic; yet perhaps that is so largely because the personal anguish underlying the scene is so wrackingly intense. As Adam and Eve take their solitary way out of Eden and into our world

268

of troubles, they face just such problems, as Michael has just explained in his brief review of human history.

Men like James Lancaster, and Fox, and Bunyan, and John Lilburne, and John Milton—the Baptists, Quakers, Diggers, Levellers, Seekers, Fifth Monarchists, Seventh-day Sabbatarians, Muggletonians, and in the largest sense free thinkers—kept what William Haller called the spirit of Puritanism alive, although they eventually scrapped much—in some cases, like the Ranters, all—of the Puritan theology. Fox sat in on Puritan churches and worship services, his new views were directed at the Puritans rather than their conservative adversaries. Fox instinctively knew who his spiritual and intellectual fathers were, where the basis of his thinking and acting came from. But the connection between what Fox preached and what centrist Puritans believe must have been as incomprehensible to the Puritan fathers as the connection between the aggressive activism of the 1960's and New Deal reform appeared to the parents of many of my students. That connection was, quite clearly, only faintly ideological; it was, primarily, a matter of stance, which is why Haller wisely used the term "spirit" in talking about Puritanism, and why I have used the term style.

The Puritans were in many ways destructive, iconoclasts, peace-breakers, regicides. M. M. Knappen and William Haller pointed out how Puritanism, which began primarily as a program for living in this world, ended by suggesting that there were no programmatic rules, external to the self, by which one could be guided.[3] And Perry Miller observed how the Puritans struck at the very roots of their analysis by progressively secularizing their arguments over time.[4] Puritanism considered as a whole shows us some elements of what Stanley Fish has called a self-consuming artifact (see chapter 4, n. 7). The thing which initially appealed to me about the Puritans was their intellectual bravery, their willingness to follow a line of argument systematically no matter how great the personal or intellectual danger involved in the process. Interminable as their prose may be, its sheer length is also a function of their hardiness, their ability to drive on through a point to its radical core. Since they were, above all, concerned with human nature, that root lay in themselves.[5] Thus, their drift was inexorably away from God; thus the Puritan epic has generated more attacks upon its God than probably any other religious poem. The Puritans were destructive for constructive and reconstructive ends; their hardiness testifies to a sense of personal well-being and their reforming zeal expresses a bone-deep faith that the world is worth a great deal—since it is worth reform. Hence the bittersweet conclusion of *Paradise Lost,* a poem above all about loss and sorrow, a poem which ends with its protagonist stepping out into the future.

The same individualistic, aggressive spirit which propelled Presbyterians and Independents into war with their king and the bishops, a spirit they had inherited from their antipapal fathers, drove Fox into confrontation in the "steeple houses" and Lancaster, at odds with his wife, to shield Fox with his body from her blows. All "Puritans," all "advanced or radical Protestants," demystified and rejected while at the same time they lovingly carried forward the work of their fathers. Rejecting the beliefs of what Fox called "professors"—Presbyterian Puritans—, judging and finally decapitating a political father, overthrowing the reign of an ecclesiastical father, or attacking and exposing a Pope in Rome: all these actions were of a piece. These fathers must have been impressive men indeed, for the sons grew up to be so much like them in the ways in which they lived in this world. No wonder Puritan writers clothed the Son in the adjectives and attributes traditionally belonging to the Father. And no wonder, on a verbal level, he ultimately acquired his Father's power.

In locating Milton at the radical end of a liberal-reformist-radical continuum, the process of my analysis from first to last, from Christ and "doctrines" to radical humanism and "uses," has followed the growth of that continuum over time, has traced the advance of that spirit or style, and has also followed what I take to be the shape of Milton's own development. The advances in Milton's thinking, it seems to me, were not haphazard but rather a microcosm of the history of seventeenth-century Puritanism. In *Paradise Lost,* Milton took one further step away from and beyond the systematic writing of earlier generations of Puritan theologians. He had already scrapped much of the programmatic ideology of the Puritans in his tracts on divorce, freedom of the press, tithing, and the Sabbath; he had become very nearly a secular republican by the time of *The Readie and Easie Way.* . . . He had, using the traditional format of the systematic summa, formulated all or at least a great many of the curious, radically Protestant views we find in *De Doctrina Christiana.* But in *Paradise Lost* Milton scrapped almost all of the technical, theological language, the well-thumbed categories, and the essentially tiresome form of systematic divinity itself. He could only take that step and dramatize rather than schematize the spirit of Puritanism so fully because he was a radical reformer. I say that for several reasons. Puritans had always wished initially to "get on top" of their world and ideas—hence the almost compulsive effort to systematize. Only a writer coming at the end of such a tradition could so successfully get on top of and dominate the implications of the Puritan style as to ignore the compulsive format and show that spirit in action. Milton handled Puritanism in the way his God treats his creatures; he could release the impulse to flower in deeds, in a story. And only a radical Puritan would be inclined to scrap the format of his fathers and innovatively create a new medium.

There was at least one further step along the radical road before him. In *Samson Agonistes,* as Stanley Fish has argued, Milton presents through his characters "two kinds of related uncertainties: an uncertainty as to the springs (or motivations) of human action, and an uncertainty as to the connection between events in the world of man and the will of God."[6] The individualistic, apocalyptic, antinomian strain remained constant there, for as Fish notes, when Samson says "Yet . . . [God] may dispense with me or thee/Present in Temples at Idolatrous Rites/For some important cause," the "Yet" by which Samson dispenses with "the Law" is "Liberating" (p. 254). Samson's gesture is antinomian; further, he dispenses with the law by stating that God dispenses with it. Such a stance underlay Milton's mature political analysis as well as his poetic vision. Indeed, Fish suggests acutely that the play almost forcibly drives the reader to a self-deifying lament—"if he were only God" (p. 263) which replicates the adventurous aims of Samson himself. A similar pressure on the reader is generated by *Paradise Lost* as well; by asking the reader to comprehend God, it effectively makes him think and see *as* God. The radical advance in *Samson Agonistes* consists in revealing the ultimate isolation and potential terror of such a point of view more clearly. By omitting God from the cast of characters, Milton underscores the terrible possibility that "no firm—that is external—basis for action exists in this world" (Fish, p. 253). The dramatic action of the epic includes God and hence implies connections (whether or not they are ever "explained") between creaturely action (which God does at least "regard") and divine response (which is portrayed for us). Admittedly, epics conventionally include gods as characters while dramas do not; when the latter include deities, they degenerate into melodrama controlled by *dei ex machina*. Consummate artist that he was, Milton no doubt perceived the generic problem when he set out, proudly, to fulfill himself in epic, brief epic, and tragedy. His was a sensibility inclined to include deities, to embrace the "big picture" in its most cosmic, absolute terms, so that limitation might well have struck him forceably. Still, it was Milton's *choice* to turn to drama, with its generically humanistic rather than potentially theocentric bias and demands. And it seems to me he could only have taken that step after the innovations we find in *Paradise Lost* and *Paradise Regain'd.*[7] The latter dramatized the problem of how a man can act on his own and yet in concert with God, the problem which Stephen Marshall raised in his discussion of kairos, the problem of recognizing and seizing that moment "apted and fitted to the doing of a business," without on the one hand being precipitous and without on the other lagging noncommittally behind. *Samson Agonistes* pressed the radical Puritan analysis and demystification so far as to raise the question whether there is in fact a God out there to work in tandem with and serve as agent for. Without a "firm" and "external basis for acting," without God dramatically present, one can rely only, in an antinomian way, on oneself.

To account for apples and oranges together, one must find the common traits between them. What unites antipapal controversialists, reformist Puritans, and the radicals is a spirit. And what accounts most successfully for the particular way *Paradise Lost* was crafted is the same spirit. This sort of analysis must resist the Arnoldian dichotomy between "literature" or "higher literature" and everything else that is written. I tried to qualify both the dichotomy and the modes of thinking which cluster around it, rather than subvert them, because obviously there is a difference between *Paradise Lost* and, let us say, the sermons of Stephen Marshall. Milton's poem is more accessible (I am speaking here not in the trivial terms of modern editions, although modern editions probably reflect the accessibility I mean) to a modern reader than those sermons. We feel immediately after reading Marshall that we need more "background"; *Paradise Lost* seems more self-contained. But, however important these differences are, and I wish to return to them in a moment, the fact remains that literary critics focus almost exclusively on those differences. There is "literature" and there is "background," "art" and "writing," and the aim is always to elucidate the former of each pair. When "background" is simply assumed without comment, the critic refers his understanding of the lines to the poem as a whole (which was not, however, *sui generis*), to the canon of Milton's writing (which was not, quite obviously, disconnected from the affairs of his society), or to literary traditions (which no writer is chosen or shaped by but rather chooses and shapes for himself). I am in effect discussing a question of "explanation," which Basil Willey has pointed out is a question really of emotional satisfaction.[8] Predominately, critics have found the greatest satisfaction by segregating "literature" from other verbal behavior and from the society in which it was written. In view of the imbalance, it seemed justifiable to list to the other side, stress the similarities between radical and centrist Puritans as well as poem and polemic, and refer Milton's lines to the activities of men around Milton as he wrote as well as to his own "nonliterary" behavior.

Strictly speaking, fully to democratize my analysis, I should have expanded my consideration of Puritan preaching in two ways. Rather than considering just four controversies, I might have gone on to show how *all* of the Puritans' specific doctrines click into place as integrated parts of a consistent whole. That would have reduplicated much previous work and been beside the point as well. For if there was a spirit or style informing all this verbal (as well as nonverbal) behavior, then a few representative issues, selected with an eye to their manifold diversity, ought to suffice. The sheer verbosity of the Puritans blocked me here as well as in the other direction in which I might have expanded, for they preached for so long, on so many occasions, that it is impossible to give more than a brief sketch of the texture of their verbal behavior. The Puritan style is always telling us not to look at it and its supposed artlessness, a fact which may explain why the tools of the so-called "new criticism" were so late applied to Milton as compared to other poets; perhaps that implicit instruction not to look at Puritan style will also serve as warrant for the brevity of my treatment. Puritan prose often resembles a tidal wave of cream of wheat flowing uphill, and I chose not to drown in it.

The Arnoldian critic of "higher literature" who denigrates the efforts of lesser pens purports to be a humanist. Like him, I believe I am explicating human behavior, and like him I assume that man by nature imposes order, partly conscious, partly unconscious, upon his life and the world he sees himself living in. Yet there are certain contradictions which creep into purely formalist or literary elitism. Often one gets the feeling that a tradition, a convention or a poem itself, rather than a man, generates this verbal order. More generally, to distinguish between "literature" and everything else written is either to assign that ordering power only to some men or else to deny it to others. Nonliterary writers implicitly become, in this view, subhuman, or else "ordering" is no longer the essential, definitive term for human nature, or else the poets are somehow superhuman, in which case the "humanist" is no longer studying human behavior. In the process of getting at the really gripping side of religious writing, the side which comes out in Fox's story about the Lancasters, the side on which ideas matter so much to human beings that they affect daily intimacies, I have had to democratize the tools of the literary critic and go searching for the patterns which inform the popular culture, the passionate polemic, as well as the lofty poem. That is easy if one treats all the verbal behavior of men democratically and their authors in the same spirit. I cannot necessarily claim that Stephen Marshall is more important than John Milton, but I cannot make the counterclaim either. Without the revolution which Marshall so obviously helped to foment, Milton's nonpoetic writing would not exist, his ideas might well not have developed as they did, and certain resonances in his poetry would be entirely lacking.

All men strike, out of the idiosyncratic interaction between their individual personality and their social surroundings, some pattern of and for themselves. To retain my examples, both Stephen Marshall and John Milton undertook to change their society. Marshall preached his terrifying sermon, *Meroz cursed*, recommending that it was "blessed" to bloody one's hands in committed pursuit of the millennium and cursed to remain neutral and not even dash "the little ones against the stones." He urged that view out of the same personal vision which rendered his sermons "occasional," a passionate response to the moment, and in the same activist's style which carried him physically before Parliament not once but many times to exhort them. Therein was a pattern, expressing a life style, and the pattern-seeking tools of the humanist can be brought to bear upon it. Milton, in contrast to Marshall, donned the singing robes in *Paradise Lost,* a gesture consistent with writing a literary version of a speech before Parliament rather than physically addressing it, with preaching divorce but not divorcing, with apologizing in Latin for regicide but no more. The members of Parliament had to listen to Marshall (or doze through his sermon), but they did not have to buy *Areopagitica.* Immediately, Marshall was politically more effective than Milton, as each man radicalized the reforming urge in his own way. To get a little, you must give up a little. For all his personal commitment, Milton wrote a poem often judged noncommitted, and forwent a kind of impact upon his society which in many ways he seems to have wished he might exert.

Nature's "world is brazen; the poets only deliver a golden" wrote Sir Philip Sidney in words which seem to confirm the Arnoldian dichotomy between art and writing, poets and the rest of humanity. Sidney himself went on to comment upon the "saucy" overtones of his remark, to wonder whether such a position did not implicitly criticize God and seek to outdo him, and to pen demonstrably "ungilded" poems and stories.[9] The formalist's notion that literary works, or more generally poets, can be insulated from the brazen world not only denigrates pragmatic accomplishment here below, but has been disputed by students of crisis psychology and utopianism; Weston LaBarre in *The Ghost Dance* (New York, 1970) for one, suggests that the effort to spiritualize, transcend, disregard, or gild the brazen occurs particularly when that brass is furnishing the trumpets of war or social dislocation, that the effort is at best an attempt to contain and control what the individual perceives to be chaotic and uncontrollable, and that at worst it is an effort to evade, escape, or regress from it. If, as LaBarre suggests, gilding is a common human response, it remains true nevertheless that some men devote more of their energy to working the brass into extremely useful items. The danger is, it seems to me, that a critic will become so enamored of a poet's golden tones that he will begin really to believe that impossible dream of living in utopian isolation, that nowhere where social strife does not affect the individual, and will thus cut the strife right out of his analysis.[10]

I do not think I demean Milton by calling him Puritan, by implying in that term his radical activism, even in his poetry, or by placing him beside Stephen Marshall. No more do I demean him by noting the potentially antisocial, antinomian pressure at work in his thought and art; nor when I point out his limitations as a political activist. Like all men, Milton gave a little to get a little. Something in his style checked both his ability to carry men with him and his ability to wield an ax. Limitations may also be virtues; the curbing impulse diffused his political effectiveness at the same time it directed the antinomian claims away from antisocial acts and into the soaring lines. And that curb also allowed Milton to state the dangers of soaring, even poetically. There are two great "soarers" in *Paradise Lost:* Milton's "song" which intended to soar "above th' Aonian *Mount*" in the very beginning and above "Olympus Hill" at the very middle of the poem, and Satan and his ambitious thoughts. Only an analysis of Milton's poetry which refers the lines not to other lines, other poems, or the poet's insulated canon but rather to the activities of mankind and to the turmoil of the society in which the poet wrote can fully face this problem. For Milton, perhaps above all poets in the history of English literature, was a committed activist who saw an intimate connection between his poetry and politics. Only a fugitive and cloistered version of Milton and his poetry would evade the awful, human possibilities both for evil and for good which Milton himself articulated in his own vision.

Appendix: THE INCREASED REFERENCE TO CHRIST IN PURITAN PREACHING

The sermons which John Wilson analyzes in his *Pulpit in Parliament*[1] seem, as he himself argues, a remarkably coherent and well-chosen sample of Puritan preaching, as useful as any sample drawn from the vast outpouring of such material in the period, significant perforce because of the situation under which the sermons were delivered, and at least a manageable basis for rudimentary numerical analysis, of which historians are now becoming enamored. Hence I shall refocus attention upon his material here.

Wilson analyzes the distribution throughout the Bible of the texts upon which the sermons were preached, arriving at the not unexpected results that many books provided a jumping-off place for Puritan preachers, but that Old Testament texts predominate over New Testament texts by a ratio of slightly over 3 to 1. Like all countable data, the texts of the sermons show some things and not others. Wilson notes that of the 55 New Testament texts, 14 were from Revelation, 9 were drawn from Matthew, 1 from Mark, and none from Romans, Galatians, Ephesians (Wilson does not mention how many texts were drawn from the other Gospels, nor does he, unfortunately, provide listings of the texts). Bearing in mind my point that the Puritans shunned the Gospels, I suspect that were one to count Biblical citations used during the body of the sermon to expound upon even these texts from the Gospels, one would find that the ratio of citations from the Old Testament, Pauline material, and Revelation would outweigh references to the Gospels by an even greater proportion.

I make that admittedly unverifiable reservation concerning Wilson's findings, which in general seem admirable, useful, and consistent with my own argument, as a caveat to counters, before I proceed to count myself. There are, admittedly, objections which can be made to the selection of any countable data, including my own.

I have selected from Wilson's Appendix II, *Calendar of Printed Sermons Preached to Members of the Long Parliament,* titles which, in my opinion, make clear references to sacred history or parts of the Bible and I have arranged them in two groups. By "clear reference" I mean a reference which would be obvious to a person familiar with the Bible but unacquainted with the content of the sermon. Thus, I have eliminated several sermons

—Marshall's *The strong helper* or *A sacred record* are just two—which I
know to be about predominantly Old Testament topics, because the titles
do not fully indicate or suggest the topics. In addition, I have not included
titles which refer to "the covenant," "God," to "the Christian," nor, obviously, the many which are entitled *A sermon preached.* Out of the 253
sermons listed in Wilson's Appendix, 9 were preached after Wilson's
terminal date of study and 27 were in some way occasional or suspect. I
have considered all 253, but, with the exception of the last 9 (for the years
1649–52), none figured in the following lists. Of these sermons, 74, in my
estimation, have clear references to sacred history or parts of the Bible in
the title.

The first group consists of sermons which refer to the Old Testament.
Included in it are references to Jerusalem which seem clearly to point to
Old Testament sources, but excluded are titles which might refer to both
the Old Testament and the new Jerusalem (e.g., Christopher Tesdale's
Hierusalem: or a vision of peace [London, 1644]—which sounds strongly
millenary). There are 49 sermons in this group.

In the second group I have placed sermons which refer to the New
Testament, Christ, or the apocalypse, omitting certain titles which sound
strongly millenary but could refer to other topics. There are 25 in this
category, or in other words there seem to be a proportionally greater
number of sermons which refer, in their shortened titles, to these topics
rather than to the Old Testament (25:49, or almost 1:2) than there are
sermons which Wilson says were preached on New Testament texts as
opposed to those preached on texts from the Old Testament (1:3).

But a more interesting point emerges if we consider these sermons not
as a single, monolithic group, but turn to the ratios between the two
groups as they change from year to year. Then we must conclude that,
assuming that the title did really announce the topic, the announced
topics of the sermons changed markedly in the 12 years covered by
Wilson's list. From 1640 through 1645, sermons referring to Old Testament
topics and themes clearly outnumbered sermons referring to New Testament topics, Christ, and the apocalypse. But beginning with 1646, sermons addressed to the latter topics outnumbered sermons on the former
in every single year.

How fairly these titles do represent the subject matter of the sermon,
and how representative these 74 sermons are of Wilson's whole sample are
both matters of dispute. However, given the curious ways Puritans could
turn discussion of a text into the most unexpected lines of argument, it
seems to make as much sense to talk about the titles of the sermons as it
does for Wilson to analyze the texts preached on. In the list which follows
I have arranged the sermons chronologically as they were preached,
showing in the first column the year (arbitrarily in old rather than new

style) and the total number of extant sermons preached before Parliament
in that year; in the second column I have first shown the total number of
identifiable Old Testament titles, then the titles themselves, and have done
the same thing for New Testament and millennial titles. The chronological
order of preaching can be seen by moving down the page from top to bottom, and back and forth from column to column as need be. For each sermon, I have given the name of the preacher and short title, but not place
and date of publication nor STC number as provided by Wilson.

Year and number preached	Old Testament	New Testament, including Christ and Revelation
1640:3	1	0
	Wilson, Thomas, *David's zeale for Zion*	
1641:19	4	0
	Bridge, William, *Babylons downfall*	
	Burton, Henry, *Englands bondage and hope of deliverance*	
	Burroughs, Jeremiah, *Sions joy*	
	Marshall, Stephen, *Meroz cursed*	
1642:25	7	3
	Goodwin, Thomas, *Zerubbabels encouragement to finish the temple*	
		Caryll, Joseph, *The workes of Ephesus explained*
	Sedgwick, William, *Zions deliverance and her friends duty*	
	Reynolds, Edward, *Israels petition in time of trouble*	
	Carter, William, *Israels peace with God*	
	Wilson, Thomas, *Jerichoes downfall*	
		Temple, Thomas, *Christ's government in and over his people*
	Vines, Richard, *Calebs integrity in following the Lord fully*	
		Whitaker, Jeremiah, *Ejrenopoios, Chris the settlement of unsettled times*
	Bridges, Walter, *Joabs counsell, and King Davids seasonable hearing it*	
1643:37	11	1
	Lightfoot, John, *Elias redivivus*	
	Cheynell, Francis, *Sions memento, and Gods alarum*	
	Marshall, Stephen, *The song of Moses*	
	Sedgwick, Obadiah, *Haman's vanity*	
	Herle, Charles, *Davids song of three parts*	
	Carter, Thomas, *Prayers prevalencie for Israels safety*	

Year and number preached	Old Testament	New Testament, including Christ and Revelation
	Newcomen, Matthew, *Jerusalems watchmen, the Lords remembrancers*	
		Hill, Thomas, *The militant church, triumphant over the dragon and his angels*
	Tuckney, Anthony, *The balme of Gilead*	
	Wilkinson, Henry, *Babylons ruine, Jerusalems rising*	
	Mewe, William, *The robbing and spoiling of Jacob and Israel*	
	Strickland, John, *Gods work of mercy, in Sions misery*	
1644:45	12	4
		Caryll, Joseph, *The saints thankfull acclamation at Christs resumption of his great power and the initials of his kingdome*
	Greene, John, *Nehemiah's tears and prayers for Judah's affliction, and the ruines and repaire of Jerusalem*	
	Staunton, Edmund, *Rupes Israelis, the rock of Israel*	
	Hardwick, Humphrey, *The difficulty of Sions deliverance and reformation*	
	Vines, Richard, *Magnalia Dei ab aquilone; set forth*	
	Reyner, William, *Babylon's ruining—earthquake*	
	Seaman, Lazarus, *Solomons choice*	
	Sedgwick, Obadiah, *An arke against a deluge*	
	Vines, Richard, *The posture of Davids spirit*	
		Woodcock, Francis, *Christ's warning-piece*
	Staunton, Edmund, *Phinehas's zeal in execution of judgment*	
	Herle, Charles, *David's reserve and rescue*	
		Strickland, John, *Immanuel*
		Ashe, Simeon, *The church sinking, saved by Christ*
	Arrowsmith, John, *Englands Ebenezer or, stone of help*	
	Vines, Richard, *The happinesse of Israel*	
1645:45	7	1
	Byfield, Richard, *Zion's answer to the nations ambassadors*	

Year and number preached	Old Testament	New Testament, including Christ and Revelation
	Woodcock, Francis, *Lex talionis: or, God paying every man* Hickes, Gaspar, *The life and death of David* Whincop, John, *Israels tears for distressed Zion* Dury, John, *Israels call to march out of Babylon unto Jerusalem* White, John, *The troubles of Jerusalems restauration*	
		Strong, William, *Humera apokalupseus. The day of revelation*
	Woodcock, Francis, *Joseph paralled* [sic] *by the present parliament*	
1646:38	2	3
	Herricke, Richard, *Queen Esthers resolves*	
		Maynard, John, *A shadow of the victory of Christ* Marshall, Stephen, *A two-edged sword out of the mouth of babes*
	Goode, William, *Jacob raised*	
		Seaman, Lazarus, *The head of the church the judge of the world*
1647:18	3	4
	Johnson, Robert, *Lux & lex, or the light and law of Jacobs house* Ashe, Simeon, *Gods incomparable goodnesse unto Israel*	
		Strong, William, *The trust and the account of a steward* Case, Thomas, *Spirituall whoredome discovered in a sermon* Hughes, George, *Vae-euge-tuba. Or, the wo-joy-trumpet*
	Manton, Thomas, *Meate out of the eater*	
		Valentine, Thomas, *Christs counsell to poore and naked souls* Sterry, Peter, *The clouds in which Christ comes*
1648:14	1	4
		Sterry, Peter, *The teachings of Christ in the soule* Bridge, William, *Christs coming opened in a sermon* Marshall, Stephen, *Emmanuell: a thanksgiving sermon*
	Bond, John, *Eshcol, or grapes (among) thorns*	

Year and number preached	Old Testament	New Testament, including Christ and Revelation
1649:6	1	Cokayn, George, *Flesh expiring, and the spirit inspiring in the new earth* 3 Owen, John, *Ouranon ourania. The shaking and translating of heaven and earth*
	Cooper, William, *[Hebrew] ierusalem fatall to her assailants*	
1651:2	0	Sterry, Peter, *The comings forth of Christ in the power of his death* Powell, Vavasor, *Christ exalted above all creatures by God his father* 0
1652:1	0	1 Owen, John, *The advantage of the kingdome of Christ in the shaking of the kingdoms of the world*
Total	49	24

Notes

1. W. Frazer Mitchell, *English Pulpit Oratory from Andrewes to Tillotson* (London, 1932), pp. 255–58, dismisses Puritan preaching as devoid of style. Morris W. Croll, *Style, Rhetoric and Rhythm*, ed. J. Max Patrick (Princeton, 1966), and George Williamson, *The Senecan Amble* (London, 1951), the two most important students of prose style in the period, largely ignore Puritans. Joan Webber, *The Eloquent "I"* (Madison, 1968), supplied a partial corrective.

2. Lawrence Stone, *The Causes of the English Revolution, 1529–1642* (London, 1972); however one might quarrel with any single point Stone makes, the questions he poses make excellent sense.

3. C. S. Lewis, *English Literature in the Sixteenth Century excluding Drama* (Oxford, 1954), p. 18.

4. John Milton, *The Reason of Church-Government Urg'd Against Prelaty*, in *The Works of John Milton*, ed. F. A. Patterson (New York, 1931–38), 3:242. Subsequent citations of Milton's work will be to this edition, abbreviated *CE*, with the exception of *De Doctrina Christiana*. In that single case, I shall use John Carey's translation (see n. 26) in the still forthcoming *Complete Prose Works of John Milton* (New Haven, 1953–) because his translation must be adopted in preference to Sumner's, which appears in CE.

5. In the unifying tradition of E. M. W. Tillyard's *Elizabethan World Picture* are B. Rajan, *Paradise Lost and the Seventeenth-Century Reader* (London, 1962 [First published, 1947]); C. A. Patrides, *Milton and the Christian Tradition* (New York, 1966); F. Michael Krouse, *Milton's Samson and the Christian Tradition* (Princeton, 1949).

6. Michael Walzer, *The Revolution of the Saints* (Cambridge, Mass., 1965) and Christopher Hill, *Intellectual Origins of the English Revolution* (Oxford, 1965), and *Society and Puritanism in Pre-Revolutionary England*, 2nd ed. (New York, 1967), treat Puritanism as a political ideology.

7. Lewis makes that point, *English Literature in the Sixteenth Century*, p. 23, and I have elaborated it, "The First English Pediatricians and Tudor Attitudes toward Childhood," *JHI* 35(1974):561–77.

8. That is, for example, the history of Puritan marriage manuals from William Perkins's *Christian oeconomie* (1595) to William Gouge's *Of domestical duties* (1624).

9. Douglas Bush, *English Literature of the Earlier Seventeenth Century* (Oxford, 1962), p. 312.

10. Abraham Wright, *Five sermons in five several styles or waies of preaching* (London, 1656). For a discussion of Wright's collection and Puritan preaching style, see Larzer Ziff, "The Literary Consequences of Puritanism," *ELH* 30(1963):293–305.

11. For the essentially bipartite form of Puritan preaching, see Mitchell, *English Pulpit Oratory*, pp. 93ff.

12. A. S. P. Woodhouse, "The Argument of Milton's *Comus*," *UTQ* 11(1941):46–71, assumes another unmediated pattern, the "segregation" of "nature" from "grace."

13. Malcolm Ross, *Poetry and Dogma* (New Brunswick, 1954). The excesses of Ross's study do not diminish the astuteness of his remarks on this matter.

14. François Wendel, *Calvin: The Origins and Development of His Religious Thought*, trans. Philip Mairet (New York, 1963), p. 224.

15. John Calvin, *Institutes of the Christian Religion*, bk. II, ch. xi, 10, ed. John T. McNeill, trans. Ford Lewis Battles (Philadelphia, 1961), p. 459. Subsequent citations will be to this edition, abbreviated "McNeill."

16. John Headley, *Luther's View of Church History* (New Haven, 1963), pp. 100–103, comments on "the Church of the Word" in Luther's thought. For a characteristic discussion by Luther of the shape of sacred history, see Martin Luther, "Preface to the

New Testament," *Works*, ed. Jaroslav Pelikan and Helmut T. Lehmann (Saint Louis, 1958-59; Philadelphia, 1960), 35:357-62.

17. For a review of the sacramentarian controversy between Luther and Calvin's disciple Zwingli, and Luther's views about the sacrament, see James Mackinnon, *Luther and the Reformation* (New York, 1962), 3:315ff.

18. John Calvin, "The Author's Preface," *Commentary on the Book of Psalms* (Edinburgh, 1845), 1:xl-xli.

19. Erik Erikson, *Young Man Luther* (New York, 1958), p. 254.

20. Edmund Wilson, "Morose Ben Jonson," *The Triple Thinkers* (New York, 1963), pp. 213-32.

21. Charles Mauron, "L'Inconscient dans l'oeuvre et la vie de Racine," *Annales de la Faculté des Lettres d'Aix-en-Provence* (1957); *Introduction to the Psychoanalysis of Mallarmé*, trans. Archibald Henderson, Jr. and Will L. McLendon (Berkeley, 1963), pp. 217-48 and passim.

22. Norman Holland, "Prose and Minds: A Psychoanalytic Approach to Non-Fiction," *The Art of Victorian Prose*, ed. George Levine and William Madden (New York, 1968), pp. 314-37; Richard Ohmann, "A Linguistic Appraisal of Victorian Style," in the same collection, provided the linguistic analysis on which Holland worked. Holland treats literary life styles in *The Dynamics of Literary Response* (New York, 1968), pp. 235-37.

23. Wendel, *Calvin*, p. 285. For Calvin's restrained handling of the Apocalypse, see *The Institutes*, bk. III, ch. xxv; McNeill ed., pp. 987-1008.

24. John Donne, *The Poems*, ed. Herbert J. C. Grierson (Oxford, 1958), 1:325.

25. John F. H. New, *Anglican and Puritan: The Basis of Their Opposition, 1558-1640* (London, 1964).

26. Cf. C. J. Stranks, *The Life and Writing of Jeremy Taylor* (London, 1952), pp. 150-61, for a careful exposition of Taylor's views; John Goodwin, *An exposition of the ninth chapter of the Epistle to the Romans: wherein ... is plainly shewed and proved that the Apostle's scope therein is to assert and maintain his great doctrine of justification by faith, and that here he discourseth nothing at all concerning any personal election or reprobation of men from eternity* (London, 1653); John Milton, *De Doctrina Christiana*, trans. John Carey, in *The Complete Prose Works* (New Haven, 1953–), ed. Don M. Wolfe, vol. 6. Subsequent citations will be to book and chapter, then to this edition, abbreviated "Yale," by page.

27. His internal, economic policies seem to have been equally simple and simple-minded; pay off political and other debts or forge new political alliances by redistributing land, but do so without altering the fabric of English society. Of course, breaking up the monasteries had a profound social, economic, and political impact, far beyond what Henry contemplated.

CHAPTER 1

1. John Milton, *De Doctrina Christiana*, bk. I, ch. xvi; Yale ed., 6:441.

2. If the dispute over bowing at the name of Jesus was not relatively a very important liturgical controversy (the sacraments, with which Malcolm Ross began, loomed, for example much larger in men's pages and expressed more directly the individual's definition of the divine nature), nevertheless, I pursue it because it shows men writing under pressure in a polarized situation where extravagant (and revealing) statements often occur, and it demonstrates more easily than sacramental dispute the connection between liturgy and *attitudes* toward the Deity. To bow or not to bow was, obviously, a question of attitude. Less central than sacramental speculation, this topic shows diverse feelings about God phrased in occasionally "unbalanced" and casually adopted terms, and shows more nakedly whither more balanced, organized, central speculation tended.

3. *The Nevv Testament of Iesvs Christ faithfvlly translated into English out of the authentical Latin ... by the English College then resident in Rhemes* (Antwerp, 1600),

p. 529. The Annotations, the doctrinal part of this polemical publication, follow, at greater or lesser length, each chapter of text and are referred to throughout this chapter as Annotations.

4. John Calvin, *Commentaries on the Epistles to the Philippians, Colossians, and Thessalonians* . . . , trans. Rev. John Pringle (Edinburgh, 1851), p. 60.

5. Thomas Cartwright, *A confvtation of the Rhemist's translation, glosses, and annotations on the Nevv Testament* . . . ([Leyden], 1618), p. 500.

6. William Fulke, *The text of the New Testament of Iesvs Christ, translated out of the vulgar Latine by the Papists of the traiterous Seminarie at Rhemes . . . with a confutation of all svch arguments, glosses, and annotations as conteine manifest impiety, of heresie, treason, and slander, against the Catholike Church of God and the true teachers thereof* . . . (London, 1601), p. 627.

7. Andrew Willet, *Synopsis Papismi, that is, a generall view of Papistrie, wherein the whole mysterie of iniqvitie and svmme of Antichristian doctrine is set downe* . . . (London, 1600), p. 1062.

8. A. S. P. Woodhouse, "Introduction," *Puritanism and Liberty: Being the Army Debates (1647-9)* . . . (Chicago, 1951), pp. 39-40, 57-60, 84-86.

9. Gervase Babington, *The workes of the right reverend father in God Gervase Babington, late Bishop of Worcester* (London, 1615), pp. 2, 246.

10. William Whitaker, *An answere to a certeine booke written by M. William Rainolds Student of Diuinite in the English Colledge at Rhemes, and entituled "A refutation of sundrie reprehensions, cauils, &c."* (London, 1585), p. 199.

11. New, *Anglican and Puritan*, p. 19.

12. Louis Martz, *The Poetry of Meditation* (New Haven, 1954), pp. 163-64.

13. George Herbert, *Works*, ed. F. E. Hutchinson (Oxford, 1941), p. 43.

14. Richard Crashaw, "Hymn in the Holy Nativity," *The Complete Poetry of Richard Crashaw*, ed. George Walton Williams (Garden City, N.Y., 1970), p. 83.

CHAPTER 2

1. A. F. Scott Pearson, *Thomas Cartwright and Elizabethan Puritanism, 1535-1603* (Cambridge, 1925), pp. 372-86.

2. Thomas Adams, *The workes of Tho: Adams* . . . (London, 1629), p. 1199.

3. Henry Airay, *Lectvres upon the whole Epistle of St Pavl to the Philippians* . . . , ed. Christopher Potter (London, 1618), p. 338.

4. The only other extant work of Airay's concerns a lawsuit which he seems voluntarily to have entered into by accepting a contested benefice. Yet, as *DNB* notes, his aims were "unselfish" and directed to the good of the parish. If entering a lawsuit suggests a contentious personality, Airay's part in this one fits a much milder man, "zealous and fervent, not turbulent and contentious."

5. Joan Webber, *The Eloquent "I"* (Madison, 1968), 7-8 and passim.

6. Joseph Summers, *The Muse's Method* (London, 1962), pp. 11-31.

CHAPTER 3

1. John Boys, *An exposition of the dominical epistles and gospels vsed in our English liturgie throughout the whole yeere*, pt. 2, *The Spring-part from the first in Lent to Whitsunday* (London, 1610), p. 122.

2. Lancelot Andrewes, *Works*, ed. J. P. Wilson and James Bliss, in The Library of Anglo-Catholic Theology (Oxford, 1841-54), 2:337.

CHAPTER 4

1. Prynne's interest in bowing dates back to his attack in 1628 on Cosin's devotions, *A briefe survay and censure of Mr. Cozens his cozening devotions* (London, 1628). In 1630, Prynne seems to have published a tract on bowing (*Short relations of the true beginning and progress of bowing.* . . .) no longer extant, to which Giles Widdowes seems to have replied. Prynne lashed out with *Lame Giles his havltings or a briefe survey of Giles Widdovves his confutation* . . . ([London], 1630), and Widdowes replied with *The*

lawlesse, kneelesse, schismaticall Puritan or a confutation... (Oxford, 1631). Page joined Widdowes in the attack on Prynne, in the same year, with *A treatise or ivstification of bowing at the name of Iesvs...* (Oxford, 1631). Prynne gave his fullest exposition, five years later, in *Certaine qvaeres propounded to the bowers at the name of Iesvs...* ([London], 1636). An anonymous tract, *Argvments against bovving at the name of Iesvs, composed about five yeares afore, by a reverened minister of the city of London for his own defence* (no place, no publisher, 1641), re-edited as *Several arguments against bowing at the name of Iesus...* (no place, no publisher, 1660), has been attributed to William Wickins by Halkett and Laing and others afterwards. Samuel Halkett and John Laing, *Dictionary of Anonymous and Pseudonymous English Literature* (1926 ed., Edinburgh and London), cite Edmund Calamy's *Nonconformist Memorial*, but in the 1775 edition of that work, edited by Samuel Palmer, 1:84, Calamy attributes only a third tract, *The warrant for bowing at the name of Jesus examined* ([London], 1660) to Wickins.

    2. William Prynne, "A Preface," *Certaine qvaeres propounded to the bowers at the name of Iesvs* ([London], 1636), sig. [A1]^r and v

    3. Sir Thomas Browne, *Religio Medici*, in *The Works of Sir Thomas Browne*, ed. Geoffrey Keynes (London, 1928), 1:12-13.

    4. Joseph Summers, *George Herbert: His Religion and Art* (Cambridge, Mass., 1954), pp. 49-69.

    5. Henry Vaughan, *The Works*, ed. L. C. Martin, 2nd ed. (Oxford, 1957), p. 412. This is, it seems to me, one of the best jobs Vaughan ever did, explicating through conceit a physical object (albeit a relatively nebulous one). The poem does move as the idea is unfolded, and there is a suggestion of ultimate redemption, for all the initial disease. Still, notice the extreme tentativeness of the ending—"If... could... perhaps at last...My God *would* give."

    6. Christopher Hill, *Anti-Christ in Seventeenth-Century England* (London, New York, 1971).

    7. Stanley Fish, *Self-Consuming Artifacts: The Experience of Seventeenth-Century Literature* (Berkeley, 1972), has a good analysis of the difficulties the reader faces in *Of Reformation*, pp. 265-306.

    8. It is, of course, the paradox of the Marxist revolutionary as well; it informed the radical millennialism of the middle ages which Norman Cohn, *The Pursuit of the Millennium*, rev. ed. (New York, 1970), has analyzed.

    9. Joseph Summers, *The Muse's Method* (London, 1962), pp. 179-80.

CHAPTER 5

    1. John Hooper, *A declaration of the ten holy comaundementes of allmygthye God* (Zurich, 1548), sig. B iii^r.

    2. Calvin, *The Institutes*, bk. II, ch. x, 2; McNeill ed., p. 429.

    3. Robert Cox, *The Literature of the Sabbath Question*, 2 vols. (Edinburgh, 1865), preface.

    4. Patrick Collinson, "The Beginnings of English Sabbatarianism," *Studies in Church History*, ed. C. W. Dugmore and Charles Duggan (London, 1964), 1:207-21.

    5. M. M. Knappen, *Tudor Puritanism* (Chicago, 1939), p. 442.

    6. Christopher Hill, *Society and Puritanism*, 2nd ed. (New York, 1967), pp. 124-218.

    7. Nicholas Bownd, *The doctrine of the Sabbath...* (London, 1595).

    8. John Dod, *A plaine and familiar exposition of the Ten Commandements...* (London, 1612), p. 3.

    9. C. A. Patrides, "Ascending by Degrees Magnificent: The Christian View of History," *Milton and the Christian Tradition* (Oxford, 1966), pp. 220-63.

    10. George Herbert, *The Works*, ed. F. E. Hutchinson (Oxford, 1941), p. 128.

    11. John Donne, *Devotions upon Emergent Occasions*, ed. John Sparrow (Cambridge, 1923), p. 4.

    12. Frank Kermode, *The Sense of an Ending* (New York, 1967).

13. John Donne, *The Poems*, ed. H. J. C. Grierson (Oxford, 1912), 1:368-69.

14. Irenaeus, *Adversus Haeresis* iv.38. I have throughout used the translation in the Ante-Nicene Christian Library (Edinburgh, 1867), vols. 5, 9. Jean Danielou, S.J., points out that for Irenaeus, Adam and Eve were "childlike," the "chief culprit was the serpent" and "that Adam and Eve had been victimized rather than sinning freely" (*From Shadows to Reality: Studies in the Biblical Typology of the Fathers* [London, 1960], p. 35). Here Irenaeus's notion of progress in history has led him to a position quite different from that of seventeenth-century Puritans, for whom Adam was before the fall the capstone of the creation, intuitively intelligent, etc. Milton's Adam is clearly not Irenaeus's, for example.

15. *PL* 7.586. Again, let me point out that the words I quote in this chapter were written in hot controversy. Asked about the words of Paul, these Puritans would almost certainly have agreed (cheerfully) that Christ came to set men free from the bondage of the Law. But if we work from what these men wrote in defense of their weekly Sabbath, or if we pause to ask whatever possessed them to seize so fiercely on this of all doctrines, we must conclude that they were far more interested in, attracted to, and excited by a rock of agelessness than they were by Christ's temporal ministry on earth and the changes that it wrought for many theologians in the process of history.

16. John Prideaux, *The doctrine of the Sabbath, delivered in the Act at Oxon., anno 1622 ... and now translated into English for the benefit of the common people* (London, 1634), p. 2.

17. John Pocklington, *Sunday no Sabbath: a sermon preached before the Lord Bishop of Lincolne at his Lordship's visitation at Ampthill in the County of Bedford, Aug. 17, 1635* (London, 1636), p. 6.

18. Edmund Warren made the point in his title, *The Jew's Sabbath antiquated and the Lord's Day instituted by divine authority* (London, 1659).

19. John Sprint, *Propositions tending to proove the necessarie vse of the Christian Sabbaoth...* (London, 1607), pp. 5-6.

20. Sir James Harrington, *Certaine qveries proposed by the king ... with an answer thereunto given and presented to His Majesty by Sir James Harrington* (London, 1647), p. 2. Harrington gave a typical, Puritanic reply when he devoted four pages of his four-and-a-half-page answer to distinguishing between the institution of the Sabbath and the institution of Easter. Concerning Easter he agreed with Charles that the Church had probably created it; but that, for him, was a mark against it (and Parliament abolished the celebration of Easter for that very reason in 1647). He denied that the Sabbath was an ecclesiastic invention like Easter, however, as Charles had assumed; rather, it was jure divino: "Your Majesty's reason upon which your query is built hath a great mistake even in the foundation of it. You being pleased to lay this for a ground that the change of the Sabbath and the institution of Easter are by one and the same equal authority and ecclesiastical decree, which with your Majesty's favor I cannot yield to, for I humbly conceive that the change of the Jewish Sabbath (the commemoration of the work of the creation) unto the Lord's day, the remembrance of that greater work (the work of redemption finished upon this day of the Lord's resurrection) was by no less than by divine authority, because the keeping of one day in seven as a Sabbath to God was not only sanctified and set apart by God's own example in the creation ... but is one of the ten commandments delivered by God's own voice on *Mount Sinai*, written by his own finger in tables of stone ... which decalogue ... is also by our blessed Savior in his Sermon upon the *Mount* declared to be the rule of his people's moral obedience unto the end of the world" (pp. 2-3).

21. Millicent Bell, "The Fallacy of the Fall in *Paradise Lost*," *PMLA* 68(1953): 863-83.

22. H. V. S. Ogden, "The Crisis of *Paradise Lost* Reconsidered," *PQ* 36(1957):1-19.

23. John E. Parish, "Pre-Miltonic Representations of Adam as a Christian," *Rice Institute Pamphlet* 40(1953):iii, 1-24.

24. Thomas Hayne, *A briefe discourse of the Scriptures...* (London, 1614), p. 41.

25. Carleton F. Brown, *Religious Lyrics of the XVth Century* (Oxford, 1939), p. 120.

26. Thomas Shepard, *Theses Sabbaticae, or the doctrine of the Sabbath* (London, 1649), p. 8. I have silently edited a reduplication in the text.

27. Stanley Fish, *Surprised by Sin: The Reader in Paradise Lost* (London, 1967). However, Fish's sense of aesthetic progress may lead him to stress unduly the "climax" of the crucifixion scene, pp. 319-26.

28. Joseph Summers, *The Muse's Method* (London, 1962), p. 204.

29. John E. Parish, "Milton and God's Curse on the Serpent," *JEGP* 58(1959):241-47.

CHAPTER 6

1. John Sprint, *Propositions tending to proove the necessarie vse of the Christian Sabbaoth...* (London, 1607), pp. 2, 56.

2. Perry Miller, *The New England Mind: The Seventeenth Century* (Boston, 1961), esp. ch. 3.

3. Thomas Shephard, *Theses Sabbaticae, or the doctrine of the Sabbath* (London, 1649), p. 3.

4. In addition to the fact that a "renaissance" and a "reformation" are by definition backward-looking, that the humanists looked to a "golden age" of classical literature, that the reformers sought their models in the apostolic church and Eden, Harry Levin has described the massive nostalgia in *The Myth of the Golden Age in the Renaissance* (Bloomington, 1969), William Haller has commented on the historiographic nationalism and root-seeking, *The Elect Nation* (New York, 1963), pp. 58-62, Lawrence Stone has added that lawyers, antiquaries, the gentry and even royalists and Laud were seeking roots in the past, *The Causes of the English Revolution, 1529-1642* (London, 1972), pp. 50-51, R. F. Jones has noticed a similar reflex in linguistic nationalism, *The Triumph of the English Language* (Stanford, 1953), and I have pointed out a similar habit of mind emerging in the new pediatric speculations (see Introduction, n. 7). Men look backward when they are afraid, as Weston LaBarre has massively documented, *The Ghost Dance: Origins of Religion* (New York, 1970), passim, but especially chapters 6-7.

5. Nicholas Bownd, *The doctrine of the Sabbath...* (London, 1595), sig. [A4]^r.

6. John Dod, *A plaine and familiar exposition of the Ten Commandements...* (London, 1612), p. 133.

7. Seymour Chatman, "Milton's Participial Style," *PMLA* 63(1968):1398.

8. William Ames, *The marrow of sacred divinity...* (London, n.d.), p. 285. A. W. Pollard and G. R. Redgrave, *A Short-Title Catalogue of Books Printed in England, Scotland, and Ireland, 1475-1640* (London, 1950) (hereafter STC), guess the date as 1638.

9. Geoffrey Bullough, "Polygamy among the Reformers," in *Renaissance and Modern Essays Presented to Vivian de Sola Pinto...*, ed. G. R. Hibbard (New York, 1966), pp. 5-23.

10. Norman Cohn, *The Pursuit of the Millennium*, rev. ed. (New York, 1970). Levin, *The Myth of the Golden Age*, also comments on this paradigm, pp. 151-54. Moreover, while analyzing the four-age theory of historical degeneration—gold, silver, brass, iron—Levin notes that discussions of the silver and brass ages were often truncated or elided (pp. 21-22). Sidney's famous comment in his *Defense of Poetry* that nature's world is "brazen, the poets only deliver a golden" seems to work that way, positing a duality rather than a four-stage process—i.e., the golden age vs. everything else that degenerated from it. Since Levin is treating only nostalgic works (nostalgically), his bipartite pattern is a truncated version of the three-fold division, involving the past and the present but not the golden future.

11. Abiezer Coppe, the Ranter, compressed much of his generally diffuse thought into the following lines, which revealingly conclude with a reference to the name Jehovah, who, it seems, is within Abiezer himself:

My *a* heart, my blood, my life, is Thine: *a* Script. est
It pleases me that *b* thou art mine.   *b* Cant. 2. Ioh, 17
I'l *c* curse thy flesh, and *d* swear th'art fine, *c* Nehe. 13   *d* Ezek. 16
For *e* ever thine I mean to be,   *e* Mal. 3. Heb. 13
As *f* I am that I am, within A. C.   *f* Script. est

(Abiezer Coppe, in Richard Coppin, *Divine Teachings* [London, 1649], sig. A2ʳ.)

12. We can speak with some confidence about Milton addressing himself to Ames's arguments, because Milton quotes Ames (although not the specific passage which links marriage to Sabbath-keeping) in his later chapter on the Sabbath (II, vii; Yale ed., 6: 706). Edward Phillips also mentioned Ames and John Wolleb or Wollebius in connection with the tract. That is not to say that Ames or Wolleb were the sole "source" for Milton's thinking; Ames merely crystalized and systematized what many Puritans thought, and Wolleb did much the same thing for advanced Protestant thought on the continent, his book becoming a standard textbook for Puritan students almost immediately after publication (John Wolleb, *Compendium Theologia Christianae* [Amsterdam, 1626]). The point is that Milton is here overtly reacting to a Puritan theory and thereby defining if not his intellectual father then his intellectual fathers.

13. James Turner Johnson, *A Society Ordained by God: English Puritan Marriage Doctrine in the First Half of the Seventeenth Century* (Nashville, 1970).

14. These examples are taken from Christopher Hill's shrewd analysis of this point, *Society and Puritanism*, 2nd ed. (New York, 1967), pp. 171–72, 177–78, 211.

15. Robert Cox, *The Literature of the Sabbath Question*, 2 vols. (Edinburgh, 1865), 2:25.

CHAPTER 7

1. Daniel Neal, *The History of the Puritans* (New York, 1863), 2:55.

2. Robert Cox, *The Literature of the Sabbath Question*, 2 vols. (Edinburgh, 1865), 1:245.

3. Daniel Cawdrey, *Diatribe triplex* (London, 1654), quotation, p. 195. Charles's views are from the work by Harrington already cited in chapter 5, n. 20.

4. Edmund Calamy, *An indictment against England because of her selfe-mvrdering divisions, together with an exhortation to an England preserving vnity and concord* (London, 1645), p. 41.

5. Lancelot Andrewes, *Ninety-six Sermons* (Oxford, 1841), 1:96.

6. Richard Gardiner, *A sermon preach'd ... on Christmas Day* (Oxford, 1638), p. 10.

7. William Jones, *The mysterie of Christes nativitie* (London, 1614), p. 12ᵛ.

8. John Boys, *An exposition of the festivall epistles and gospels, vsed in our English liturgie* (London, 1613), p. 70.

9. John Day, *Day's festivals or twelve of his sermons* (London, 1614), p. 20.

10. John Donne, *The Sermons of John Donne*, ed. Evelyn N. Simpson and George R. Potter (Berkeley and Los Angeles, 1953), 6:185, 97.

11. Several pressures seem to be at work on Calamy. Clearly he is fascinated by "national divisions" because he explicates them at length before turning to a plea for unity. Unity, of course, means that the diverse should meet and mesh in *his* position. The divisions thus become a proof of the rightness of Calamy's position, separation a way to keep the truth so pure of old. In addition, Calamy may have had in mind the pressures from the nascent left flank of the revolutionary movement and have been attempting to consolidate opposition to the king.

12. Richard Crashaw, "Hymn in the Holy Nativity," *The Complete Poetry of Richard Crashaw*, ed. George W. Williams (Garden City, N.Y., 1970), p. 81.

13. John Langley, *Gemitus Columbae: The mournful note of the dove ...* (London, 1644), p. 15.

14. Thomas Thorowgood, "To the honourable House of Commons," *Moderation*

iustified, and the Lord's being at hand emproued ... (London, 1645), sig. A2^r and v.

15. Louis Martz, *The Poetry of Meditation* (New Haven, 1954), pp. 163-64.

16. L. C. Martin, "Introduction," *The Poems of Richard Crashaw* (Oxford, 1957), pp. xxxiii–xxxviii, is vague about dating either Crashaw's formal conversion or the composition of the volume of 1648. However, it seems unlikely that our vagueness about these dates seriously hinders us from concluding that he had indeed converted by the time he recast the poem.

17. David Daiches, *Milton* (London, 1957), p. 38.

18. Arthur Barker, "The Pattern of Milton's Nativity Ode," *UTQ* 10(1940-41):174.

19. And besides, Lowry Nelson, Jr., *Baroque Lyric Poetry* (New Haven, 1961), pp. 32-52, has done an excellent and thorough analysis of tense and time scheme in the poem, from which my discussion has, throughout, profited.

20. Rosamond Tuve, *Images and Themes in Five Poems by Milton* (Cambridge, 1957), p. 37; Martz, *The Poetry of Meditation*, p. 166.

CHAPTER 8

1. C. V. Wedgwood, *Poetry and Politics under the Stuarts* (Cambridge, 1960), p. 3.

2. Joan Webber, *The Eloquent "I"* (Madison, 1968).

3. Stephen Marshall, *A right understanding of the times* ... (London, 1647).

4. Samuel Mather, *The figures or types of the Old Testament*, 2nd ed. (London, 1705), p. 55.

5. William G. Madsen, *From Shadowy Types to Truth: Studies in Milton's Symbolism* (New Haven, 1968), ch. 2.

6. Eric Voegelin, *The New Science of Politics* (Chicago, 1952), chs. 4 and 5; Norman Cohn, *Pursuit of the Millennium*, rev. ed. (New York, 1970), pp. 179-94.

7. Jean Danielou, S.J., *From Shadows to Reality: Studies in the Biblical Typology of the Fathers* (London, 1960), p. 31.

8. Eric Auerbach, "Figura," *Scenes from the Drama of European Literature* (New York, 1959), pp. 11-76.

9. H. R. MacCallum, "Milton and Figurative Interpretation of the Bible," *UTQ* 31(1962):397-415.

10. John Calvin, *Commentary on the Epistles of Paul the Apostle to the Corinthians*, trans. Rev. John Pringle, 2 vols. (Edinburgh, 1848; reprinted Grand Rapids, Michigan, 1955), 2:175.

11. Hobbes stated the problem succinctly: "No man can have in his mind a conception of the future, for the future is not yet. But of our conceptions of the past we make a future" ("Human Nature," *English Works*, ed. W. Molesworth [London, 1841], 4:16).

12. Irenaeus, *Adversus Haeresis*, iv.38, Ante-Nicene Christian Library (Edinburgh, 1867), 9:42.

13. Augustine, "Against Two Letters of the Pelagians," *Saint Augustine's Anti-Pelagian Works* (A Select Library of the Nicene and Post-Nicene Fathers, ed. Phillip Schaff, vol. 5) (New York, 1887), p. 420. Hereafter, I shall cite both sections of the work and volume and page of this edition, abbreviated *NPNF*.

14. In book II of the *Confessions*, Augustine stated this problem of human time and God's eternal plan in its most well-known form. The highest reality is the eternal knowledge of God concerning providential history, and the difficulty which Augustine there treats at length is man's inability to comprehend history in its relation to this timeless plan. I choose the less famous formulations of this point because, written in controversy, they show more clearly the strategic nature of Augustine's argument.

15. John Calvin, *The Institutes*, bk. II, ch. xi, 10; McNeill ed., p. 459.

16. Thomas Taylor, *Christ revealed or the Old Testament explained* (London, 1635), p. 208; emphasis mine.

17. Stephen Marshall, *A sermon of the baptizing of infants* (London, 1644), p. 12.

18. Thomas Cooper, *The blessing of Japheth, prouing the gathering in of the Gentiles and finall conuersion of the Iewes* (London, 1615), p. 2.

19. Thomas Wadsworth, *Mr. Thomas Wadsworth's last warning to secure sinners* ...

(London, 1677), p. 2.

20. John Dod, *A plaine and familiar exposition of the Ten Commandments...* (London, 1612), p. 128.

21. W. A. [William Aspinwall], *Thunder from heaven against the backsliders and Apostates of the times, in some meditations on the 24 chapter of Isaiah...* (London, 1655), p. 6. Concerning the identity of William Aspinwall, *DNB* notices three William Aspinwalls in the mid-seventeenth century: an Independent divine, a Quaker, and a Fifth Monarchist. One wonders whether they might not have been the same man. *Thunder from heaven* contains learned exegesis of Hebrew, and references to Buxtorf, which suggest the training of an Independent divine; the author speaks of having visited America, a trip *DNB* assigns to the Quaker; the author further mentions a commentary he has written on Daniel (one is listed by *DNB* and *BMC*), and Daniel is one of the chief lodes for millennial speculation. Also strongly millennial is his comment that "the most glorious manifestations of Christ's kingly power both in Church *and state* will be reserved for his ancient people the Jews when they are called home again" (emphasis mine). As there was a strong element of millennialism in Quaker writing, and also in many cases in Independency, the three men might well be one in various stages of "radicalization." But whether one, two or three men, the positions held are all relatively extreme—certainly so in *Thunder from heaven*, which is an attack upon Cromwell from the left.

22. Lewes Hughes, *A looking-glass for all true hearted Christians...* (London, 1642), pp. 3-4.

CHAPTER 9

1. John Calvin, *Commentaries on the Epistle of Paul the Apostle to the Romans*, trans. Rev. John Owen (Edinburgh, 1848; reprinted Grand Rapids, Mich., 1955), p. 437.

2. Matthew Poole, *Annotations upon the Holy Bible*, 3rd ed. (London, 1696), vol. 2, sig. Cc2^r, col. 1.

3. Thomas Cranmer, *The First and Second Prayer-books of Edward VI* (London, 1910), p. 102.

4. John Stockwood, *A very fruitfull and necessarye sermon of the moste lamentable destruction of Jerusalem...* (London, 1585), title page.

5. Thomas Lushington, *The resurrection of our Saviour rescued from the soldiers calumnies...*, ed. Edward Hyde (London, [1741?]), p. 3.

6. Francis Tayler, *A godly, zealous and learned sermon upon the 18, 19, 20, 21, verses of the 10. chapt. of the Romaines...* (London, 1583), sig. c4^r.

7. John Foxe, *A sermon preached at the christening of a certaine Iew*, trans. James Bell (London, 1578), sig. B3^v.

8. Edward Spencer, [*An epistle to the learned Manasseh ben Israel in answer to his dedicated to the Parliament* (London, 1650)], p. 2. British Museum copy wants title page; information supplied by *BMC*.

9. Thomas Sutton, *Lectures vpon the eleventh chapter to the Romans...* (London, 1632), p. 384.

10. Henry Finch, *The world's great restauration, or the calling of the Jewes and (with them) of all nations and kingdoms of the earth, to the faith of Christ* (London, 1621).

11. Andrew Willet, *Hexapla, that is a six-fold commentarie upon the...Epistle... to the Romans...* (London, 1620), pp. 488-91, 510-11; cf. *De vniversali et novissima Ivdaeorum vocatione, secvndum apertissima in Divi Pauli prophetiam, in vltimas hisce diebus praestanda liber vnus* (Cambridge, 1590).

12. Thomas Draxe, *The worlds resurrection or the generall calling of the Iewes. A familiar commentary upon the eleventh chapter of Saint Paul to the Romaines...* (London, 1608); Thomas Cooper, *The blessing of Japheth...* (London, 1615), pp. 53–55; Elnathan Parr, *A plaine exposition upon the 8, 9, 10, 11 chapters of the Epistle of Saint Paul to the Romans...* (London, 1618); Thomas Sutton, *Lectures vpon the*

eleventh chapter to the Romans . . . (London, 1632); William Prynne, *A short demurrer to the Jewes long discontinued remitter into England* . . . (London, 1655), pp. 65-66, 89-90.

13. Thomas Thorowgood, *Jewes in America, or probabilities that the Americans are of that race* (London, 1650), pp. 22-23.

14. Robert Maton, *Israel's redemption, or the propheticall history of our Saviour's kingdome on earth* . . . (London, 1642). Maton reissued the work as *Israel's redemption redeemed or the Jewes generall and miraculous conversion to the faith of the Gospel* . . . *clearly proved* . . . (London, 1646). The second edition includes the text of the original, Petrie's criticisms, and Maton's rejoinder. Broken up into sections, and therefore a bit disconnected, the work does show the debate between a Fifth Monarchist and a Scots Presbyterian clearly.

15. Edward Nicholas, *An apology for the honourable nation of the Jews and all the sons of Israel* (London, 1648); Thomas Collier, *A brief answer to some of the objections and demurs made against the coming in and inhabiting of the Jews in this Commonwealth* (London, 1656); Moses Wall, "Some discourses upon the point of the conversion of the Jewes" in Menasseh ben Israel, *The Hope of Israel*, 2nd ed. (London, 1652).

16. Finch, *The world's great restauration*, pp. 2-3. Significantly, Joseph Mede, brilliant expositor of Revelation and a man who probably did much to bring the millennial note of Puritanism to the fore (his book went through three Latin and two English editions between 1626 and 1650), despite the obviously scholarly and restrained approach he personally took, agreed with Finch: "God forgive me if it be a sin, but I have thought so many a day" (quoted by Moses Margoliouth, *Notes and Queries*, 2nd series, 2:12).

17. William Laud, *The Works of the Most Reverend Father in God Wm. Laud* . . . in the Library of Anglo-Catholic Theology, vols. 56-64 (Oxford, 1847), 1:16.

18. I do not wish to enter the debate whether Bacon was or was not a Puritan; I wish only to remark a similarity of method and intellectual analysis.

19. William Haller, *The Elect Nation: The Meaning and Relevance of Foxe's Book of Martyrs* (New York, 1963).

20. Perry Miller, *The New England Mind: The Seventeenth Century* (Boston, 1961).

21. John Bunyan, *Grace Abounding to the Chief of Sinners*, ed. Roger Sharrock (Oxford, 1962), p. 101.

22. John Goodwin, *An exposition of the nineth chapter of the Epistle to the Romans* . . . (London, 1656); Milton, *De Doctrina Christiana*, bk. I, ch. iv; Yale ed., pp. 168-202.

23. Edward Lane, *Look unto Jesus or an ascent to the holy mount to see Jesus Christ in his glory.* . . . *At the end is an Appendix shewing the certainty of the calling of the Jevvs* (London, 1663).

24. Thomas Manton, *The Complete Works of Thomas Manton*, 22 vols. (London, 1870-75), 18:242.

CHAPTER 10

1. Theodore Beza, quoted by Thomas Thorowgood, *Jewes in America* . . . (London, 1650), sig. c4^v.

2. Thomas Collier, *A brief answer to some of the objections and demurs made against the coming in and inhabiting of the Jews in this Commonwealth* (London, 1656), p. 24.

3. D. L., *Israel's condition and cause pleaded or some arguments for the Jews* . . . (London, 1656), p. 2.

4. Thomas Calvert, "To the Christian Reader," in Rabbi Samuel, *The blessed Jew of Morocco or a blackmoor made white: Being a demonstration of the true Messias out of the law and prophets* (York, 1648), sig. A3^v.

5. John Lightfoot, *The harmony, chronicle and order of the New Testament* . . . (London, 1655), pp. 194-95.

6. John Lightfoot, *The Whole Works of... John Lightfoot,* ed. J. R. Pitman (London, 1815), 12:441.

7. George Hickes, *Peculiam Dei: A discourse about the Jews as the peculiar people* (London, 1681), p. 21.

8. Leo Solt, "Puritanism, Capitalism, Democracy, and the New Science," *American Historical Review* 73(1967):18-29.

9. John Bunyan, *Grace Abounding to the Chief of Sinners,* ed. Roger Sharrock (Oxford, 1962), pp. 43-54, esp. 43, 50, 52.

10. Perry Miller, "The Marrow of Puritan Divinity," *Publications of the Colonial Society of Massachusetts* (Feb., 1935), p. 299.

11. Basil Willey, *The Seventeenth-Century Background* (Garden City, 1953), esp. pp. 11-16; Don Cameron Allen, *The Legend of Noah: Renaissance Rationalism in Art, Science, and Letters,* Illinois Studies in Language and Literature, vol. 33, Nos. 3-4 (Urbana, 1949).

12. Zevedei Barbu, *Problems of Historical Psychology* (New York, 1960), pp. 145-79. Barbu argues that the social psychology of the English nation was shaped, in part at least, by the dislocations of the Reformation. He might just as easily be talking about post-Reformation, Protestant Europe, since he supplies no counterexample to show how this response was specific to the English. The paradigm he articulates, however, can, if restricted to the Puritans, suggest usefully why they were such compulsive theologizers.

13. Edmund Calamy, *An indictment against England because of her selfe-mvrdering divisions...* (London, 1645), p. 40.

14. John Vicars used and translated the phrase in the title of his Puritanic, providential history of the civil wars, *Jehovah-Jireh, "God in the Mount," or England's Parliamentarie-chronicle, containing a most exact narration of all the most material proceedings of this renowned and unparalleled Parliament...* (London, 1644), title page. In ch. 12, I shall notice how crucial the phrase or its English version were in organizing Vicars's strange account.

15. John F. Wilson, *Pulpit in Parliament: Puritanism during the English Civil Wars 1640-1648* (Princeton, 1969), pp. 255-74.

CHAPTER 11

1. Richard Harwood, *King David's sanctuary or a sermon preached before His Majesty the fourth of Febr: 1644...* (Oxford, 1644).

2. Joan Webber, *The Eloquent "I"* (Madison, 1968), esp. ch. 2.

3. The phrase is N. J. C. Andreasen's, "Donne's *Devotions* and the Psychology of Ascent," *MP* 62(1965):207-16. Andreasen delicately qualifies Louis Martz's argument, *The Poetry of Meditation* (New Haven, 1954) that specific devotional manuals explain or inform this or that poem or piece of prose, by suggesting that a general frame of mind (which would, quite possibly, appreciate the same patterns in manuals of devotion) underlies not only Donne's *Devotions* but pieces with a similar rhythm. Martz has taken a great hammering for his thesis, yet it must be granted that the ultraconservative, Counter-Reformation, Roman Catholic sources which he studied do resemble each other in their underlying rhythm. C. L. Barber, *"A Mask Presented at Ludlow Castle:* the Masque as a Masque," *The Lyric and Dramatic Milton,* ed. Joseph Summers (New York, 1965), pp. 35-63, and Angus Fletcher, *The Transcendental Masque: An Essay on Milton's Comus* (Ithaca, 1971) have both remarked on the rhythm of ascent in that genre. Particularly revealing is the way Barber, in order to demonstrate that *Comus* conforms to the terms of the genre, must read the first five lines of the poem backwards, commenting on how we are first located in "'this dim spot,/Which men call earth,' that far above it are 'regions milde of calm and serene ayr,' and beyond these, 'the starry threshold of Joves court'" (p. 48), quoting first lines 5-6, then 4, then finally line 1. Neither study convinces me entirely that the young arch-regicide-to-be fitted into a genre with such obviously Royalist and/or reactionary overtones, but that is a question I cannot pursue here.

4. Madan suggests that this sermon was probably preached, but not before the King nor in Oxford. That it was printed in London further suggests it was a hoax. Falconer Madan, *Oxford Books* (Oxford, 1865-1931), 2:1364.

5. Again Madan speculates (*Oxford Books*, 2:1272) that this sermon was a London forgery.

6. Jasper Mayne, *A sermon concerning unity & agreement, preached at Carfax church in Oxford, August 9, 1646* ([Oxford], 1646).

7. George Wilde, *A sermon preached upon Sunday the third of March in St. Maries Oxford...* (Oxford, 1643).

8. Walter Curle, *A sermon preached at the publike fast at S. Maries in Oxford, the tenth of May, 1644...* (Oxford, 1644).

9. John Sprint, *Propositions tending to proove the necessarie vse of the Christian Sabbaoth...* (London, 1607), p. 7.

10. Henry Ferne, *A sermon preached before His Majesty at Newport in the Isle of VVight, November the 29, 1648...* (London, 1649), p. 1.

11. George Hickes, *Peculiam Dei...* (London, 1681), p. 21. Simon Patrick, *Jewish hypocrisie, a caveat to the present generation...* (London, 1660), had developed much the same analysis.

12. Henry Leslie, *The martyrdome of King Charles, or his conformity with Christ in his suffering...* (The Hague, 1649), p. 12.

13. Fletcher's one-sentence review of "the curve of historical change between Skelton and Dryden" leaves a good deal to be desired as it transcends or transmogrifies (like the authors Fletcher is considering) the facts of history: "absolute monarchy went through a *steady rise* under the Tudors and James I, a *sunburst* under Charles I..., an *eclipse* with the Civil War, a *metamorphosis* during the Commonwealth and Protectorate, a *delicate revival* with the Restoration, and a final *transmogrifying* at the moment of the Glorious Revolution" (*The Transcendental Masque*, p. 56, emphasis mine). Lawrence Stone, *The Causes of the English Revolution, 1529-1642* (London, 1972) provides a much sounder analysis and corrective to Fletcher's extraordinary terms.

14. Ben Jonson, "Ode to Himself," *The Complete Poetry of Ben Jonson*, ed. William B. Hunter, Jr. (New York, 1963), pp. 386-88.

15. Christopher Hill, "Society and Andrew Marvell," *Puritanism and Revolution* (London, 1958), pp. 337-86.

16. Fletcher, *The Transcendental Masque*, p. 58.

CHAPTER 12

1. Michael Walzer, *The Revolution of the Saints* (Cambridge, 1965), pp. 270-97.

2. Stephen Marshall, *Meroz cursed...* (London, 1641).

3. Stephen Zwicker, *Dryden's Political Poetry: the Typology of King and Nation* (Providence, R.I., 1972), has traced out messianic arguments that linked the kings of England with Old Testament figures, in a way which Norman Cohn has explained, in *The Pursuit of the Millennium*, rev. ed. (New York, 1970), pp. 19-36, 108-126. Elizabeth called forth a great deal of this, but as the Stuarts drew farther away from their subjects, the fire seems to have gone out of this *topos*, except for the inner coterie.

4. *Areopagitica*, in CE, 4:340.

5. Thomas Cooper, *The blessing of Japheth...* (London, 1615), p. 34.

6. Stephen Marshall, *The strong helper...* (London, 1645), pp. 22-23.

7. Stephen Marshall, *A sacred record to be made of God's mercies to Zion...* (London, [1645]), p. 16.

8. Stephen Marshall, *The right understanding of the times...* (London, 1647), p. 40.

9. Edward Spencer, *An epistle to the learned Menasseh ben Israel...* (London, 1650), p. 2.

10. Arise Evans, *Light for the Jews or the means to convert them, in answer to a book... called the Hope of Israel... by Manasseh ben Israel... shewing the time of*

King Charles' coming in . . . (London, 1656). Stennet's tract was reprinted by the American Sabbath Tract Society (New York, 1848). According to the reprint, the original edition was published London, 1658.

11. Frank Kermode, *The Sense of an Ending* (New York, 1967).

12. J. R. Hale, "Incitement to violence? English divines on the theme of war, 1578–1631," in *Florilegium Historiale: Essays presented to Wallace K. Ferguson*, ed. J. G. Rowe and W. H. Stockdale (Toronto, 1971), pp. 368-99, gives excellent background on the subject. The following section appeared in somewhat modified form as part of "Puritan Soldiers in *Paradise Lost*," *MLQ* 35(1974):376-403.

13. Walzer, *The Revolution of the Saints*, pp. 270-97.

14. Richard Sibbes, *The Complete Works*, ed. Rev. A. B. Grosart (Edinburgh, 1862), 2:232.

15. John Davenport, *A royal edict for military exercises* (London, 1629), p. 18.

16. Josiah Ricraft, *A survey of England's champions and truth's faithful patriots . . .* (London, 1647), p. 68. *England's worthies, under whom all the civill and bloudy warres since Anno 1642, to Anno 1647 are related . . .* (London, 1647), attributed to John Vicars, was amazingly similar.

17. Thomas Adams, *The sovldier's honovr* (London, 1617), sig. B[1]^V.

18. Thomas Sutton, *The good fight of faith* (London, 1624), p. 15.

19. Simeon Ashe, *Good covrage discovered and encovraged . . .* (London, 1642), pp. 8, 14.

20. The two sermons, preached in 1645 before Parliament and published by order of same, are the two extant copies of a three-sermon sequence on consecutive texts. Cf. John F. Wilson, *Pulpit in Parliament* (Princeton, 1969), pp. 84, 244-45, 265.

21. John Vicars, *Jehovah-Jireh, "God in the Mount," or England's Parliamentarie-chronicle . . .* (London, 1644).

22. Michael Wilding, "The Last of the Epics: The Rejection of the Heroic in *Paradise Lost* and *Hudibras*," in *Restoration Literature*, ed. Harold Love (London, 1972), pp. 91-120. Wilding seems to be correct about the anti-Puritanic *Hudibras*, which demonstrates, in a different way from the Royalist texts I have already considered, the way in which anti-Puritans retreated from the world; Butler did so by damning worldly militarism and the heroic code which derives from it. Stanley Fish, *Surprised by Sin* (London, New York, 1967), ch. 4, is much closer to the mark in his analysis of the curious sort of heroism which Milton defines through the angels.

23. The phrase is A. J. A. Waldock's, *Paradise Lost and its Critics* (Cambridge, 1947), p. 105.

24. [James Heath], *A brief chronicle of all the chief actions so fatally falling out in these three kingdoms: viz., England, Scotland & Ireland, from the year 1640 to this present twentieth of November, 1661 . . .* (London, 1662), p. 1. Edward Phillips, Milton's nephew, extended this work after Heath's death.

25. *Readie and Easie Way . . .* , CE, 6:123.

26. William Riley Parker, *Milton: A Biography* (Oxford, 1968), p. 370.

CHAPTER 13

1. Joan Webber, *The Eloquent "I"* (Madison, 1968).

2. Henri A. Talon, *John Bunyan: The Man and his Works*, trans. Barbara Wall (Cambridge, 1951), p. 132.

3. Roger Sharrock, "Introduction," in John Bunyan, *Grace Abounding to the Chief of Sinners* (Oxford, 1962), p. xxxii.

4. John Donne, *Devotions Upon Emergent Occasions*, ed. John Sparrow (Cambridge, 1923), p. 4.

5. Cf., for example, "Hymne to God my God, in my sicknesse," ll. 12-15.

6. James Thorpe, "Introduction," *The Pilgrim's Progress and Grace Abounding* (Boston, 1969), p. viii; Thorpe astutely makes my point when he remarks that "there are several ways in which one can describe its structure."

7. Stanley Fish, *Self-Consuming Artifacts* (Berkeley, 1972), pp. 224–64, makes much of that point about lack of progress in Bunyan's prose.

8. In *Pilgrim's Progress*, Christian visits a bloodless cross very early in the story; that cross removes a burden from Christian's back, but as his many further trials manifest, solves little and is in no way decisive.

9. Mention of Holy Sonnet VII prompts me to observe that it, like many of Donne's poems, moves from a contemplation of eternity back down to a consideration of time. Quite obviously, that is precisely the opposite of the pattern of ascent I have been tracing here and labeling "Anglican." As with my discussion of Royalist sermons, my point is not that all Donne's poetry conforms to a single pattern, but rather that there are certain patterns in it which Milton, for example, would never use. "Those are my best dayes, when I shake with feare," Donne concluded Holy Sonnet XIX, one of his best, even if most crabbed; the line is different, in its tentativeness, from "They also serve who only stand and wait." Indeed, it is that tentativeness which is the whole point of Holy Sonnet VII, where the speaker cannot, because of his human limitation, have the final vision here and now. Only such tentativeness, one must suppose, can precede the final ascent which, if not stated here, is nonetheless implied.

10. N. J. C. Andreasen, "Donne's *Devotions* and the Psychology of Ascent," *MP* 62(1965):207–16.

CHAPTER 14

1. Let me be explicit. I believe Milton thought he was divinely inspired. I do not believe that in fact he was. Certain gestures of faith which Milton made I cannot follow. Indeed, this claim of his troubles me deeply; such claims have generally caused more trouble than good. Norman Cohn, *The Pursuit of the Millennium*, rev. ed. (New York, 1970), gives many examples of the troubles. William Kerrigan's fine study, *The Prophetic Milton* (Charlottesville, 1974), which appeared too late for me to profit as much as I might, still does not allay my reservations on this point.

2. George Fox, *The Journal*, ed. John L. Nickalls (Cambridge, 1952), pp. 52, 159, for example; cf. p. 47, where Fox attacks Ranters for believing that they are God.

3. James Turner Johnson, *A Society Ordained by God: English Puritan Marriage Doctrine in the first half of the Seventeenth Century* (Nashville, 1970). John Demos, *A Little Commonwealth* (New York, 1970) discusses Plymouth Plantation family life. See also Leven L. Schucking, *The Puritan Family*, trans. Brian Battershaw (London, 1969), and Edmund Morgan, *The Puritan Family: Essays on Religion and Domestic Relations in Seventeenth-Century New England* (Boston, 1944).

4. W. R. Parker, *Milton: A Biography* (Oxford, 1968), pp. 368–84, 433–50 and passim seems to me at once sympathetic and acute when he portrays Milton arranging controversial battles for himself which a blind man could win. Milton's sonnet to Cyriack Skinner compresses in a few words Milton's attempt:

What supports me dost thou ask?
The conscience, Friend, to have lost [his eyes] overply'd
In libertyes defence, my public task,
Of which all Europe talks from side to side.
This thought might lead me through the worlds vain mask
Content though blind, had I no better guide.   [I, pt. 1, 68]

5. Joan Webber, *The Eloquent "I"* (Madison, 1968).

6. H. R. MacCallum, "Milton and Sacred History: Books XI and XII of *Paradise Lost*," *Essays in English Literature from the Renaissance to the Victorian Age Presented to A. S. P. Woodhouse* (Toronto, 1964), pp. 149–60, explicates "loops of time"; quotation from Summers, *The Muse's Method* (London, 1962), p. 204, where he also speaks of "movements of unredeemed history."

7. Summers, *The Muse's Method*, ch. 3.

8. As I remarked above, I am compelled by the analysis of Summers and Fish on these matters.

9. Michael Wilding, "The Last of the Epics," *Restoration Literature*, ed. Harold Love (London, 1972), pp. 91–120.

10. Admittedly, many fine writers have ignored the question of political commitment—e.g., C. S. Lewis, Anne Ferry, Summers, Fish—a silence which may tacitly depoliticize the poetry. John Diekhoff, for one, openly argued for Milton's depoliticization in ways which have become fairly standard; he explained why Milton taught "virtue" in *Paradise Lost* by asserting that the Puritan revolution had undertaken "to force freedom upon the world" and that Milton finally recognized that during the Revolution he had "had hold of the wrong end of the stick. . . . The system of ethics must precede the politics. . . . The first step toward political freedom is to make men just" (*Milton's* Paradise Lost, *a Commentary on the Argument* [New York, 1946], pp. 146, 149). William Riley Parker, *Milton: A Biography*, pp. 591–95, has a similar, extended discussion of what Milton "learned" during his recovery from politics. Most recently, Hugh Richmond, *The Christian Revolutionary: John Milton* (Los Angeles, 1974), spiritualizes and thereby depoliticizes the term "revolutionary." The position of a man like Diekhoff is only partly apolitical, since it might be adopted and used by elitist, or reactionary thinkers.

11. Virgil, *Aeneid*, 12:951–52; *Loeb Classical Library* (Cambridge, 1928), 2:64.

12. William Riggs, *The Christian Poet in* Paradise Lost (Berkeley, 1972).

13. Anne Davidson Ferry, *Milton's Epic Voice: The Narrator in* Paradise Lost (Cambridge, 1967), did not address herself directly to my point, yet in practice had constantly to deal with it.

14. William Empson, *Milton's God* (Norfolk, Conn., 1961), p. 10.

CHAPTER 15

1. Fish calls attention to a process of expanding definition, *Surprised by Sin* (London, 1967), pp. 57–68.

2. Peter Berek, "'Plain' and 'Ornate' Styles and the Structure of *Paradise Lost*," *PMLA* 85(1970):237–46, analyzes the "plain style" of God and poses good questions about it.

CHAPTER 16

1. Seymour Chatman, "Milton's Participial Style," *PMLA* 63(1968):1398.

2. Thomas Carter, *Carter's Christian commonwealth or domesticall duties deciphered* (London, 1627), p. 1.

3. William Gouge, *Of domesticall duties* (London, 1622), p. 31. The answer Gouge gives (really a nonanswer) runs thus: "This extent is to be restrained to the generality of the things in question. As in other places where the Apostle saith *all things are lawful for me*, he meaneth all indifferent things, for of them his speech was in that place. And where again he saith, *Whatsoever is set before you, eat*, he meaneth whatsoever good and wholesome meat, for of that he spake" (pp. 31–32). His discussion of the question ends there, in utterly turgid and generalized prose.

4. James Turner Johnson, *A Society Ordained by God* (Nashville, 1970).

CHAPTER 17

1. Millicent Bell, "The Fallacy of the Fall in *Paradise Lost*," *PMLA* 68(1953):863–83.

2. H. V. S. Ogden, "The Crisis of *Paradise Lost* Reconsidered," *PQ*, 36(1957):2.

3. J. M. Evans, *Paradise Lost and the Genesis Tradition* (Oxford, 1968), pp. 249–71, comments on the ways in which Milton's emphasis upon work in Eden tends to blur any sharp distinction between pre- and postlapsarian life. Peter Lindenbaum, "The Anti-Pastoral Pastoral: The Education of Fallen Man in the Renaissance," Ph.D. diss. (University of California, Berkeley, 1970), ch. 5, elaborates. Evans thought this stress on work in Eden idiosyncratic to Milton, "the real originality" of Milton's vision (p. 265), but Nicholas Bownd, *The doctrine of the Sabbath* (London, 1595), p. 5 and John

Dod, *A plaine and familiar exposition of the Ten Commandements* (London, 1612), p. 128 are only two other Puritans who also believed in it.

    4. 9:5-6; I have always assumed that for Milton "tragic" means something more than merely "sad." However, the way in which the narrator talks about the state wherein

God or Angel Guest
With Man as with his Friend, familiar us'd
    To sit indulgent   [9:1-3]

and its contrast to his present topic of "foul distrust, and breech/Disloyal . . . revolt,/ And disobedience" (9:6-8) do not really suggest that purgative theory of tragedy which Milton articulated in his preface to *Samson Agonistes*, "Of that sort of Dramatic Poem which is call'd Tragedy." The change seems to be little more than from "happy" to "sad," at least in the immediate context. Whatever we make of "tragic," however, the point of interest lies in the contrast drawn between this new subject and epic and/or romance.

    5. *Pace*, C. S. Lewis, *A Preface to Paradise Lost* (London, 1942), pp. 96-97. It is our sense of Satan which, formed by comparisons, degenerates.

    6. Northrop Frye, *The Return of Eden* (Toronto, 1965), pp. 102-3.

    7. Summers's good analysis of the opening of book eight (*The Muse's Method* [London, 1962], pp. 154-57), which serves to exonerate Eve from the charge of sheer stupidity, helps us to see how Adam's sin is prepared for before the fall—how his psychology remains constant. But Summers's analysis also, it seems to me, serves to call our attention to the separation which occurs here. Eve may have a more recognizable motive here than she does when she suggests they separate in book nine, but the basis of that motive, Adam's inattention to her (twice the narrator comments that no one was looking at her, since if they had, they would have wished her to stay [8:43, 62-63]), remains inexplicable in terms of temporal causality. Further, the narrator asks, "O when meet now/Such pairs, in Love and Mutual Honour joyn'd?" (8:57-58). Obviously, the answer is, not any longer in our world. But the implied contrast between "then" and "now" serves ultimately to remind us that, at this moment, Adam and Eve are not joined *either*; "then" is not so different from "now," unfallen from fallen; the scene works together with book nine as much as it contrasts with it, and Eve's decision to part company is as remarkable here as it is later.

    8. Wayne Shumaker, "The Fallacy of the Fall in *Paradise Lost*," *PMLA* 70(1955): 1185-87, 1197-99, replying to Millicent Bell, seems to forget the difference between the two questions when he writes, "What cause, the Heavenly Muse is asked, 'Mov'd our Grand Parents/ . . . to fall off/From their Creator, and transgress his will,/ . . . Who first seduc'd them to that foul revolt?' The answer comes immediately" (p. 1197).

CHAPTER 18

    1. John Goodwin, *An exposition of the ninth chapter of the epistle to the Romans* . . . (London, 1655).

    2. It is commonplace to notice parallels between Milton's ordering of topics and that of other theologians like Ames and Wollebius. One would like to see this sort of structural analysis pushed farther; is there a "Puritanic" ordering of topics? To what extent is Milton idiosyncratic? And, again, what significance inheres in the ordering? All of these questions would require comparative study of theologians of quite different sensibilities.

    3. Sumner, who translated both *"poenitentia"* and *"resipiscentia"* with the single world "repentant," contributed to the fuzziness; Carey seems fairer to Milton's thought when he uses two words—"penitence" and "repentance." Still, "penitence" was not a word Milton frequently used throughout his authorial career, as a glance at the Index of the Columbia edition of *The Works* makes clear, and one wonders whether Milton may not himself, in his prose, have used "repentance" ambiguously.

    4. It has been customary to consider books eleven and twelve as a unit, rather than relating them to book ten; much excellent comment, pointing to what I take to be

basically Puritanic structures, patterns, and concerns, has emerged from this analysis, e.g., F. T. Prince, "On the Last Two Books of 'Paradise Lost'," *Essays and Studies* 11 (1958):38-52; John E. Parish, "Milton and God's Curse on the Serpent," *JEGP* 58 (1959):241-47; Rosalie L. Colie, "Time and Eternity: Paradox and Structure in *Paradise Lost*," *Journal of the Warburg and Courtauld Institutes* 23(1960):127-38; Summers, *The Muse's Method* (London, 1962), ch. viii; H. R. MacCallum, "Milton and Sacred History: Books XI and XII of *Paradise Lost*," *Essays in English Literature from the Renaissance to the Victorian Age Presented to A. S. P. Woodhouse* (Toronto, 1964), pp. 149-68; and Fish, *Surprised by Sin* (London, 1967), ch. vii.

5. Carey, in his translation of *De Doctrina*, editorially parallels these lines to Milton's discussion of "repentance," and "regeneration," pp. 453, 461, but does not cite 10:1097 in his discussion of "penitence."

6. Edward S. Le Comte, *Yet Once More: Verbal and Psychological Pattern in Milton* (New York, 1953), pp. 28-29.

7. Thomas Hayne, *A briefe discourse of the Scripture...* (London, 1614), p. 41, and Guillaume de Salluste du Bartas, *Bartas: His Devine Weekes and Works* (1605), trans. Joshua Sylvester, ed. Francis C. Haber (Gainesville, Fla., 1965), p. 398, might both be added to the example of Bullinger noticed in this connection by John E. Parish, "Pre-Miltonic Representations of Adam as a Christian," *Rice Institute Pamphlets* 40(1953):iii, 1-24. Less literary examples abound in chance passages throughout Puritan preaching.

AFTERWORD

1. George Fox, *The Journal*, ed. John L. Nickalls (Cambridge, 1952), p. 130. The explanation of Mrs. Lancaster's motives was written by Ellwood, who placed it, as I have done, after the telling of the fight. I have followed Fox's longer version of the altercation rather than Ellwood's edited and slightly more snappy version.

2. When Huck Finn describes the Grangerford's living room, he notes that they have a Bible and *"Pilgrim's Progress*, about a man that left his family, it didn't say why." *The Adventures of Huckleberry Finn*, ch. 17. *The Writings of Mark Twain*, Hillcrest ed. (New York and London, 1869-1909), 13:141.

3. M. M. Knappen, *Tudor Puritanism* (Chicago, 1930); William Haller, *The Rise of Puritanism* (New York, 1938).

4. Perry Miller, "The Marrow of Puritan Divinity," *Publications of the Colonial Society of Massachusetts* (Feb., 1935), p. 299.

5. Christopher Hill, *Anti-Christ in Seventeenth-Century England* (London, 1971), has brilliantly traced out how men located Antichrist first at Rome, then crossing the channel to advise the king, then among the Presbyterians and Independents. Ultimately, in the 1650's, radicals decided he was within themselves, inside each man.

6. Stanley Fish, "Question and Answer in *Samson Agonistes*," *Critical Quarterly* 11(1969):237-64.

7. By noticing the secular and demystifying pressure at the root of Puritan analysis, I add one further reason to believe that *Samson Agonistes* was written last rather than, as has been argued by W. R. Parker among others, *PQ* 28(1949):168, in 1647-53 before *Paradise Lost.*

8. Basil Willey, *The Seventeenth-Century Background* (Garden City, 1953), pp. 11-16.

9. David Kalstone, *Sidney's Poetry* (Cambridge, 1965), argues that Astrophel's "significant activity is the discovery of conflict" (p. 180) while Peter Lindenbaum, "The Anti-Pastoral Pastoral," Ph.D. diss. (University of California, Berkeley, 1970), chs. 2 & 3, notices the antiescapist elements in the *Arcadia*. In the *Defense of Poetry*, Sidney shows his own sensitivity to the charge that fashioning a golden world to replace the brazen might seem to amount to calling God's providence into question; he defends himself against a "saucy comparison" in the sentences immediately following.

10. Harry Levin, *The Myth of the Golden Age in the Renaissance* (Bloomington, 1969), conscious of Mircea Eliade's studies (p. 3), still opts to consider only the

"primitivistic" rather than "millennial" elements of his subject and comes thereby to imply that all Elizabethan Englishmen happily dreamt of the golden age out of mere exuberance rather than as escape.

APPENDIX

1. John Wilson, *Pulpit in Parliament: Puritanism during the English Civil Wars 1640-1648* (Princeton, 1969), Appendix II, "Calendar of Printed Sermons Preached to Members of the Long Parliament," pp. 255-74.

Index

Names in italic type are those of writers, primarily sixteenth- and seventeenth-century writers, whose work is analyzed in the text. Numbers in boldface type refer to lines in *Paradise Lost*. Anonymous books are indexed by short title, place, and date; other titles, whose authors are here indexed, may be found in text or footnotes (except works by Milton, which are indexed).

THE JOHNS HOPKINS UNIVERSITY PRESS

This book was composed in Baskerville text and Palatino Italic display type by Horne Associates, Incorporated, from a design by Susan Bishop. It was printed on 50-lb. Publishers Eggshell Wove and bound by Universal Lithographers, Inc.

LIBRARY OF CONGRESS CATALOGING IN PUBLICATION DATA

Berry, Boyd M.
    Process of speech.

    Includes index.
    1. Milton, John, 1608–1674. Paradise lost. 2. Puritans—England. 3. Preaching—History—England. I. Title.
    PR3562.B4   821'.4   75-36933
    ISBN 0-8018-1779-X